MELVILLE'S REVIEWERS

Melville's Reviewers

BRITISH AND AMERICAN
1846-1891

by

HUGH W. HETHERINGTON

NEW YORK / RUSSELL & RUSSELL

To my wife, Grace

PREFACE

FIELDS

The fields from which have been gathered the reviews and notices of the books of Herman Melville are the actual files of the magazines and newspapers. Since during his lifetime, 1819-1891, few magazines and practically no newspapers were indexed, and since such general indexes as Poole's give perhaps fifteen per cent coverage, and of magazines only, I have located what was said in print about his books by leafing through the bound volumes, as I suppose have the other harvesters.

I have often therefore been a pilgrim to the libraries best stocked with the middle-sized volumes of old magazines and the huge volumes of old newspapers. The latter are much harder to find. The files of newspapers, except of the most prominent, are in two sorts of libraries only—the very greatest, and those in the home towns or cities. As few realize, really complete files of nineteenth-century newspapers are rare, or in some cases nonexistent, even in the home libraries. As for microfilming, the only pertinent newspapers which in 1951, when I did much of the scanning of newspapers, had been microfilmed *in toto* were the *Times* of London, the New York *Times,* and the New Bedford *Mercury*. My fortunate chancing on the fact that the files of certain papers in the New York Historical Society Library were more nearly complete than those found elsewhere led to some of my most exciting discoveries, the *National Intelligencer* and *Tribune* reviews of *Moby-Dick*.

The richest fields, of course, have been the mammoth libraries. It is difficult to say whether my harvesting was better in the New York Public Library or the Library of Congress. I found less than I had hoped in the British Museum: first, before I went to London in 1957 I had already scanned many British newspapers in American files, particularly in the Boston Public Library and the Library of Congress; and second, the heavy bombing during World War II of the wing of the British Museum Newspaper Depository in Colindale containing the provincial newspapers had destroyed many of the files. Yet Colindale was not an entirely barren field. I would have gone further, however, with my examination of British provincial papers if in the considerable time I was giving to the project I had found more reviews of Melville's works.

Other libraries which have been rewarding fields include those of Yale University, Columbia University, Harvard University, the University of Michigan, the University of California at Los Angeles, Union Theological Seminary, and the American Antiquarian Society, the Huntington Library, the Boston State Library, the public libraries of Boston, Los Angeles, Nantucket, New London, of several Long Island towns, and the fine one in New Bedford. My debt to the gracious staffs of these libraries is great.

THE HARVESTERS

There were about a dozen excerpts from reviews in Meade Minnegerode's *Some Personal Letters of Herman Melville and a Bibliography* (1922), and a half-dozen additional in O. W. Riegel's sketchy "The Anatomy of Melville's Fame" (1931, in *American Literature*). I can say honestly, however, that the real harvesting began with my dissertation, *The Reputation of Herman Melville in America* (Michigan, 1933—published in microfilm by the University of Chicago, 1946). This contained over a fourth numerically of the items I now have, including a considerably larger proportion of the items which have, after all, proved the most important. I included a number of British reviews because the influence in America of British criticism was immense, especially before the Civil War. Charles R. Anderson, in two articles which he later summarized in *Melville in the South Seas* (1939), showed he had done some real gleaning after *Typee* and *Omoo*. Willard Thorp in *Herman Melville: Representative Selections* (1938) gave some clues about an English group of admirers of Melville in the eighties which I have been able to pursue further. Ben Kimpel in his judicious *Herman Melville's Thought After 1851* (unpublished dissertation, North Carolina, 1942) contributed a few more reviews. Mentor L. Williams turned ingeniously to unexploited sources for "Notices of Melville's Novel in Religious Periodicals 1846-49" (1950, in *American Literature*).

The inspired research of Jay Leyda enabled him to incorporate into *The Melville Log* (1951) about three fourths of the total number of reviews and notices I have in my book. About two of these three fourths he could have amassed by working back through secondary sources by then available, as I had also done independently, but the other fourth he must have dug out of the original periodical files. Thus he is indeed a major harvester. In "Another Friendly Critic for Melville" (1954, in *New England Quarterly*) he added about ten new items. Good summaries of the early reputation of individual books, based mostly on the *Log,* were given by William Gilman in *Melville's Youth and Redburn* (1951), by Merrell R. Davis in *Melville's Mardi* (1952), and by Elizabeth S. Foster in her edition of *The Confidence-Man* (1954).

Since the day in 1950 when I saw the *Log* in proof sheets, I have renewed my search and have located additional reviews and notices, amounting to about a fourth of those now in my book. I have also examined the originals of nearly all of the approximately fifty per cent of the items in my book which I did not myself discover. My "Early Reviews of Moby-Dick," in the *Moby-Dick Centennial Papers* (1953), published by the Southern Methodist University Press, offered about fifteen reviews I had just discovered, besides those already known. Since then I have found nine more reviews of Melville's masterpiece. A side fruitage of my search was my "A Tribute to the Late Hiram Melville" (1955, in *MLQ*), a study of previously overlooked shockingly inadequate obituaries, which, however, took me beyond the limits of my present book, Melville's life span.

In my dissertation I made a very few breaks in the great wall of anonymity surrounding the reviewers. Leyda made many more, and was able to give with certainty the identities of a number and to suggest plausibly the identities of many others. Perry Miller in *The Raven and the Whale* (1956) sought to relate the opinions of the reviewers to their political and personal biases, and turned up with one new review—of *Typee.* His province was the Americans only, while mine includes the British as well. I have found out who wrote some more of the reviews, especially British, and have made suggestions as to who wrote others. Many of the old reviewers will always remain, I fear, unknown, but far more acquaintanceship with these gentlemen has been gained than at first seemed possible.

At the risk of arousing muttering of "scissors and paste," I have used a basic chronological order because I believe such an arrangement would after all be most useful. I have attempted to bring out trends and significances without departing far from chronology, a method which has been more difficult than might be supposed.

ENCOURAGERS

Pre-eminent among my enhearteners, as he is among the harvesters, is Jay Leyda, who gave a whole day to the revival of my spirits in the dark time when it seemed to me that the *Log* had presented Melville's early reputation as fully as I could ever aspire to do. In that stimulating day he taught me more about research than all the universities had; called my attention to the great, still-unharvested field, the newspapers; and helped me to prepare a little device, so simple it seemed strange I had not thought of it before, so efficacious it seemed almost a wizard's wand, which has enabled me to discover hundreds of items.

There have been many others. John Brooks Moore first led me to read Melville, while the "revival" was still in its infancy. Robert W. Babcock criticized constructively my dissertation. Others whose encouragement or assistance has been invaluable at various times include Clara M. Bollinger, Faith Lawrence, Martha Engh, Russell Thomas, Robert and Mame Sterritt, Orwin Rush, Wilson Walthall, Wilson O. Clough, my sister Mrs. Frank E. Welles, my cousin Thomas J. Nelson, my father George Hetherington, my mother Anna Jones Hetherington, my aunt Alice Hedges, my wife Grace Irvine Hetherington, John K. Mathison, Ann Winslow, and Jack Allen, and the distinguished Melville scholars Luther S. Mansfield and Tyrus Hillway. My parents-in-law Arthur and Ida May Irvine provided a fund which has facilitated my work. Thanks also are due to Dean Ottis H. Rechard of the College of Arts and Sciences and Laurence L. Smith, Head of the Department of English of the University of Wyoming, who supported my application for two sabbatical leaves which made possible the latter part of the research and the writing of this book; and to Dr. Smith and Dean Robert H. Bruce of the Graduate School of the University of Wyoming, who made possible a reduction of teaching load which enabled me to give the manuscript a final polishing.

I also wish to acknowledge my indebtedness to the Ford Foundation for generous aid in the publication of this book by a grant under its program for assisting American university presses in the publication of works in the humanities and social sciences.

H. W. H.

The University of Wyoming
Laramie, Wyoming

CONTENTS

LIST OF ILLUSTRATIONS

MELVILLE'S REVIEWERS

Chapter I: REVIEWERS BRITISH AND AMERICAN

"The opinion of Washingon Irving . . . of Bryant—is a mere nullity in comparison with that of any anonymous sub-sub-editor of the Spectator, the Athenaeum, or the 'London Punch' "—Edgar Allan Poe.

VOICES FROM ALBION

If Melville's reviewers could come back to life, many of them would be surprised to find themselves figuring in this book. Here, however, they are: those who did and those who did not admire Melville; those who did and those who did not write with skill and insight. Not present, of course, are those who have eluded my search for many years through many great libraries, those who waited to write until Melville was dead on September 28, 1891, and, with a handful of exceptions, those who were neither British nor American.

"American" has been taken to include Canadian and Hawaiian. A few French reviewers whose comments were reprinted in America have been introduced, but aside from these only the British and American reviewers seem to have come to Melville's attention. At any rate, the interesting though perhaps less relevant subject of his Continental reviewers must be left to other investigators.

By having his first six books published in London before they were published in New York, Melville received more money than if he had reversed the process. As he soon found out, however, he was thus committing his reputation, far more than has in recent years been realized,[1] to the mercies of the professional book-tasters of Edin-

1. Perry Miller's central thesis in *The Raven and the Whale* (New York, 1956) that Melville's "reputation was to be saved or destroyed in New York" (p. 246) can well bear reappraisal.

burgh, Dublin, and London. There was nothing the American brethren of these reviewers awaited more eagerly—especially when an American book had appeared first in England—than their mail from the British Isles.

Nearly eight years before Melville wrote his first book, *Typee,* the already great impact of the British reviewers on the American, and on the United States public, had been dramatically accentuated by certain events of April 23, 1838. There had already been much excitement about the approaching great race between two steamships, the *Sirius* and the *Great Western,* owned by rival British companies.[2] That April morning, down on the Battery in the Port of New York, the "crowds of water gazers," which one "Ishmael" often saw there, had gathered in much larger numbers than usual, to greet the *Sirius,* which had arrived at dawn. In the afternoon the *Great Western* puffed up the harbor. Which ship had really won the honors? The *Sirius* had got there first, but had taken eighteen days from Cork, while the *Great Western* had come from Bristol in only fifteen days.[3] The New York newspapers took sides. An employee of aggressive Colonel James Watson Webb's *Courier and Enquirer* stole temporarily the *Great Western's* mail, containing the London papers of April 6, and quickly got out a foreign news edition, on that very day illustrating how the steamships were to stimulate the pirating of British materials. Such a theft was hardly cricket, James Gordon Bennett in his *Morning Herald* informed the *Courier.* The hot-blooded Colonel recompensed the *Great Western* by espousing her claims, while Bennett spoke out for the *Sirius.* The *Sirius* never again came to New York, but the *Great Western* was put into regular transatlantic service and on her second return crossing to Liverpool reduced her time to twelve days and a half.[4] By 1851 the American steamship *Arctic* was to make an eastward crossing in nine days and a half.[5]

It was thus no longer necessary to wait for news from Europe the nearly thirty days the sailing vessels usually required. Bennett declared in the *Herald* on April 26, three days after the end of the great race, that the consequences which would "follow from the event, and the grand scale in which it is likely to be followed up,"

2. David Budlong Tyler, *Steam Conquers the Atlantic* (New York, London, 1939), p. 55.
3. *Ibid.,* p. 52.
4. *Ibid.,* p. 66.
5. *Ibid.,* p. 183.

would "open up quite a new era in the philosophy of commerce, arts, and social life."[6] The Atlantic had been shrunk to less than half its former size—for business, for diplomacy, and for the evaluating of new books.

When several weeks later the *Great Western* left New York on her first return trip, a company of gentlemen including General George Morris accompanied her as far as Sandy Hook, where they were taken off by the pilot. "It may perhaps have occurred to the general at the time," says Henry A. Beers, that here "was what would work a change in the conditions of American journalism. It was now possible to get the freshest supply from the London market within a fortnight and the news of Europe before it was cold."[7] Morris's friend Nathaniel Parker Willis, later to be his partner in the successful conduct of the *Mirror* and the *Home Journal,* frankly proposed to profit by plundering the new harvest from Europe in a periodical to be called the *Pirate,* which he actually did soon launch under the subdued name of the *Corsair,* though for a voyage of only a year.[8] Willis was to become one of Melville's most admiring reviewers.[9]

Bennett may have exaggerated the influence of the steamships on the cultural interrelations of the two continents, but the halving of the time it took the mails to cross the Atlantic did make for changes in the world of readers and reviewers of American books published in London—a world in which opinion could fluctuate from day to day and in which such a substantial advancing of the date of the arrival of new London literary journals could make a difference. Now there was a doubled likelihood that when an American book came out first in London, American readers would see a British review even before they had seen a copy of the American edition of the book itself— before they had a chance to make up their own minds about it and before there had been a chance for them to have their minds made up for them by the press of Richmond, Boston, or New York. American critics and readers would be more likely than ever, consciously or unconsciously, to heed a British judgment if it were twelve days old instead of thirty. To his brother Gansevoort in London, who had recently crossed on the *Great Western,* Herman wrote in 1846 soon after the English publication of *Typee,* urging him to send "*every*

6. *Ibid.,* p. 56.
7. *Nathaniel Parker Willis* (Boston, New York, 1885), p. 239.
8. *Ibid.,* pp. 241-242.
9. See below Chapter VI, footnote 22.

notice of every kind that you see or hear."[10] Evidently Herman's impatience could scarcely brook the fortnight these London pronouncements would be in transit on a steamship. How could he have waited out the month a sailing vessel would have taken?

British periodicals were the more widely read in America because they were actually sold at a higher price in London itself than in New York, where an avid reader could subscribe to five leading British magazines for ten dollars a year, and for even less by "clubbing."[11] New Yorkers were obviously subjected to a barrage of British opinions of a new book days before the provincials were, in times when by today's standards transportation across our country was slow, whether by train, or by river or canal boat.

Americans who did not buy the English journals found they could still read many English articles in the United States newspapers, where they were frequently copied in whole or in part. At least two magazines also, in the absence of international copyright, found it possible to subsist for years chiefly by the reprinting of such articles— the New York *Eclectic Magazine,* and the better known *Littell's Living Age.*[12] Begun in 1844, *Littell's* offered some fiction, but it was "the more serious material from the *Edinburgh,* the *Quarterly,* the *Westminster, Blackwood's* . . . that was responsible for the great appeal of *Littell's*".[13] *Harper's Magazine,* created in 1850, filled many pages with borrowed British items, though later it became less eclectic.[14] All three of these magazines reprinted British commentaries on Melville; indeed, *Littell's* offered five of the most ambitious of the British critiques on his works.

It seems, however, that the "Greeks" were not satisfied: they must introduce into the "Trojan" citadel a veritable wooden horse, named, most suitably, the *Albion.* The founder of this magazine, Dr. John S. Bartlett, was born in Dorsetshire, became a surgeon in the British Navy, arrived in America as a prisoner in the War of 1812, came to New York, and "conceived the idea of establishing an English newspaper in the United States—a journal which should give to British residents on this continent a true exposition of public affairs, and a

10. Quoted in Merrell R. Davis, *Melville's Mardi: A Chartless Voyage* (New Haven, 1952), p. 19.

11. Miller, p. 12.

12. *Littell's* survived until 1941, a very long life for an American magazine.

13. Frank Luther Mott, *A History of American Magazines, 1741-1850* (New York, 1930), p. 748. Mott says the circulation of *Littell's* was never large, but it was steadily successful for many years.

14. Joseph Henry Harper, *The House of Harper* (New York, 1922), pp. 85-87.

general view of the news, politics, and literature of the United King-
dom"[15]—not unlike the modern Paris edition of the New York *Herald
Tribune*. In 1822, sixteen years before the first transatlantic steamship, Bartlett started his project as the weekly *Albion;* he carried it on
until 1848, when the ownership and editorship passed to William
Young, born in Deptford, England, who conducted it until 1867, in
the spirit of its founder.[16] The *Albion* lasted until 1875, thus surviving
by many years several of the periodicals which have received much
more attention from the Melville scholars. It had, however, with the
sole exception of the New Bedford *Mercury,* the most complete American series of notices and reviews of Melville's books, beginning with
Typee and including all down through *Israel Potter*. In January,
1847, the *Southern Literary Messenger,* evidently regarding with satisfaction the presence of the wooden horse with its belly full of non-
Yankees in the Yankee stronghold, bestowed this tactfully phrased
compliment upon the *Albion*: "It combines all classes of intelligence
from every country, furnishes much entertaining and instructive
literary matter of a high order, and is neutral to all kinds of parties."
If this Richmond dictum was to be credited, the horse, with his eyes
fixed upon London, was ready to buck off any contributor with
Whig or Democratic bias who tried to stay on his English saddle.

Always on the eastern horizon were those "courtly muses of Europe" to whom, Emerson in 1837 had said, "we have listened too long";
now right at hand were all these chances of exposure to English
judgments of books. No wonder respect tended to become ac-
quiescence. Poe wrote the classic description of the salaams performed
by Americans toward the Mecca that was London. He thus etched
with acid his "disgust" at American subservience to British criticism:
"It is not too much to say that, with us, the opinion of Washington
Irving—of Prescott—of Bryant—is a mere nullity in comparison with
that of any anonymous sub-sub-editor of the Spectator, the Athenaeum,
or the 'London Punch.' It is not saying too much to say this . . .
we day after day submit our necks to the degrading yoke of the cru-
dest opinion that emanates from the fatherland."[17] Events were to show
how neatly, at least in the case of Melville, Poe had hit the nail on the

15. A. Everett Peterson in *DAB*. The full title, as of 1847 was "The Albion:
British, Colonial, and foreign Weekly Gazette (*Coelum, non Animum Mutant, Qui
Mare Currunt*)."

16. *Appleton's Cyclopaedia*. Mott refers to the *Albion* as chiefly eclectic; but the
reviews of Melville were original, so far as I know.

17. *Broadway Journal*, October 4, 1845, quoted in "Marginalia," *Selections from
Poe's Literary Criticism*, ed. John Brooks Moore (New York, 1926), p. 76.

head—or rather had hit two nails on the heads—in this one blow; for not only was Melville turning his fame over to London to receive its first fashioning, but to a remarkable extent he was turning it over to the *Spectator* and especially to the *Athenaeum*. Among factors which made these two weeklies so formidable were their promptness, their thoroughness, their coverage, and their longevity. The only journal on either side of the Atlantic which was to have a more complete series of reviews of Melville's works than the *Athenaeum* was the New Bedford *Mercury*. No New York organ, not even the British-oriented *Albion,* was to be so continuously diligent in scrutinizing his productions. Poe's touch about *Punch* was obviously a bit of satirist's license; at any rate *Punch* ignored Melville completely.

Although the Duyckinck brothers, Evert and George, were certainly no mere echoers of English views, it is difficult not to conclude from an examination of the policies and particularly the format of their New York *Literary World* that they hoped it would be the American *Athenaeum*. They successfully emulated the London organ in coverage of new books and in promptness of reviewing, indeed in both respects—and, it may be said in quality also—outstripping all American competitors. Their imitation of the *Athenaeum's* format was amusingly precise: like it the *Literary World* was a weekly, a quarto, in some years exactly the same size, had three columns to the page, and often began with a review of a book. The type was very similar, and the set-up of the volume indices strikingly alike in appearance; the full title of the American weekly was an obvious echo.[18] Unfortunately the *Literary World* was no *Athenaeum* in length of life.[19] The effort of the *Literary World* to ape the appearance of the *Athenaeum* was no isolated case: Mott goes so far as to say that "American magazines were, in the main, simulacra of those of London and Edinburgh."[20]

In urging that *Typee* be issued in London at the same time as in New York, Thomas L. Nichols told Herman's brother Gansevoort that he "felt sure that the reviews of the English press would make its American success," and that he "was not at all sure that the process could be reversed."[21] Nichols certainly seemed sure the English re-

18. The full titles were: *The Athenaeum: Journal of English and Foreign Literature, Science, and the Fine Arts; The Literary World: A Journal of American and Foreign Literature, Science, and Art.*

19. *Literary World* (1847-1853); *Athenaeum* (1828-1921, and to date as *Nation and Athenaeum*).

20. *Op. cit.,* p. 393.

21. Nelson F. Adkins in *New England Quarterly,* V (April, 1932), p. 348, gives extracts from Nichols' *Forty Years of American Life* (New York, 1863, 1874).

viewers would be pleased with the book. What if they were not? At any rate it is clear he feared their power. In June, 1835, the *Knickerbocker* had objected to the "absolute sway of English criticism over our tastes and opinions," and had exclaimed, "We would like very much to see one of our critics pluck up sufficient courage to question the orthodoxy of a bull of the pope of London or Edinburgh."[22]

Nichols and the *Knickerbocker* were speaking for New York, but New England agreed. Edwin Percy Whipple, a then much-admired Bostonian critic, lamented in the *North American Review* for January, 1844: "If the *Quarterly Review* or *Blackwood's Magazine* speaks well of an American production, we think we can praise it ourselves."[23] For a Cambridge view, there was the *Fable for Critics* (1848), wherein Lowell several times satirized the American veneration. In the most sarcastic passage in the poem, he represented Cornelius Mathews as having publicly accused all successful American authors of having toadied to John Bull, and then as privately confessing that we were always "licking the critical shoes" of "some two penny editor over the seas" since it was the "whole aim of our lives to get one English notice": "My American puffs I would gladly burn all . . . / To get but a kick from a transmarine journal." Again, Lowell had Apollo tell the American critics they would all crowd about and claim they knew Sylvester Judd (author of the recent transcendental novel *Margaret*) "If some English critic should chance to review him." Apollo summed it up thus: "Your literature suits its each whisper and motion / To what will be thought of it over the ocean."

Virginia concurred. It was probably the editor, poet John Reuben Thompson, who in the *Southern Literary Messenger* for April, 1850, exclaimed with disconsolate irony: "At last we have a literature. It is but recently—within a few weeks—that the fact has been established to our entire conviction, and we hasten to announce it to such as are in darkness and know it not. The source of the Q. E. D. the reader will be at no loss to conjecture. It is transatlantic. No American argument on the subject, of course, could amount to a demonstration, but the dictum of the English press settled the question forever."[24]

22. Quoted by Mott, p. 406.
23. Quoted by Mott, p. 406. *Graham's Magazine* (April, 1853), said that Whipple had a "greater intellect than Emerson and a surer one than Carlyle." This great mind does not seem to have shown any awareness of the existence of Melville.
24. For further evidence of this subservience, see the *New Englander*, I (September, 1848), 456.

Evidence of the great and rapid effect of English reviews on Americans came also from Philadelphia, where the *American Courier* for March 30, 1850, stated that "The numerous favorable notices and extended extracts in the London papers" of *White Jacket* "have doubtless so sharpened the appetite of the reading public near the agencies of the English papers as to cause a rush as soon as it is known that Harpers of New York have issued it." That the *Courier* was unaware that the Harpers had nine days earlier published the book showed how the eyes of eager American readers who were so benighted as to reside elsewhere than in the metropolis were as likely to be fixed on the bookish doings around Trafalgar Square as on those in Manhattan. The *Courier's* next remark illustrated the way Americans often sampled new books: "The portions we have already devoured in the English papers give an earnest of a treasury of nautical amusement and interest when we shall have leisure to devour the whole."

Melville himself was extremely sensitive to English opinion, and took the greatest satisfaction in crowing when an offspring of his brain was handled more considerately across the ocean. In a letter in 1847 to Evert Duyckinck he called a copy of a flattering English review Duyckinck had sent him "frankincense," and continued, "Upon my soul, Duyckinck, these English are a sensible people. Indeed to confess the truth, when I compare the reception of Omoo in particular, with its treatment here, it begets ideas not very favorable to one's patriotism."[25] Several times, indeed, Melville rather jumped to the conclusion—as he did here in the case of the reception of *Omoo*—that the English had really been more favorable. In his long and losing battle with the critics, which, despite some moments of triumph, seemed to him to be more and more leading to utter defeat, nothing wounded him more deeply than what they did in London to his *Mardi*.

Few Americans actively concerned with literature were happy over this dependence on British judgments, except some author or publisher when a book did get a nod from London. What was nearest to an organized protest came from a group known as the Young Americans, the germ of which was the Tetractys Club, formed in New York in the spring of 1836. As the name indicates, there were originally four members, Evert A. Duyckinck, William Alfred Jones, Jedidiah B. ("Jerry") Auld, and Russell Trevett. Soon there was added a fifth,

25. Quoted in Davis, p. 36.

Cornelius Mathews, who apologized for spoiling the name of the club, but soon became its most militant participant.[26] Occasionally attending the meetings were Evert's young brother George and the latter's school friend William Allen Butler, who became a very distinguished lawyer. Their most determined enemy was Lewis Gaylord Clark,[27] who voiced his opposition in the *Knickerbocker*, which he edited from 1834 until its demise near the end of the Civil War.

With the exception of Mathews, who burned to produce the great American novel, they knew they were primarily critics rather than creative writers. Of them all Jones was the most gifted critic;[28] though their mainstay was Evert Duyckinck, who wrote smoothly and was certainly able to recognize true merit, who as reader for Wiley and Putnam's exerted real power in the realm of letters, and who had the tact and tolerance to maintain friendships with men of varying backgrounds. They controlled or launched several magazines; the height of their influence came during their guidance of the *Democratic Review* during 1845 and 1846 and of the *Literary World* from late 1848 until 1853. At the end of 1846 the by-then-famous author of *Typee* was taken into their fraternity.[29] All the Young Americans so far mentioned (except Trevett, the most obscure, and Mathews, the most self-centered) helped to enhance Melville's fame, as also did Margaret Fuller, with whom they were on good terms. A number of others who were more or less associated with the clique do not seem to have shown any interest in Melville.

Politically they inclined to the left, adhered to the Democratic party, invoked Jefferson, espoused the welfare of the people. Their main objective, however, was to further the development of a distinctively American literature, described in their more expansive hours as somehow embodying the vastness of their country and the splendor of her destiny.[30]

Tough-minded novelist William Gilmore Simms, their chief Southern satellite, in a letter to Evert Duyckinck in 1845, showed that he clearly envisioned the peril to their program of the servility to British judgments of American books. He wrote that the authors of America might "do wonders yet" if they could work together: the first step

26. John Stafford, *The Literary Criticism of "Young America"* (Berkeley, 1951), p. 17.
27. Miller, p. 71.
28. Stafford, pp. 28-32.
29. Miller, p. 167.
30. Miller, p. 111.

must be to "disabuse the public mind of the influence of English and
Yankee authorities," who had "fastened our faith to the very writers,
who least of all others, possess a native character," such as Longfellow
and Irving.[31]   Thus he scented collusion between a certain type of
Yankee critic and the British critics.   It is true that the inner New
York circle of the Young Americans seems to have been less acutely
conscious of the American subservience to British opinions than were
Simms of Charleston, Poe—self-styled a "Virginian"—, Lowell of
Brattle Street, and Thompson of Richmond, who were at times on the
circle's periphery.   Perhaps one had to get out of the rotary mutual
congratulations of Gotham to get a perspective on how formidable were
the English critics, though the New Yorkers were sufficiently disturbed by the limitations of American literature itself.

HABITS OF BRITISH AND AMERICAN REVIEWERS

During the early part of the century, in English speaking countries
at least, anonymity in reviewing reigned supreme.   I have found not a
single British review or periodical article dealing with Melville signed
with a real name before 1874.   Three bore the pseudonyms of men
whose real names have now been determined.   I know of one lone review, two articles, and two or three published letters about Melville
signed with real names in America.   On this side of the Atlantic
a small percent of the reviews were signed with one or more initials,
and these it has nearly always been possible to identify; thus the "R"
who several times reviewed Melville in the New York *Tribune* was
certainly George Ripley.   More than in England, there were in America by the mid-century feeble symptoms of a rebellion against anonymity; yet the "really elegant magazines," including the *Atlantic* and
Putnam's, "clung to the purer view of the ministry of letters" by
cloaking the reviewers.[32]   More of the reviewers, however, have by
various means been unmasked with absolute or relative certainty
than had once seemed possible.   Before my recent efforts much more
work had been done on identifying the American contributors than
the British.

Anonymity meant that the editor or editors assumed responsibility
for the opinions expressed in a magaine and scrutinized and revamped
the contributions.   Poe spoke of the judgments of the "anonymous
sub-sub-editor."   Melville in *Pierre* said it was "editors of all sorts"

31. This letter, dated July 15, is quoted by Stafford, p. 32.
32. Algernon Tassin, *The Magazine in America* (New York, 1916), p. 315.

who had extravagantly bestowed on "The Tropical Summer: A Sonnet" such "generous commendations." Thus it can be assumed that the reviews, especially the great majority which were completely anonymous, were usually colored by the editors' tastes.[33] Furthermore, it was certainly more likely that a man known to have been the "literary editor" wrote or reshaped a notice than that the general editor did so, particularly in the English publications with large staffs. In outlying America surely the general editor and the "literary editor" were often one and the same.

Another prevalent habit was extensive quoting. The excuse was that the review was a substitute for the book, in days when the cost of books was relatively high;[34] actually indolence was probably one reason for the habit, to which the British were, if anything, more addicted than were the Americans. It was an aim of the conscientious and idealistic Young Americans to cut down on this quoting.[35]

It is not so easy as some have maintained to decide how much puffery was present in a given review. Of the two main motives for puffery—to please the publisher and to please the author—the latter, in the case of a cisatlantic writer, especially one as politically unimportant as Melville, could hardly have been a powerful motive in London. The only strong reason for the British to bestow unmeant compliments upon Melville would be to remain in the good graces of his English publishers, John Murray and later Richard Bentley, who were both indeed formidable. British journalists were much inclined to ignore an American book if it was not published in London, but there were exceptions.

In his own land Melville did have three groups of special pleaders. First there were the newspaper editors in the smaller towns where or near where he or members of his family resided or had resided. Second there were personal or family friends. Beginning with *Mardi,* his first book after his marriage, a number of noticers did avow respect for his father-in-law, but some of these said flatly they could not tolerate the book even though its author was the son-in-law of the Chief Justice of Massachusetts. Lastly, and most important, there were the Young Americans.

33. Stafford (p. 9) tells how Emerson's review of young Channing's poems was mutilated so that he hardly recognized it, and then was published without Emerson's name—in the *Democratic Review.*

34. *Moby-Dick* sold for $1.50, while a transatlantic passage, second class could be had for $12.00.

35. Stafford, p. 13.

That Melville had another special pleader in America in the Democratic press, and especially a predisposed enemy in the Whig press has recently been claimed.[36] Perhaps we should look at the reviews themselves before we adjudge this dubious theory. No one, however, has even suggested that London decisions as to the merits of his books depended on his political affiliations.

Most of the differences between the British and American reviewers came from the greater professionalism of the British, made possible by the fact that British magazines with literary interests were, as shown by their longer lives, more stable than were the American. Their staffs were changed less frequently, also. To consider four magazines which were particularly interested in Melville, compare the life spans of the *Spectator* (1828–) and *John Bull* (1820-1892) with those of the *Knickerbocker* (1833-1865) and the *Democratic Review* (1837-1859).[37] The American market helped the British more than vice versa; the absence of international copyright helped to starve the American magazines but weakened the British far less.

The British reviewers tended to be more thorough and analytical, to be more concerned with aesthetic values, to be more aware of literary conventions. The American custom of inserting into newspapers skimpy notices by persons who obviously, or often even admittedly, had read only a few pages or none, seemingly did not prevail as widely in England. There the trend was to do a professional job on a book or not discuss it at all, as is usual today in America also. No British reviewer of Melville admitted, as from time to time an American did, that he had not had time to read a book, even in some cases where his comments were so meagre as to arouse suspicion that he had not and that his professionalism had thus degenerated into a mere pose. All in all, however, the comparative American amateurism was

36. Miller, p. 234 and *passim*.

37. Six British magazines are today survivors from early to middle nineteenth century (*Quarterly Review, Blackwood's, Spectator, Athenaeum, Chambers', Saturday Review*) as against only three American (*Harper's, New Englander*—now *Yale Review*—and *Home Journal*—now *Town and Country*—, besides the *Saturday Evening Post* from the eighteenth). The *North American Review*, which paid no attention to Melville, did live 124 years. Of those now deceased, among those which reviewed Melville, ten British, arranged in order of decreasing life span are *Gentleman's Magazine* (176 years), *Dublin Review* (93), *Westminster* (90), *John Bull* (72), *New Monthly* (64), *Eclectic Review* (63), *Dublin University Magazine* (47), *Atlas* (46), *Literary Gazette* (41), *Critic* (20); and ten American are *Godey's* (68), *Albion* (53), *Knickerbocker* (32), *Hunt's* (31), *Democratic Review* (22), *Graham's* (19), *American Review* (7), *Literary World* (6), *Columbian* (5), *Sartain's* (5). (*Union List of Serials*.)

one cause for the deference of the American public to the transmarine pronouncements.

Although I have not examined the British provincial newspapers as comprehensively as I have the American, I have gone through a considerable number of London newspapers, and some provincial also, to find almost none of the hasty little notices characteristic of the American provincial press. The importance of these superficial American notices may be questioned; I am offering them, however, for what they may reveal of the contributor's opinion of the author's previous works and of the general attitude of the public.

Ten years before the writing of *Typee*, Edward S. Gould had in 1836 in a lecture in New York scathingly attacked American reviewers, outlining six reasons why they were entirely too lenient.[38] The situation even then may not have been quite so bad as Gould thought, and there had been some improvement in the ten years since, particularly because of the work of the inner circle of the Young Americans. One of the main aims of the Young America critics was to become more professional, as indeed they did, especially Evert Duyckinck, and even more so William Alfred Jones. Stafford says that during the forties Jones "might truthfully be called a professional literary critic."[39] Then there were the excellent contributions of Lowell and Poe, who both may surely be said to have evinced real professionalism. A limited number of the American reviews of Melville did bear comparison with even the best of the British. Yet the professionals were still in the minority in America; and the Young Americans, contrary to the impression given by some recent writers,[40] actually were responsible for a very small proportion of the reviews of Melville. If his works had been reviewed more frequently by them, or reviewed at all by Poe, Lowell, or even Whipple, the general impression produced by Melville's American reviewers would have seemed comparatively less amateurish.

There were occasionally symptoms of British condescension toward

38. Published in the *Literary and Theological Review* on April 9, 1836. The six reasons for lenience were: (1) Gifts of complimentary copies; (2) Indulgence for personal friends; (3) Lenience toward colleagues on the same journal; (4) Fear of offending the author's admirers; (5) Desire to encourage American literature; (6) Indolence. Interestingly enough he did not mention pressure from the publishers, an indication this may have been less developed in America than in England (Quoted by Mott, p. 407).

39. P. 28.

40. Miller, *passim*.

the literary products of the New World. Some British reviewers found in Melville faults they regarded as typically American: "go aheadism"; disregard of the rules of composition; energy, force, imagination unchecked by discipline, balance, art. The majority of the British critics, however, said nothing about typically American sins; and a few commended his writing as having a freshness or magic that had not been achieved by their own authors.

On the other hand, in the American commentators obvious and explicit patriotism was not common, though loyalty to one of their own undoubtedly in some cases affected, consciously or unconsciously, their judgments. Furthermore, the lack of an international copyright law, which led to the pirating of all kinds of English literature, good and bad, and thus put the indigent American at a great disadvantage, aroused the nationalism of the American press, and, said Duyckinck in 1845, "It was determined, however unconsciously, that all the geese that should be produced this side of the Atlantic should be called Swans."[41] Duyckinck soon came to regard Melville as really a "Swan," and would have said that, in Melville's case, the patriotism was only a stimulus to giving him the approbation he really deserved.

In the discussion of Melville's reviewers as set forth in the following chapters, it has not seemed worth while to dwell on negative results. A very few cases of failure to review a book I have pointed out where the omission seemed of special interest, but for the most part the reader is invited to note for himself the absence of reviews which might have been expected. Many newspapers, both British and American, seem to have totally ignored Melville. I have leafed through, for reviews of all his prose works, those newspapers and magazines which reviewed any one of his books, and which had apparently not been so scrutinized by other investigators. This procedure was not carried out so rigorously for Melville's poetical works, chiefly because the results were usually negative. Most of the magazines in America which had noticed his prose, were dead before the time of his first volume of poetry, *Battle Pieces* (1866), a considerable proportion of the magazines having been Civil War casualties.[42]

41. Quoted by Stafford, p. 15.

42. Tending to invalidate negative results from newspapers is the fact that even in the best files of that period there are some missing days. Where I have noticed missing days, I have checked other files of the paper if they could be found.

INVITATION FROM PARLIAMENT TO PLAY FAIR

Before 1838, John Bull had given the American author full opportunity to win what success he truly deserved in Great Britain, for an American book, whether first published there or not, could be copyrighted there. Uncle Sam, however, did not play the game fairly, for in the United States a British book, wherever first published, could not be copyrighted. The situation in America was hard on both the British and the American writer. An American publisher had only to buy a single copy of a successful British book and then proceed to print it. To issue an American book, however, the American publisher had to pay the American writer something for his manuscript. Thus the British books were printed and sold in America for less than in England itself, where the publisher had to remunerate the British author. The British writer was deprived of all revenue from the American sales; and at the same time the American writer was subjected to crushing competition from the underpriced copies of the works of famous and established British writers.[43] The authors of both countries made efforts to secure redress; but Congress could not be stirred to action.

Parliament could not change the American set-up, but it could change the British in such a way as to try to bring the cousins across the ocean to their senses. In 1838 Parliament, as noted earlier, passed a bill allowing the author of a book first published in a foreign country to have British copyright provided that country conferred similar privileges on English authors. Certainly this embodied a fair enough proposition. Congress, however, failed to respond, and so from then on American books first published in America were as unprotected in England as English books were in America.[44]

Nathaniel Parker Willis, outraged at this new evidence of Congressional indifference, declared his intention, in December, 1838, in a prospectus for his proposed *Pirate,* not only to skim for it the cream from the journals of Europe, but also "as to original American productions" to do "as the publishers do, take what we can get for nothing . . . holding, as the publishers do, that while we can get Boz and Bulwer for a thank-ye or less, it is not pocket-wise to pay much for Halleck and Irving."[45]

43. Beers, p. 241.
44. Richard Rogers Bowker, *Copyright: Its History and Its Law* (Boston and New York, 1912), p. 310.
45. Beers, p. 240.

In spite of the new 1838 law, there was still a loophole for the Yankees astute enough to see it, as did Irving, Cooper, Prescott—and Melville. If an American book was published *first in England,* it could still be copyrighted there. Such was the situation for eleven years, during which Irving and Cooper, and Melville on a smaller scale, garnered pounds sterling by the mere maneuver of prior London publication, followed shortly, so as to get some dollars also, by American issuance and copyright.

The loophole, however, was plugged on June 5, 1849, when in the quietly handled case of *Boosey* vs. *Purday,* it was decided in Exchequer that a foreigner could have no copyright in England even if his book was first published there. Richard Bentley, who had published *Mardi,* and was in the process of getting out *Redburn,* lost no time in informing Melville of this decision; almost within a fortnight, on June 20, he wrote him about it, adding this gambit to Melville and his compatriots: "Why not at once with dignity come into the international copyright act?"[46] What could poor Melville, or all the American authors for that matter, do about it, but go on striving vainly, as they already had for years, to secure reciprocating American laws?

Apparently the new decision did not at once go into effect; or for some time was not considered to be in effect; for Bentley, late in 1849, did accept the manuscript of *White Jacket* and, more than a year later, that of *The Whale* (to be rechristened far more picturesquely in New York). In a letter inserted in the *Times* on January 25, 1850, he stated that he had "become the purchaser of" what he "firmly" believed "to be the copyright" of *White Jacket* "for a considerable sum."[47] (This amount was £200.)[48] Perhaps a gentleman's agreement between English publishers to respect each other's rights in American books for which they had paid good money had survived the 1849 decision or was set up after it, and was, temporarily, being honored.[49] In the fall

46. Bernard R. Jarman, "With Real Admiration: More Correspondence between Melville and Bentley," *American Literature,* XXV (November, 1953), 307-313.

47. Jay Leyda, *The Melville Log* (New York, 1951), p. 362. Hereafter cited as *Log.*

48. Leon Howard, *Herman Melville* (Berkeley and Los Angeles, 1951), p. 147.

49. To take at its literal face value Willis's commentary on "International Copyright" in his *Home Journal* for January 12, 1850, is to conclude that such an agreement had a formal existence, had been regarded as really binding, had survived or been set up after the new court decision, and had been abandoned before the end of 1849. Willis wrote of the "recent English repudiation of copyright" thus: "It has been a rule among publishers abroad that an agreement of prior publication, between one of their number and an American author, should be as valid as the legal copyright of an English author. To punish us for our wholesale thieving of English books,

of 1850, however, *Punch* declared, obviously referring to the *Boosey* vs. *Purday* case or some subsequent confirmatory court ruling, that "The recent decision of the Chief Baron had decided that a foreigner can have no copyright in England; and as Americans are foreigners, English copyrights in American works are good for nothing."[50]

It is not clear why the United States government, even if indifferent to defrauding foreign writers of the American income which was justly theirs, let so many years pass before it provided the financial protection which would have been so beneficial to the development of the literature of the young nation. True, American publishers did sometimes make rather niggardly voluntary payments to British writers—conscience money—thus a little mitigating the injustice. One American publisher, George Palmer Putnam, was a real campaigner for international copyright as early as 1836; but for decades a great obstacle was the opposition of the powerful House of Harper,[51] although it claimed that it did at last side with the angels.[52] It was not until May 3, 1891, that Congress finally participated in the international copyright law,[53] too late to help American authors when they had needed it most. They now welcomed it, of course. But by this time the new nation had grown relatively more powerful economically, and the London book market was comparatively less important financially. American books were approaching the British in sales appeal. For Herman Melville, therefore, who had lately been made almost wealthy by inheritances, and who had barely five months to live, the new law was hardly the boon it would have been in the impecunious days of forty years before, when he had been reported in the *Times* as having "wearily hawked" *White Jacket* from "Picadilly to Whitechapel."[54]

---

they have broken up this protection, by mutual consent, and now an American author can no more sell a book in England than Dickens can sell one here—justly enough." On the other hand, Willis could have been unaware as to how much the abandonment of "protection" was merely a result of the court decision (passage from Willis in *Log,* p. 361).

50. *Log,* p. 397.

51. George Haven Putnam, *George Palmer Putnam* (New York, 1912), p. 172.

52. Harper, p. 109. Harper also claims his house voluntarily paid British authors, but Putnam (p. 162) says it did not do so.

53. Harper, p. 109.

54. *Log,* p. 362.

Chapter II: TYPEE

"He seemed to write like a giant refreshed."—London *Morning Chronicle* (1851), referring to *Typee*.

BRITISH RECEPTION

If his first six books had not been issued by an arrangement whereby each came out originally in England a few weeks before it did in America, the story of Melville's reputation, as well as of his finances, would have been vastly different. Yet it was partly the result of apparent ill fortune that such strategy was carried out for his first book. He had begun by offering the manuscript of *Typee*, in the spring of 1845, to several American publishers, including Harper and Brothers. They had all declined it on the ground that the tale could not be true and was therefore of little value.[1] That summer, however, Thomas L. Nichols was delighted with the "sailor boy's writing." He urged Herman's brother Gansevoort, who had just been appointed Secretary of the United States Legation to England, to take the manuscript with him to London to try its fortunes there. Nichols pointed out the advantages of prior British publication.[2]

Gansevoort accomplished his mission, but not at once. In October he showed part of the manuscript to John Murray, who immediately appreciated its dramatic verve, but "scented the forbidden thing—the taint of fiction."[3] Gansevoort labored to convince this powerful publisher that it was a real sailor's real tale, not the concoction of a "practiced writer" which Murray smelled.[4] Melville made changes to give his yarn more informative value, and maintained in his preface that

1. Zoltan Haraszti, "Melville Defends Typee," *More Books*, XXII (June, 1947), 205-208.

2. Adkins, quoting Thomas L. Nichols, *New England Quarterly*, V, 348.

3. Emily Morse Symonds (George Paston, pseud.), *At John Murray's* (London, 1932), p. 51.

4. *Log*, p. 199.

while some things might seem strange, he had stated "such matters just as they occurred." For weeks Murray hesitated, but on December 3, 1846, he accepted the manuscript, though it was not yet complete.[5] It went to press with the blessing of Washington Irving, then in London, who breakfasted with Murray and Gansevoort, stayed on after Murray left, listened to the brother's reading from it, and declared it "exquisite" and "graphic."[6] In more ways than one it was well launched, for Murray was the most influential of British publishers.

Eighteen days before it came out in New York, Melville's first book made its premiere appearance in London, on February 26, 1847,[7] under the title *Narrative of a Four Months' residence among the Natives of a Valley of the Marquesas Islands,* as a number in "Murray's Home & Colonial Library," a non-fiction series. Melville had made his bow before the world not as a novelist but as a travel writer. Naturally enough, therefore, his assertion that he had told only the truth aroused comment; and his claim that he was reporting actual facts invited scrutiny of both his satire on the missions and his deflation of civilization; and his treatment of sex disturbed a few—thus leading to four controversies all involving some divergence from purely aesthetic evaluation.

A young author's first review! Gansevoort did not have to wait long for it. It had already appeared on February 21, seven days before the book itself. How eagerly Gansevoort must have picked up the copy of the London *Athenaeum,* which contained it, and mailed it to the even more eager Herman.

Henry Fothergill Chorley was honest; he was incorruptible; he was prompt—Murray must have facilitated his promptness by sending him a pre-publication copy—and he was severe. For sixteen years, as a chief reviewer for the revered and feared *Athenaeum,* Chorley had made the major contribution to building up its reputation for being above puffery.[8] It was he who pronounced the first press judg-

5. Symonds, *loc. cit.*
6. *Log,* p. 202.
7. Meade Minnegerode, *Some Personal Letters of Herman Melville and a Bibliography* (New York, 1922), p. 105. This was only Part I; Part II did not appear until April 1. Melville had submitted the title beginning *"Typee: A Peep at Polynesian Life"* later used by Wiley and Putnam, but Murray had changed it without consulting the author (Davis, p. 14).
8. Richard Garnett in *DNB.* Chorley was on the staff of the *Athenaeum* from 1833 to 1866. He failed as a novelist, but succeeded with his books on music, and was respected as a reviewer. This review of the *Narrative* certainly had the tone of the reviews of *Mardi, White Jacket,* and *The Whale* identified as Chorley's by Leslie A. Marchand, *The Athenaeum: A Mirror of Victorian Culture* (Chapel Hill, 1941), p. 192.

ment on the *Narrative,* as he did on so many other books. The main
burden of his remarks, sandwiched into columns of summary and
quotation, was suspicion of the reality of the tale. Poor Murray!
Chorley, however, found "stirring adventure," and asserted that
whether it was true or not, no one would surely "refuse thanks to the
contributor of a book so full of fresh and richly colored matter," thereby evidently consoling Gansevoort, who described this critique as
"favorable."[9]   Chorley displayed British condescension in declaring
"Mr. Melville's manner is New World all over," but showed his interest by continuing his synopsis on February 28.

Murray was only one of a number of Britishers who questioned
the authenticity because of hesitance to accept so good a book as the
genuine work of a common sailor. Chorley did not make this point,
but a week later it was very possibly Thornton Hunt,[10] unconven-
tional but not untalented eldest son of Leigh Hunt, who in the serious
Spectator, on February 28, solved the problem to his own satisfaction,
but hardly to Melville's: the book just wasn't too good, indeed just the
kind of undisciplined writing to have originated in an American
forecastle.   Thus his lower rating of the book made easy his own
suspension of disbelief. "Had this work been put forth as the production of an English sailor we should have had some doubts," reasoned
the *Spectator's* critic, but there were two reasons why an American
sailor author was a possibility. First, across the Atlantic no employment was invested with "caste discredit," and it seemed "customary
with young men of respectability to serve as common seamen, either
as a probationership to the navy or as a mode of seeing life." Cooper
and Dana were examples. Second, the system of popular education
gave "the American a greater familiarity with popular literature and a
readier use of the pen than is usual with classes of the same apparent
grade in England." "Striking" as was the style, there was nothing in
the book "beyond the effects of a vivacious mind, acquainted with
popular books, and writing with the *national fluency;* or a reading
sailor spinning a yarn; nothing to indicate the student or scholar."
Although he found some parts "very interesting," his was the lowest
rating given the *Narrative* as literature by the secular British. The

9. Diary, in *Log,* p. 204.

10. Beginning in 1840, Thornton Hunt regularly contributed for twenty years
to the *Spectator.* His father tried to make an artist of him, but he had
turned instead to criticism (W. A. J. Archbold in *DNB*). Walter Graham says Robert
S. Rintoul was proprietor and manager of the *Spectator* "with editorial assistance from
Thornton Hunt" (*English Literary Periodicals* [New York, 1930], p. 328).

Spectator, a weekly, was very supercilious about everything American, and often expressed a low opinion of the American mentality in, for example, such a statement as that Bayard Taylor had "that superficiality which seems a general characteristic of the American mind."[11]

John Forster was perhaps the contributor to the London *Examiner,* the following week, on March 7, who confessed initial suspicion, but felt, "on closer examination" not "disposed to question the authenticity," converted by the "thorough impression of reality" and by the reason given in the *Spectator*: educated Americans did, like Dana, go before the mast. Yet, unlike that journal's writer, the *Examiner's* found no faults and thanked Murray for "this clever book." "The Devil is not so bad as he is painted, says the proverb. Cannibals are not so unpleasant as we think, says Mr. Melville," he remarked in obvious enjoyment. In his entertaining summary, which revealed he had read with gusto, he admired especially Toby—"quite a character in his way, and most cleverly sketched"; "young ladies, though in summer costume of Paradise, coquettish and fantastical, delicate and ladylike, as Parisian belles"; and the ending, for there were "few narratives of escape" more interesting or dramatic.[12]

For the London *Atlas,* on March 21 and 26, the verisimilitude, which had persuaded the *Examiner* that Melville had himself done the deeds as well as written the words, was in itself sufficient. The *Atlas* did admit amazement at so well educated a sailor; yet unlike the *Examiner* had been finally "convinced from internal evidence that it had not been rewritten by any other hand than the author's." The *Atlas* even sympathized with Tommo's jumping ship, and relished an American's strictures on French policy. The book was as "remarkable" for its "distinctive" and "lively" style as for "the novelty of the

11. January 30, 1847. In reviewing Ticknor's *Spanish History,* the *Spectator* said that "Americans fail altogether in mere belles lettres" (January 12, 1850). Again, "there is a general resemblance throughout the Union in lathy lankness, in taste in tobacco chewing, in dress, in manners . . . or . . . 'no manners'" (September 20, 1851). The *Spectator,* however, was to take the side of the North, generally unpopular in England, in the Civil War (William Beach Thomas, *The Story of the Spectator, 1828-1928* [London, 1928], p. 185).

12. The reviewer of the *Narrative,* and also of *Omoo* and *Mardi* may well have been John Forster, who had been appointed "chief critic on the *Examiner* both of literature and the drama in 1833," and was editor from 1847 to 1856. He was notable as a biographer, especially of his friend Dickens, nearly all of whose manuscripts he owned (Charles Kent in *DNB*). It is less likely that the reviewer was Albany Fonblanque, the editor until 1847, who was a friend of Mill. The *Examiner* was the "chief organ of intellectual radicalism" (Richard Garnett in *DNB*).

facts it records." Offering a detailed and appreciative synopsis and a column of quotations, the *Atlas* added that if "we were to extract all the amusing things," "we should . . . copy the whole book."

Meanwhile that was almost what the Manchester *Guardian* was doing. The nineteenth-century mania for publishing extracts in newspapers reached a culmination, apparently, in Manchester, for the *Guardian* printed extensive quotations on March 18, and 25, and on April 8, 11, 15, 18, and 25. On April 18 it had carried two unconnected excerpts from the *Narrative* on different pages, all without one word of criticism.

It was the book's very excellence which caused *John Bull,* a weekly newspaper, in a brief notice on March 7, to question that it was written by an American sailor. The defense of Lord George Paulet "would almost justify the suspicion that the work is not written by an American at all," and "When, too, we consider the style of composition, so easy, so graceful, so graphic, we own the difficulty we feel in believing that it is the production of a common sailor." Yet it was "bewitching," and whoever the author was, concluded *John Bull,* "he has produced a narrative of singular interest," in which he had delineated "with so much power" the customs of the island people.

A month later, on April 6, it was probably Samuel Phillips who in the *Times* of London was at one with *John Bull* in finding the high quality a basis for skepticism.[13] Melville must indeed be "a very uncommon sailor, even for America, whose mariners are better educated than our own. His reading has been extensive . . . his style that of an educated man." Getting rid of Toby, the only possible credible witness, was suspicious. Phillips found a few inconsistencies; yet Murray had not offered "a more interesting book . . . hardly a cleverer." Phillips deigned to find it "full of the captivating matter upon which the general reader battens," and "endowed with freshness and originality . . . that cannot fail to exhilarate the most enervated and blase of circulating library loungers"; yet of "evidence against the smartness and talent" he found "none."

The weekly London *Critic* had carried an article eight good-sized pages long, in three installments, on March 7, 14, and 28, the first and

13. Samuel Phillips "about 1845 . . . obtained an appointment on the staff of the 'Times' as a writer of literary reviews," a post he kept until he died in 1854. W. P. Courtney says his reviews were written with "vivacity" and perceptivity (*DNB*). "Of the regular reviewers only one is known for certain in the earlier years, Samuel Phillips, who joined the staff of the *Times* in 1845" (*The History of the London Times 1841-1884* [London, 1939], p. 468).

third containing only approbation. The *Critic* took pains to show the story was true. There was some exaggeration, yet "generally there is a *vraisemblance* that cannot be feigned . . . the writer . . . though filling the post of common sailor is no common man." "His clear, lively, and pointed style," the "skillful management of his descriptions," and his "philosophical reflections" had at first led the *Critic* to suppose it was "ghost written," but it "had since learned on good authority, that this was not the case," that it was "the *bona fide* production of the brother to one of the gentlemen officially attached to the American Legation, and his alone." Evidently Gansevoort was still doing his duty! For the artistry, the *Critic* had a handsome encomium: "This is a most entertaining and refreshing book . . . The picture . . . of Polynesian life is incomparably the most vivid and forceful that has ever been laid before the public." Indeed, it was "one of the most brilliantly colored and entertaining" books "that has for a long while" appeared.

Beginning in March and culminating in April, there was a veritable debate in London about Melville's case for Polynesian culture. In the March 7 *Examiner,* there had been noted with genial sympathy the "kind of pantisocracy, or social millennium in little," in which were "no evil passions, malice or hatred: therefore no malicious legislation. Plenty to eat, nothing to do, and a delicious climate. Wives with Heaven knows how many husbands; husbands content with ever so small a share of a wife, and no surplus population. Inducements to South Sea colonization which we think it almost dangerous to set forth."

The *Critic,* however, took the negative, and on March 14, in the second installment, the only one of its three not completely complimentary, had decried two "blemishes" in an attractive book: the "censure of the missionaries" and the thesis of the superiority of primitive life. Also in April, Simmond's *Colonial Magazine* joined the negative by disparaging "the high strain of admiration for savage life and uncivilized customs" as endangering "inexperienced youth," and quoted with disapproval the today-famous paragraph ascribing the felicity of the Typees to the absence of money. Nevertheless, *Simmond's* concurred with the majority in finding this book one of the "most interesting" in Murray's Library; the adventures and the "glowing pencilling of savage life and scenery" possessed "charm calculated to rivet the reader's attention as strongly and continuously as" *Robinson Crusoe.*

Also in April the affirmative was upheld with more vigorous arguments in *Douglas Jerrold's Shilling Magazine*. Editor Jerrold, who conducted his short-lived magazine without much assistance, no doubt himself reviewed the *Narrative*. Jerrold, novelist, author of dramas which had their day on the stage, was handsome, fiery, vivacious, and witty; partly as a result of early hardships, which included service in the navy as midshipman from the age of ten to twelve, he was full of indignation against "shams, abuses, inequalities," and injustices.[14] His magazine, he announced, was published "for the good of the people."[15] He wrote about the new book characteristically, with deep concern for the poor, with sparkling wit, and also with some insight into economics.

It was natural that Jerrold was the first Englishman to applaud the "No Money" paragraph, and though he did not mention *Simmond's,* he seems to have been refuting its condemnation. He was inspired by the ringing phrases of Melville's paragraph to embroider enthusiastically on its theme: "No corn-laws, no tariff, no union workhouse, no bone crushing, no spirit crushing, no sponging houses, no prisons. . . . Here the bosom of nature unscarified by the plough, offers up spontaneously her goodliest gifts . . . Surely Rasselas, had he had the good luck to stumble on it would not have gone further in his search after happiness." Jerrold thought that Melville had, if anything, understated his case for his cannibals, as "man eating is not confined to the Anthropophagi of the South Seas." They at least "devoured only their enemies"; but "there is nothing which man in a civilized state has a keener appetite for than his particular friend." Indeed it was "impossible to read this pleasant volume without being startled at the oft-recurring doubt, has civilization made man better and therefore happier?"

Jerrold was also one of the stoutest vouchers for authenticity: "What will our juvenile readers say to a *real* Robinson Crusoe, with a *real* man Friday?" Furthermore, the book was "one of the most captivating" he had ever read; and although there were "little pretensions to author-craft," there were "life and truth in the descriptions and a freshness in the style . . . which is in perfect keeping with" the material.

Phillips also, in his above-mentioned review in the *Times* of April 6, revealed receptivity to the Utopian theses in an admonishment, sure-

14. J. A. Hamilton in *DNB*.
15. Graham, p. 293.

ly religious in spirit, to the missionaries: "The author . . . has written a charming little book . . . with a laudable Christian purpose. Let it be regarded as an apology for the Pagan; a plea for the South Sea Islanders [to the?] governments, and missionaries, who understand so little the sacred charge which God commits to them, when He places in their hands the children of His favored sunny regions; may they learn from fiction a lesson which experience hitherto has failed to teach them . . . viz., that if it be necessary for Christianity to approach the Heathen, it is equally necessary that it should approach him reverently and tenderly."[16] This seems to have been the only British defense, before 1856, of the deprecation of the missionaries in the *Narrative*.

On the other hand, in an eleven-page April assault, a critic in the *Eclectic Review* took the negative on all four of the controversies. First he derided the rosy picture of Typeean society as "strikingly opposed to all, which our knowledge of human nature and experience of its state in other regions would lead us to expect . . . We smile, if a deeper feeling be not enkindled, at the favorable light in which our author contrasts savage with civilized life." Second, he defended the missionaries against the "implications" of Melville, who had clearly aimed "to connect the Christian missionary with the atrocities practiced on savage tribes"; these atrocities had been perpetrated, but not by religious men. Third and most violently, he denounced the immorality: "We pass over the account given of the reception met with from the natives [when the Marquesan girls swam out and boarded the whaler, to the delight of the sailors], simply remarking that it affords an apt, but most humiliating illustration of the profligacy practiced on such occasions. There are grounds on which we demur to the desirableness of such facts . . . being communicated to the public." Yet, perhaps such revelations were needed, because they explained why the missionaries had been disparaged by some visitors, "whose anger has been aroused by the obstacles opposed to their criminal indulgences." And fourth, he declared the "overdone levity" of Toby—about being eaten—shook his "confidence" in the account's "authenticity." It all added up to the most pejorative of the British

16. The rather unusual point of view in this paragraph, religious, yet revealing a breadth that suggests the writer has compared the merits of various religions, and that he was not devoted specifically to the spread of Christianity, is accounted for if Samuel Phillips indeed was the reviewer, for he was of Jewish descent, born in England (*DNB*).

reviews, one unique in granting to the *Narrative* no values or charms whatever.

After April, the interest of the British press in the *Narrative* diminished, but during the rest of 1846, discussion did continue, especially about its veracity, against which two humorists, along with an unyielding skeptic, took the stand. The first humorist, an advocate of the book as an achievement in belles-lettres, was *G. A. a'Beckett's Almanac of the Month* for June, which in a hoax headed *Alleged Forgery*, told of how an "individual, who gave the name of Herman Melville was brought up on a charge of having forged several documents" representing that he had resided in the Marquesas. The evidence was "conflicting," but it "was obvious that whether the papers were forgeries or not, the talent and ingenuity of Herman Melville were, of themselves, sufficient to recommend them very favorably to a literary tribunal."[17]

On August 8, the *Athenaeum's* die-hard Chorley was not converted even by the July 1 resurrection of Toby,[18] whose letter to the Buffalo *Advertiser* he quoted to add that "every reader must decide for himself" as to the value of this "somewhat unexpected testimony" to the "authenticity" of this "clever work." On October 3, Chorley, noticing the publication of *The Story of Toby*, made clearer than ever that his own decision was a "Nay." He could only say what he "had said before—it deserves to be true. We vouch for the verisimilitude—but not the verity."

The other agnostic humorist, probably William Jerdan, expressed himself on December 20, in the London *Literary Gazette*. "A mob of contemporary periodical brethren have dwelt at much length upon the wonderful adventures and extraordinary revelations of" the *Narrative,* he said—"But as we happened to fancy the name of Melville to be equivalent to that of Sinbad the Sailor, we . . . abstained from noticing this clever and entertaining production; and as an apology for which, we beg Mr. Melville to accept this explanation, and do us the honor to dine with us on the 1st of April; we intend to ask only a small party, Messrs. Crusoe, Sinbad, Gulliver, Munchausen . . . and a few others."

During the last six months of 1846, however, at least three believers came forth, not counting *Chambers' Edinburgh Journal,* which carried

17. Quoted by Russell Thomas, "Yarn for Melville's *Typee*," *Philological Quarterly,* XV (January, 1936), 16-29.

18. See later in this chapter for an account of Toby's reappearance.

without comment extensive selections on August 8 and October 17.[19] In July the *Gentleman's Magazine* briefly revealed a liking for the book; implied acceptance of its veracity; declared it "most interesting, most affecting, and most romantic"; and asked nostalgically "Ah! thou gentle and too enchanting Fayaway, what has become of thee?"

Two magazines turned seriously to the *Narrative* for information about the South Seas. In August, 1846, the Catholic *Dublin University Magazine* viewed it as true, and divided a long article between it and *Adventures in the Pacific* by John Coulter, M.D., a British whaling surgeon, who also had visited the Marquesas and seen cannibals. The *Dublin* assumed Melville's book as well as the surgeon's had real documentary value. It was patronizing toward the "non-descript young American whose passion for adventure" caused him to go whaling; but he was "entertaining" and also creditable as an eye-witness of a "primitive people": the "main interest" of his work was in "his personal narrative, but its value as a contribution to knowledge arises from his minute account of this tribe." Both authors wrote "easily" and "well."

A contributor to the London *Quarterly Review* in October, in eighteen pages, mostly appreciative summary and quotation, took the *Narrative* as genuine, and accepted the author's facts, but not all his inferences. Even if "rather an acute than a profound observer," he was to be commended for his timeliness in offering such an informative account before "the Polynesians were destroyed by advancing civilization." Yet he demurred at the author's attempt to defend cannibalism, and declared he was guilty of hastening to "important conclusions from experience, which though undoubtedly great, is after all but partial," in attacking the "whole system of colonization . . . without discrimination." Thus he was not altogether a convert to the Typeean Utopia. But he did find the book eminently readable and delightful, especially the "account of the approach of the vessel to the land of promise," under a climate of "'delightful lazy languor'" which recalled a "fine passage" in the "Lotus Eaters." Finally, "with regard to the literary merits" there could be "but one opinion": "The style is clear, manly, and lively; the vivacity of the author is combined with

19. Melville assumed that these excerpts in *Chambers'* indicated it thought his tale true. An interesting symptom of the world-wide fame of the *Narrative* was the appearance, without critical comment it is true, of a very detailed summary of it, reprinted from a British periodical, in the *Adelaide Miscellany*, Adelaide, Australia, on June 2, 1849.

the refinement of the gentleman." Recommending the tale "cordially,"
he thanked "the author" for the "amusement and information."

It became routine, as Melville's other books came out, for reviewers,
whatever they thought of them, to pay high tribute to the first. Probably the most glowing of all prefaced the London *Morning Chronicle's*
review in 1851 of *The Whale:*

> The power and skill of the new literary enchanter were at once ad-
> mitted. With a bursting imagination and an intellect working with
> muscles which seem not to tire, Herman Melville bid high for a high
> place among the spirits of the age. There was never an author more
> instinct with the flush of power and the pride of mental wealth . . . Not
> merely a man of talent but of genius . . . And his style was thoroughly
> characteristic. Its strength, its living energy, its abounding vitality were
> all his own . . . He bounded on and on, as if irresistibly impelled by the
> blast of his own inspiration, and the general happiness of phrase, and
> the occasional flashes of thought rendered in the most deliciously perfect
> words, were subsidiary proofs of the genuineness of the new powers with
> which he addressed the world.

This probably remains to this day the most extravagant eulogy Melville's first book has ever received.

Much less a devotee, William Harrison Ainsworth, under the pseudonym "Sir Nathaniel," in 1853 in the *New Monthly Magazine,* was
still one to favor the first book. Referring primarily to the *Narrative,*
he said that although the muses had "scarcely patronized sea-faring
verse," by them nevertheless "must have been inspired—in fitful and
irregular afflatus—some of the prose-poetry of Herman Melville's sea
romances. . . . He has snatched a quill from a skimming curlew. . . ."
Yet he was convinced now they were "more or less imagination."[20]

The discussion about fact and fiction in the *Narrative* was to be
reopened by *Omoo.* One of the last British comments on the *Narrative* before its author's long obscurity, was very skeptical. The *Dublin
University,* in March, 1856, had renounced its 1846 implied profession
of faith to the extent of even thinking "Herman Melville" might be
a *nom de plume,* as would be expected of an author who loved "mysti-

---

20. He was moved to compare them with "Locksley Hall," from which he quoted
the famous escape passages. ("American Authorship No. IV: Herman Melville,"
Colburn's New Monthly Magazine, XCVIII [August, 1853], 300-308.) This was twice
reprinted in America: in the *Eclectic Magazine* (not to be confused with the English
Eclectic Review), XXX (September, 1853), 45-62; and in *Littell's Living Age,* XXXVIII
(August 20, 1853), 481-486.

fication." *Typee,* and also *Omoo,* had large infusions of fiction, but were admirable for their "glowing language."[21]

The most important British defense of Melville's case against the missions came on July 1, 1856, in a journal sympathetic toward America, the *Westminster Review.* Therein it was probably John Chapman who assessed the value of missions, both Protestant and Catholic, in fifty carefully reasoned pages.[22] He cited the *Narrative,* first, to show how the missionaries in Hawaii intensified the caste system, with its gap between the wealthy chiefs and the miserably poor, and second, to illustrate the luxurious lives of the missionaries, who deprived the natives of their natural supplies with the pretext that it was good for them to go to work.

What had been the results of the four controversies? Three had viewed with sourness Typee Valley as a Utopia (*Simmond's, Critic, Eclectic*); one, with measured disapproval (*New Quarterly*); but there were three ardent fans (Phillips, *Examiner,* Jerrold). One attack on the censure of the missions (*Eclectic*) was overbalanced by two defenses (Phillips, *Westminster*). Only three were shocked (*Spectator* —"sea freedoms," *Simmond's*—"voluptuous scenes," and the outraged *Eclectic*), but the other fourteen had with no sense of guilt given themselves up to enjoyment. And by 1856, the British score stood at nine on the affirmative side and eight on the negative, on the proposition: Resolved that one Herman Melville has told the truth.[23]

But the score then stood two negative to fifteen affirmative[24] on the proposition: Resolved that one Herman Melville has written in his *Narrative* a book original in matter and charming in manner. What

21. "A Trio of American Sailor Authors," XLII, 47-54, reprinted in *Littell's Living Age,* XLVII (March, 1856). The author was obviously not the same as the one who originally reviewed the *Narrative* in the *Dublin.*

22. "Christian Missions: their Principle and Practice," *Westminster and Foreign Quarterly Review,* X (n. s.), (July 1, 1856), 1-51. John Chapman was editor and proprietor in the fifties. Some of the contributors were Froude, Mark Pattison, and later Walter Pater and George Eliot. It was "on principle extravagant in its praise of anything that it considered truly American" (William B. Cairns, *British Criticism of American Writings, 1815-1833, University of Wisconsin Studies in Language and Literature,* No. 14, [Madison, 1922]). See also Graham, p. 252. Leyda suggests Chapman was the author of the article (*Log,* p. 517).

23. This is counting thus: as believers, the two non-commenting extractors; as two votes the obviously different first and later critics in the *Dublin;* as a doubter the rather noncommittal *Simmond's;* and not including any articles which were primarily reviews of later books.

24. This is counting as negative as to merit the *Spectator,* whose position was perhaps not quite so extreme.

did it matter, was the composite British query, if in a work so full of the "pride of mental wealth" (*Chronicle*), reality was tinted with the hues of the imagination?

AMERICAN RECEPTION BEFORE OMOO

Under the title by which it is now known, *Typee: A Peep at Polynesian Life* was published in New York by Wiley and Putnam on or about March 17, 1846.[25] Like John Murray, George P. Putnam thought he was sponsoring "a work of fact."[26] Although the four debates about the book which were continuing in England were not long in getting started in America, the first few notices were skimpy, uncontroversial, and amiable. There was a noncommittal mention of *Typee* in the Boston *Traveller* on March 20, but the first known judgment from the American press came on March 21 in the New York *Anglo American,* which laconically pronounced the book "delightful, interesting."[27] On March 23 there were two items, a meagre but well-disposed notice in the Boston *Advertiser* and a review in the New Bedford *Mercury*. As the Boston paper could spare but twenty-four words, the review from New Bedford was the virtual beginning of Melville's American reputation. It was an auspicious commencement; the *Mercury* prefaced a synopsis by declaring, "This is a singularly attractive and delightful work," and the "descriptions of Polynesian Life" have "a careless elegance of style which suits admirably with the luxurious and tropical tone of the narrative." Among the extracts the *Mercury* chose was the significant "No Money" passage, which, however, it did not explicate or judge.

The *Mercury* refuted what it undoubtedly knew was one of the chief British reasons for questioning the authenticity of *Typee,* and thus put into print what was to be, for the most part, the American position on this point: although, the "elegance" of Melville's writings "bespoke the practiced and accomplished writer rather than the inmate of the forecastle," such "instances of rare talent and superior

25. *Log*, p. 207. March 17 was the date of deposition of the book at the office of the Southern District of New York. As the first known American review was on March 23, and even the first published extract did not appear in America until March 21—in the Albany *Evening Journal*, it is probable that the actual date of publication was a few days later than March 17. On March 27 this Albany paper had three additional extracts. Minnegerode, p. 105, is surely inaccurate in saying that the British publication was simultaneous with the American.

26. According to Diary of Gansevoort Melville (*Log*, p. 212).

27. The *Anglo American* condensed the *Athenaeum* review of *Typee* and published it part on April 4 and part on April 11.

learning are, however, by no means of rare occurrence among the motley groups who man the numerous whaleships from our ports." Coming from the largest of the American whaling ports ("nowhere in all America will you find more patrician-like houses . . . one and all . . . harpooned and dragged up hither from the bottom of the sea," we read in *Moby-Dick*), this evidence was both convincing and pertinent, as the *Dolly* in *Typee* is a whaleship.

Another aspect also of the veracity of *Typee* shortly found an American defender. The New York National *Anti-Slavery Standard,* on April 2, had been suspicious enough to check Melville's account of the Typees, with Captain David Porter's,[28] to find that Melville's "exactly corresponds with that of Captain Porter's which he says he had never seen." The *Standard* liked the book very much, finding it "curiously charming and charmingly curious."

Meanwhile the fame of *Typee* in America was being rapidly augmented during the last days of March and during April by a succession of notices and reviews from delighted readers who had not thought of wondering about the literal veracity. These included eminent and even major literary figures, residing in various states. Massachusetts at first showed more interest than did New York. In the Boston *Advertiser* on March 23 was this lone sentence: "This is quite an interesting volume, and gives a pleasant and detailed description of the manners and customs, the climate, fruits &c of these islands." Nathaniel Hawthorne in the Salem *Advertiser* for March 26 declared *Typee* "lightly but vigorously written," with the "narrative . . . skillfully managed."

In New York, Charles Fenno Hoffman on March 30 in the *Gazette* and *Times* pronounced it "one of the most delightful and well written narratives that ever came from an American pen. Mr. Melville has made the subject of Typee henceforth wholly his own by his felicitous mode of showing off its wild and noble charms." First of the professing admirers of Fayaway, Hoffman quoted the engaging description of her functioning, scantily clad, as the mast of a canoe. On April 4 in the *Albion,* British-oriented New York weekly, a critic, very likely the editor Dr. Bartlett, obviously assumed the readable book was a genuine report: "A few months' residence in

28. *Journal of a Cruise Made to the Pacific in the Frigate Essex, in the Years 1812, 1813, and 1814,* 2 vols. (Philadelphia, 1815). Anderson, *Melville in the South Seas* (New York, 1939), p. 130, shows that Melville was indeed somewhat indebted to Porter. The review in the *Standard* was signed "B" and may possibly have been by Charles F. Briggs, who had some connection with this magazine.

the Marquesas has" been the basis for "two volumes of interesting and curious matter, and the description of a country and place but little known." They were "written in a very easy, familiar style—and as the adventures they record were often 'spun as yarns' to relieve the weariness of a night watch at sea—we may hope they will be read to amuse the fireside circle on shore, and we cheerfully recommend them."

The *New York Illustrated Magazine* for April revealed belief as well as enjoyment: "This is one of the most interesting, amusing, and original books of adventure we have read for many a day. Get it and read it by all means, as we are willing to risk the price of the book that you will find in it something that you never read of or thought before—besides it is by an American sailor."

Virginia was heard from. Probably it was the editor, Benjamin Blake Minor who in the April number of the *Southern Literary Messenger,* took *Typee* to be a historical document of value, saying it contained "many curious and interesting matters—observed and gathered three years since, by the author, in Polynesia," a region "destined to a rapid rise in Historical and Geographical importance."

Then came Ohio. The Cincinnati *Morning Herald* on April 4 seemed to assume the actuality of this "very captivating book." To a quite complete summary the *Herald* appended: "The description of the natural scenery is highly wrought and the book contains extremely entertaining notices of the customs of the islanders. It is decidedly a pleasant book, but not knowing Mr. Melville, we must say it is also a wonderful book."[29] Was there here a faint suspicion?

Credence in Melville's report of "his own adventures" characterized the longest uncensorious American article devoted exclusively to *Typee,* in April in the Whig *American Review,* which has been ascribed to George Washington Peck merely because he did the next year review *Omoo* in this magazine.[30] A careful comparison of the two reviews shows they could hardly have been by the same man.

Beginning by calling it "an interesting narrative" the critic of *Typee* in this periodical continued: "The style is plain and unpretending, but racy and pointed [What praise could be higher?], and there is a romantic interest thrown about the adventures which to many readers will be highly entertaining. We cannot yield assent to many of

29. On April 7 this Cincinnati paper published an extract, "A Typee Beau."
30. Miller, p. 159. The "rabid disapproval" of the passages quoted ascribed by Miller to this reviewer is not in any way implied or expressed. Leyda (*Log,* p. 217) does suggest Peck may have written this review of *Typee.*

the author's remarks about the Missionaries of the Sandwich Islands, which we think are prejudiced and unfounded; but his adventures carry on them an air of truthfulness and fidelity." It was just Melville's account of his adventures, particularly his amorous ones, which was to stir Peck to express so violently his disbelief as well as stern moral censure. The above protest about the missionaries was the only remark in the whole nine pages of this *Typee* review which could possibly be considered hostile, except a wisecrack at the end. Lacking Peck's hysterical prudery, this critic had certainly read *Typee* with amused enjoyment. His detailed summary was entirely good-natured, and his remarks about the extracts were invariably pleased and tolerant. He referred to the narrative of the invasion of the ship *Dolly* by swimming island girls merely as "an astonishing spectacle." Without comment he quoted those passages which were just the ones to horrify Peck: the portrayal of the minute examination of the two white boys by the unchaperoned Typee damsels; the description of Fayaway in the "summer garb of Eden"; and the scenes of bathing with Fayaway. Such scenes, which the next year Peck did not quote, and would have thought pernicious to quote, were then decried by him as "venomous" and calculatingly designed to "excite unchaste desire."

The careless jollity, to be described by Peck as "cool, sneering wit" merely entertained the *American Review* peruser of *Typee*. True, there was a touch of acid in his concluding remarks, but also appreciation of the essential comedy, the turning of "terrors and hardships," as Edward R. Rosenberry puts it, to "comic account," the perception that "the unmistakable keynote in Melville's comedy of hardships is a gastronomic one."[31] In good spirits the reviewer ended by wondering how Melville could resist the temptation to return to the adoring Fayaway, but then recalled the waiting "hopeful gourmands": "If he does return, we can only express the hope, in the language of Sydney Smith to a Missionary Friend on his departure for New Zealand, that he may not disagree with the stomach of the man that eats him." This reviewer had, what Peck lacked, a sense of humor, and could even jest about missionaries.

A big day for *Typee* was April 4, the date of five American reviews, two of which have been discussed; the other three were more impressive. One was by George Ripley, who in highly commendatory mood said in the *Harbinger* that he had overcome his doubts about authenticity. Margaret Fuller, the same day in the New York *Trib-*

31. *Melville and the Comic Spirit* (Cambridge, 1955), p. 12.

une, was not so sure about that, but was one of the most enthusiastic American reviewers. *Typee* was for her "a very entertaining and pleasing narrative, and the Happy Valley of the gentle cannibals" compared "very well with the best contrivances of the learned Dr. Johnson." Melville could make "pretty and spirited pictures" and "had a quick and arch manner." Was she hinting at fictionization? At any rate, as will be seen, she was sure the author had told nothing but the truth about the missionaries. Horace Greeley, much delighted with Miss Fuller's talents, had recently given her the position of literary critic. Her praise of *Typee* in his great Whig newspaper would surely be widely heeded.[32]

Probably Hiram Fuller wrote the review of *Typee* in the New York Evening *Mirror* on that same April 4. Fuller, a "far-away cousin of Margaret Fuller,"[33] who had assisted him in a Providence school, had left his successful teaching career in 1844 to come to the metropolis to try his luck at journalism, and was now editor of the *Mirror.* He may have talked the book over with his cousin, for like her he tended to bracket it with famous imaginary voyages, yet was delighted with it as such.

Fuller, if it was he, now in the *Mirror* indeed doubted the book's literal veracity, but in implying that he detected fictionizing actually composed a glowing tribute to the author's talents. He saw and applauded heartily the main serious point, that the gentleness and happiness of the Typees were a reproach to the Western World; and he enjoyed the tone of comedy. He said—

This book has the *vraisemblance* of Robinson Crusoe—we hope it is at least as true. Certainly, if it is not, we shall set the writer down as second only to Defoe. It is asserted to be a description of matters of fact— an unvarnished tale of a sojourn among the cannibals. But what cannibals. We think seriously of recommending a trial of the effect of eating one's neighbors, as a humanizing diet for some of our war-breathing legislators. A decided improvement would it be if they could be brought to the temper of the Marquesan cannibals. And what tales of Arcadian life! Chateaubriand's Atala is of no softer or more romantic tone— Anarcharses scarce presents us with images more classically exquisite. The

32. On April 4 and 11, the *Anglo American* reprinted the suspicious *Athenaeum* review. On April 11, *Littell's Living Age* reprinted the reviews from both the *Athenaeum* and the believing *Spectator.* Thus was illustrated the prestige of these two English magazines in the United States.

33. Beers, p. 273. Mott, p. 329, calls Hiram Fuller "a relative of Margaret Fuller." See also *DAB.* Miller, p. 129, denies this relationship.

man Friday of the romance is a model of humanity, devotion and good humor—a philosopher in *tapa*—a tattooed stoic [Kory-Kory].

The "peculiar piquancy of a residence among" the leading men of the Marquesas consisted "in a knowledge that they will eat you up literally and not figuratively if you quarrel with them." Since so few have been faced with such a situation, he rejoiced "that the lot fell to one who could use his pen so admirably as our author."

As with *John Bull* and Phillips, the critic's doubts resulted partly from his seeing the author as a man of the world: "His style has a careless elegance which suits admirably with the luxurious tropical tone of the narrative," and we suspect "the author to be at least as well acquainted with the London clubhouses, as with the forecastle of a merchantman." At any rate it was "a delightful book." Thus, like some Londoners who also were not sure they were reading straight autobiography, the *Mirror's* critic was willing to let the boy author of so entrancing a production have his joke if he wished.[34]

Meanwhile Walter Whitman, as he then styled himself, in the Brooklyn *Eagle* for April 15, although uncertain as to the percentages of romance and reality, had declared the book charming entertainment: "A strange, graceful, most readable book . . . It seems to be a compound of the 'Seward's Narrative' and 'Guidentie di Lucca' style . . . As a book to hold in one's hand and pore dreamily over of a summer day, it is unsurpassed."

No such tolerance—humorous like the supposed Fuller's or dreamy like Whitman's—was displayed by the acrimonious George Washington Peck on April 17 in the *Morning Courier and New York Enquirer,* who made the element of romancing the basis for the harshest secular condemnation *Typee* received on either side of the Atlantic. Thus the reviewers in the *Mirror* and *Courier,* the only Americans of the lay press who made explicit their doubts of authenticity, came to diametrically opposite conclusions as to merit. Both papers were Whig, if that proved anything.[35] There were evidently Whigs who were,

34. The style of this review does suggest the authorship of Nat Willis; but he was close enough to the Melville family, as we shall see, to know Herman had never been near a "London clubhouse"; hence Fuller is the more likely author. Could Willis have helped with the *first* part of the review?

35. Fuller's *Mirror* had been professedly non-partisan at first, but Fuller was in 1847 to support for the presidency the Whig candidate, Zackary Taylor, who rewarded him with an appointment in the Navy Department (*DAB*). According to Frank Luther Mott, *American Journalism,* rev. ed. (New York, 1950), p. 261, the *Courier* was the chief Whig paper prior to the debut of the *Tribune* in 1841, and remained for some years after that one of the most important.

and Whigs who were not amused. Of the latter breed was Peck of the *Courier*. He admitted that *Typee* "is written in an exceedingly racy and readable style, and abounds in anecdotes and narrative of unusual interest"; but it was his "candid opinion" that "in all essential respects, it is a fiction,— a piece of Munchausenism—from beginning to end. It may be true that the author visited, and spent some time in, the Marquesas Islands; and that there may be foundation for some parts of the narrative. But we have not the slightest confidence in any of the details, while many of the incidents narrated are utterly incredible. We might cite numberless instances of this monstrous exaggeration; but no one can read a dozen pages of the book without detecting them."

Something to this effect had been said by the British although by no means so acidly; but Peck made an entirely different deduction from that made in London and in the *Mirror*: "This would be a matter to be excused, if the book were not put forth as a simple record of actual experience. It professes to give nothing but what the author actually saw and heard. It must therefore be judged, not as a romance or poem, but as a book of travels—as a statement of facts,—and in this light it has . . . no merit whatsoever. Parts of the work claim to be historical, in giving an account of the missionary labors in the island, the proceedings of the French etc.: but the spirit of fiction in which the whole is written deprives these of all reliability."

This severe writer in the *Courier* was surely Peck,[36] who had recently become night editor. Although the outraged "morality" was absent, yet here were the dripping vitriol, the dogmatic incredulity with which it is known Peck was to tackle *Omoo*. Naturally enough, the most hostile lay reviews of *Typee* and *Omoo* were from the same pen.

Nathaniel P. Willis was still a contributor to the *Mirror,* which he had conducted jointly with Morris and Fuller from October, 1844, until the early summer of 1845, when Fuller had become sole owner and manager.[37] Willis had been quite an intimate of Gansevoort Melville, whom he had seen much of in London about the time the *Narrative* came out, and had perhaps met Herman in Boston in March, 1846, and, if not then, before long.[38] Three years later in

36. Leyda suggests Charles F. Daniels (*Log,* p. 211), but Miller (p. 216) rightly, I think, assumes it was Peck. Peck's having done the *Courier* review makes even less likely his having done the *American Review* article on *Typee* wherein the veracity *was* granted.

37. Beers, p. 273, and *DAB*.

38. Davis, pp. 7-8.

his *Home Journal* Willis said, "Herman Melville talks Typee and Omoo, just as you find the flow of his delightful mind on paper." Although Melville was to fail in an attempt to get a rebuttal into the *Courier,* he evidently had little difficulty persuading the amiable Willis to vouch for the book. In the *Mirror,* wherein space had been given to a skeptic, Willis in his usual vivacious style wrote on May 9:[39] "We are requested to state, on the authority of the writer himself of this universally read, though suspected book, that the work is a genuine history of actual occurrences, and not by any means the fiction it has been represented. The misbelief in the story arises from the actual poverty of most persons' imagination . . . People who live in our cold country have a hard time believing . . . It is unfair to class Melville with Sir John Mandeville because he has had the good luck to live with Fayaway in Typee, while other mortals have grown wizen over anthracite." It was a defense both whole-hearted and adroit, with a telling thrust at stuffy Peck and the *Courier,* whose editor Colonel Webb had in his paper ridiculed Willis as a mere "boudoir" writer of works which were only fit to "make the papillotes of ladies' chambermaids." Willis may not have had a great intellect, but there was one thing he understood, and that was women—and men who didn't. There was a basis for the rumors of Nat Willis's success in youth with the ladies of Florence and Rome and other European cities which his enemies—especially Colonel Webb, and perhaps George Peck—assiduously circulated about the town, although, as his enemies would not admit, he had reformed when he had married.[40] Nat Willis was clever. How well he must have known George to have been able to diagnose his animus against *Typee* as a symptom of sexual jealousy, even though the prim New England bachelor had not betrayed such jealousy in his review of that book. But the correctness of Nat's diagnosis seemed more obvious when the next year Peck's animosity burst into a veritable flame when he read *Omoo.* (The *Mirror* was to publish a rejoinder to Peck's attack on *Omoo.*) To have Peck in the detested

39. Willis's authorship of this paragraph is established by a passage (quoted by Davis, p. 28, but omitted in the *Log*) in a letter Melville wrote on September 2 to Murray: "—Accompanying this you will receive a paper (formerly conducted by Mr. P. Willis) which contains an article with regard to the genuineness of Typee which I wish you to observe." The reference to N. P. Willis as "Mr. P. Willis" is a characteristic piece of Melvillian carelessness in such matters. The paper "formerly conducted" by Willis was, as I have explained, the *Mirror,* and not, as Davis suggests, the *Home Journal,* which Willis was still conducting, as he was to do almost until he died in 1867 (Beers, p. 347). Davis says he was unable to find a review of *Typee* in the *Home Journal* and I also failed to find one.

40. Beers, pp. 242, 119-125, 321.

Courier scout *Typee* as a "monstrous" lie was almost enough to arouse Willis to reassess it as true, even if he had not been impelled to do so by his fondness for Melville.

What a churlish reaction to a young writer's *jeu d'esprit* was Peck's article! Understandably enough, over a month later Melville was still acutely distressed by what he called "that obnoxious review" in a letter on May 23,[41] wherein he revealed a plot to have his own refutation published anonymously as supposedly from a well-disposed reader of the book, in the *Courier* itself. The doubting review in the *Mirror* did not annoy Melville enough to cause him to mention it in this letter; and apparently he was not satisfied merely to be defended in Willis's recantation for the *Mirror,* as he did not then refer to that either. No, nothing would do, to establish the book as a "genuine narrative," but to have it declared such in the offending *Courier.* The *Courier,* however, evidently refused the space. Melville was the more concerned because he had heard the "malicious notice" had "been copied into papers in the Western part of the state."

What those provincial papers did, whose copyings I have been unable to locate, he might disregard, but he must have been exasperated when he found the noisome item copied in the May number of the journal which, in Whig circles at least, had been for a decade considered the leading American literary monthly, the *Knickerbocker.* The editor, Lewis Gaylord Clark, has been credited with inditing the very peculiar notice in which the copying was done.[42] Can it have been Clark himself who penned this, the most self-contradictory article in the whole chronicle of Melville's reviewers? Clark, if it was he, after admitting having "perused this very entertaining work with a great deal of pleasure from the very easy gossiping style of the author, and his constant and infectious bonhommie," even though "frequently struck . . . with the idea that the writer was occasionally romancing," went on to say, "In this impression we are confirmed by the capable critic of the 'Courier and Enquirer' daily journal, who says of this work . . ."—and then quoted in its entirety Peck's review. Peck had by no means accused Melville of "occasionally romancing,"

41. Zoltan Haraszti, pp. 203-208. The letter was addressed to Alexander Bradford, who had been a law partner of Gansevoort Melville before the latter went to London.

42. Clark's authorship is suggested by Leyda, *Log,* p. 216, and assumed by Miller, p. 159. If Melville had seen the *Knickerbocker* item by May 23, he would surely have mentioned it in his letter of that date. Here we have an illustration of how late in the month an issue of a magazine could come out in those days.

but of deliberate falsification which had rendered his work "of no great merit whatever." Could it have been Clark who admitted reading "with a great deal of pleasure" what his admired *Courier* critic had declared was totally devoid of both reliability and value? One could hardly have blamed Melville at this point if he recalled Poe's very low opinion of the *Knickerbocker* and its editor.[43]

On April 25 William Gilmore Simms had found *Typee* charming and truthful in a brief review in the *Southern Patriot*. It was, he said, "a very curious and interesting narrative of savage life, and well deserving perusal." It reminded him of delightful books "of his boyhood," including voyages by Cook and Byron: "The scenes, the circumstances are quite as fresh, and the regions of the world in which they occur are still quite as novel and unexplored as the day of their first discovery by voyagers of Europe. We have every reason to believe that Mr. Melville is a veracious chronicler, though he tells a very strange story."[44]

Peck and the echoers of his doubts were still very much in the minority in America, and May added five to the growing list of professed believers. In that month, four magazines and one newspaper endorsed the genuineness of *Typee,* and all admired it. If among the five there was touch of suspicion, it was in the Albany *Argus* on May 26, which noted the romantic coloring, yet seemed to believe it a reliable portrayal of a "segment" of the earth. It was "a decidedly interesting book—embodying valuable information and amusing narrative . . . The Typee tribe had the reputation of savage and fierce cannibals. But his sojourn there (involuntary as it was) seems to have been far from unpleasant. His descriptions of their percular deism, their almost dream-like way of passing life—their voluptuous climate, their wars, their peculiar polygamy [actually, polyandry], and the remarkable beauty of the natives, add much useful information to the History of the Polynesian Isles." There was "a tinge of romance throughout," which gave it the "charm of a beautiful novel," for "some of the events are 'passing strange.' "

Also in May, the *Democratic Review* and *Graham's Magazine* raised the question of veracity, yet cast their votes in favor of Melville

43. Poe said that "under King Kong the Second, in the august person of one Lewis Gaylord Clark," the *Knickerbocker* had become a "realm of outer darkness, of utter and inconceivable dunderheadism" (E. A. Poe, "The Literati," *Works,* J. A. Harrison, ed. [New York, 1902], XV, p. 181).

44. Given entire in *Letters of William Gilmore Simms,* eds. Oliphant, Odell, and Eves (Columbia, S. C., 1953), Vol II, p. 158.

and recommended the book. The *Democratic* had a few sentences for what was "perhaps . . . the most interesting of Wiley & Putnam's deservedly popular 'Library of American Books.'" "The scenes," were "described with peculiar animation and vivacity . . . that must task the credulity of most plain matter of fact people . . . yet they are without doubt faithfully sketched" as well as "amusing." *Graham's* noted, sympathetically, Melville's case for the Typees, and pleaded the cause of his truthfulness: "If the truth about the savage nations were not always a little stronger than civilized fiction can be, we should sometimes be inclined to compliment him for his strength in drawing the long bow of travellers; but his descriptions are doubtless transcripts of facts, not imagination, sounding as they do, 'as bad as truth.' Those who desire a 'Peep at Polynesian Life,' had better by all means obtain his work." The reviewer may have been Thomas Buchanan Read.[45] Those who are willing to credit Melville's ethnology were on the right track, as is now known.[46]

The problem of authenticity was given no thought by the two other May reviewers, both of whom merely told of their enjoyment. The *Merchant's Magazine and Commercial Review* adjudged that *Typee* would be "popular" and appeared to find it, for all its colorfulness, reliable enough: "The perfect *sang froid* exhibited in his intercourse with the cannibals, and ease with which he seemed to regard the delights, hopes, and fears of his Polynesian life give a particular richness to the book. . . . The faithfulness of the descriptions and narrative give it a peculiar charm, and few can read without a thrill the glowing pictures." For the delighted *Godey's Lady's Magazine and Book* in May, *Typee* was merely the most attractive of travel books: "It is extremely interesting—the regions in which the author makes his observations being untrodden ground, and the scenes striking to an unusual degree. American travellers surpass all others in the liveliness and freedom of their descriptions." There could be a patriotic attitude toward our literature among Philadelphians as well as among the Young Americans of New York.

Yet in the letter of May 23 already referred to, Melville showed bitter dissatisfaction with the Americans. He declared that he "could not but feel heartily vexed that while the intelligent Editors of a publication like that [*Chambers' Edinburgh Journal*] should endorse the genuineness of the narrative—so many numbskulls on this side

45. Suggested by Leyda, *Log,* p. 216.
46. Anderson, p. 190.

of the water should heroically avow their determination not to be
'gulled' by it. The fact is, those who do not believe are the greatest
'gulls'—full fledged ones too." Melville had perhaps seen some skeptical American notices which I have not found, but it is likely he was
mainly venting his pique at Peck. Actually, after the gracious recantation in Fuller's paper, Peck remained the one and only "heroically" professing secular American doubter, unless he added Peck's echo, Clark,
and even that made only two. There was in May one vocal enough
religious doubter, the *New York Evangelist,* to be discussed later.
There had been only three others who mentioned "romancing" but
not in disparagement. On the other hand, there had been six actual
defenses of the truth of the book, besides eleven items in which credence was clearly implicit or explicit. As of May 23, the American
score might be totalled,[47] even including the mildest doubters, as six
against to sixteen for authenticity, and in England five against to only
five for. This was the first of several times when Melville allowed
one virulent attack to color his whole outlook.

He should have been cheered by the appearance before long of
another champion, a popular American woman journalist. In London, most of the questioners had acted like gentlemen, but only in
New York did a lady come to his rescue. Expressing wonder why
she had "never chanced" upon the book before, Sarah Jane Lippincott
signed with her *nom de plume* Grace Greenwood a supposed affidavit
in the *Home Journal*: "While luxuriating in its perusal, I looked back
upon myself in my ante-Typee-cal existence with positive commisera-
tion. There are those who doubt the authenticity of his charming
narrative. 'Oh, ye of little faith!' I have a solemn conviction of its
truth—a pertinacious belief in the entire work—an humble, unques-
tioning reliance on the word of the author." Such gallant support
must have shown Melville that the Americans had not all deserted
him.

We do know Melville's spirits were immensely raised by the arrival in the lists on July 1 of the most powerful of all imaginable
allies in his battle to convince the world he had not lied. Toby,
Tommo's pal in jumping ship and in Typee Valley, who to get help
for his lamed friend, had gone over the mountains and had not been
heard of since—Toby was disclosed to be alive, as Richard Tobias
Greene of Buffalo, New York, and ready to fight by Tommo's side.

---

47. These calculations include the notices in the May numbers of American
magazines, some of which might not yet have been published. The proportions,
however, would be little different if the May numbers were not included.

Picture Tommo's joy to find in the Buffalo *Commercial Advertiser* for July 1 a letter from Greene, who had been roused by the attack on *Typee* as "too romantic to be true" on May 9 in the New York *Evangelist,* offering public testimony to his old shipmate's veracity. Consequent events followed fast. Toby's letter was reprinted on July 3 in two rival Albany papers, the Democratic *Argus* and Whig Thurlow Weed's *Evening Journal.*[48] To Tommo, Toby wrote a more detailed report, revealing that he had been lured, with promises of help for his friend, onto a whaler which promptly sailed away; a copy of this second letter appeared in the Buffalo paper on July 11, and was reprinted in Weed's paper two days later. The *Courier* now finally gave in, and on July 11 reprinted Toby's first letter with a fairly adequate brief recantation. Before July was over, Tommo and Toby met, four years and a week after parting. Meanwhile on July 12, the Boston *Puritan Recorder,* unaware of Toby's resurrection, attested: "The author has 'spun a yarn' that will not only interest the seaman; but many a landsman will hold on to the book until he has read the last page."

Melville on July 15 clearly enjoyed writing the still suspicious Murray about Toby, and telling him about the revised edition already planned by Wiley and Putnam, to contain Toby's story as a "Sequel."[49] Actually Melville was to send the "Sequel" to Murray to publish first because of an unexpected delay in getting out the revised American edition. Melville must have seen some recent comments from the still faithful or newly converted which I have not located, when he wrote on September 2 to Murray: "They believe it here now—a little touched up they say but true."[50]

Toby's reappearance did not, however, convert the Washington *National Intelligencer's* critic, who reviewing *Omoo* on May 26 and 28, 1847, discussed *Typee* at length, having overlooked it the year before. He asked, "What sailor will not stand up for the yarns of a messmate ashore?" What was the proof of Toby's identity? He preferred to believe Toby was "made a *rôti suffoqué* of, was boucanisé a la Polynésiènne." How hard-hearted! Yet the *Intelligencer,* a very influential

---

48. Weed added the comment that Toby's testimony only increased "our doubts"; but three days later, after a protesting visit from Melville, published a half-hearted retraction (Davis, p. 22). Davis gives a detailed account of the plans for the revised edition. Weed was the first real political boss of New York state.

49. *Log,* p. 222.

50. *Log,* p. 226.

Whig paper with a long, distinguished history, was to prove a great admirer of Melville.

The approach of the *Intelligencer's* reviewer recalled the London reviews, which he had obviously digested. There was the condescension, the urbanity, the denial of literal veracity, but all in such terms as to be highly flattering to *Typee* as an achievement in belles-lettres: "Typee was not intended or expected to be scrupulously matter-of-fact, but is justifiably embellished as in a 'Sentimental Journey.' . . . There was a debate about its actuality in England . . . Melville has shown himself an adept in sustaining the *illusion of truth* . . . we read it with as much delight and faith as we read Grimm's fairy tales. The author, of course, maintains the authenticity—that is his business." More fully than any other contemporary reviewer, he gave detailed arguments— some sound—to show that "Typee was but a very agreeable and fanciful sea romance"[51] yet finally adjudged it "a literary performance of great merit and beauty."

It remained for Charles Anderson to divide the old question, "Did Melville tell the truth in *Typee?*" into its two logically component questions: "Is the book correct ethnologically?" and "Are its events literally autobiographical?" Because no reviewer quite achieved this analysis—which, after it has been pointed out, seems so obvious—one, thinking of ethnology, would affirm the book's veracity, and the next, thinking of autobiography, would deny it, or more justly, hint at romantic coloring. To the first question, Anderson has shown the answer is essentially "Yes." To the second, his answer, and that of others, has been "Yes," but with qualifications. The second question may never receive a complete answer. Melville was sincere, says Rosenberry, in his assertions that he had told of the events just as they had occurred, as his quick resentment at disbelief revealed: "it was at least the brand of truth that came naturally to his countrymen in reporting wonders."[52] As to more tangible points, it is now certain he was in Typee Valley three weeks, and five days, instead of four months as

51. He tried to establish five points: (1) There was poetic exaggeration in the height of the cliffs [True]; (2) The alighting of the boys in the palm trees was fantastic [I have seen similar alighting done in the movies and by mountain climbers]; (3) No one would go into a valley of man eaters [The book makes it clear the boys did it quite unintentionally]; (4) The account of the manners and customs was scanty [Perhaps, but it has been shown to be mainly correct—Anderson, p. 156-78]; (5) The actions of the natives were obviously concocted to give "thrilling interest" [undoubtedly, partly true].

52. *Op. cit.*, p. 11.

in the book.[53] Robert S. Forsythe's comment made twenty years ago
is still essentially valid: "Melville was not attacked even by the most
skeptical of the reviewers" for "the chief liberty taken—it may well be
the only liberty"—that with time.[54]

Evidently Melville did not feel the deep resentment toward those
who pilloried him as a "traducer of missions," that he did toward "the
parcel of blockheads," as he described them to Murray, who were not
sure he had ever been "at the Marquesas." Yet the onslaught made
on his first book by the American journals of professional piety was a
terrific one. These lumbering organs, however, got into action slowly,
and so it happened that the first two American allusions to the evaluation in *Typee* of missionary efforts had been in support of Melville.
They had both come on the same day, April 4, and both from transcendentalists. Indeed, a low enough opinion of missionaries had been
shown in "Self-Reliance" by Emerson himself.

George Ripley's defense was the milder of the two. He wrote in the
Harbinger that Melville had not impeached the honesty of the aims
of the missionaries, but only regarded them as injudicious, and that
other bad Caucasian influences had come in, especially in the Sandwich
Islands. As for the sketch of the missionary's wife drawn in her
carriage by natives, Ripley said that "equally menial and desecrating
menial servitude and caste distinctions can be found near and within
our metropolitan churches."

The other defense came from Margaret Fuller, who may well have
discussed the book with her friend Ripley, as they were in essential
agreement. Her barbed and witty comment on the missions comprised
almost half her review in the *Tribune*. Melville was correct about
them, she thought. She suggested that the "sewing circles now engaged in providing funds for such enterprises" should read "beginning
p. 249. vol. 2nd, in Chapter XXVI and make inquiries in consequence,
before going on with their efforts." She added ironically: "Generally
the sewing circles of the country villages will find this the very book
to read while assembled at their work. Othello's hairbreadth 'scapes
were nothing to those by the hero in the descent of cataracts, and
many a Desdemona might seriously incline her ear to the descriptions
of the lovely Fayaway." The brilliant feminist undoubtedly enjoyed
penning this thrust at conventionally pious women. Had she not
shown excellent pedagogy in piquing the ladies' curiosity by assigning

53. Howard, p. 52.
54. "Herman Melville in the Marquesas," *Philological Quarterly*, X (January,
1936), 15.

them a specific page for reading? These two were the only Americans, before the appearance of *Omoo,* who are known to have seconded Melville's judgment on the missionaries.

Most other secular critics were either uninterested or glad enough to evade the problem. Hoffman in the *Gazette* noted Melville's severity in describing the missionaries but turned the matter over to those "better qualified to judge than we secular journalists." He did say that the "representations" of a man of Melville's fine family background would awaken attention. The only lay demur was an incidental one from the *American Review.*

The religious attacks in the United States were not numerous—I have found only five which antedated *Omoo*—but they were vituperative. The first blast had come on April 9 in a long article signed "H. C."[55] in the New York *Evangelist,* a Congregational newspaper. Prevaricating fictitiousness was the central charge, along with immorality: "If this be not sheer romance (which there is reason to suspect), it is the extremely exaggerated, but racily written narrative of a forecastle runaway from an American whaleship," who like the fish in the fable "jumped out of the frying pan into the fire. He had life among the Marquesean cannibals to his liking; a plenty of what pleases the vicious appetite of a sailor, or of sensual human nature generally." Then came strong resentment about the missions: "The book abounds in praise of the life of nature, alias savageism, and in slurs and flings against missionaries and civilization. When the author alludes to or touches matters of fact at the Sandwich Islands, he shows the sheerest ignorance, and utter disregard of truth."

Quaintly enough, "H. C." assumed the moral superiority of America to that great center of iniquity, London: "The work was made, not for America, but for a circle, and that not the highest, in London, where theatres, opera-dancers, and voluptuous prints have made such unblushing walks along the edge of modesty as are . . . rather more admired than we hope they are among us. We are sorry that such a volume should have been allowed a place in the 'Library of American Books' [Wiley and Putnam's]. It can only have been without reading it beforehand, and from deference to the publisher on the other side." Here was another aspect of the British market which some thought would influence an American author.

55. This signature indicates that the author was not, as Leyda (*Log,* p. 210) suggests, the Reverend George B. Cheever. This newspaper had been founded in 1832 to "promote revivals and missions, temperance and other reforms" (Mott, *American Magazines,* p. 373).

The religious sectarians gave *Typee* a bad time in July by taking it to task in three of their publications. The *Christian Parlor Magazine,* a similarly embellished, but less worldly rival of the "ladies' books,"[56] outdid the *Evangelist,* in a ten-page attack in July, under the heading, "Typee: The Traducer of Missions." The editor and probable reviewer was the Reverend Darius Mead, who "catered to the sentiments and prejudices of the fundamentalist devout."[57] "An apotheosis of barbarism! A panegyric on cannibal delights! An apostrophe to the spirit of savage felicity!" was the preacher's opening charge. There was no reason to doubt his assertion that he had "read this book word for word." He had expected information; but he was "soon disappointed"; for "instead of a calm and unbiased view," the book was "a tissue of misrepresentation, and detraction of the devoted men and women who have exiled themselves" to carry "the blessings of the gospel to some of the most degraded and benighted children of Adam." Literary charms, indeed, he found: "With a lively imagination and a good and often graceful description, together with a somewhat happy strain of narrative, he has written an attractive history of personal adventure and unwilling abandon among the happy and sequestered Typees." Ordinarily, he would not have regarded such a trivial work "worth an extended notice," but its publishers and its dedication to Justice Shaw "had given it respectability."

Melville, however, according to the *Parlor Magazine* reviewer, was guilty of "the most palpable and absurd contradictions." He expressed skepticism as to whether the author had ever seen the Marquesas and gave extensive passages from Wilkes in confutation. To show how horrible had been the original status of the Polynesians, he called attention to Wilkes's story of how "on February 11, 1840, Messrs. Hunt and Lythe, with their ladies, missionaries to Carolib or Goat Island were witnesses to a cannibal entertainment" at which at least thirty persons were eaten. "Mr. Hunt saw eleven bodies brought in and one cooked and eaten within two yards of him."[58] The parting

56. *Ibid.,* p. 745. The *Christian Parlor* aimed to combat the "overwhelming flood of impure and corrupting literature."

57. Mentor L. Williams, "Notices of Melville's Novels in Religious Periodicals 1846-1849," *American Literature,* XXII (May, 1950), 119-127. On July 31, Rufus Anderson, secretary of the American Board of Commissioners of Foreign Missions, added a postscript to a large book order sent to Wiley and Putnam: "I have read *Melville's* 'Typee' with great regret that it bears the respectable name & sanction of your House" (*Log,* p. 224).

58. Commodore Charles Wilkes, *Narrative of the U. S. Exploring Expedition 1837-1842,* 5 vols. (Philadelphia, 1845).

shot was that whether the book was "true or false, the real or pseudonymic author deserves a pointed and severe rebuke for his flagrant rages against civilization."

Equally harsh, though not so long-winded, was William C. Bourne, in the July *New Englander*,[59] representing the Congregational orthodoxy of which Yale was still a stronghold. The "free and easy style" of *Typee* first made him suppose the "errors" were "unintentional" but he soon decided the author was "actuated, either by a perverse spirit of intentional misrepresentation, or that he is utterly incapable, from moral obtuseness, of an accurate statement . . . he was fretted out of humor with civilized life . . . what he remembered of the Islands of the Pacific had become a sort of confused mass in his own brain. . . . If he meets a native female Islander, she is a goddess; if a missionary's wife, she is a blowsy, red-faced oppressor of the poor native—reducing him to the state of drudge. . . . Of the truths of general history, he seems to know nothing . . . whenever civilization comes in contact with savage life, there the savage wastes away. . . . For the first time seeing this fact, he gives his own crude explanation of it . . . and would have the world then receive his volume as a work of authority."

Contemptuous as he was, Bourne had to admit the book was "not without literary merit. It is a very companionable one. As a specimen of the lighter writing of the day, it is entitled to notice"; but his final blow was a bracketing of Melville with the Mormons: "But as to the writer's ability to treat on some of the matters of his volume, it would rank well with Joseph Smith's competency to give an exegetical work on the book of Genesis."

In July also, a spokesman for a more liberal church, in the Boston *Universalist Review*, chastised the errant writer more briefly and tactfully.[60] Granted, the book was "very interesting," and instructive too, if there "were not a strong coloring of the romantic thrown over the descriptions, and an evident attempt in the management of the narrative." How much was fact and how much imagination? Yet the pictures "seemed to bring the objects before our eyes." A philosophical disagreement with Melville's judgment of the missions followed: this

59. Williams carelessly classifies this magazine as "lay" (*op. cit.*). Mott says "It was one of the best of the religious quarterlies" (p. 315). He also says it was characterized by "congregationalism in theology," by "adherence to strictly orthodox morals," and that it was "the child of Yale" (p. 313). Bourne's known authorship of the later attack on *Omoo* in this magazine surely justifies the assumption that he wrote in similar vein about *Typee*.

60. The editor of the *Universalist and General Quarterly Review* was Hosea Ballou, II (Mott, *American Magazines*, p. 372).

reviewer suspected "that the voluptuousness . . . in the valley of Typee, had somewhat affected his own taste; and if so he would be apt to regard as evils many of those changes introduced by the missionaries, which would appear to others as improvements. Indeed we must not look for unmixed advantages in any state of social progress . . . . In judging of the results of the enterprise, great care ought to be taken not to fix on the partial inconveniences, and even downright evils to the exclusion of the general good with which they are naturally connected."

Last and bitterest of the religious attacks on *Typee* alone, was the five-page review in May, 1847, in the orthodox Boston *Christian Observatory*,[61] which, fortunately for its equanimity, was unaware of the recent publication of the even more anti-missionary *Omoo*. The *Observatory* was nearly unique in declaring *Typee* meagre not only in "truth" but in "literary merit." The style was "vivacious," but "the attempts at wit are so constant and laborious, that they are far from pleasing to a chaste mind."

The main aim of the *Observatory* was to refute Melville's thesis that the culture of the Typees was superior to that of "Christian communities." Melville was actually setting up the "Typeean system of morals and religion" as better than that of Christianity as "judged by the fruits of both." The gospel, forsooth, had conferred nothing! Indeed ". . . let us eat raw fish, and have a plurality of husbands . . . let us now and then taste a little human flesh!" "All this depreciation of Christian communities, compared with cannibals," the author "justified on the ground that thousands in Christian lands live contrary to the gospel! A man who reasons thus has little knowledge of Christianity." Throughout, the missionaries were "disparaged and ridiculed," their work described as "fruitless and mischievous," but missionaries were "more worthy of respect and confidence than is Melville," to prove which point the *Observatory* cited Wilkes. English missionaries had triumphed in the East, in spite of attacks in "reputable literary journals," attacks "marked by wit and learning, and rhetorical skill, to which" *Typee* "can make no pretensions."

Melville's first two books were ultimately to arouse the greatest religious tempest, outside of New England, in Hawaii. The comments of the *Polynesian*, edited in Honolulu by the Reverend Mr. James J. Jarvis, tended always to be tinged with jocularity, which later became

61. According to the "Introduction" to the 1847 volume, the policy of this magazine was based on "the good old Scriptural orthodoxy of New England," and the Congregational form of church government.

much more sarcastic. Its first reaction, on October 3, 1846, was rather frivolous, a protest against the aspersions cast on the inelegance of the missionary ladies' equipages by Melville, who would "be astonished at the present display of . . . fashion in these turnouts," though the costume of the human steeds had improved "not a whit." Was the missionary reviewer here approving Melville's satire?[62] On October 17, the *Polynesian* reprinted the New Bedford *Mercury* review, remarking that while some critics had wondered whether *Typee* was "genuine," they united in considering it "clever."

No American lay writer for the press seems to have raised the slightest objection to *Typee* on moral grounds during 1846. Of the four religious commentators even, two hinted protests, and only one made a direct attack. The Christian *Parlor Magazine,* pious competitor of *Godey's Lady's Book,* had satirized Melville's preference for savages by pretending to be so gripped by his art as to be forced to burst into this apostrophe which Freud would no doubt have regarded with great interest. "Come, oh yearning soul of the angelic Fayaway, let me henceforth be the chosen partner of thy tabooed pleasures. . . ." The *Parlor* saw the author as one of those deserters from vessels "whom Wilkes blames for introducing vices." That was all, in a long review.

The sole frontal attack in 1846 on the immorality had thus been that of the *Evangelist,* whose most explicitly accusing sentences were these: "We have long noted it as true in criticism, that what makes a large class of books, bad, immoral, and consequently injurious, is not so much what is plainly expressed, as what is left to be imagined by the reader. Apply this rule to the work in hand, and while everyone will admit it is written with an attractive vivacity, and (except what is palpably lies) with great good humor, it cannot escape a severe condemnation."

What a different ethical air had been breathed by a critic, a bit Puritan, but flexible, who had found in the author a "freedom of view—it would be too harsh to call it laxity of principle—which renders him tolerant of codes of morals that may be little in accordance with our own," but such as were "proper" to a young sailor and which made "his book the more wholesome to staid landsmen." The critic was Hawthorne.

---

62. Reverend Mr. Samuel C. Damon, on October 15, said in the Honolulu *Friend* that he was hoping to get a copy of *Typee,* of which he had been led to entertain a favorable opinion.

George Ripley, in the *Harbinger,* had been one of the two Americans who had explicitly endorsed the Utopian implications in *Typee,* which have so appealed to modern critics, especially Lewis Mumford.[63] The *Mirror* had shown approving interest, but of the other American journals, only the religious had noted Melville's defense of the Typee way of life, but they had condemned it as anti-Christian.

Ripley had considered the Marquesan culture as not only alluring, but even instructive. The basis of this ideal society was that "there is *abundance for every person,* and thus the most fruitful cause of the selfishness and crime of our enlightened and philosophic situation does not exist there. Here is the lesson which the leaders of this nineteenth century may learn from the Typee." An even higher degree of felicity could be attained with our "greater refinement and intelligence and our higher religious development" if we only had equable distribution of wealth. "Let associated, cooperative labor once take the place of the drudgery of our gloomy manufactures, the dullness of our agriculture, and the poverty of our cities, and we shall no longer need to look to the islanders of the South Seas for examples of social virtues and happiness." Until the disastrous fire of March 3, the *Harbinger* had been published at Brook Farm, and Ripley was still managing to get it out at nearby West Roxbury.[64] His meditation on *Typee* showed that his transcendental and Fourieristic hopes for the regeneration of mankind had survived the end of his experimental colony.

The other serious and appreciative student of Typee Valley as a Utopia was the *National Anti-Slavery Standard* (in its May 27, 1847, review of *Omoo*), which as could be expected, had a different basis for its approbation.[65] It seconded the broader implications: "In truth, Typee resolved 'the problem of the age,' and proved that happiness was not only possible without the aid of pastry cooks, lawyers, tailors, and clergymen, but that men would be happier without these excrescences of civilization." Its main concern, however, was to show how the Utopian strain was virtually anti-slavery propaganda, because the cannibals were really more humane to their enemies than the Southerners to their slaves:

It proved another important fact, the most important of all facts for Americans, that Slavery is not . . . indigenous to the tropics. It is true

63. *Herman Melville* (New York, 1929), p. 68. "Typee is Melville's Walden," says Mumford.

64. Mott, *American Magazines,* p. 764.

65. The review of *Omoo,* like that of *Typee,* was signed "B."

that the Typees eat their enemies, but then they do not eat them alive; they have the humanity to wait until their victims are dead before they begin to feast upon them. Here we reverse the rule, and feed on each other while living. One dead enemy was sufficient to feast a whole tribe of Typees; but with us a hundred slaves hardly suffice to furnish food for one Southern family. The Typee munches the muscles and tendons of his dead enemy between his molars, but inflicts no pain upon him; but with us the Calhoons, Clays, and Polks, feed daily upon the sweat, the tears, the groans, the despairing hearts, of living men and women; they do not eat the insensible flesh of their dead slaves, but they lacerate it when alive with whips and cauterize it with hot branding irons. We would advise our readers who are sick at heart, from reading the daily reports of the murders committed by our army in Mexico; or of the inhuman cruelties of our slaveholders at the South; or of the daily outrages upon the rights of humanity practiced by Christian judges, and lawyers in the Halls of Justice, to turn for relief to the amiable savages of Typee, whose greatest cruelty consists in devouring the body of an enemy who has been killed in a hand to hand scuffle.

The *Standard* also liked the novelty: "New, fresh, devil may care; free from the dry, stale, and wearisome conventionalities of trained literature" was this book, "not made from the pickings from other books, but from the personal observations . . . of the author." This spicy review seems to justify the claim of Edward Everett Hale that the *Standard* was a "brilliant *exception*" to the "proverbial dullness" of "organs of causes."[66]

AMERICAN REACTION TO *TYPEE* AFTER *OMOO*

More than with Melville's later books, the reaction to *Typee*, in both countries continued, as the years passed, to be favorable. Reviewers fell into a kind of tradition of beginning by allusion to its dramatic success, along with eulogy, often extravagant, of its delights. Especially when they were puzzled by the book at hand, they looked back with nostalgia to Melville's first fruitage. Among a vast number of illustrations, a few will suffice. The comment of the *Columbian Magazine,* in a review of *Omoo,* has become almost common coin: "The author of *Typee,* like Byron, went to bed unknown to find himself famous when he got up in the morning. *Typee* has been read, we suppose, by every man, woman, and child in the Union who undertakes to keep pace at all with the march of current literature." The *Democratic Review* described *Mardi* as written "in the style of *Omoo*

66. *James Russell Lowell* (New York, 1898), p. 172. Lowell was then an associate editor.

and *Typee*, books that made the multitude crazy with delight." Colonel Greene of Boston, before executing *Mardi*, said that the reputation of the author of *Typee* and *Omoo* was high, but "we have always thought it not so high as it ought to be"; for these works were not only graceful but powerful, and the reviewers had not "done justice to his knowledge of human nature." The *Southern Literary Messenger*, before crucifying *Pierre*, said, "Few books ever rose as rapidly and deservedly into popular favor as *Typee*."

The resurrection of Toby, and the continuation of Melville's adventures in *Omoo*, a more autobiographical work, settled the doubts about actuality—except for the few die-hards, chiefly British. The second book, however, added fuel to the fires of the evangelicals who took offense at his deflation of the missions, and of the few who were bent on detecting licentiousness.

Even though it was a small minority numerically who expressed in print resentment of Melville's criticism of the missions, and even fewer who spoke against his frankness, they must have made an impression on his publishers, for before many months after the first edition, Wiley and Putnam brought out a revised expurgated edition. Bernard de Voto discovered that there had already been second and third issues of the first American edition, and that there were three successive stages of increasing bowdlerization, culminating in the revised edition.[67] Melville may have not been consulted about the changes in the later issues of the first edition. Meanwhile, it was a bit of a joke on Murray that he brought out a reprinting of the first English edition with no changes except the addition of the "Story of Toby."[68]

In the new preface Melville wrote for the revised edition, he gladly seized the opportunity to reaffirm the truth of his tale; but he also minimized the importance of the alterations. (Did he want to believe them minor? Did the publishers feel this was politic?) According to the new preface "several passages, wholly unconnected with" the main adventure "have been rejected as irrelevant. . . . Here and there some slight modifications of style have also been added." Actually someone had performed what was little less than a mutilation—removal of all attacks on the missionaries, the French, and the evil effects of civilization. Nor were the "modifications of style" really "slight," as they included the removal of many specific

67. "Editions of Typee," *Saturday Review of Literature*, V (November 24, 1928), 406. The bibliography of the second edition is complex, and only the main aspects are given here.

68. Minnegerode, p. 109.

descriptions of sexual life and of native costumes—or lack thereof.[69]

There was no widespread interest in these changes. I have found only one press comment—indeed a peppery one—on the "moral" expurgations in the revised edition. They were by no means thorough enough to satisfy a Honolulu contributor, probably the Reverend Mr. Samuel C. Damon, on June 1, 1847, in the *Friend*:[70] "If the author had erased other passages, we think he would have shown good judgment and exhibited a 'sober second thought.' " Thereby he could have suppressed "those glaring facts respecting his habits of gross and shameless familiarity, not to say licentiousness, with a tribe of debased and filthy savages of Marquesas. . . . In Chapter XVII, revised edition, there is the following remark, 'Bathing in company with some troups of girls formed one of my chief amusements!'—Scores, aye, hundreds of passages might be quoted, showing that the writer sunk lower than the debased people among whom he took his temporary abode."

On the other hand, the deletion of sections exposing the missions was vigorously condemned by a seconder of Melville's censure of Protestant proselyting, the *United States Catholic Magazine and Monthly Review*, in November, 1847: "Let it be remembered that in the second edition of *Typee*, the passages reflecting most severely upon the Sandwich Island missions were expunged. And whoever may thus have aimed to prevent the dissemination of truth, that hypocrisy might flourish a little longer, let him be held up to deserved ridicule and scorn."

Harper and Brothers, to whom by then Melville had assigned the exclusive American rights to *Typee*, issued a reprinting of the revised edition about May 25, 1849,[71] thus eliciting statements from two religious magazines. The *Evangelist* on July 5, repeated what it had said about the first edition, admitting the "literary merit" and "poetic genius," but deploring the "degraded moral tone," the "slanderous attacks on the missionaries," the "unquestioned falsehood from beginning to end"; yet did not specifically note the expurgations. The *Biblical Repository and Classical Review* for October 1849, found in this "entertaining writer" some "romantic exaggeration," and applauded the fact that "the good sense of the author" and the "moral

69. Haraszti, p. 208. See also Minnegerode, pp. 110-123, wherein detailing of the revisions requires thirteen pages.

70. The *Friend* was self-described as "Semi-Monthly Journal devoted to Temperance, Marine and General Intelligence, Published and Edited by Samuel C. Damon, Seaman's Chaplain."

71. *Log*, p. 305.

sentiments of the world," had "constrained him . . . to strike out those parts which related to missionary operations in Tahiti and the Sandwich Islands, which contained assertions reckless and charges gratuitous and false."

There was secular approval, too, of these excisions. The *American Review* in August, 1849, may not have been aware of the nature of the changes: "This is a very elegant edition of the popular work of Mr. Melville, with his own revisal and improvements." Nor aware in December was *DeBow's Commercial Review of the South and West,* which merely remarked that the "extraordinary popularity" had called for a "revised edition" of a work which combined "the attractiveness of elevated romance" with "truthful views of life in the far distant isles. . . ." But *Sartain's Union Magazine,* also in November, was aware: "Among the improvements is the omission of certain parts relating to Tahiti and the Sandwich Islands, which in their original form gave much discontent without being at all necessary to the completeness of the narrative." The book was "one of the choicest collections of adventures extant." Thus no one seems to have commented explicitly on the absence of the "voluptuous" passages in the Harpers' edition.

The other known commentator on the 1849 edition was quite unconcerned about morality and religion. It was probably Dr. J. G. Holland who on July 7, 1849, had said in the Springfield *Republican*[72] that it was "no small merit to have written a book so consistent in its details, and so plausible and harmonious in its plot that the reading world is wholly undecided whether it be entirely true or entirely false."

Because the opinions of the French critic Philarète Chasles were reprinted by the Duyckincks and others in America, they might be considered part of Melville's American reputation.[73] Chasles came to the conclusion (truer for England than for America, and probably true for France) that Melville's first two books had been generally

---

72. For this and other items from this paper I am indebted to an article by Jay Leyda, "Another Friendly Critic for Melville," *New England Quarterly,* XXVII (June, 1954), 243-249. Holland became Associate Editor on May 24, 1849.

73. "Voyages réels et fantastiques d'Herman Melville," *Revue des deux mondes,* n. s. 2 (15 mai, 1849), 542-570. Some of his materials on *Typee* had already been used in "Sejour des deux Américains chez les Taipies, dans L'île Noukahiva," *Journal des débats* (22 juin, 1846). Extracts from the *Revue des deux mondes* article were translated and inserted into the Boston *Daily Advertiser* on June 15, 1849, and into the Albany *Argus* on June 18; and George Duyckinck translated the whole and published it in two installments, on August 4 and 11, in the *Literary World.* For later publication of this Chasles material in America, see below, Chapter IV, footnote 44.

received as fictions, and that Toby had convinced nobody: "Toby se porte caution de Melville qui se porte caution de Toby . . . Mascarille répand de Jodelet et Jodelet de Mascarille." The gallery was thereby amused, and there was a piquant introduction of "des Hazards de jeu" into the domain of literature. He had decided, nevertheless, that these books had told the truth; for *Typee* and *Omoo* were the "voyages réels" of his 1849 Paris article, while *Mardi* was the "voyage fantastique." He had made his deduction first from internal evidence: "J'y voyais un écrivain moins habile a s'amuser d'un rêve et jouer avec un nuage que gêne d'un souvenir puissant qui l'obsède." The young author used violent Rubens-like color, and strained for dramatic effect, but he was basically veracious. Then Chasles had chanced on external evidence also. He had met an American citizen (identified by Leyda as Thomas Gold Appleton), who assured him Melville was a real person—apparently this had been questioned in France as well as in England—and reported testimony of Melville's cousin (identified by Leyda as Robert Melville, two years Herman's senior) that Herman had recounted real experiences.[74] Chasles agreed with the cousin that *Omoo* was a "pâle contre-epreuve," while such things in *Typee* as the meeting of the boys with the savages had the "qualité de vie."

What were the final words on *Typee* from the chief American critics who were aware of its author? The Duyckincks in their *Cyclopaedia* (1856) ascribed the great success of this "glowing picturesque narrative" largely to the realization of the growing importance of the Pacific. Fitz-James O'Brien twice, in 1853 and again in 1857, published essays in *Putnam's Magazine* in each of which he assessed Melville's works to date.[75] Clearly his favorite was *Typee*. In the earlier essay he advanced a theory (surely disproved by Melville's later work even if partly true for *Typee*): "Matter is his god. His dreams are material. His philosophy is sensual"; and offered in substantiation Melville's obsession with beautiful women. It was "this sensual power"

74. The cousin claimed to have seen Melville's *"Rough Notes"* on his voyage in the hands of Justice Shaw, but they have never been found, and Melville said in the preface to *Omoo* that he had kept no journal (Anderson, p. 189). Professor Charles E. West, a former teacher of Melville, who had instructed him at the Albany Classical Institute, had been disturbed that his pupil who had been notable for truthfulness had sent out such a pack of lies as *Typee,* and was relieved when an ancient mariner who had been to Typee Valley assured him they were facts (*Log,* p. 286).

75. "Our Young Authors—Melville," February, 1853: "Our Authors and Authorship—Melville and Curtis," April, 1857. As the first article was in the very first number of *Putnam's* it may well have been widely read.

that held the "secret of Mr. Melville's first success." (Did not O'Brien here mean what today we would mean by sensuous?) He confessed his relish of the Fayaway scenes, and noted the Utopian implications. In his second essay he still ranked *Typee* first, and spoke of the intensity of the vicarious experience it afforded. It revealed "a man's large nature, and quick sympathy with all things beautiful and strong" and "in style and form . . . a rare degree of ripeness and perfection."

Typee was becoming, in a way in which none of Melville's other books did in that century, a part of the national legend. "Grace Greenwood," in the *Saturday Evening Post* for October 9, 1847, cleverly used the Typeean Utopia as a medium through which to project her satire on the shabby treatment of authors in America (especially as a result of the absence of copyright legislation). She indited a supposed letter from Melville in which he said that he had no personal complaint, as his book had sold better than he had expected, but that he found a painful contrast between the humble status of the poet in America and of the poet in Typee land, who was given a choice lodge, abundant poeepoee, the "choicest bit when an enemy is dished up," a body servant "degraded to present position" for writing a "cutting review" of the poet, and an entranced audience for his public chantings. William Ellery Channing produced in 1847 his "The Island Nukeheva," eight pages of heroic couplets more notable as eulogy of the romantic delights and ideal life in Typee Valley than as poetry.[76] Melville was among the literary and other lions at Anne C. Lynch's gay New York party on Valentine's Day, 1848, where his Valentine, composed by Bayard Taylor, expressed the hope that "some guardian angel" would *"Taboo"* from every ill the "Bright painter of these tropic isles."[77] In Massachusetts *Typee* had been read aloud in 1846 in the Longfellow household;[78] on Long Island, Joann Miller, friend of George Duyckinck, was "enamoured" of it;[79] and even out in the High Sierras, "Dame Shirley" called it in her published letters in 1851 a "beautiful romance."[80] It became the prey of a plagiarizer.[81] It was read and reread as it was by a brilliant and perceptive woman:

76. *Poems, Second Series* (Boston, 1847), pp. 144-152.

77. The Valentine was published in the *Home Journal* for March 4.

78. *Log,* p. 223. Fanny Longfellow, a summer boarder with "Typee's cousin" Robert near Pittsfield, headed a letter "Melville Hall, Typee Valley" on July 28, 1848 (*Log,* p. 278).

79. *Log,* p. 299.

80. Van Wyck Brooks, *The Times of Melville and Whitman* (New York, 1947), p. 142.

81. *Log,* p. 313.

"I have just read again Typee. It is a *true history,* yet how poetically told—the divine beauty of the scene, the lovely faces & forms—the peace & good will—& all the golden splendor & enchantment glowing before the dark refrain constantly brought as a background—the fear of being killed and eaten—the cannibalism in the olive tinted Apollos around him—the unfathomable mystery of their treatment of him." So Sophia Hawthorne wrote to her mother in the autumn of 1850 from the Berkshire Hills.[82]

Nothing could show more clearly its vogue than the protests from those who thought things had gone far enough. Lowell groaned in September, 1848, "I am heartily sick of Typee"—a pun: he was also sick of proof-reading.[83] Donald G. Mitchell in the *Lorgnette* for 1850 satirized the prevalence of the "Jane Eyre malady" and the "Typee disorder."[84]

Other evidence that *Typee* continued to remain during its author's lifetime his best known book, came from the printers. It was reprinted, before 1891, ten times in America and seven in England, definitely outstripping its nearest rival, *Omoo,* which was reprinted seven times in America and six in England.[85]

Evidence of the hold *Typee* took on the popular mind included the symptoms of various sorts of the fascination of what Channing called in his poem "the sweet shape of Fayaway." Travellers to Typee tried to locate Melville's characters, but especially his inamorata. Their reports showed the current interest in the love story, even if they were inconclusive in proving or disproving the real existence of the girl. Lieutenant Harry A. Wise, U.S.N., saw in November, 1848, "a damsel named Fayaway from Typee Valley," ironing the trousers of the French official, but decided finally she might not be the "genuine Fayaway" after all.[86] Highly educated Alfred G. Jones was in Typee Valley on August 24, 1854, where he met Te Moena (Melville's

82. Eleanor Melville Metcalf, *Herman Melville: Cycle and Epicycle* (Cambridge, 1953), p. 91.

83. *Letters of James Russell Lowell,* ed. Charles Eliot Norton (New York, 1894), p. 141.

84. The *Lorgnette or Studies of the Town by an Opera Goer* (New York, 1850), I, No. 12, 227. It was a collection of papers which had appeared serially during the year. Later Mitchell became well known as "Ik Marvel," author of light essays, including *Reveries of a Bachelor.*

85. Minnegerode, pp. 124, 132.

86. *Log,* p. 281. Wise later worked these items up into his popular *Los Gringos* (London, 1848), wherein he paid tribute to the charm and to the correctness of Melville's pictures of island life (p. 325).

Mowanna), and also an interpreter who had lived on the islands twenty-five years, and who recalled Melville himself, as well as, among others of his characters, the then dead Kory-Kory and Mow Mow, but "no Fayaway," as indeed their language did "not admit of such a name."[87] E. K. Drayton, physician of the U.S.S. *St. Mary's,* visited Nukuheva in 1855, and remarked on the "romance" of *Typee* as contrasted with the "reality" of Polynesian life.[88] "R.S.," probably a British naval officer, reported that in the fall of 1867, on a tour of the Marquesas, he found Melville's account of Typee "well known," and "was told that Fa-a-wa and a daughter of Melville's were still living."[89]

The marriage of Melville on August 4, 1847, to Elizabeth Shaw resulted in some amusing illustrations of the impression Fayaway had made on the American imagination. The New York *Tribune* quipped on August 7 that "the fair forsaken Fayaway" would undoubtedly now bring a suit for breach of promise against "Mr. HERMAN TYPEE OMOO MELVILLE." Thus it was possible, even in 1847, and even in the *Tribune,* to view Melville's "sins" in a merely humorous light. This squib was copied out in Honolulu on March 18, 1848, in the *Polynesian,* without acknowledgment of source and with this elaboration which showed it was there taken more seriously: "We think the case a plain one and have no doubt the fair one would gain her suit . . . if she had a good lawyer." The *Polynesian* wondered at Melville's "inconsistency" in exchanging "his delightful fairy" for one nurtured in "odious" civilization. Melville's Marquesan love continued to intrigue the Americans in Hawaii; on April 1, 1847, the Reverend Mr. Samuel C. Damon, in his Honolulu magazine, the *Friend,* had remarked that even "the gentle charms of Fayaway" could not keep Melville in Typee; and on April 1, 1850, "earnestly recommended" that "the dashing Melville, who has won such laurels among the literati" should "take a trip with his young bride to the scenes of his earlier days—it may be the gentle Fayaway would stand upon the beach to extend a cordial welcome."

87. Mabel Wise, "Traces of Melville in the Marquesas in the Journal of A. G. Jones, 1854-55," *Bulletin of the New York Public Library,* LII (July, 1948), 362-369. Jones, with degrees from Harvard and Columbia, was clerk to Captain Theodorus Bailey, U. S. N. He testified that the Typees were indeed cannibals and had by then killed nearly all the Happars.

88. In the New York *Spirit of the Times,* May 24, 1856. (Norris Yate, "A Traveller's Comment on Melville's 'Typee,'" MLN, LXIX [December, 1954], 581-583).

89. Reported in a letter published in the *Athenaeum* on April 25, 1868. Clarence Gohdes, "Gossip About Melville in the South Seas," *New England Quarterly,* X (September, 1937), 527.

An encounter of a far more pleasing sort—if also frustrating—was envisioned by George W. Curtis, who in his "Summer Notes of a Howadji," written in 1851 on the shores of Lake George, told of dreaming he was "a Typeean, a Herman Melville," and ran "to catch a moonlight glimpse of Fayaway," to see only the "rippling brilliance of a rapidly fading boat."[90]

And Fitz-James O'Brien centered the most glowing of nineteenth-century American tributes to Melville's first book around an unabashed evocation of the loveliest of the Polynesians—"Fayaway, charming, smooth skinned siren, around whose sunbrowned form the waves lap and dimple like the longing touches of a lover's fingers. What luxury untold it must have been to live with thee beneath the shady place of Typee. To dance with thee in the moonlight in front of the deep-caved hut; to hunt with thee for strange flowers in the deep silent woods, or sail with thee on the wave when the sunset painted our tappa sail with finer hues than the work of Gobelins."[91] That was in 1853. Titus Munson Coan, self-described as a "Hawaiian-American," complained that in his 1859 interview with Melville, "the shade of Aristotle rose like a cold mist between myself and Fayaway."[92]

CONCLUSION

As to the literal truth of *Typee,* just before the re-entrance of Toby, the British tally had been a tie. The remaining months of the year brought forth two more of each persuasion, leaving the British score still a tie, seven to seven. The American pre-Toby statistics were six doubters (including the politest) and sixteen believers. Before the year 1846 was over, two with religious bias had joined the unbelievers; on the other side, at least five printings of Toby's own letter, and the recantation of the *Courier,* could be figured in at year's end. Calculations including the subsequent few years would give similar British-American ratios. The British were certainly much more inclined to distrust the tale, often because of aristocratic bewilderment at a literate man before the mast.

The extent of the assault on *Typee* as licentious has been much exaggerated, especially by its author's first biographers. There were just two secular protests, both mild: one in London (*Simmond's*—one or two "voluptuous scenes might have been expunged"); and one in Washington (the *Intelligencer*—somewhat more prissy). Thus

90. Published in the *Tribune,* September 11 (*Log,* p. 428).
91. See Footnote 75.
92. *Log,* p. 605.

only religious magazines were outraged, and not even all of them. In America the moderately disturbed included three of these (*Biblical Repository, Universalist*—"voluptuousness" again—*Christian Parlor*); only three were really shocked (*Evangelist*—what "was left to be imagined," *Christian Observatory,* and most violently the *Friend*—"shameless familiarity . . . with . . . filthy savages"). Geographically the horrified trio represented New York, Boston, Honolulu.[93] To match this display of American prudishness, Great Britain had a sole case, indeed more up in arms than any American (*Eclectic Review*—such "profligacy!").[94]

The contrast between the minds of two centuries is vividly illustrated in the reactions to the love story of Tommo and Fayaway. To the twentieth it seems nearly incredible that anyone could have found this delicately portrayed romance shameless and lascivious. How amazed would the nineteenth have been to learn that critics would some day be troubled because Tommo was too well-behaved! Vernon L. Parrington says: "There is no likelihood that this young man will succumb to Queen Hautia; he is always on guard. If he needs any advice at this period, it is that of Koheleth: 'Be not righteous overmuch.' "[95] Even more startled would the nineteenth have been to hear Richard Chase: "The hero's attachment to Fayaway cannot be regarded as a completely sexualized one. She remained a wraith of youthful erotic fantasies, as her name indicated."[96]

To turn again to 1846, from the British laymen came one mild objection to, and one vigorous defense of, the judgment on the missions (that is, in *Typee* alone); from the Americans one demur, two secondings. Thus the most clear-cut difference between the British and American responses was the considerably bigger storm raised over here by Melville's "voluptuousness" and by his censure of the missions. The contrast is reflected in the refusal of Wiley and Putnam to issue even one unexpurgated reprinting, even though Murray had done so.

93. The *Polynesian* was not aroused to its extreme denunciation of *Typee* until it had seen *Omoo.*

94. Anderson is right in insisting that the reaction was in general more favorable than has been realized, and that the sanctimonious condemners were much in the minority. His implication that only the religious doubted the authenticity is inaccurate. His remark that such doubts as the British confessed were indirect compliments is justifiable, but does apply to a few Americans also (pp. 180-181).

95. *The Romantic Revolution in America* (New York, 1927), p. 262. See also Mumford, p. 55.

96. *Herman Melville* (New York, 1949), p. 12.

What was said of Melville's broader criticism of the culture of the West, of so much interest to moderns?[97] In England two secular and one religious journals objected briefly to the Utopian implications, but Phillips approved and Jerrold was really sympathetic. In America three religious magazines felt called upon to defend civilization as Christian, but the *Mirror* gave Melville a nod of approbation, and real support for him came from two sources, Brook Farm and the abolitionists. For 1846 there was no real contrast between British and American reactions to his reappraisal of the Occident, though in the following years a few more Americans than British voiced agreement with him. In both countries it had been the reformers who had found in *Typee* nourishment for their dreams of an earthly Eden.

In England as in America strictures on literary grounds were virtually nonexistent. There was only one low British estimate, based on finding symptoms of lack of education in a book which was nevertheless pleasing (*Spectator*), but there was one accusation of a touch of an opposite sort of fault—slickness (Phillips). The only completely adverse British journal was religious (*Eclectic*), and even it granted that he who began to read the book could not help finishing it.

There was only one entirely hostile American secular notice (Peck's), and even he admitted the style was "readable," and his paper later carried something in retraction. None of the religious journals (save only the *Observatory,* the next year) denied the aesthetic merit; indeed they thought it was the very charm and vivacity that made it so dangerous. Anderson's generalization that the American praise was "heavy and patriotic" and the British "light and urbane"[98] has much truth, though some Americans did achieve suavity (Margaret Fuller and the *Intelligencer,* at least).

The full glory of the original emergence of Melville before the world has by no means been realized in recent years. The moderns have perhaps been so dazzled by the Melville revival that they have not perceived the remarkable brilliance of his nineteenth-century debut. His contemporaries, however, were well enough aware of the nearly unique enthusiasm with which his first book had been greeted. On December 20, 1851, the London *Morning Chronicle* began: "When the author of 'Omoo' and 'Typee' appeared, we were happy to hail a new and bright star in the firmament of letters. There was vast

97. V. F. Calverton, *The Liberation of American Literature* (New York, 1932), p. 272.
98. *Op. cit.,* p. 181.

promise in these finely imagined fictions .... He seemed to write like a giant refreshed .... The power and skill of the new literary enchanter were at once admitted."

What were the reasons for the remarkable appeal *Typee* had for its first public? Interest in the South Seas was being heightened by explorers and missionaries. Then attention had recently been called to the friction between England and France resulting from the French occupation of Tahiti and the Marquesas. Melville's siding with the British pleased in England, though less in America.

More important, there was the originality—of substance and form. The *Morning Chronicle* in 1851 declared the author of *Typee* had proved himself refreshingly different from "the banal followers of Marryat," when "He took a new subject and treated it in a new fashion. " He turned away from the old Atlantic scenes of "naval romance to something new—the Pacific . . . with its eternally sunny skies . . . an ocean Eden . . . such was the semi-fairy world into the gorgeous midst of which Herman Melville, like a potent and beneficent magician hurled his readers." In similar vein Fitz-James O'Brien wrote in 1853 that *Typee* came from the press when "public taste was wearied and sickened by didactic novels and journals of travel through fields explored many times before. It presented us with fresh and delightful incidents from beyond the seas, over which was thrown an atmosphere soft and glowing." In 1857 he said *Typee* was a relief after such recent things as "travels in the holy land full of Biblical rapture." "We were weary of sea novels . . . We knew exactly what" the sailors "ate, what they drank, and at what hour they ate and drank it." But Melville "gave us something new . . . by a happy mixture of fresh land scenery, with some clever ship life he produced an amalgan that was loudly welcomed by the public, sea and shore mingling harmoniously together like music chords."

There was a statement in the *Intelligencer,* which whatever priggishness it revealed, was a valid analysis of another cause of the vogue of *Typee*: it was "skillfully prepared" to delight a generation "highly-sensuous and wonderloving, much rejoicing in its refinement and morality, but exceedingly content to be helped to an ideal sojourn with barbarism and an ideal plunge into such a state of Nature as the loosest voluptuary may sigh for."

What did these explanations by three contemporaries have in common? All three found in *Typee* deliverance: the *Chronicle,* a geographical one, from gray Atlantic skies; O'Brien, a literary one, from didactic travelogues and convention-ridden sea fictions; the *Intelligencer*, though not entirely in approval, from repressive Victorian morality. *Typee* provided relief, escape, if you will. Deliverance, then—a deliverance which gave its readers a sense of the lifting of the onerous taboos of the Occident, the outward token of which was the vicarious divesting of their own voluminous and restrictive garments as Tommo and Fayaway stripped to bathe together in the limpid tropical lake.

It was a sort of more exotic frontier, too, to which Melville took them in that year 1846, when the South Seas were newly discovered by poetic fancy and frontier attitudes were peculiarly dominant.[99] Novel and alluring variations of the main tenets of that frontier philosophy, individualism, democracy, optimism—a more free-roving and relaxed individualism; a softer democracy based on easy abundance for all in the happy valley; a dreamier optimism enhanced by visions of unmarred and unconcealed and symmetrical human forms against palms and mountains and seas—all these were offered by the traveller from the Marquesas to a fettered generation. They were receptive.

99. Lewis Mumford, *The Golden Day* (New York, 1926). Carl Russell Fish, *The Rise of the Common Man* (New York, 1927), p. 9.

Chapter III: OMOO

"Melville is the greatest writer of the age in his way."
—*Noah's Weekly Messenger* (1847), reviewing *Omoo*.

BRITISH RECEPTION

Although many more in England than in America had considered
Typee wholly or partly fiction, Murray decided to give Melville
another chance. The British publisher must have concluded that the
first book had been successful enough to justify his risking some
murmuring about the romancing in a second.

Murray saw, moreover, that Melville had given to the new manuscript a more factual and less extravagant tone. The second book
did follow its author's beach-combing days much more closely than
the first had his weeks among the cannibals. Charles Anderson
proves that *Omoo* was "perhaps the most strictly autobiographical of
Melville's works."[1] Although he finds departures from autobiography
in pointings, telescopings, expandings and even in indebtednesses to the
books of other voyagers, Anderson is surprised to discover that so
often the book stuck so close to what Melville saw and did,[2] and that
many of the characters were so similar to real inhabitants of Tahiti
as to be easily identifiable by later travellers. There were enough
minor divergences, indeed, between the living and the telling, to lead
Leon Howard to say that *Omoo* "was a convincing narrative of what
might have been had the runaway Melville been a little more bold
and a little more carefree than he actually was."[3] Anderson's thesis,
nevertheless, that *Omoo* was the least fictionized of his works still
seems valid. Melville had made a greater effort this time to give
those who wanted a narrative of real experience their money's worth,

1. *Melville in the South Seas*, p. 179.
2. *Ibid.*, p. 307.
3. *Herman Melville*, p. 101.

and thus to justify his book's inclusion in Murray's Home and Colonial Library.

At any rate, that is where it was to stand; and *Omoo: A Narrative of Adventures in the South Seas* became a member of that most decorous company of books of non-fiction when it was published in London on March 30, 1847,[4] the day it received the first known British press notices. Something of an event the publication was. It was greeted on April 10 by reviews in no fewer than four London journals, besides extracts in a fifth. One was in the *Athenaeum,* by the poet and dramatist, John Abraham Heraud,[5] whose harsh censure must have seemed to Melville an ill omen. Poor Murray again! In spite of Melville's new restraint, here, made so soon, was the old annoying charge of fictionization. Heraud pointed out that the author asserted "incidentally the authenticity of his narration—without any direct answer being given to the doubts which have been thrown on the reality of his former narrative," and went on sarcastically: "Doubtless we shall hear more of the author's adventures:—for, though the *vraisemblance* of history is well preserved, there are in the style and about the narrative indications of romance that suggest a power of prolonging these adventures to any extent for which a public may demand them." There were to be a dozen such agnostics about *Omoo,* but Heraud was to remain, as far as is known, unique in those years in declaring it tedious: "About an island so frequently described our adventurer has nothing new to tell us. . . . We pass over many sailor like tricks and humours; the rather, since they follow in arbitrary succession,—not sustaining any connected interest, and therefore at times, in spite of smartness of narrative, growing even wearisome and even dull." Poor Herman! Yet he should have been cheered by the three other London reviews on that same day, all much more favorable.

One was from the other member of the pair of big guns of English reviewing, the *Spectator,* wherein it was perhaps Thornton Hunt who granted that *Omoo,* though lacking the "novelty of subject" of *Typee,* was still, "unlike most sequels . . . equal to its predecessor" and had "sufficient freshness," as it derived interest from the author's "fluent vivacious style" and "natural aptitude" for description and narration. Evading the autobiographical dilemma, he made a

4. Davis, *Melville's Mardi,* p. 34.

5. Leslie A. Marchand, *The Athenaeum: A Mirror of Victorian Culture* (Chapel Hill, 1941), p. 215. Heraud was dramatic critic for the *Athenaeum.* He was a disciple of Schelling, the German philosopher, and was a friend of Carlyle (*DNB*).

thrust at the licentiousness, one of three such British remonstrances:
"As in Typee, there are a few free passages, that might as well have
been omitted." Obviously, "free" was for the Victorians a heavily
loaded word.

In the third April 10 London review, in the *People's Journal,* very
likely it was editor John Saunders,[6] Chaucerian, and later novelist
and successful dramatist, who was briefly enthusiastic, implying belief
in the actuality by remarking that a "new type" of author was spring-
ing up, "adventurers able to describe their experiences." To a summary and quotations he appended: "It would be difficult to imagine a
man better fitted to describe . . . such a life and such scenes." He
relished Melville's gusto and his characterization of Doctor Long
Ghost, who indeed is the central character and picaresque hero.

Britannia made the fourth Londoner to comment on *Omoo* that
April 10, revealing laconically its liking: "The writer, without being
a copyist, has caught the spirit of Cooper's nautical style; and by a
free bold style of description, and perhaps some romantic license in
dealing with his facts, gives great animation to his pages." *Britannia*
found the portrayal of Tahiti "melancholy" in its emphasis on disease,
diminution of numbers, and the presence of "the vices of both civilization and barbarism with the virtues of *neither.*"

British interest in *Omoo* was further evinced on April 10 by excerpts in other journals. The London *Critic* gave *Omoo* two large
pages on April 10, and three on April 17, which consisted entirely of
quotations with no comment.[7] The Manchester *Guardian,* the champion quoter from *Typee,* began on that day a generous series of extracts from *Omoo* (not as extensive as from the first book), continuing on April 14 and 24. Can any inference be drawn from the
fact that the *Critic* quoted "Tahitian Sermon" and "A Half Christian,"
even though it had regarded the milder reflections on the missionaries
as "blemishes" in *Typee,* or that the *Guardian* quoted "Tahitian
Churches"? Did absence of comment from both imply assent to

6. According to the masthead, *People's* was "edited by John Saunders." He had
only the year before got out his admirable edition of the *Canterbury Tales*—a busy
year for him, as that same year he had founded *People's* (G. Le Grys Norgate in
DNB).

7. Leyda's description of these items in the *Critic* as "reviews" is inaccurate (*Log,*
p. 240, 241). The following were the extracts in the *Guardian:* "A Dinner Party
in Imeeo," "Tahitian Churches," "A Polynesian Dance," "Polynesian Hospitality," and
"A Daring Harpooner." The *Critic* offered "Little Jule," "The Doctor," "Killing in
Sport," "Tattooing," "Ship's Plagues," "Tahiti," "Tahitian Girl," "A Tahitian Sermon,"
"A Half Christian," "Native Dance," "Dinner Party at Imeeo," "The Cocoa Nut,"
"A Partoowye Family," and "Visit to Queen Pomaree."

actuality? All in all the new book had created quite a stir, predominantly pleasant, in England on this day.

Two days later, on April 12, *Bell's Weekly Messenger* gave a most cordial though slightly fatherly welcome to "this Sequel to *Typee,* which had excited extraordinary interest." *Bell's* professed faith in Toby: "Toby confirmed all essential particulars"; and added that the adage "Truth is stranger than fiction" could be applied even more to *Omoo,* readers of which would experience "intense delight." It noted Melville's strictures on the French; and wished that he had "spoken with more respect of the missionaries" and had not "mentioned so openly the names of individuals [Melville indeed had, and in derogation, as in the cases of Consul Wilson and Dr. Johnstone]. But these perhaps are merely errors of taste . . . excusable in a young American, who appears to be more than usually endowed with the roving dispositions of his countrymen"—*Bell's* could not resist a touch of the common British condescension, but handsomely concluded that *Omoo* would "be a rich treat to all those who delight in stirring adventures graphically and pleasantly narrated," and would be even more popular than *Typee.*

Thus three of the old controversies which had surged around *Typee* were already instigated within two days after the ink was dry on *Omoo*: veracity, obscenity, and the missions. Yet only Heraud had disparaged the book on aesthetic grounds; and, to make a trio of the only three British journals who combined plaudits for the literary qualities of *Omoo* with acceptance of it as a true history, *People's* and *Bell's* were joined on April 17 by *John Bull.*

John Bull began warmly: "They who have read the *Marquesas* will expect much of this work, but . . . they will not be disappointed"; and extolled the artistic values: "Nothing can exceed the interest which Mr. Melville throws into his narrative; an interest which arises mainly from two causes, the clearness and simplicity of his style, and the utter absence of all approach to prolixity. He dwells on no subject long enough to exhaust it; and yet his rapidity is never at the expense of sufficient fulness to place every subject distinctly before the reader. Where there is occasion, too, he is sly, humorous, and pungent as he needs be." The style of *Omoo* has seldom been admired more highly. *John Bull* also revealed complete confidence in the book and offered the first defense I have found of its picture of the religious situation: "The author's account of the island, of the natives, of the proceedings of the French, and of the conduct of the missionaries (whom he is not inclined to spare) form by far the most valuable and interesting portions of the work."

I have discovered only two British references to *Omoo* in May. *Chambers' Edinburgh Journal* implied indirectly both approbation and belief, saying that there was in the *Marquesas* a "certain originality ... both in manner and matter" that was "very captivating," and "the things in the narrative were evidently true, whatever may be said of the persons"; so naturally the author had "been encouraged to make a second appearance"; and gave five long excerpts. Also in May the *Nautical Magazine* and *Naval Chronicle* evidently considered the "Description of a Ship's Forecastle" in *Omoo* accurate enough to copy.

Although strongly mistrusting that it was a bonafide report, yet in the following months four Britons delighted in *Omoo*—the critic of the *Literary Gazette* and Samuel Phillips, both of London, and John Wilson of Edinburgh, and the *Dublin Review's* contributor. The latter three agreed that a book so vivacious and adroit could not possibly be the product of an American common seaman.

Of the four the *Gazette's* critic was briefest and least ardent. Clearly he was the same one who had laughed loudest of all at the idea that *Typee* was a true story; he was now the only one to consider the fictitiousness of *Omoo* too obvious to need demonstration. Very likely he was the editor, William Jerdan.[8] He said Melville had here carried on his "Imaginary adventures in the Pacific in the same Crusoe-ish vein as his Typee," while "some of the sketches of character are very happy, and the descriptions of the island graphic, truthful, and effective." He gave extracts.

Under his well-known pseudonym "Christopher North," John Wilson,[9] later admired as a philosopher, was to give Melville much attention in *Blackwood's Magazine,* beginning that June in one of the longest of the articles on *Omoo*. He showed great enjoyment of the author's personality, but also the typical British suspicion that a man who wrote so well had a quarter-deck background. "There is nothing improbable in his adventures, save their occurrence to himself, and that he should have been a man before the mast on board South-Sea traders, or whalers, or on any ship whatever. His speech be-

8. Internal evidence indicates that the series of reviews of Melville in the *Gazette* beginning with *Typee,* and ending with *White Jacket* was by the same person, probably William Jerdan, editor from 1817 to 1850 and sole proprietor from 1842 to 1850, who had some standing as a literary critic (Sidney Lee in *DNB*). One of the chief cynics about the truth of the first two books, he, save for some reservations about *Mardi,* thought them all meritorious as literature.

9. See Chapter V, Footnote 6.

trayeth him." His tone was too refined and well-bred for one who had spent his days in the low company of merchant seamen. " 'Herman Melville' sounds like the harmonious and carefully selected appellation of an imaginary hero of romance"—a remark which, as we shall see, was to have a number of American repercussions. Perhaps, said Wilson, he had been a maritime officer or a rich gentleman traveller.[10]

But such considerations diminished not a whit Wilson's partiality for the company of this raconteur, and he phrased his detailed summary in terms of jocular approval. He had been puzzled by seeing "Omoo, by the author of Typee" advertised in the newspapers. "With Trinculo we exclaimed, 'What have we here? a man or a fish? dead or alive?' " Were they elephants, conspirators, or what? But soon "We found ourselves in the entertaining society of Marquesan Melville . . . perusing an excellent book."

Particularly the characterizations fascinated Wilson (as they did many others), who praised the "portrait gallery," and declared Long Ghost "a jewel of a boy, a complete original, hit off with uncommon felicity . . . a practical wag of the first order." Melville himself, "to judge from his book, must be exceedingly good company." At "terse and true" description this "prime fellow, this common sailor Melville" excelled, "placing the scene before us in ten words."

Wilson noted with relish many incidents, particularly the yarns about what happened in the "Calabooza Beretanee," on Zeke and Shorty's plantation—"full of rich, quiet fun"—, at the court of the queen of Tahiti, and the "capital story" about Bembo's whaling. "There is a world of wild romance and thrilling adventure in the occasional glimpses of the whale fishery afforded us in Omoo; a strange picturesqueness and piratical mystery about the lawless class of seamen engaged in it," said Wilson and concluded by declaring that he "looked forward with confidence and interest to an account of what befell" Melville on board the whaler, the *Leviathan,* on which he left Tahiti. Although he was probably annoyed to have the reality of his very name itself questioned, Melville must surely have been enheartened by this genial admirer who, with remarkable clairvoyance, urged him to project his most vivid memories, those of whaling days, into

10. Wilson argued that Melville was higher socially than he represented himself. How, otherwise, did he know all about the French system of navigation, and the cabin of the commander of the French Flagship, since "he says he was in fetters during the time he was on board" and that he left the ship at nightfall on the fifth day, unless he was an honored guest of the captain instead of a despised merchant seaman? Now we know there is some departure from strict autobiography here and that he had read up about the French.

the great book which even then was perhaps taking shape in his imagination.

There were two minor London items in July. The *Examiner* on July 10 revealed, incidentally, admiration for Melville's dramatic powers and considerable confidence in the "reality" of his adventures.[11] On July 31 *Hogg's Weekly Instructor* copied from *Omoo* two extracts, "Gale," and "Tahiti."

On September 10 another important advocate of *Omoo* as a literary production spoke out, and at length, Samuel Phillips, in the *Times* of London. He questioned the veracity, however. He granted the author "had visited the spots he describes," but, like Wilson, denied he was a common sailor, and raised a new doubt—whether he was an American. "Common sailor he is not," began the "puzzled" Phillips, who gave as the reason for wondering about his nationality his "many easy references to English literature and to London"— complimentary enough to Melville but hardly to Americans. *Omoo* was "not a whit less charming than *Typee*" nor "one shade more authentic." The case was opposite from that of *Robinson Crusoe;* that seemed true, while *Omoo* and *Typee* professed to be genuine histories, yet seemed "incredible," as the "illusion" was "not perfect." Yet *Omoo* was a good book, eminently readable: "Let him write as much as he will, provided always that he writes as well as now, and he shall find us greedy devourers of his productions. He has a rare pen for the delineation of character; an eye for the humorous and picturesque which is worth a Jew's ransom;[12] for the description of natural scenery he is not to be beaten, either on this side of the Atlantic or the other . . . and a gift . . . for quiet and stinging satire." Phillips joined Wilson, *People's,* and other *aficionados* of the Long Ghost, quoting admiringly the description of this renegade medico and of other figures. With such "characters the little Jule could not fail to be the scene of interest and striking adventures."

Phillips revealed his Jewish background in endorsing Melville's exposure of the blunders of the Christianizers. Europeans did "not know how to improve the conditions of their fellow creatures. . . .

---

11. In a review of John Coulter's *Adventures on the Western Coast of South America.* The *Examiner* said that "This book goes far to prove the reality of Herman Melville's adventures in the same scenes; and . . . has the same wild peculiarities of incident, almost the same glow of colour in descriptions, and not a little of the dramatic force of character and dialogue, which attracted to Mr. Melville so much admiration and so many doubts."

12. This somewhat trite expression might have come naturally to the mind of an unorthodox Jew, as Phillips was.

Mr. Melville's account of the missionary doings agrees with all that has reached us from trustworthy travellers." He has "given us a true picture." Finally Phillips was sure Melville would "favor us with further adventures" which he would await "with impatience" and receive "with pleasure." "He is a companion after our own hearts; his voice is pleasant"; and "we are sure" his face is "a cheerful one."

In the longest British review of *Omoo*, the *Dublin Review* contributor in December agreed essentially with Wilson and Phillips, indeed being very well-disposed toward this "most interesting and romantic 'Adventure,'" only seeming Laodicean after the encomiums of the other two. He quoted a portrayal of Long Ghost, but without explicit praise.

Like Wilson he stated the familiar British dilemma about the supposed low caste authorship, wondering "how such a book came to be written by one 'before the mast,' as he describes himself to be; or how one capable of so thinking, reflecting, and inditing could have gone before the mast! And in a whaler, of all ships. . . ." Like Phillips, he doubted the writer was American, but for a different reason: his lack of "anti-Anglican prejudice" and his "severe criticism of the French."

For the literary qualities he had only esteem: "Throughout . . . there runs a vein of humor and irony, combined with great powers of observation and expression which renders it highly entertaining, and . . . engrossing." Also he sympathized with the objections to the missionaries, and concurred with Melville's disapproval of the reverend lawmakers' abolition of "wrestling, footracing" and other sports and their crusade against "short kilts." "The sacred cause . . . which the missionaries advocate . . . is impotent before the evils which accompany . . . it."

Omoo was definitely a success with the British reviewers in 1847. As to its authenticity, five made evident their doubts (Heraud, *Gazette*, Wilson, Phillips, *Dublin Review*), but the latter three on the flattering grounds that the author exhibited too much education and skill in writing to have been a common seaman, the latter two indeed thinking the book too good to be the product of any American; seven were noncommittal on authenticity; and only four actually vouched for the truthfulness of the tale (*People's, Examiner, John Bull, Bell's*). One took the writer to task for licentiousness, and that only in passing (*Spectator*). There was one mild reprover about the missionaries (*Spectator*), and three even vigorously seconded Melville's censure

(*John Bull,* Phillips, *Dublin Review*). After fourteen journals had expressed approval of *Omoo* as a literary production (and three others had published extensive extracts without comment), Melville could well afford to forget the sole journal which had been censorious on aesthetic grounds (*Spectator*), and even that one might have sung a different tune if its comments had not antedated the encomiums in so many other distinguished journals. According to an editorial in the New York *Tribune* for October 6, 1847, the reception in England had been "even more favorable than in America" as *Omoo* had been "reviewed eulogistically, by nearly every literary journal of respectability in Great Britain." Melville, on October 29, wrote to Murray expressing his "gratification at the reception it has been honored with in England."[13]

As so often with Melville's books, although the immediate British reaction to *Omoo* was favorable, the delayed reaction was less so. True, the *Gentleman's Magazine,* in April, 1848, offered a brief and typically British doubting compliment: "We do not know how much of this narrative is authentic and how much is embellished; but it is very entertaining and very pleasingly written." But after its year of good fortune in the Mother Country, *Omoo* got there two of the most terrific blasts so far directed at its author's books. The first came in March, 1848, from the *English Review*.[14]

Seven acidulous pages in the *English Review* illustrated what outraged Victorian "moral" squeamishness was capable of when thoroughly aroused. *Omoo* was to receive one more severe English trouncing on this score, by the *Eclectic Review*, though both these rebukes had already been outdone in America, as will be seen, by George Washington Peck. Mainly exercised by the immorality of *Omoo,* the *English Review* took a few side shots at *Typee.* Admittedly both books had many merits: Melville conveyed "much curious and interesting information"; he was justified in his "warm indignation against the cruelty and rapacity so often practiced by the Europeans on the islanders"; he everywhere treated the English "with candour and friendliness," which made "the task of censuring him doubly painful"; he was right that the savage, because nearer nature and not cursed with the fearful concept of future punishment, may be happier than the corrupt "civilized" man; and (thank Heaven!) he had enough

13. *Log,* p. 263.
14. In an article entitled "Polynesia," in which Melville's books were compared to their disadvantage with J. Coulter's *Adventures on the Western Coast of Africa* and *Adventures in the Pacific.*

decency to denounce "the infidels of France." Nor was the *Review* upset about the missionaries.

Throughout the article, however, was an almost continuous barrage at Melville's supposed pornography. The *Review* was in fine fettle in such a reprimand as this: "There is . . . a laxity of moral feeling, an absence of religious principle throughout both works, which there should not be; and the jesting tone, or the unoffensive expression [*sic*] which accompany or veil the most objectionable passages, make them yet more pernicious. In *Typee* these things are less apparent, though the work is deserving of censure. In *Omoo,* however, the cloven-foot is much too visible to be mistaken, despite the commonplace declarations of respect for religion and morals."

The *Review* quoted the account of the island girls' invasion of the ship, in order to say: "The strange mixture of genuine licentiousness and affected morality which this passage exhibits, is both painful and ludicrous. . . . Melville's delicacy leaves us somewhat in the dark while his innuendoes allow us to imagine almost anything we please." The thought had never entered his head "that he might have attempted to enlighten the minds of his hosts [hostesses?] on 'temperance, righteousness, and judgment to come.'" Long Ghost was dismissed as "a thoroughly unprincipled scoundrel," described by an author who had "scarcely a good word to say for any individual, whether . . . Polynesian or European" whom he saw. As for his meeting only one true Christian, "neither he nor his companions were such as were likely to meet Christians." The *Review* copied the account of the Lory-Lory, a native girls' dance, to pronounce it "though highly interesting . . . sufficient to condemn the author to far more than *earthly* shame and contempt." So the *Review* was glad to turn away from pages which were calculated to "lower the tone of thought and feeling of all those who are carried away by the liveliness and good nature of the author."

With equal revulsion from the moral degradation of *Omoo's* author, the London *Eclectic Review* in November, 1850, devoted over five closely-printed pages to a scornful refutation of his case against the missionaries. The acrid tone may be illustrated by the charge that if "falsehood" is overthrown today, it will "return" tomorrow: "'Omoo' illustrates this. . . . We were under the illusion that the abettors of infidelity and the partisans of popery had been put to shame by the repeated refutation and exposure of their slanders against the 'Protestant Missions' in Polynesia; but Mr. Melville's productions prove that shame is a virtue with which these gentry are totally unacquainted and they are sharpening their missiles for another attack." Although cogent at some points, the *Eclectic's* rebuttal was interpenetrated throughout with the *ad hominem* fallacy. The *Eclectic* occasionally answered Melville's arguments directly but usually set them aside because he was a "prejudiced, incompetent, and *truthless* witness." The *Eclectic* declared his evidence valueless because, first, he was a voice of "popery," and what was worse, he resorted to quoting from a Greek Orthodox, Kotzebue;[15] and second, he was shamelessly immoral. A summary of his two books was offered as adequate proof of the wickedness of this "roving sailor," who "cohabited with a native girl, named Fayaway. We shall not pollute our pages by transferring to them the scenes in which this wretched profligate appears, self-portrayed, as the chief actor." Later he became that despicable thing, a "beachcomber," acquired a "dissolute companion" (poor Long Ghost!) and engaged in "adventures" which "he describes in a manner exceedingly attractive to every devotee of the sensual." Melville, moreover, had "traduced the activities of the London Missionary Society."

It is hoped that, if he could not laugh at the bitter reviling from these two pious reviews, Melville had not lost the clippings from the numerous respectable British journals which in 1847 had frankly enjoyed his gaiety and geniality. He can hardly have been cheered, however, to discover that in his own country, both *Littell's Living Age* —with alacrity, on November 16—and the *Eclectic Magazine*—almost as promptly, in December—both found the *Eclectic Review's* assault worth reprinting in full.[16] How eager these American magazines seemed to be to copy an adverse English judgment on an American book!

The final words, however, from Britain on *Omoo* before the long silence were good ones, and from commentators obviously unaware of its supposed obscenities. Ainsworth in August, 1853, and the *Dublin University Magazine* in 1856 were both hard on Melville's later works;

15. To the charge of Kotzebue that the missionaries had "forbidden innocent pleasures" and imposed a system which "cramped mental power," the *Eclectic* offered as an adequate reply the statement that Kozebue was here describing the religion of the Church of England, an example of a slightly different type of fallacy of evading the question.

16. Graham, p. 239, calls the *Eclectic Review* "a sectarian religious organ of the dissenters." The term "eclectic" in its title was not used strictly as that term is now commonly applied to magazines, as its articles were evidently mostly orginal. The American *Eclectic Magazine*, however, was, like *Littell's*, primarily a reprint medium.

but Ainsworth spoke of the "breadth and finish" of the characterizations in *Omoo;* and the Irish critic lauded it along with *Typee*.[17]

Especial reassurance that Melville was not an ethical pariah, came in July, 1856, when, as we have seen, *Typee,* and to an even greater extent *Omoo,* were quoted copiously, along with other reputable books, by the *Westminster Review* in a dignified article questioning the value of missions. Passages from *Omoo* were therein used to illustrate the snobbishness of the missionaries, who were terribly upset by poor Herman's lack of fine clothes; to demonstrate the extortion of agricultural produce from the poor by the missionaries; to prove the insincerity of conversions, as in the case of the native girl who was "mickonaree in the mouth" but not "in certain other respects"; and to reveal the bad effects of the abolition by the missionaries of innocent native pleasures without providing any substitute relaxation or occupation. Thus the last article of any note on *Omoo* during Melville's lifetime, on either side of the Atlantic, approved its main serious theme. The book, moreover, continued to be read in England, where Murray brought out after 1847 six more reprintings before Melville's death.[18]

AMERICAN RECEPTION

No American book was ever launched in America with more brilliant fanfare from the American press than was *Omoo*.[19] To begin with, its New York publication, by Harper and Brothers on May 1, 1847,[20] was preceded by more advance mentions and printings of extracts than was that of any of Melville's other books. The first press comment from one who had probably read the book was one sentence—introducing an excerpt—in the New York *Mirror* on the publication day, which set the pitch for the American reception by declaring "that the author has lost nothing of the freshness and vigor

17. See Chapter II, footnote 20.

18. Minnegerode, p. 133.

19. The *Literary World* had on April 16 announced *Omoo* as "just ready." A note in *Yankee Doodle* was a straw in the wind indicating the question of authenticity would be raised: "Important if true—Mr. Mellville's forthcoming work Omoo." On April 24 both the *Literary World* and the *Anglo American* printed extracts, as did the New Bedford *Mercury* on May 1. On this day the Albany *Evening Journal* expected a new work by the author of "delightful" *Typee* to be "interesting and instructive."

20. According to an advertisement in the New York *Commercial Advertiser* for April 27 (repeated May 1), *Omoo* was to be published on May 1. John Wiley was finally afraid to publish *Omoo*, despite pre-publication changes, probably expurgations, made with the advice of Duyckinck, his reader (Howard, p. 102).

of style, which, as much as the novelty of subject, gave so great a popularity to Typee."

The very next day, May 2, Melville was proclaimed "the greatest writer of the age in his way" by Mordecai M. Noah, who according to Mott was "a brilliant writer, and a successful playwright."[21] Editor Noah was surely the contributor to the *Sunday Times and Noah's Weekly Messenger* of a paragraph long enough to be considered the earliest American review of *Omoo*. As far as I know, before Noah no one had placed Melville on so lofty a pedestal, nor was anyone after him to do so on the evidence of *Typee* and *Omoo* only. Aside from this flamboyant dictum, Noah's little review was, in enthusiasm and confidence in the story's veracity, merely typical of the American reaction to *Omoo*, which "marvelous as some of the stories are, is evidently a narrative of important facts. Some of the anecdotes . . . are very entertaining, and . . . the interest never flags." In a "charming style" it not only furnished "amusement" but acquainted the reader "with many facts hitherto allowed to slumber in obscurity. Melville . . . has deservedly been styled the 'De Foe of America.'" The same day the New York *Atlas* predicted that *Omoo* would be more successful than even *Typee*.

Noah seems to have started a veritable shower of brief but cordial newspaper compliments which occurred during the following week. Two came on May 3, one from the Whig *Albany Journal,* in which probably editor Thurlow Weed, having read only a fourth, felt he could say the new work "fully" justified "the expectations . . . raised" by *Typee*. The materials in *Omoo* would have failed to "interest in the hands of an ordinary writer," but Melville's "talents and genius" imparted "life and spirit to even commonplace occurrences. He throws a charm around everything. . . . Even the rotten old ship . . . becomes in the plastic hands of our Author, a beautiful 'thing of life' with which the reader falls in love . . . . Mr. Melville excells most other writers . . . in truthfulness. . . . He clothes Forecastle . . . Yarns in their appropriate drapery. He exhibits the Sailor in his 'toggery' and makes him eat and talk naturally [apparently German capitalization rules prevailed in Albany]." Two extracts followed. Also on May 3 the New York *Mirror* had learned that the sequel to *Typee* contained "even more astonishing recitals," and predicted popularity.

21. Noah was "a self appointed 'Judge and Governor of Israel,'" who had "planned 'Ararat,'" an early Zionist movement, designed to settle Jews on Grand Island, in the Niagara River." He was connected with several papers, and his successful plays were military melodramas (Mott, *American Journalism,* p. 182n).

On May 4 the Boston *Daily Advertiser* after a friendly summary adjudged the style "very good" and the "narrative amusing."

On May 5 four newspapers told how much they liked *Omoo*, in Boston the *Bee* and the *Post*, in New York the *Evening Post*, in Brooklyn the *Eagle*. The *Bee* found it "abounding in passages of wit, humor, romance and poetry . . . with all the mellow elegance of style" of *Typee;* declared it would be popular; and said that while it resembled somewhat *Two Years Before the Mast*, it was "a much more racy and captivating work" and contained "many good stories"—illustrated by the Doctor's rope-to-man's-chest trick. The *Evening Post* decided that *Omoo* had "all the liveliness" of the popular *Typee* and would "be much read."

I have found only six Americans who printed questions about how true was Melville's new tale. Two of these were among the four who otherwise praised it on May 5. One was the Boston *Post's* Colonel Greene, whose suspicions did not diminish his pleasure. He did regard the title as "heathenish and cattleish," but continued that it was "unnecessary to discuss" whether or not Melville had "ever visited the places he describes," "but if he have not, his books are worthy of a place with Robinson Crusoe and Gulliver. If he have . . . he has the descriptive power in greater abundance than any traveller of the age. That all in his book is actually true we can hardly believe, but he imparts a great deal of information tallying with the reports of former voyagers," and also "gives us an array of characters as interesting as those of romance with acuteness and power." The Colonel relished Doctor Long Ghost, and found "the Tahitian girls . . . sprites of fun, softness and beauty."

Whitman in the Brooklyn *Eagle* the same day also doubted the reality and was almost the only one who qualified his profession of pleasure with an intimation that the book was hardly of great significance, even if it did provide "the most readable sort of reading": "The question of whether these stories be authentic or not has, of course, not so much to do with their interest. We therefore recommend this 'narrative of adventures' . . . as thorough entertainment—not so light as to be tossed aside for its flippancy, nor so profound as to be tiresome. All books have their office, and this a very side one."

The Washington *National Intelligencer* on May 26 found it hard to believe that a man so refined as Melville could have associated on terms of "cooperation and sympathy" with such "abandoned villains"—the nearest any American came to the contention of at least five British that no man so educated could have demeaned himself by going before the mast. This was only one of several times the *Intelligencer* seemed to be echoing the British.

Such qualms were, as has been seen, highly exceptional in the United States, where the current of enthusiasm conjoined with complete faith rolled along. The two Thomases of May 5 were outvoted within five days by no fewer than six who regarded the tale as real, of whom five virtually took oath it was indeed after the fact.

Less adulatory than some, the Baltimore *American* on May 6 seemed sure *Omoo* was reliable, pointing out that *Typee* "described the South Sea Islanders in their savage state," *Omoo* "as they are affected by intercourse with civilized foreigners and . . . the missionaries." The style was "agreeable, and the scenes . . . instructive as to Polynesian character." The Boston *Daily Evening Transcript,* the same day, was a much more ardent admirer, as well as a particularly strong voucher for the veracity in these "random recollections of the romantic points of some months of hardy adventures in those distant localities, the minute circumstances of which are here so pleasantly detailed."[22] Anything by the author of *Typee* would have a "rapid sale"; but Melville had by no means merely repeated himself. *Omoo* had "the marks of an originality which could only rise from a personal acquaintance with the scenes which the talented author so happily depicts. While evidently truthful to the eye, it is no less exciting to the mind, than the wildest romance, and consequently must leave everywhere a pleasing impression, which its easy and natural style does so much to enhance."

Three believing praisers found their way into print in New York on May 8. The *Albion* was explicit in faith: "*Omoo* and *Typee* are actually delightful romances of real life"; and cordial in admiration: Melville had "more than sustained his widely spread reputation. . . . There is a freshness and novelty in the graphic sketches" of island society not found in other travel "writings."

On the same day,[23] the *Anglo-American* was even more emphatic as to both belief in and admiration for "this curious and fascinating

22. The reviewer could have been Cornelia C. Walter, known as the "brilliant lady editor of the *Transcript*" (Mott, *American Journalism,* p. 217), whose editorship was terminated in 1847 by her marriage; or it could have been Epes Sargent—dapper and elegant—who had worked on the *Mirror,* and succeeded Miss Walter as editor of the *Transcript* (William B. Cairns in *DAB*).

23. Also on May 8, the New York *Mirror* printed an extract. *Yankee Doodle* implied scepticism in a May 8 squib in referring jocularly to "Omboog, or three months residence in the Moon" (*Log,* p. 244).

narrative": "It abounds in all attractive things; not a chapter but is replete with interest; not a sentence but glistens. 'Typee' was something rare; but 'Omoo' is still rarer. In descriptive power both works are truly remarkable. The enchanting scenery of Polynesia is presented to the very eye itself, as if suffused with rays from illuminated roses. There is, nevertheless, a direct, straight-forward air about the narrative . . . which precludes the conclusion that any of the incidents, however, uncommon, are mere fictions. . . . 'Omoo' is destined to create a prodigious sensation."

Evert Duyckinck, in the *Literary World,* made the third of the May 8 advocates. Therein, and in a somewhat more enthusiastic and polished article in the New York *Evening Mirror* on May 21,[24] he presented three main points. First he vouched for the truth of *Typee,* and by implication of *Omoo.* He summarized the contrast between the foreign and American attitudes justly: although abroad it was thought the author was a "veteran bookmaker, who, being master of a brilliant style, had ingeniously fashioned a most readable piece of Munchausenism while sitting in his library, his work was at once recognized as a genuine narrative in the city where it was published." He had talked with a naval officer who had been at Tahiti, and who had declared "that in reading 'Omoo' he actually imagined himself on the spot." Second, he lauded the writing: "It is the warmth, the tropical luxuriance, the genial flow of humor and good nature—the happy enthusiasm, gushing like a stream of mellow sunshine from the author's heart—all these and a thousand nameless beauties of tone and sentiment are the captivating ingredients of 'Omoo.' Who can follow our young adventurer in his wanderings . . . and listen to his pleasant discourse without feeling completely regenerated?" Finally Duyckinck declared that "deserving of serious consideration" was the "testimony of this candid and impartial witness" as to the limitations of the missionaries.

The May 10 review in the Newark *Daily Advertiser* occupies a unique place in the chronicle of press comment on Melville, because

24. Leyda suggests and Miller assumes that Duyckinck was the author of both articles (*Log,* pp. 243, 245; Miller, pp. 203, 207). Miller argues that even though Duyckinck had been superseded in May as editor of the *Literary World,* and "had assured his brother he wrote nothing for the magazine from the moment he was ousted . . . he must have left in the office the review which appeared on May 8." Miller misdates the second article as for May 22 and exaggerates the difference in enthusiasm between the two articles. It is possible that the author of the *Literary World* review was the new editor, Charles Fenno Hoffman, but internal evidence points to Duyckinck as the reviewer.

its author was the only one, British or American, who in his reviews asserted he had himself been in the South Seas. He was willing, as an eye witness, to attest to the general verity of the book and of Melville's interpretation of the effect of the impact of the missionaries on Polynesia, as well as to the "romantic interest and agreeable style" which entitled the author to be considered among the "rivals of De Foe":

But what particularly interests us is the fact we have some right to judge of the truthfulness as well of the picturesqueness of its descriptions of life and manners in the South Seas. It was our fortune . . . to run through a few years since very much the same career of nautical vagabondage so faithfully and picturesquely detailed in the bewitching yarns of Mr. Melville; only excepting, of course, the paradisaical sojourn in the wondrous valley of Typee. . . . How the public have received Mr. Melville's "experience" I do not know—but for ourselves, a whilome cosmopolite and impartial observer of things in the South Seas, we do not hesitate to give him a grip of approval, and repeat the oft-pronounced but, till his genial spell awaked old associations, the almost forgotten encomium *matai*.

During the next few days, some minor items revealed continued interest in *Omoo* outside of New York City. American concern about English opinion was again shown when the Albany *Evening Journal*[25] on May 12 took satisfaction in proving that *Omoo* had admirers in London by quoting the *Spectator,* which was also quoted on May 15 in the Union College *Parthenon.* Evidently some serious Union student, having decided that *Omoo* was enjoyable but trivial, added that like *Typee,* it would "be pleasure-giving to lazy voluptuaries, who are found in college as well as elsewhere."[26] The Boston *Recorder* for May 13 had one sentence about "This . . . very entertaining sketch of his wanderings by a wild rover of the seas."

Toward the end of May came an upsurge of discussion of *Omoo* beginning with Duyckinck's May 21 defense, already considered. The *American Literary Gazette* reported on May 22 that *Omoo* "was selling rapidly." On May 26 and 28 the Washington *National Intelligencer* presented what was the nearest approach to a disparaging American criticism of *Omoo* on aesthetic grounds, but still tinged with moral qualms. Questioning the actuality of both *Typee* and *Omoo,*

25. The entry was entitled "*Omoo*: Who Reads an American Book?" The comment was that "such questions are no longer asked, because American Books, 'that are books,' have not only readers but admirers in England."

26. That some professor was not the writer was indicated by the subtitle: "A Semi-Monthly Magazine Conducted by the Students of Union College."

the writer for the *Intelligencer* declared *Typee* superior in "sustaining the *illusion of truth,*" yet quoted copiously to illustrate the many "beauties" of *Omoo*. He was shocked that Melville had sunk—or pretended to sink—to mingling with such low associates as Long Ghost, "an unprincipled vagabond, hardly less witless than worthless," who might "do very well for a strange figure in a fiction," but could not be regarded with "admiration or amusement"; and "as a principal character" was "a complete failure."

No literary faults were found by the New York *Evangelist,* which on May 27 became the fifth American skeptic as to the reality of *Omoo*. The *Evangelist* admitted with candor the book's delights: "These lively sketches steal one's favor and approbation in spite of himself. They are so graphic and spirited, and narrate scenes of such strange and surpassing interest, that the reader is borne along . . . without stopping to inquire how much is true or false, or what reliance is to be placed on the author's most deliberate statements. But on arriving at the end and looking back the conviction speedily arises that it is but little else than romance." Not unexpectedly the *Evangelist* said finally that "the author's mendacity is sometimes flagrantly visible, as well as his spite against religion and its missionaries."

On the same day "B." in the *National Anti-Slavery Standard* declared Melville's picture a true one, and liked *Omoo* though it "contained nothing so purely novel" as did the "bewitching" *Typee*. Yet in *Omoo* "The sketches of sea life and character, are very lively and accurate, and the insight which it gives of the state of society in the half Christianized islands of the Pacific, entertaining and instructive." Melville's volumes were "corroborated" by other travellers. On May 29 *Littell's Living Age* reprinted the quite positive reviews from the *Spectator* and the *People's Journal.*[27]

By June the new book had come to the attention of the general and commercial magazines. *Hunt's Merchant's Magazine* was noncommittal as to merit, but seemed not to question the veracity. The *Columbian Magazine* merely gave the "place of honor to the most popular of the recent issues of the press." *DeBow's Commercial Review* remarked that Melville had been "favorably known to the world by his brilliant and spirited 'Typee,'" which he "has now continued in a similar vein." Clark, in the June *Knickerbocker,* thought that "Without being equal . . . to its popular predecessor," *Omoo* was "yet

27. It is rather appalling to think what the *Christian Observatory* might have said in its May number about *Omoo,* if it had not been unaware of that work.

a very clever and entertaining work," and declared that "the author professes to describe merely what he has seen; and so evidently natural are his pages, that we are bound to take him at his word, and to believe . . . that the reflections in which he occasionally indulges are spontaneous, and such as would suggest themselves to the most casual observer. 'Omoo' has already passed to a third edition." Benjamin Blake Minor,[28] in the *Southern Literary Messenger,* showed himself also no skeptic and somewhat more of an admirer: Melville had "enjoyed a new and interesting field of adventure," but "with his animated and vivid style, humorous vein and sailor-like spirit, might venture to lead his readers, with renewed pleasure, even over well beaten tracks." *Godey's Lady's Book,* in July, though relishing the "vivid descriptions of natural scenery that seem as though touched by the pencil of the painter," found the author's "great talent . . . in his sketches of character," some of which were "exquisite": "Dickens has nothing more amusing in his Pickwick Papers than the portraits of Zeke and Shorty, and the whole story of the sojourn in the valley of Mortair is capital."

At once more enthusiastic and also more censorious than any of these six June commentators, was Horace Greeley, whose estimate of the literary qualities, in a letter published on June 24 in the New York *Weekly Tribune,* could scarcely have been more favorable. *Omoo* dispelled any "illusion" that "the fascination of 'Typee' was due to its subject," and proved the author "a born genius, with few superiors either as a narrator, a describer, or a humorist. Few living men could have invested such scenes, incidents, and persons as figure in 'Omoo' with anything like the charm they wear in Melville's graphic pages; the adventures might have occurred to anyone, as others equally exciting have done to thousands of voyagers in the South Seas; but who has ever described them so well?" Greeley also pronounced both books "doubtless in the main true narratives . . . worthy to rank in interest with Robinson Crusoe," but as we shall see presently, he had an exceedingly grave charge to make.

As in the case of *Typee,* the discussion about the accuracy of *Omoo* was blurred by the failure of most to realize clearly that there were two distinct problems involved, whether the author was reporting actual adventures, and whether his picture of conditions was correct. During the first year *Omoo* was before the public, however, only six reviewers expressed doubts on either score, four on the first,

28. Identified by Leyda, *Log,* p. 248.

and two on both. These six, however, were heavily outvoted. Settling aside a noncommittal few, there were at least nine who surely implied complete credence. There were at least ten who, usually without separating the two problems, definitely affirmed their belief. The judgment of the tenth, the *Mirror* on October 6, half a year after the publication of the book, may be taken as a sort of final word from the secular reviewers as to the veracity. Concerned only with the second problem, the *Mirror* granted that although Melville's books were not "sources of statistical information," they were just as much needed: "They are to such works what landscape paintings are to maps. One gives particulars, and the other general truths. A landscape drawing of Tahitian scenery might be untrue in all its particulars, and yet enable us to form a perfectly correct idea of the general characteristics of that region, but a map would be utterly useless if not strictly correct in all its lines. Mr. Melville has performed for us the duty of the landscape painter."

Although the great majority of Americans found nothing in *Omoo* to offend, its supposed licentiousness caused in lay journals a bigger tempest in America than in Britain, and a bigger one than *Typee* did in either country. More also of the religious journals took *Omoo* to task on this score in America than in Britain. The storm did not break in America until June, 1847.

The first reproof was gentle, administered in the June *Southern Literary Messenger* by editor Minor: "There appears at times rather a license in the tone and spirit of the book, but from a sailor under such circumstances, this might be expected." The next reproof was much more severe, and came from a person whose opinion carried weight, Horace Greeley, who in his above-mentioned letter to the *Tribune* in June charged that *Omoo* as well as *Typee* was "unmistakably diseased in moral tone, and will very fairly be condemned as dangerous reading for those of immature intellects and unsettled principles. Not that you can put your finger on a passage that is positively offensive; but the tone is bad, and incidents of the most objectionable character are depicted with a racy lightness which would once [when?] have been admired but will now be justly condemned. A penchant for bad liquors is everywhere boldly proclaimed, while a hankering after loose company, not always of the masculine order is but thinly disguised and perpetually protruding itself through the work."

Greeley, however, ranked the book higher than did Minor, for its charm and vivacity, which, indeed, made its depravity the more insidious. A few days later he delivered a temperance lecture at Sault Ste. Marie.[29]

The long essay, in the *American Review* for July, by George Washington Peck[30] is a kind of inverted classic, and has achieved a sinister fame among students of Melville. Unlike Greeley, who could speak of the "charm" of Melville's "graphic pages," Peck declared that the "venerous" strain in *Omoo* debased it in its entirety. He began by saying he was examining a piece of "cheap literature," and continued acrimoniously:

The reckless spirit—the cool sneering wit, and the perfect want of *heart* . . . make it repel almost as much as its voluptuous scenery painting and its sketchy outlines of stories attract. . . . Every sentence is so smart and comes off with such a bang. We do not like that a man should exhibit no earnestness in his character. . . . His heart is hard . . . he prefers painting himself to the public of his native land as a jolly, rollicking blade —a charming graceless ne'er-do-well. . . . He is what a plain New Englander would call a 'smart scamp.' The phrase is a hard one, but it is certainly well deserved. . . . He gets up voluptuous pictures, and with cool deliberate art breaks off always at the right point so as without offending decency, he may stimulate curiosity and excite unchaste desire . . . with the most incredible accounts and dark hints of innumerable amours with the half-naked and half-civilized or savage damsels of Nukuhiva and Tahiti.

His account of his amours, charged Peck, was incredible for three reasons: (1) He claimed that he was always successful. Even the "best of us" might have done as he represents himself as having done, but "should we have come home and told of it?" (What an ingenuous admission of the hypocrisy of the "Victorian" moral pose!) (2) He "couldn't have had the physical ability" to "play the gay deceiver at such a rate among those brawny islanders." (3) "We don't believe the girls were beautiful. He is welcome." Thus was launched an entirely novel attack on Melville's veracity.

Peck lamented: "It seems necessary nowadays for a book to be vendible, that it be venomous, and indeed venerous . . . or it must be effeminate—pure because passionless." Witness such books as *Omoo*, on the one hand, and the "namby-pamby Tennysonian poetry we

29. Mentor L. Williams, "Horace Greeley Reviews *Omoo*," *Philological Quarterly*, XXVII (January, 1948), 96.

30. This review was signed "G. W. P."

have of late had so much," on the other. With righteous pity Peck took leave of one who "at the worst" is "no such chief of sinners that we need single him out for special condemnation. Have we not Don Juan? Is not the exhaustless invention of Gaul coining millions out of 'nature's frailty?' When we consider the crimes of some of the modern novel-writers, Omoo seems but a 'juvenile offender.'" At least Peck did not, like the *English Review*, predict for Melville a fiery hereafter. Lowell considered Peck important enough to introduce him into *A Fable for Critics*, as a target of satire for giving mere "Pecks" at new books and objecting to anything "peculiar and strong."[31]

The vigor of Peck's onslaught on Melville had been exceeded by his virtuous wrath in the presence of the more egregious iniquity of George Sand, in the *American Review* for May, 1847; and in June, 1848, in the same magazine at great length he condemned *Wuthering Heights* as "disgusting" and "coarse." Melville's amours continued for years to haunt Peck's imagination; he was to exclaim in the *American Review* for November, 1852: "Naked women were scattered profusely through the pages, and the author seemed to feel that in a city where the ballet was admired 'Typee' would be successful." To this he appended an interesting footnote: "Mr. Cornelius Mathews was, we believe, the first to designate this prurient taste under the happy and specific head of 'the ballet feeling.'"[32] Peck died unmarried.[33]

Peck was an editor of the *Morning Courier and New York Enquirer,* in which he had dismissed *Typee* as a tissue of lies, and it was not surprising that on July 14 his *American Review* barrage was seconded thus in that newspaper: "*Omoo* and *Typee* . . . which have attracted a great deal more of attention . . . than they have deserved, are reviewed in a just and highly interesting paper by G. W. Peck . . . .This article evinces uncommon critical acumen and a clear sighted, discriminating sympathy with what is sound and healthy in literature and morals."

Young America, however, came to Melville's defense. Even in the virtuous year 1847, Peck had gone too far. Jerry Auld, a lawyer and

31. Miller, p. 216, admits that his thesis that the opinions of the reviewers were chiefly determined by political bias could not account for such "frenzy" as Peck's. Miller's remark that Peck's "hatred for Melville obviously had a motive deeper than political hostility, although that was a strong element" is something of an understatement.

32. In a review of *Pierre*.

33. Sidney Gunn in *DAB*.

member of the original Tetractys Club, in a letter to the New York *Evening Mirror* for July 21,[34] offered a vigorous rebuttal:

How was it possible for Mr. Colton [editor of the *American Review*] . . . to admit so execrable an article into his magazine as the disgusting and spiteful review of Omoo? We should have supposed that the voice of the public would have outweighed the captious snarlings of any small clique. . . .

We happened, like the vast majority of readers here and abroad, to read Omoo with feelings of unmixed delight; we shared in the exuberant jollity . . . the illusion was perfect, and the incidents and scenes as vivid and natural as ever words painted. But the critic comes, and in a pet demolishes poor Omoo, calls him a reckless liar and shameless pander, and brands every delighted reader as a fool and sensualist. . . . We never dreamed of sensuality in the perusal, and no one has made the accusation but this oversensitive and querulous mortal.

But if Omoo is free from the guilt of pandering to a depraved taste, so is not the reviewer. Finding a fair chance to disgorge on the public a little of his own filth, in the pleasant disguise of a moralist and conservative, he launches forth as much disgusting loathsomeness and personal blackguardism as could be crammed in . . . his few pages.

The grossness and spite of the reviewer, indeed, is the protection of the author, but if indecent flippancy deserved reproof, it justifies our defense. And yet . . . this affected jumble of smutty morality and personal abuse finds favor in an austere paper famous for stern conservatism [the *Courier*].

Peck had met his match in this battle of wits, in lawyer Jerry Auld.

Young America talked back to Peck yet once more. Another original member of the Tetractys Club, Evert Duyckinck, on July 24 in *Yankee Doodle* took up arms: "A writer, whose initials (G.W.P.) make him known as one of the assistant editors of the *Courier & Enquirer* newspaper, takes Mr. Herman Melville to task, in the last number of the *American Review* in high parsonical style, for the freedom of his 'Omoo.' Mr. P. is not entitled to the throwing of the first stone, and if he had made up his mind to lynch 'Omoo,' he should have selected cleaner shot . . . to pelt it with." Here is another example of the heavy Victorian loading of the word "free," an opprobrious epithet Duyckinck indicated *Omoo* did not deserve.

34. This letter was signed "J. B. A.," the initials, according to Leyda, of Jedidiah B. Auld (*Log*, p. 251).

Meanwhile the New York *Eclectic Magazine* in July reprinted John Wilson's article in *Blackwood's,* in which, unaware of the lubricity in *Omoo,* he had revealed his enjoyment of the book, in spite of asking whether there actually was a person named "Herman Melville." The Albany *Daily Knickerbocker,* consequently, on August 4, told "friend Blackwood," that Melville, a man of good "heart" and "mind" and "physical organization," had proved he really existed by "having married the beautiful and accomplished daughter of Chief Justice Shaw of Massachusetts." Indeed the wedding had taken place that very day.

To Editor Greeley, as has been seen, the moral lapses of *Omoo* were no laughing matter. This was further shown on October 2, when he published in his *Tribune,* no doubt gladly, a letter from William O. Bourne. Although Bourne's central concern was the slander on the missionaries, he took a very sharp side slap at the vices, especially lechery, he detected in Melville: "His contempt for the con- stituted authorities and the consuls and officers—his insubordination— his skulking in the dark where he could not be seen by decent men —his choice of low society—his frequent draughts of 'Pisco' or other liquors—his gentle associations with Tahitian and Marquesan damsels —and the unsullied purity of his life and conversation [subtle irony!], all entitle him to rank as a man, where his absurdities and misrepre- sentations place him as a writer—the shameless herald of his own wantonness, and the pertinacious traducer of loftier and better men." Naughty Herman! All that drinking!

Once more Melville's loyal friend the *Evening Mirror* came to his rescue, on October 6, and in an editorial rebuked Bourne: "The Trib- une of last Sunday contained a very ill-natured and bigoted notice of Herman Melville's two works, Typee and Omoo, from a corre- spondent, who in his zeal to defend the missionaries of the Sandwich Islands from the imputations . . . in these volumes, is guilty of very gross and palpable unfairness." The writer in the *Mirror*—perhaps editor Fuller—thought it scarcely worth while to refute directly the charge of licentiousness—and tippling—and contented himself with emphasizing the predominating "excellencies" of the works.

The reproof Bourne got from Fuller stimulated him to reply: it seems he had the last word in the continental United States about the lewdness of *Omoo,* in a long article in the January, 1848, *New Eng- lander,* a strongly Calvinistic magazine, published in that stronghold of orthodoxy, New Haven. Therein Bourne, concerned chiefly with defending the missions, spoke sharply about the wanderer's morals: "If Tommos and Long Ghosts play their insidious words into the ears of Ideeas and Loos"—Tahitian damsels—it would be a long time before "pure religion" could be established in those isles. He insinuated that there were travellers who were disappointed at having their licentiousness restrained and therefore condemned the missionaries. "The unfinished records of the love scenes of our *modern* Boccaccio, which leave the reader in a state of not very uncertain surmise as to the secret incidents, we commend to the conscience of the author."

From Hawaii a westerly wind soon blew in, an ill wind for Melville but not for Bourne—unless he resented being plagiarized. In the Honolulu *Polynesian,* on March 18, 1848, the Reverend Mr. Charles E. Hitchcock, with many words and much venom, admitted having enjoyed Melville's writings, "mingled, we must confess with regret at his unblushing avowal of licentiousness and its kindred vices." Those "familiar" with the South Sea Islanders knew "what value to place upon his *truthful* description of . . . his pure, lovely, and unsophisticated Fayaways and Kory-Korys." Indeed "The account of his intercourse with this degraded and licentious people, though in glowing terms, does not fail to convey . . . the naked truth regarding his real principles and character." He was about as reliable "in matters of history" as "Baron Munchausen."[35] Hitchcock copied liberally and without acknowledgment (as a rival paper, the Sandwich Island *News,* pointed out with triumphant sarcasm a few days later), from Bourne's letter to the *Tribune.*[36]

There was evidence from the bookstores of the continued success of *Omoo* despite Peck and his abettors. Peck announced smugly in July that *Omoo* had been forgotten, but he was wrong. William E. Cramer had recently severed his connection with the Albany *Argus* —in which he had vouched for the truth of *Typee*—and moved to Milwaukee. There he had established the *Daily Wisconsin,*[37] wherein he declared on July 1 "that 'Omoo' . . . is obtaining so wide a success

35. Given in Anderson, p. 184.

36. On March 23 the *News* revealed its discovery that "most" of the article in the *Polynesian* was "claimed" by a "certain correspondent of the N. Y. Tribune" (*Log,* p. 274). Much of it *was* lifted from Bourne. It should not be forgotten that two American magazines, the *Eclectic Magazine* and *Littell's Living Age,* toward the end of 1850, kept the controversy alive by both reprinting the vigorous flaying of *Omoo* as lies and profligacy in the London *Eclectic Review.*

37. Davis, p. 15, says that in early 1846 Cramer was co-editor of the *Argus;* Leyda, *Log,* p. xxiv., tells of his move to Milwaukee and establishing his paper there, later that same year. Cramer was a friend of the Melvilles.

that already, three editions have been exhausted," and added that he was "proud" both as a personal friend of the author and as an American, to see work from his pen winning its way to public favor." The Harpers got out four reprintings before the end of the year.[38] Nor did Peck anticipate that *Omoo* would be eulogized by so influential a voice as that of Phillips of the *Times,* in September, from which on October 30, in the New York *Tribune,* "P," its London correspondent, quoted at length to add: "'Omoo' has met with a most favorable reception in England; indeed an elaborate review of it in the Times of the 24th ult. would alone secure it a wide circulation." "P" undoubtedly meant circulation in America too, in those days when British judgments of American books aroused such American respect—a respect illustrated by Cramer's November comment in his paper on the *Times* review: "It is gratifying that . . . *Omoo* is received with highest encomiums in England."

The presentation of the ineffectiveness of the missions in *Omoo,* although so much more explicit than in *Typee,* aroused the American religious less than might have been expected. The *Christian Observatory* in May, 1847, attacked *Typee,* unaware that *Omoo* had appeared. The earliest press allusions to Omoo's report on the missionaries had evinced concurrence. Thus Duyckinck, the first of all, had found in *Omoo* a "greater amount of reliable information" than in all the "missionary wares . . . palmed off on the credulity of the public." According to Duyckinck, because Melville had defended the poor savage, he had been branded an "Atheist"; but reports of "glorious revivals" were indeed "nonsense." The American public had heard only one side, "and the bare intimation of another is an outrage not to be tolerated"; but Melville had the courage to give that other side.

Next had come the Newark *Advertiser* critic, also in May, who had felt that, as an eye witness, he had a real basis for declaring *Omoo* told the truth. The very thing, in fact, that had convinced him of the "perfect creditibility" of Melville was "his account of the character of the Tahitian nation, as developed under the two-fold influence of sailors and missionaries." This critic had been "often mortified" by the "evident incredulity" of "well-meaning supporters" of the missions when he had "stated facts" about the "present conditions of these interesting converts,"—facts "which, with the missionary Heralds and Intelligencers before them, in the face, we may say of Moses and the prophets, were not to be believed, though one should rise from the dead.   The account of Captain Wilkes, and others convinced us that our government officials, for reasons best known to themselves, are accustomed to observe these matters only through the eyes of the missionaries.   We were glad, therefore, to see a plain and honest statement of things with which a month's stay in Tahiti made us too well acquainted."   And even Greeley had thought Melville's "candid testimony" about the missions had value.

The *Evangelist,* on the other hand, had objected in May to Melville's "spite against religion and its missionaries"; and Peck had taken a shot at him for "many a covert sneer" at the missionaries; but the first real blasts against *Omoo* were the two from W. O. Bourne, in October, 1847, in the *Tribune,* and the next January, in the *New Englander.*   In both, as we have seen, he denounced Melville's "wantonness," but his main objective was to refute the strictures in *Omoo* on the missions.   His method, particularly in the *Tribune,* was to begin by discrediting the witness: "The habits and associations of Mr. Melville, as he himself exposes them, prove that he is utterly unqualified to act as an intelligent observer."   Bourne did argue directly in the *Tribune* that, first, the missionaries *had* done much to promote arts and industries, and second, that they should not be censured for forbidding their children to associate with the "gross, diseased" native children.   Would Melville allow colored children to go to school with his own?

In the *New Englander* Bourne was less personal.   His main contention now was that the condition of the "children of nature" was so "impure and vile" before the coming of the missionaries that it was "unreasonable to expect general refinement, intelligence, and purity of sentiment and life in the course of one generation."   To show the benefits of missions, he quoted Darwin's *Voyage of a Naturalist.* Not the general influence of the white man, as Melville contended, but the preaching of the gospel, had done away with idolatry, and had stopped wars and destruction of forests.   But did not Bourne play into Melville's hands in his peroration: "In our civilized and Christian land, how many there are who present no better aspects of moral character than the half-reclaimed Tahitian or Hawaiian"?

In this second article Bourne attacked Catholicism, citing Commodore Wilkes's statement that the Hawaiians themselves saw Catholicism as a step toward idolatry.   Thus, though he did not refer to it explicitly, Bourne was undoubtedly replying to the dignified defense of Melville's case against Protestant missions in November in the *United States Catholic Magazine and Monthly Review,* which had reasoned that as a Protestant and an on-the-spot observer, his conclusions carried weight. *Omoo* corroborated *Typee:*

Some doubts were cast upon the authenticity of "Typee" by those who believe that all testimony against the South Sea Protestant missions must be fictitious. But the publication of "Omoo" by Mr. Melville, had decided that he deals in truth, and is only gifted with the power of describing most vividly the exquisite garden spots he has visited. It surprises us that any one reading "Typee" should suspect it of being a fable, or imagine that his statements regarding the Sandwich Islands were only a flight of fancy . . . his account is corroborated by the uniform evidence of disinterested travellers, and by the admission of the missionaries themselves, as will appear in the course of this article.

The Catholic magazine had also applauded Melville's satire on the Protestant efforts to clothe the heathen. "No wonder he recommends the Marquesans be sent to the United States as missionaries."

A Unitarian reviewer (signing himself "E.B.H.") for the Boston *Christian Examiner* for May, 1848, made an effort to be fair to the various disputants, in a long article entitled "Catholic and Protestant Missions." He emphasized that the "chief authority" used in the "present busy attack on Protestant missions is Mr. Melville," as his books had been "favorably noticed and largely used by" the *Catholic Magazine.* This Unitarian placed little reliance on Melville's contentions, because Melville himself had removed them from the second edition of *Typee,* and because they were inconsistent and contradicted by other observers; and pointed out that not "all his assertions" were "against the missions, but some of them strongly in favor."

Out in Honolulu, the main aim of the Reverend Mr. Hitchcock, so exercised over Melville's morals, was to refute in the *Polynesian,* on March 18, 1848, his case against the missions. Melville's literary gifts were indeed great: the more the pity, for he held "both Catholic and Protestant missionaries up to scorn—the former as lustful and winebibing, the latter as bigoted sectarians, political meddlers—doing nothing for agriculture." Melville had, regrettably, condescended to reiterate "petty scandalous reports, and to deal in insinuations respecting Missionaries . . . people as much superior to him in a moral point as he is intellectually superior to the degraded natives with whom he associates on terms of such close intimacy."

The *Polynesian* was supported by another Honolulu resident, Samuel C. Damon, who on April 1, 1848, in the *Friend*

argued that it was the missionaries who had made some islands safe
for sailors where formerly they had been in danger of massacre. Melville tried a residence among people who had not been enlightened by
the missionaries, but found it intolerable: "Yet how many readers have
been found to credit every word Melville has written in praise of the
Marquesan savages, and discreditable to his missionary countrymen,
while they will not read the testimony of old and truthful missionaries
who have spent twenty or thirty years in doing the people good. A
run-away, dashing sailor understands the whole subject of missions;
what he says must be so, he *has been there!* But the old and ex-
perienced missionary, with withered locks, he alas! is deceived
by the natives; oh he is laboring to perpetuate a *humbug!*" Damon
was not yet done with Melville, and continued his sarcastic banter two
years later on April 1, 1850, suggesting that "our anti-missionary
friends try settling in the Feejeean or Marquesan groups." Melville
should by all means himself return. Why linger among "the fashion-
able circles of New York or Boston"? He should embark for Isles
where " 'with lavish kindness . . . the gifts of God are strewn,' " but
"where there are no . . . evidences of Christianity."

Melville had, however, a Hawaiian defender too. On December
10, 1849, out in Honolulu H. R. Hawkins, Jr., in a letter to his father,
who had it printed in the Lansingburgh *Gazette,* March 14, 1850, said
he would not try to describe islands "so often described by more
fluent pens, *instance* Typee and Omoo. All that Melville ever told
about the Missionaries in this part of the world, you may take for
Gospel."[39]

On May 1, 1849, a contributor, perhaps Charles F. Briggs, to
Holden's Dollar Magazine, remarked that the "account of the missionaries" in *Omoo* "has been pronounced by those, who ought to be
qualified, as grossly exaggerated or wholly untrue"—at least he hoped
it was untrue, for Melville represented "a condition of society which
would be disgraceful to any civilized being."

As Mentor L. Williams points out, the reception of *Typee* and
Omoo in the religious journals depended somewhat on the denomination. The orthodox evangelical churches were bitter against Melville;
the more liberal, such as the Unitarian and Universalist, were disap-
proving though more open-minded; the Catholics were glad to see ex-
posures of the failure of Protestant missions.[40] Duyckinck's Episco-

39. Log, p. 368.
40. "Notices of Melville's Novels in Religious Publications, 1846-49," *American
Literature,* XXII (May, 1950), 119-127.

palianism undoubtedly reinforced his personal friendship and inclined him to uphold Melville's strictures.

CONCLUSION

With only six doubters out of perhaps forty reviewers in America, as compared with six out of fifteen in England, it is clear the literal veracity of *Omoo* was called into question far less often over here. Obviously it was harder for the less democratic society to imagine a common seaman with Melville's gifts. To Murray, who had pestered him for "documentary evidence" that he had been in the South Seas, Melville wrote on March 25, 1848, "Bless my soul, Sir, will you Britons not credit that an American can be a gentleman, & have read the Waverley Novels, tho every digit may have been in the tar-bucket— You make miracles of what are commonplaces to us."[41] The British doubters, however, usually admitted that if indeed he had served before the mast, his writing deserved but the higher plaudits.

The closeness of *Omoo* to autobiography, as well as its continuing to be of interest, was shown, during the first decade after its appearance, by four travellers to Tahiti, who, in varying moods, described encounters there with some of its characters. In 1851 Edward Lucett, an ill-natured Englishman, admitted having been put in the stocks in the English Calabooza on Papeete, where, he claimed spitefully, Melville ridiculed him and attacked him with a bowie knife.[42] He also accused Melville of leading the mutiny on the *Lucy Ann*. Both accusations have been disproved by Anderson and others.[43] Lucett admitted *Omoo* was a "spirited narrative," but its author was a "reckless loafer." Another Englishman, Robert Elwes in 1853 told of having met Dr. Johnstone, who, angry at Melville's satiric portrait of him, was threatening to sue Murray.[44]

41. *Log*, p. 274.

42. Lucett's *Rovings in the Pacific, from 1837 to 1849* (London, 1851) was discovered by Daniel Aaron, "An English Enemy of Melville's," *New England Quarterly*, VII (December, 1953), 562-567, and, independently, by Anderson.

43. Anderson, pp. 235-236, proves that Melville had left the island of Papeete four days before the supposed knife incident, and thinks Lucett's attacker was "Salem" rather than Herman. Melville participated in the mutiny but did not lead it (Robert F. Forsythe, "More upon Herman Melville in Tahiti," *Philological Quarterly*, XVII [January, 1938], 1-17; Ida Leeson, "The Mutiny on the Lucy Ann," *Philological Quarterly*, XIX [October, 1940], 370-379).

44. *A Sketcher's Tour Around the World* (London, 1853), p. 222. Discovered by Forsythe. Melville spelled the name "Johnson."

On the other hand, Lieutenant Henry A. Wise, U.S.N., in 1849 was jocular.[45] He had been in Tahiti in November, 1847,[46] where he also had met Dr. Johnstone, whom he says Melville "immortalized" in *Omoo*, but who was not amused at his immortality and intended to prosecute the British publisher. Wise praised *Omoo* for its accuracy and charm, and reported that Long Ghost was in Sidney or digging gold in California.[47] The humorous mood again prevailed in the American Edward T. Perkins, who in 1854 recounted having some years before discovered Willie the carpenter, who owned to being the lover mentioned by "Mr. Omoo," but resented his "insinuating that scamp of a Long Ghost offered to do my courting for me." The girl in question, now Willie's wife, was present and recalled the Ghost.[48]

The great majority of the journalists in both countries avoided the problem of Melville's picture of the missions. Among those who were interested in England, Melville's censures found at least four seconders (*John Bull*, Phillips, *Dublin*, *Westminster*), and two who replied to him, one mildly (*Spectator*), one acrimoniously (*Eclectic*). In America the missionaries had got more attention from the press, as four applauded Melville (Duyckinck, Newark *Advertiser*, Greeley, *Catholic Magazine*), while there were rejoinders—two moderate demurs (from *Examiner*, *Holden's*), a passing "Peck," and two real blasts (from *Polynesian*, Bourne).

It has been easy to let one's whole conception of the reception of *Omoo*—as did some of Melville's first biographers[49]—be permeated by the toxin emanating from such an outburst as the *Eclectic Review's*. It is true, moreover, that the very possibility of the publication, in a prominent American secular magazine and in a great newspaper, of

45. *Los Gringos* (New York, 1849), p. 358.

46. Wise's *Journal*, in *Log*, p. 281.

47. *Los Gringos*, p. 358. I discovered this book (Hugh W. Hetherington, *The Reputation of Herman Melville in America*, unpublished Doctoral Dissertation, Michigan, 1933, p. 502). It was reviewed by N. P. Willis on October 13, 1849 in the *Home Journal*, with an allusion to Melville's "delightful mind"; by Ann G. Lynch on October 27 in the *Literary World* as affording a treat in the way of gossip about Melville; and, disapprovingly, on November 8 in the New York *Evangelist*, with a thrust at Wise for taking Melville as his model in an account that was also "probably fiction."

48. *Na Motu: Or Reef Rovings in the South Seas* (New York, 1854), p. 323. It was reviewed with pleasant nods at *Typee* and *Omoo* in the *Athenaeum* for November, 1854 (*Log*, p. 493). A German visitor to Eimeo had heard of Zeke and Shorty (*Log*, p. 404).

49. Raymond M. Weaver: *Herman Melville* (New York, 1921), pp. 244-245. Mumford, p. 75. Anderson, p. 180, points out how distorted was their picture of the reception.

such horrific remarks as Peck's and Greeley's about a book that now seems so innocent does illustrate a certain facet of "Victorianism." A historian says: "On the matter of sexual relationships the code of the thirties and forties was exceptionally strict. Violation of this code was almost the sole meaning attached to the word immorality . . . . This code was accompanied by a prudery which was almost universal. . . . Probably at no period was an ankle so exciting."[50] If any of Melville's books was to arouse this kind of censure, it was naturally *Omoo*, recently characterized as "the most rakish and uninhibited."[51]

In spite of everything, most of the American journalists were merely entertained. Including a probably Peck-controlled seconder of Peck, there were only five Americans of the press, besides one Hawaiian, to whom it even occurred that there was anything indecent in *Omoo*. That left at least thirty-six in the ranks of the non-shocked.[52] If thirty-five out of forty-one Americans failed to detect in *Omoo* the pornography Peck found there, perhaps the American public of a hundred years ago was not as prudish as has been supposed. The great majority thought *Omoo* harmless enough. One said specifically that it gave "delight in a sufficiently instructive and innocuous" way (Boston *Transcript*); one even wished the author "had told more of his own adventures with the fair Tahitians" (Colonel Greene); and *Godey's Lady's Book* betrayed no sign of fear that its fair and sheltered readers were in jeopardy from *Omoo*.

The proportion across the Atlantic was almost exactly the same. There only three made any sort of allusion in the press to the supposed obscenity, one only incidentally (*Spectator*), and two with virulent denunciation (*English Review* and *Eclectic Review*), leaving seventeen (including four who offered extracts only) who were quite oblivious to the lurking moral perils. The author's joviality was particularly relished by three (Wilson, Phillips, *Dublin*). Out of twenty Britons, seventeen were merely amused.

Adverse criticism of *Omoo* on purely literary grounds was almost totally absent in both countries. The characterization met with nearly unanimous approval. Naturally Doctor Long Ghost was the center of attention. He had only three detractors, all American (Peck, *National Intelligencer*, Bourne). On the other hand, this light-hearted joker and lover had three *aficionados* in America (Boston *Bee*, Colonel Greene—"an actual creation"—, Duyckinck—"a capital character"), and

50. Fish, p. 152.
51. Rosenberry, p. 20.
52. Assuming that in no case did one person write for more than one journal.

three in England (*People's*, Phillips, Wilson—"a jewel of a boy, a complete original."). Thus by no means unappreciated at his debut was this figure, recently described by Rosenberry as Melville's "greatest comic creation and one of the funniest characters in our literature."[53]

Objections to the style came from the tiniest minority on both sides of the Atlantic. One American disliked writing which was "so smart" (Peck, of course); one implied *Omoo* was more pleasant than important (Whitman); a collegian consigned it to lazy students. A lone Briton found it "tedious" (Heraud). Some of the religious organs did not discuss the style. That was about all: everybody else was enthusiastic about the manner, the British urbanely, the Americans sometimes patriotically. In London there was found in *Omoo* "an eye for the humorous and picturesque" (Phillips); "pungent" writing (*John Bull*); "descriptions terse and true" (Wilson). In Richmond it was found "vivid" (*Southern Literary Messenger*); in Boston "more racy and captivating than Dana" (*Bee*); in New York invested with "charm" (Noah, Greeley); containing "not a sentence but glistens" (*Anglo American*). In Honolulu, a year after the publication of *Omoo*, an admission was made by a derider of Melville's morals and religion which was altogether typical of the contemporary judgment: "As works of fiction . . . abounding with graphic sketches of seafaring life, Typee and Omoo are unequalled. The vividness of forecastle revelations . . . the genial flow of humor and good humor . . . are truly delightful" (*Polynesian*).

As was to be expected for a sequel, the reasons for the triumph of *Omoo* included some of those which brought about the triumph of *Typee*—the romance of a newer and more exotic frontier, vicarious relief from repressions. Phillips in the *Times* could "strongly recommend" that "the reader take a cruise with Omoo, the Doctor, and Jermin" and "invigorate his soul with the healthy breezes of the South Pacific," a good change, "from the wearisome, insipid, and monotonous doings of our sadly enervated and too political generation."

Doctor Long Ghost and his pal who was to tell the tale, as they sauntered gaily and lazily through the islands were certainly individualists and optimists, living their own version of democracy in shattering and escaping from the totalitarianism of the whaling vessel. With the profound appeal made to man's craving for myth by its story of a white man who both loves and fears his cannibal captors, an appeal more cogent than anything in *Omoo*, *Typee* was to make

53. *Op. cit.*, p. 20.

finally a deeper impression on the nineteenth-century mind. Yet the immediate success of *Typee* with the reviewers was no greater than that of *Omoo,* for what it lacked in myth-potency, it made up for partly by surpassing *Typee* in geniality and humor, as even the *Polynesian* had to allow. What so irritated Peck ("cool, sneering wit") and also Greeley ("the tone is bad—incidents of most objectionable character depicted with racy lightness") was obviously the very mood of humor and good fellowship which a hundred years later was to arouse the enthusiasm of Rosenberry, but also appealed to nine out of ten of the gentlemen of the press, even in 1847, when two distinguished Britons concurred in declaring the author a genial companion, a "prime fellow" who "must be exceedingly good company" (Wilson), "a companion after our own hearts" (Phillips). In 1847 as much as or perhaps even more than today, there was a welcome for something none too common in literature, the spirit of comedy.

Chapter IV: MARDI

". . . extraordinary ideas in a still more extraordinary and extravagant style."—London *Morning Post* (1847), reviewing *Mardi*.

BRITISH RECEPTION

When Melville offered *Mardi* to Murray and to the public, he was gambling, and for high stakes. Murray had had fair warning. On March 25, 1848, nearly a year before it was finished, Melville had written candidly to Murray that his original plan for his forthcoming book had been to write a "bona-fide narrative" of "his adventures in the Pacific, continued from 'Omoo,' " but that now he had changed his "determinations," and that the "reiterated imputation of being a romancer in disguise" had "pricked" him into a resolution to show what a "real romance" from him would be like.[1] Here he accounted for a contrast between the first and later parts of *Mardi,* a book beginning with a voyage on a whaler in the real Polynesia, but then becoming a romantic quest for the lost white maiden Yillah, symbol of the form of happiness man most desires, and then turning into a journey through Polynesian islands, by now transformed into allegorical representations of the countries of the world.

When the manuscript finally reached the English publisher some ten months later, it had a preface in which Melville boldly restated what he had told Murray, and added that he "wanted to see whether the fiction might not be received for a verity." *Mardi* was thus declared an experiment, and experimental indeed it was, in ways far more profound than as a mere test of credulity. Although he lost with Murray, who promptly declined this professed fiction, Melville was still to have his chance with the readers, for his agent was able

1. *Log,* p. 274.

to find another London publisher within ten days;[2] and *Mardi: and a Voyage Thither* was published in three volumes by Richard Bentley on March 15, 1849.[3] Had Melville lost with the public?

The London reviewers gave it considerable attention. On March 24 three important London literary journals led the procession. Very likely it was the editor, William Jerdan, a man much interested in literature,[4] who in his *Literary Gazette* confessed sheer bewilderment: Melville "took in many of the knowing ones in his former work; but we fancy the present will puzzle them more. It has pozed us, and is a 3 vol. metaphor into the application of which we can only now and then catch a glimpse. It has struck our head like one of those glancing blows which set everything glancing and dancing before your eyes like splintered sunrays; and amid the sparkle and glitter you can discern nothing distinctly. Yet the images are brilliant, and upon the whole you wonder how aught so luminous can be so dark. ... As for giving any idea of it we can give none ourselves."

He pronounced "superb" the "adventures" of Taji and the Norwegian harpooner Jarl in the opening chapters, which he summarized. "The sharks and other fish" were "described in the manner of" the *Ancient Mariner*. He perceived in each of the roaming chapters "an allegorical theme dressed up with those pieces of scenic and personal description, of which the author is master ... and yet allusive (though we must say ... too vaguely) to matters of universal note and the business of life." Offering a few quotations, he left this "strange" *Mardi* to its "doubtful fate."

Henry F. Chorley, says Richard Garnett, could "not readily recognize excellence in an unfamiliar form" and his criticism had tended to become more and more acidulous.[5] Sour disapproval of something

2. *Log*, pp. 291-292.

3. The London *Morning Herald* on March 15 carried the announcement that "Herman Melville's Mardi" was published that day by Richard Bentley. The publication was also announced in the London *Morning Post* of the same day. Davis, *Melville's Mardi*, p. 97, basing his statement on advertisements in the *Gazette* and *Spectator* gives the date of publication as March 17, but these weeklies would probably be less precise as to a date. A vigorous advertising campaign was carried on. *Mardi* was advertised in the *Herald*, beginning on March 12, every day up to and including March 20, and on March 22, 23, 26, 28, April 3, 4, 11, 18, 21, 23, 26, 28, 30, May 4, 12, 16, 18, and in the *Morning Post* on March 12, 13, 14, 15, 17, 21, 23, 28, 29, 30, April 5, 19, 21, 24, 28.

4. Sidney Lee in *DNB*.

5. *DNB*. The identification of Chorley as the reviewer of *Mardi* is made by Marchand, p. 192, who gives him as the reviewer of *White Jacket* and *The Whale* also.

that was most unusual was certainly the keynote of his March 24 *Athenaeum* review of *Mardi*. He first censured the writing: "The affectation of its style, in which are mingled many madnesses" indicated that the author had "been drinking at the well of 'English bewitched' of which Mr. Carlyle and Mr. Emerson are the priests." The book consisted, Chorley maintained, of "frantic romance, with dry little digressions." If it were "meant as a pleasantry, the mirth has oddly been left out—if as an allegory, the key of the casket is 'buried in ocean deep'—if as romance, it fails from tediousness—if as a prose poem, it is chargeable with puerility." Few would finish it, he declared.

The beginning, however, was not bad: "In spite of all its tawdry faults of style, the commencement of the story impressed us strongly in a strange witch-like way." Quoting the account of the capture of the brigantine, Chorley admitted that few would "contest the power of the picture—but very shortly after this the romance ends and the harlequinade begins." The rescue of the maiden was told, he granted, "with considerable spirit." "But as we proceed the improbability deepens; the author trifles with his tale for some purpose too deep for our plummet to fathom . . . and . . . becomes more and more outrageous in the fashion of his incidents and the forms of his language . . . . Matters become crazier and crazier—more and more foggy—page by page—until the end—which is no more an end than the last line of Coleridge's *Kubla Khan*—is felt to be a happy release. . . ." Chorley was to show even more acerbity toward *Moby-Dick,* although he was to like *White Jacket*.

As its pages were large and its print fine, the two-page review of *Mardi* which the *Atlas* carried on March 24 was among the longest, and was, on the whole, a tribute, though with reservations, to the author's genius. "The immense variety of subjects and of information" today, said the *Atlas,* offered "peculiar temptations to the romancing philosopher" and led this author, "a man of imagination" to "invest" what he saw when he travelled with "the fancies of his own mind"; and thus the work was "a compound of 'Robinson Crusoe' and 'Gulliver's Travels,' seasoned throughout with German metaphysics of the most transcendental school": "The great questions of natural religion, necessity, free-will, and so on, which Milton's devils discussed in Pandemonium, are here discussed on a rock in the Pacific Ocean by tattooed and feathered sceptics. They are treated with much ingenuity, and frequently with a richness of imagination which disguises the triteness of the leading ideas. Politics take their share in the work —not often well, sometimes most absurdly illustrated." The "great merit of the work," however, was "its fanciful descriptions of nature amid all her variations." A chapter about "the passage of the boat through the sea monsters of the pacific is about the cleverest and tersest description of animated nature we ever encountered." The style was striking, being "that of the true German metaphysician—full of tender thoughts and false images—generally entertaining—often ridiculous—attaining sometimes the brightest colorings of fancy, and at others talking the most inaffable [*sic*] bombast."

The *Atlas* gave a quite complete summary of the plot and illustrative quotations, with this judgment: "Altogether we regard this as a remarkable work. When a man essays a continual series of lofty flights, some of his tumbles will be absurd; but we must not be thus hindered from admiring his success when he achieves it."

A week later, on March 31, it was perhaps editor John Forster who in the London *Examiner* adjudged *Mardi* the product of the misdirection of notable talents, which, however, were at times clearly revealed. There were no doubts about the veracity of this book, he said, ironically: "From first to last it is an outrageous fiction; a transcendental Gulliver or Robinson Crusoe run mad. . . . A heap of fanciful speculation, vivid description, satirical insinuations, and allegorical typifications are flung together with little order or connexion; and the result is a book of which the interest is curiously disproportioned to the amount of cleverness and ability employed in it."

On the other hand, the *Examiner's* reviewer liked the pictures of the sharks and the author's "taste in dreams," and declared the best parts were the digressions, which were "examples of thoughtful writing, and very extensive reading, much in the manner of Sir Thomas Browne, and with a dash of old Burton and Sterne." The political discussions were "sensible," especially the one granting that even in America "poverty was servile before wealth." Melville himself considered the *Examiner's* review (and, less justifiably, the *Gazette's*[6] also) favorable; perhaps he too regarded his digressions of more merit than the central allegory, as does Rosenberry, who finds they especially embody the "Rabelaisian abundance and variety that make *Mardi* the source book of Melvillian thought and the bewilderment and delight of Melville enthusiasts from Hawthorne on."[7]

6. *Log*, p. 300.
7. *Op. cit.*, p. 76.

At least seven London journals reviewed *Mardi* during April. They may be arranged in an order of ascending approval as follows: the *Spectator, Britannia, John Bull,* the *Critic,* the *Morning Post,* the *New Monthly Magazine and Humorist,* and *Bentley's Miscellany*—the *Spectator* voicing utter damnation, and *Bentley's* expressing belligerent advocacy.

The *Spectator,*[8] which tended to be fearful of new directions, contained, on April 21, the most crushing British condemnation of the year. Melville had now attempted "wildly nautical romance," but with indifferent success because he had neither the "mind nor mental training requisite for fiction"; and in aiming to become "what he is not, he spoils what he is," said the *Spectator.*

"The expansion" of the circumstances preceding the rescue of Yillah "by the most vulgar and obvious tricks of writing" constituted the "Voyage Thither" of the title. After the arrival at Mardi, occurred "adventures that defy description to depict their absurdity or their total lack of interest." Something intended "for a kind of Circean magic" was "derived from the Arabian Nights." There were many "poor witticisms, and remarks even poorer, on currency, wars, and what not" apparently designed "for allegorical satire, as if Mr. Melville had Gulliver's Travels in his eye. To this borrowing there would have been no objection, had it been properly done. . . . it is not plagiarism that is the ground of censure; it is the manner in which the 'conveyed' goods are disfigured and deprived of value without gaining any character in place of what is left out." The first part was, indeed, tolerable, but even that was not "too good." The *Spectator's* judgment of the book as merely blunderingly incompetent and imitative, set its article apart from nearly all the other censurings of *Mardi,* which centered rather on the excesses of fantastic invention.

Britannia, in a long review on April 14, had been considerably more sympathetic. Melville here was more ambitious than in his first books, for he had attempted "to give reality and shape to the mythology of the Pacific" but "under the disadvantage of writing in prose, and in the form of a three volume novel." "The first volume was by far the best," thought *Britannia:* "The whole account of this voyage over the waters of the Pacific is singularly attractive. While the appearances of sea and sky, in all their changeful beauty, are given with perfect fidelity . . . as seen from an open boat . . . there broods over the account a vague air of mystery, a feeling of solemn awe, which

8. Thornton Hunt may have been the contributor.

all men experience in solitude, and which . . . is an apt preparation
for the scenes which follow. To the fidelity of representation which
has been so justly admired in 'Omoo' and 'Typee' there is added here
something of that sentiment of the marvelous and of that shadowy
terror which characterize 'The Ancient Mariner.' "

Unfortunately, according to *Britannia,* the following two volumes
were less successful. The "opening of the mythological" part of the
story was "striking," marked with "vivacity of . . . fancy" and "rough
poetry," and touches of "magical splendour," but "Afterward the interest declines until at last little more remains than a residuum of
clever rhapsody."

Characteristically, *Britannia* pronounced Melville's faults typical of
his country and undertook to give him good advice: "Like other
American authors we could name, Mr. Melville has power and originality, but he wants taste and discernment. . . . We strongly advise the
author in the future to confine himself to more real and practical subjects. It requires genius of a rare order to deal with supernatural influences. He has strength but not delicacy, and it is rather by way
of admonition than of disparagement that we say he has but indif-
ferently succeeded in a line which we think is very little suited to his
talents."

John Bull, on April 21, was the only Briton to essay an interpretation of the allegory, remarking after a clear enough summary, that
the story was "evidently intended for an allegory." Yillah was the
"soul's high romance, and its ideal happiness, before it has become
effaced by contact with a base world." Hautia was a "personification
of selfishness, of gross desires, and of material enjoyment." These in-
terpretations would seem reasonably satisfactory. *John Bull* found in
the allegorical representation of the world "much keen satire."

In the same paragraph in which the literary qualities were commended, however, *John Bull* reprimanded the author severely—for
lack of orthodoxy:

While it is impossible not to admire the brilliance of coloring with
which the whole tale is invested, and the striking truth of many of the
allegorical remarks and frequent home thrusts, we cannot but express
our profound regret that a pen so talented, and an apparatus so fascinating
. . . should have been made use of for the dissemination of sceptical
notions. To introduce the Savior of Mankind under a fabulous name,
and to talk down the verities of the Chrstian faith by sophistry . . . is a
grave offense, not against good faith alone; and we could heartily wish
Mr. Melville had confined himself to the lively and picturesque scenery

of which his pencil is a master, and, if he pleased, to such subjects as offer a fair scope for the indulgence of his satirical vein, without introducing crude metaphysics and unsound notions of divinity into a craft of build far too light for carrying so ponderous a freight.

The *Critic* on April 1 declared that it "was ascertained now" that everything in *Typee* and *Omoo* was "nothing but a beautiful dream." Although "the author has not lost a jot of his skill in sketching," and "although his fancy is equally fertile, his imagination equally glowing, his pictorial power equally brilliant," *Mardi* would attract less attention because there would not be the excitement of guessing whether it was true or not, as it was so palpably fiction. *Mardi,* however, was "not purely a romance," but rather "an extraordinary mixture of all kinds of composition and of the strangest variety of themes . . . strung together by the slight thread of a tale which is not very intelligible . . . it will not be read for the tale but for the interspersed passages of great interest and beauty"—much what the *Examiner* had said. The *Critic* thought *Mardi* would "better please the refined and thoughtful reader" than its predecessors, but that it would prove "less interesting to the mere seeker after amusement"; and summed up: "Beyond question it is a production of extraordinary merit."[9]

Although the London *Morning Post* on April 30 did not praise *Mardi* as highly as some, it also found less to object to. Melville voyages, said the *Post,* "to a Utopia of his own creation in . . . unknown latitudes, where he calls into existence imaginary tribes and nations, of whose fabulous manners he details to us an exciting description" and where he communicates to us "extraordinary ideas in a still more extraordinary style." Although it was "utterly impossible to follow our author and his companions in their charming wanderings . . . upon every fitting occasion hits are made at the foolish importance attached in society to mere conventionalities." There were "an infinite number of episodes . . . and speculation . . . immeasurably fantastical." He "has something to say upon every conceivable subject." Indeed he took us "through a gorgeous dream . . . in which . . . the most stupendous . . . phenomena of nature are exaggerated beyond limit by the insatiable appetite of human fancy"; yet "everything" was "treated in a new way" and there was "such a commingling of learning and imagination and of shrewdness and quaintness as entitles it to the designation of a useful as well as entertaining production." This was the only critic who found *Mardi* "useful"!

9. Miller inaccurately refers to this review as "an unfavorable notice" (p. 248).

By far the longest of the reviews of *Mardi* was the almost entirely favorable one in the April *New Monthly Magazine and Humorist.* The author can hardly have been the editor, W. Harrison Ainsworth, who later was to dismiss *Mardi* so scornfully, as will be seen. The *New Monthly* critic thought the germ of Melville's book was the story found in the *Gesta Romanorum,* in Purchas, in Southey's *Thalaba,* and in Mandeville, of a garden or paradise "which the magician Aladdin made the means of destruction, by persuading his victims that death in his service was only a step to a more beautiful paradise"; only that in *Mardi,* the traveller, Taji, kills the magician, Aleema, and saves the victim. The reviewer had prepared with evident relish a very long summary, which was out of proportion in giving the first part in much greater detail, with nothing about the final chapters. Referring to the beginning of the quest of Taji for Yillah, he said, "Like the preface to a pantomime over, the serious business of the book commences at this point." He did trace the journey to a few of the allegorical islands, but found it "impossible to follow Taji" and his companions in "their delightful wanderings." He objected to Babbalanja's unorthodox theology, but his final words about this "very remarkable book" were these: "The style is, unfortunately, too frequently objectionable, and there is a want of consecutiveness in the narrative; but there is a mixture of quaintness and shrewdness, and of learning and fancy, which imparts a charm to every page, however desultory."

Bentley's Miscellany, the publisher's organ, also in April, defended *Mardi* almost passionately, arguing in terms that suggest the aesthetic of Benedetto Croce, that the author's extravagances were forgivable because of his successful creation of an exotic and captivating world: "He endeavors . . . to build up for fancy a distant home in the ocean . . . . In the development of this design he is guilty of great extravagance; but while floating between heaven and earth, creating archipelagos in the clouds, and peopling them with races . . . strange and fantastic . . . he contrives to interest us in his creations, to excite our passions, to astonish us with the wild grandeur of his imagination, and to excite in us a strong desire to dream on with him indefinitely." And Yillah was a "sweet creation, like the wept of wish-ton-wish."

It was true that "occasionally the author determines to display his learning when vanity gets the upper hand of him" and then "bewilders his judgment." Yet in manner as well as in matter, unconventionality had been part of the artistic triumph. He had indeed abjured "all connections with the rules and principles of style," but justifiably, because his language suited his subject: since the aim was to "create an Utopia in the unknown latitude of the Pacific," plain and ordinary language and ideas "would hardly have been congruous." This "highly exaggerated style" would not have done for "probable events" but was "the right thing here":

Everywhere there is freshness, originality, or a new way of treating old things. The sea is not the cold sea of the north . . . but a warm fluid rolling over coral reefs . . . clear to depths of many fathoms, and embracing as it flows innumerable verdant isles. . . . No wonder his imagination runs riot in luxuriant descriptions. . . . He deals with materials very different from those of the ordinary novelist and writer; wild and fabulous he is and full of Utopian fantasies. But in his company we at least escape from those pictures of society which differently brushed up and varnished have been presented to us a thousand times before.

Thus, *Bentley's* concluded, though there was much to object to, the book could nevertheless be recommended because the "agreeable greatly predominates over the contrary." Melville had probably not seen this review when on June 5 he wrote to Bentley: "The critics on your side of the water seem to have fired quite a broadside into 'Mardi.' "[10]

Again for May, as for March and April, the picture was one of checkered shadows and lights, only this month the shadows predominated more, for no one liked *Mardi* as well as had the *Post*, the *New Monthly*, or *Bentley's*. I have found three May reviews, all from London. Of these three, *Sharp's London Journal* on May 15 was the earliest, and completely negative, charging that the book "aims at many things and achieves none satisfactorily; but its main intention is to be a mild satire on the whole world and its ways, and a preaching of certain transcendental nonsense which is meant for *bona fide* transcendental philosophy. There is little or no story; and after the first volume . . . the labor of reading is perfectly Herculean, and . . . remarkably unprofitable. What our transatlantic friends think of this new production of their favorite, we are at a loss to imagine."

The *Morning Chronicle* came forth next, on May 19, with a long and cleverly written but repetitious article, the thesis of which was that *Mardi* might have been a very fine book but was not, that it was the

10. *Log,* p. 306. The excerpts from this review in the *Log* (p. 295) make it seem a *great* deal less favorable than it actually was. Howard, p. 132, evidently having read only Leyda's excerpts selects as summarizing the review a sentence which by no means does so, and thus makes it seem adverse, as it was not.

product "of a fascinating gentleman" but was not "a fascinating book"; its author was "not a genius perhaps, but a superlatively clever and highly-read man, endowed with very considerable powers of fancy, and a curious and very rare talent for a species of writing which is at once enthusiastic and epigrammatic—which burns . . . with an intense and richly-colored glow of poetic ardor and with the more glittering, but paler fires of an artful rhetoric. . . . But . . . we have risen from the perusal of . . . as much as human endurance could get through—with the feelings which we think we should experience were we to behold a powerful and graceful fencer tilting at the empty air, lunging at an imaginary adversary, and parrying impalpable and aerial thrusts, until his eye reeled and his arm failed, and the strong and artistic athlete sunk wearily down, overcome in a needless, meaningless, and maniacal strife."

The *Chronicle* had "some difficulty in describing the extraordinary imaginary *olla podrida* of which the last two volumes . . . are made up." The first volume was "excellent, all instinct with great delicacy, and told with high graphic and poetic power. But the instant that the boat touches the magic ground of 'Mardi' all is changed": "The author throws off all control . . . and riots . . . in a chaos of incoherent poetry and vague satire—a mental cloudland, full of bright flashes and dark vapours; but the hues and lines of the picture, the poetry and the satire . . . so worked and whipped and mashed up together, that the coolest and clearest-sighted reader will hardly be able to tell after fifty pages or so whether the book before him be composed of sublime poetry or bedlamite ravings."

There was "no attempt at consistent, natural satire." "Here and there you caught a glimpse of the author lashing the vices and follies of the nations of the earth," but all was lost in "rolling hazes of bombast and turigd poetry, or rather prose run mad." It was "a wonderful and unreadable Compound" of Ossian and Rabelais, or *Utopia* and *Oceana*, of Gulliver and *Cook's Voyages*. There was evidence of "great imaginative strength," but "rendered absolutely nugatory" by the absence of "method" and "common sense."

Finally, the *Chronicle* sought to give Melville guidance. The first volume of *Mardi* did indeed inspire "strong hopes." If he would put "tether soaring spirit" and not try "to invent a new world," he would be "not only one of the most original authors of the day, but one of the most fanciful, the most brilliant, and the most delightful."

The *Illustrated London News,* on May 26, however, called *Mardi* a work "of especial excellence," even though it was "one of the most grotesque volumes . . . met with in a long time." All the difficult subjects of modern discussion were taken up by "the feathered savages . . . of the Pacific." "The very idea of the book" the *News* scarcely knew "whether to admire or condemn"; yet it contained "some of the finest nautical description that the world has ever seen"; and "the observations and illustrations, as the monsters of the deep are encountered, are expressed in language elegant and expressive, sometimes even beautiful to the last degree." The conversations were "intended to satirize European belief and practice, after a Pacific fashion; and . . . are . . . often highly quaint and ingenious, still more often absurd and ridiculous." The *News* concluded, however, that "the latter are regularly forgiven for the former; we are quite content to take the book, with all its merits and deficiencies, as one of the most extraordinary."

John Wilson, as "Christopher North," discussed *Mardi* in *Blackwood's Magazine* for August.[11] He had hoped for more in the vein of *Typee* and *Omoo* and was "sadly disgusted on perusal of a rubbishing rhapsody, entitled *Mardi.*" He was at least the fifth Briton who was "quite pleased" with the first part of the work, though he thought even that was inferior in "nautical fun" and "character delineation" to the first part of *Omoo.* He concluded acidly: "What trash is all this!—mingled, too, with attempts at a Rabelaisian vein, and with strainings at smartness—the style of the whole being affected, pedantic, and wearisome exceedingly." This was the last British review—if it be considered a review—of *Mardi.*

Of the fourteen 1849 British reviews, five which admitted the charm of the opening chapters were negative in final judgment (*Chronicle, Britannia, Gazette,* Chorley, Wilson). One disliked the total effect but relished the digressions (*Examiner*). Two among the more tolerant detected transcendentalism as a taint (*Atlas, Examiner*). Five mentioned the allegory, four disparagingly (*Gazette,* Chorley, *Atlas, Spectator*), but one sympathetically (*John Bull*). Of the fourteen reviews only two were totally adverse (*Sharpe's, Spectator*). "How extraordinary!" was the keynote of most of the comment, whether positive or negative. Five, after balancing faults and merits, concluded that the obverse of fantasticality was originality and ruled

11. In a review of *Kaloolah* by Jonathan Romer, which he thought much better than *Mardi.*

in the book's favor (*Critic, Atlas, New Monthly, Bentley's, News*). A seventh, though greatly disturbed by the impiety, completely approved the literary qualities (*John Bull*). One virtually found no faults (*Post*). Although *Mardi* was not exactly greeted with a London ovation, the immediate British critical reaction was less hostile than it has been represented as being, for example, by Howard, who disregards the five most favorable reviews.[12] Miller's conclusion that the "English reviews . . . said it was no book at all" is too hasty a generalization.[13]

As in the case of others of Melville's books, the final British reaction to *Mardi* was more adverse than the first. Incidental allusions to it in reviews of the later books were uncomplimentary to an unusual degree. Only three really significant British items after 1849 have come to light, and all are crushing. One of the latest blows was dealt by the critic who in the *Morning Chronicle* in 1851 reviewed *The Whale* not without some sympathy. Obviously the same as he who had damned *Mardi* in this paper, he now took a long paragraph to reiterate his objections to it, lamenting the change from the charming *Typee* and *Omoo* to this "Melancholy rodomontade—half raving, half babble—animated only by the outlines of a dull, cold allegory." Ainsworth in August, 1853, in his *New Monthly Magazine,* was just as harsh. He liked the first part, but quoted with amazement the American G. W. Curtis's praise of the whole book as a piece of "unrhymed poetry." "Cis-Atlantic criticism," he declared in highly sarcastic vein, had rather compared it to "Foote's 'What, no soap? So he died and she very imprudently married the babe.'" Whether this satiric thrust is any more intelligible than the book he was denouncing for unintelligibility, the reader can decide for himself. Could the *Dublin University Magazine* in January, 1856, be considered less severe? The *Dublin* did admire the "powerful pictures of sea life" in the first part and delighted in the "gorgeously poetic style," but pronounced the latter chapters "little better than insane ravings."

Thus poor *Mardi*, though admired at its debut in England somewhat more than has been realized, passed soon there under a heavy cloud of disparagement into total oblivion. It was not reprinted there until 1923.[14]

12. *Op. cit.,* p. 132.
13. *Op. cit.,* p. 246.
14. Hetherington, p. 493.

AMERICAN RECEPTION

Melville's friends Evert and George Duyckinck made a brave effort to give *Mardi* a good launching on its American voyage. They were now in a better position to do so, for after a year and a half during which the *Literary World* had been out of their hands, they were, in October, 1848, able to purchase it. Evert heralded the advent of *Mardi* with a series of three extensive and highly commendatory articles in their magazine.[15] The first, on April 7, antedated the American publication by the Harpers in three volumes, which took place on April 14,[16] and occupied the place of honor on the generous-sized front page. *Mardi*, according to Evert, was "an onward development . . . of all the fine literary qualities" of *Typee* and *Omoo*, but "the invention is bolder, the humor as strong, sometimes more subtle, while the felicitous descriptive power at once tells the story and insinuates a thousand compliments to the reader's understanding."[17]

Mardi, continued Duyckinck on April 14, answered in the affirmative the question whether there was anything more in the author of *Typee* than a clever writer of travel stories, for it was "not only a very happy genial production in the best mood of luxurious invention, but a book of . . . curious thought and reflection," recalling Rabelais.

To the poetic beauties of *Mardi*, Duyckinck brought warm approbation in his third article, on April 21. Fayaway was "mere earthiness" before Yillah's "spirituality," and "The descriptions of . . . Williamille, of its hanging groves and sequestered gardens, of its regal device of the twin palaces of the Morning and Afternoon . . . are in the highest style of invention, oriental richness, and moral truthfulness to the whole race of man. . . . Indeed we despair of giving in any way an account of the contents of this well-filled book, laden deep as a Spanish argosy with many an ingot of gold and silver in the hold."

Duyckinck was much interested in the political allegory, and lauded Melville for daring to tell America unpleasant truths about herself in his satire; but he thought the underlying philosophica

15. They had announced *Mardi* as early as December 18, 1848, and had run a advertisement describing it as "glowing" and "dramatic" on February 10. It was advertised on April 12 in the *Commercial Advertiser*.

16. According to an advertisement in the *Morning Courier* on April 13, the Harpers would publish *Mardi* on April 14. This is the date given by Davis, p. 99 .

17. An extract, "Taji sits down to Dinner with Five-and Twenty Kings," took up a large part of this article. This extract was copied from the *Literary World* b *Littell's Living Age* on April 28.

meaning was what was most significant: "*Mardi* probes yet deeper
. . . the individual world of man, the microcosm is to be explored and
navigated." The author was no lounger, but a man in earnest: "*Mardi*
is a species of Utopia—or rather a satiric voyage in which we discover human nature. There is a world of poetical, thoughtful, ingenious moral writing in it which Emerson would not disdain—gleams
of high raised fancy, quaint assemblages of facts in the learned spirit
of Burton and the Doctor . . . it is an extraordinary book." Duyckinck admitted that the "discourse sometimes gets lost in the clouds,"
but concluded that this "capital essayist" was "an author of innate force
and steady wing . . . with whom the public, we trust, may walk hand
in hand, heart in heart, through many years of goodly productiveness."

The next American press comments, after Duyckinck's first article,
and also antedating the April 14 publication, must have made him feel
he was not failing in his efforts to give *Mardi* a good start. They appeared on April 13, in two Whig newspapers which had been pitted
against each other in the battle over the morality of *Omoo*, the *Morning Courier and New York Enquirer* (con), and the *Evening Mirror*
(pro), but which now concurred in lauding *Mardi*. The *Courier's*
sole sentence could scarcely have been more flattering: "Mr. Melville's
new production will be found to fully sustain the brilliant reputation
of his previous works—redolent of stirring interest, glowing and picturesque in style, and powerfully dramatic in its construction as a
work of art." Excessive praise, perhaps, but no more so than the
Mirror's, which was more specific:

A great pleasure is in store for the literary world. Mardi, with all its
fascinations, its unique style, its beautiful language, its genial humor, its
original thoughts, its graphic descriptions, its poetic flights, its profound
reasonings, its gentle religious teachings, its inimitable shows, stretches
before us like a new world, and the mental eye can never weary of gazing
upon its strangely beautiful landscape. Here are points of interest for every
mind. The scholar can feast upon its classic allusions, the man of erudi-
tion can add to his store, the divine find food for thought and discussion,
the poet luxuriate in scenes of pure fancy, the little child find entertainment, and genius salute the author as the rising sun. It remains for the
future to appoint Melville his niche in the Temple of fame.

Could editor Hiram Fuller, so good a friend of Clark, chief enemy
of the Young Americans, have written this glowing encomium?[18]

18. Miller (p. 129) says that Fuller "became more and more a friend of Clark. . . ."
Miller did not know of this review in the *Mirror*, as it is not in the *Log*, and was

Within three days after the publication of *Mardi*, three other American newspapers noticed it with hasty friendliness. The Boston *Transcript* on April 16 said that "Our correspondent who found fault with us for comparing Melville to De Foe will see that the parallel holds" for *Mardi*. The same day the New York *Commercial Advertiser* "anticipated from such portions as" had been read "that the same liveliness of style, with quite as much romance of circumstances, will be found" in it as in *Omoo*. The Hartford *Courant* on April 17 predicted that it would "fully realize the expectations of those who were delighted with" Melville's previous works.

So far there had not been a single cavil in America, but on April 18, in the Democratic Boston *Post,* surely from the pen of the editor Colonel Charles Gordon Greene, came the first hostile review, a long one allowing to *Mardi* scarcely a redeeming feature. After a bulging paragraph of the highest imaginable praise for *Typee*, Greene opened up full blast on *Mardi*, a "poor production" in which he was "bitterly disappointed":[19] "The 'Voyage Thither' is interesting enough, though even this is almost spoiled by the everlasting assumption of the brilliant, jocose and witty in style. After the arrival at 'Mardi' the book becomes a hodge-podge, reminding us of the *talk* in Rabelais, divested of all its coarseness, and, it may be added, of all wit and humor."

No one, declared Greene, would believe the assertion in the preface. "He had better stick to his 'fact' which is received as 'fiction,' but which puts money in his purse, than fly to 'fiction' which is not received at all." It would probably sell and be read, but anyone who liked it would be a "wonder": "It . . . lacks incident and meaning. The conversations are like nothing one ever read or heard, and if they have any significance, are too recondite, at least for our intelligence to follow. Sometimes it seems . . . a satire upon matters and things in general, but this is soon dispersed by the appearance of a mass

---

discovered by me. Clark's hostility to the Young America movement is a main thesis of his book. The *Mirror's* review was quoted from in an advertisement on April 21 in the *Courier!*

19. The four acidly derogatory reviews in the *Post*, of *Mardi*, *White Jacket*, *Moby-Dick*, and *Pierre*, and the three approving ones, of *Omoo*, *Israel Potter*, and the *Piazza Tales* read as if they were by the same person, and there is good evidence that editor Greene wrote the review of *White Jacket*. See Chapter VI, footnote 20 below. He founded the *Post* in 1831 and conducted it until he sold it in 1875. He was an active Democrat (*Appleton's*). His more learned brother Nathaniel did contribute to the paper, but after the end of his term as Democratic appointee to the Boston Postmastership in 1849, sailed in the fall of that year to Europe for a twelve years' residence ("Obituary" of Nathaniel Greene, Boston *Post*, December 1, 1877).

of downright nonsense. The characters are 'legion' and uninteresting—the whole book is not only tedious but unreadable. In a word
'Mardi' greatly resembles Rabelais emasculated of everything but
prosiness and puerility." Five days later Melville wrote his father-
in-law that *Mardi* had been "burnt by the common hangman in the
Boston *Post.*"[20] That particular punishment was not inflicted on
the poor book in the April 18 review. I have scanned the *Post*
carefully without finding a notice in which the book was consigned
to just that cruel fate. Probably here was just another case of Melville's extreme sensitiveness to harsh treatment of *Mardi,* this time
finding an outlet in his extravagant dramatization of the implications
of the April 18 review.

At any rate, after this blow from Boston, it was well for Melville's
morale that his new book was spoken of with high enthusiasm by
five American journals, and by another with at least approval, before
April was over.[21] The first was the New Bedford *Mercury,* which
on April 20 declared that the "author of 'Typee' and 'Omoo'" was
"so well known" that "the appearance of a new work from his
singularly fascinating pen will be cordially welcomed"; it quoted from
Mardi's first chapter; and referred "our readers to the work itself for
the subsequent details of 'Perils round the stormy capes,' the 'landing
at the island of Guam,' 'a dinner with four-and-twenty Kings' . . .
and adventures of all sorts by sea and land, through some 700 or 800
pages of unique and graphic descriptions, mingled with genial humor,
philosophy and originality of thought, altogether inimitable."

Almost equal approbation came the next day, April 21, from
editor William Young—probably the reviewer—in the *Albion,*[22] who
found in *Mardi* "an infinite fund of wit, humor, pathos, and philosophy"; the "same charming powers of description already evinced . . .
in 'Typee' and 'Omoo,' while the range of the subject is far more comprehensive, and the abilities of the author are in consequence farther
developed"; and "a lively, pungent, instructive, and exceedingly clever
bundle of his thoughts and imaginings." One of the few Americans
to raise objections to the writing, the *Albion's* reviewer yet thought
the book contained ample compensations: in the "style we notice a

---

20. *Log,* p. 300.

21. In its tri-weekly edition for April 16 the *National Intelligencer* quoted with no
comment Duyckinck's first flattering review in the *Literary World,* which included the
chapter about the twenty-four kings, and inserted the whole again in its weekly edition
on April 28.

22. *Albion* had on April 14 published selections from *Mardi.*

too habitual inversion, an over-straining after antithesis and Carlyle-isms, with the not-infrequent sacrifice of the natural to the quaint. These defects, however, are spots in the sun; and we welcome Mardi to a place on all bookshelves and a cupboard in the chambers of memory." A charmingly domestic metaphor!

No such qualms about the style or anything else troubled Nathaniel P. Willis—surely the writer in his *Home Journal* on the same April 21 who revealed here the characteristically Willisian penchant for flatter-ing literary allusion and ebullient romantic enthusiasm which Melville more than once aroused in him. He professed *Mardi* was wholly en-gaging: ". . . a good book from a man of genius being like Keats' thing of beauty:—'a joy forever.'" *Mardi* was "in a higher vein" than *Typee* and *Omoo,* "still richer in description, fuller of incident, with more humor, wit, character," and "will undoubtedly" be "here and in England . . . the book of the season."

Brave in the face of British condescension toward American let-ters, Willis reminded readers of the "ecstasies into which the London press was thrown" by *Typee,* and thought *Mardi* "will increase the wonder." It was not the first book "which America has sent across the water of late years to enrich the London market"; and "Naturally we may expect greater freshness and fertility of invention from the American writer, and such books as 'Typee' and 'Mardi' are evidence that the expectation will not be disappointed." Willis declared—

Mardi is an exquisite book, full of all oriental delights. It is not at all like Typee in its plan, but it is something like it in feeling, though the interest is of a higher character. We . . . will . . . introduce the reader to what we predict will turn out the favorite character . . . of the book— a virgin rescued from the hands of a party of priests about to lead her to sacrifice. Her whole life has been in their hands; they have told her stories of her infancy of a mystical poetical character, fed her on "The honey dew of Paradise" till her whole existence seems supernatural and devoted . . . . We quote this, as a whet to the feast in store: [the chapter "Yillah in Ardair"].[23]

On May 5 in the *Home Journal* Willis briefly reaffirmed his high opinion of *Mardi,* wherein one need not try "to separate fact from fiction, as the author confessedly writes" here "for the single purpose of making a charming book, although there are authentic phenomena

23. Under its banner, the *Home Journal* carried this: "By Morris and Willis." Willis did most of the writing, as his partner Morris was the business manager (Beer, p. 103). It was probably Willis who had written with similar ardor about *Typee* in the *Mirror.*

recorded. The large class who delight in records of travel and graphic narrative, will enjoy 'Mardi' in the highest degree."

That Willis was respected in Richmond as a critic was shown on April 27 in that city's *Republican and General Advertiser*,[24] which thought *Mardi* bid "fair to be the rage of the reading world the next season." *Typee*, which with its truly American "freshness and originality" was as a "bubbling stream" for readers who had "burned up their brains in the hot beds of the Eugène Sue and Lytton Bulwer school of literature," had been a tremendous success: but, said the *Republican*, the author had now produced a work "which in the opinion of the best critics is superior to 'Typee,' and is destined not only to create a great sensation, but to shed a still broader blaze of light on that funny question once asked in England,—'Who reads an American Book?' We subjoin from the 'Home Journal' edited by Morris and Willis, the following editorial notice of 'Mardi.' It must be a rare work which elicits such commendation from such critics."

The New York *Atlas* on April 22 had briefly revealed its admiration of "a wonder of Polynesian adventure, equalling in its characteristics the merits of Ellis and the beauties of Sir John Singleton." The Newark *Daily Advertiser,* on April 24, was certain that Melville had reached a new high in a work which, equalling *Typee* and *Omoo* "in wild interest and picturesque beauty" possessed—"a higher degree of merit—exhibiting through stirring and diverse scenes an intimate acquaintance with human nature, and an unlooked for love of high philosophical speculation. The author's romances of the real appeal mostly to the love of the sensuous and the adventurous; this his ideal romance, addresses also the imagination and reasoning faculties . . . on the whole a remarkable book. . . ."

The New York *Literary American* on April 28 liked *Mardi* without regarding it necessarily as an advancement, indeed "could find little difference between the supposed true narratives and the professed romance," as they were "all marked by the same off-hand facile style, the same engrossing marvelous incident, and the same knowledge of the sea"—characteristics which had contributed to the young writer's "decided" success. A "few hours" could not "be spent more pleasantly than in reading this Polynesian Romance, which contains, no doubt, a faithful portraiture of the manners of the people, and is a *rara avis* in both plan and execution."

24. The editors were Oliver P. Baldwin and Robert F. Gallagher.

Besides the Boston *Post,* only one journal refused to concur in the nearly unanimous April verdict in favor of *Mardi.* No Devil's Advocate, like Colonel Greene, but only a mild dissenter was the Worchester *Palladium* on April 25. Referring to the preface, the *Palladium* said that Melville's "dissatisfaction with his success in authorship" was shown in his not drawing "the line vividly between truth and fiction" and thus marring his performance. The author of *Mardi* had "many attractive qualities": "He is ever watchful, sprightly and ready, to catch materials . . . wherever he finds them . . . in . . . nature, or in the manifestations of the world of spirit, of mind, of sentiment"; yet, although the book had its "peculiar merit," the *Palladium* thought the public would not consider it "an improvement upon his former productions." "Many might read it "for something to carp at . . . ."

The next month opened with some fervent if strange praise on May 2 from the Boston *Daily Bee,* which had on April 28 contained this single sentence: " 'Mardi' which we are now reading is thrillingly interesting." Now, four days later, the *Bee's* was the most curious of all the reactions to the problem of fiction and truth. Melville had offered this romance, the *Bee* said, to see whether the "fiction might not, possibly be received for a verity." Indeed that is just how the *Bee* received it:

> Notwithstanding . . . the preface, we can scarcely realize that the characters portrayed in the pages we have managed to find time to read are not real personages. Honest Jarl, that hardy ole norseman—Samoa and Anatoo, the "model couple"—the real Borabolla—the transcendental Babbalanja—all must have been real personages, or the author never could have given us such life-like portrayals of them and of their peculiarities. And the lovely Yillah too; why where in the brain could such a lovely portrait of waking beauty have been taken from as this—read it, and then buy the book: [Quotation: description of Yillah].

Melville must have been amazed. What did he think of this notion that the creator of the symbolical Yillah and the esoteric Babbalanja had met them in the flesh in Tahiti or the Marquesas?

After enjoying nearly a month of virtually all favorable American reviews, Melville discovered on the front page of the New York *Daily Tribune* for May 10 a long condemnation of *Mardi* signed "R" and thus from the pen of George Ripley, who was later to admire *Moby-Dick.* Ripley exclaimed that his "reading faculty" had never been "so near exhaustion" or his "good nature" as a critic "so severely exercised" as in "the attempt to get through this new work by the author of the fascinating 'Typee' and 'Omoo.'" If he had never heard of Melville he would soon have laid it aside "as a momentous compound of Carlyle, Jean-Paul, and Sterne, with now and then a touch of Ossian."

Melville's first two books were based on personal experience, "ever revealing the soul of a poet and the eye of a painter"; the present "aims at a much higher mark and fails to reach it." Ripley agreed with so many of the British that the first part was "excellent," for "therein Melville is himself—and this is saying a great deal"; but after he arrived in Mardi, he was presented with "a tissue of conceits . . . expressed in language that is equally intolerable for its affectation and its obscurity." "The story has no movement, no proportions, no ultimate end; and unless it is a huge allegory, bits of which peep out here and there, winding its unwieldy length along, like some monster of the deep, no significance or point. We become weary with the shapeless rhapsody, and wonder at the audacity of the writer which could attempt such an experiment with the long-suffering of his readers." Melville exhibited promise as well as "excellent performance," but had left his true "sphere," and should return to "the transparent narration of his own adventures."

The next day, however, there were kind words from Virginia. The Richmond *Enquirer* on May 11 ended an altogether affirmative brief notice by remarking that *Mardi* "abounds in very spirited and graceful sketches of land and ocean, of the pursuit of the whale. . . ." And the May *Hunt's Merchant's Magazine* could "conscientiously commend" *Mardi* "to the attention of every reader." The "recollection of the thrill of pleasure" with which Melville's first two books were read would, *Hunt's* hoped, lead to "further acquaintance with the original mind of their gifted author." *Mardi* would ". . . more than fully repay a careful perusal. The style is unique and cannot be described. It is peculiarly the author's own. He has started a new track and disdains the beaten path. The language possesses all the polish of an Irving with all the spirit of a Scott. The matter is truly poetical—philosophical as Plato, yet beautifully imaginative as Moore; the treatment thoroughly dramatic. As a whole, it is a master stroke of genius."

The pendulum was swinging, and another commentary published in Richmond this month was very negative. The May *Southern Literary Messenger* carried a letter from the New Yorker Park Benjamin pronouncing *Mardi* a "failure": "The attempt was considerable; the labor of production must have been great, since every page fairly reeks with 'the smoke of the lamp.'" *Typee* and *Omoo* were fine,, but in *Mardi* ". . . there is . . . a continual straining after effect, an effort constantly at fine writing, a sacrifice of natural ease to artificial witticism." Melville had been "overfed with praise," and had to "write up to" his reputation.[25]

Three American magazines contained discussions of *Mardi* in June. Charles F. Briggs in the June *Holden's Dollar Magazine* was certainly inconsistent.[26] Complimenting the style of *Typee* and *Omoo*, he said that *Mardi* "had been written with more care and ambition," but that it "abounds in the same traits of a generous and frolicksome nature, and is as graceful, pure, and glowing . . . ." Indeed it was "elegant and most entertaining." It was perhaps after reading only the first part that Briggs penned these praises and after reading to the end that he wrote with some self-contradiction the following: "The great defect of Mardi is the apparent want of motive in the composition; it is . . . difficult . . . to guess at the aims of the author; if he had any satirical intentions, they are so cunningly covered up that we cannot discover them; there is no story to interest, but a dreamy kind of voluptuousness, and an ecstatic outburst of abandoned animal impulse . . . there are also affectations of style and rhapsodical episodes, which puzzle the reader, and after going all through the ['elegant and most entertaining'?] volumes, he at last lays them down with a wonder as to the author's meaning, and a bewildered feeling of having been in a dream. Perhaps this was the very object aimed at by Mr. Melville, and if so he has been very successful."

Bayard Taylor, later to be famous as the American Marco Polo of the age, was then a protégé of Willis, who had helped him to finance his first trip abroad, a vagabond expedition the fruitage of which was his profitable *Views Afoot* (1846), dedicated to Willis.[27] Taylor perhaps wrote the comments in the June *Graham's Magazine*[28] wherein

25. Given in *Log*, p. 305.

26. Briggs's authorship is suggested by Leyda (*Log*, p. 305) and assumed by Miller (p. 249), who gives the month incorrectly as March. On June 16 the *Literary World* published an extract from *Mardi*. On June 30 the Philadelphia *Courier* in its Semi-Annual Pictorial Issue carried a quotation from Duyckinck's review.

27. Beers, p. 298.

28. It is more than possible that this contributor to *Graham's* was Taylor, who had composed the gracious Valentine for Melville for Anne Lynch's party the year before, and was to have dinner with Melville the next year (*Log*, p. 395). In the late summer of 1848 Taylor had been offered the editorship of *Graham's* at a good salary and had eagerly accepted; but the finances of *Graham's* were shaky, and he ended up by taking in September a "nominal editorship" which did not require him

like Willis, he set *Mardi* far above *Typee*: " 'Mardi' is altogether the most striking work which Mr. Melville has produced, exhibiting a range of learning, a fluency of fancy, and an originality of thought and diction, of which 'Typee' with all its distinctness and luxuriance of description gave little evidence." Truly prophetic, he continued: "At the same time it has defects indicating that the author has not yet reached the limits of his capacity, and that we may hope from him works even better than the present," since *Mardi,* although it lacked 'unity and fusion," was "full of those original touches which indicate original genius."

Mrs. Sarah Josepha Hale had in her "Editor's Book Table" in the June *Godey's Magazine and Lady's Book* a curiously noncommittal notice, but she revealed her low opinion of the new book when in her "Editor's Book Table" the next February she called *Redburn* "a sensible book, and one that will do more for the author's reputation than ten thousand such as 'Mardi.' "

Outstanding was Young American William Alfred Jones's[29] article on *Mardi* in the July *Democratic Review* since his was, besides Duyckinck's, the only favorable American review of length, and because he gave the religious theme more careful thought than did anyone else. Jones, later Librarian of Columbia College, was pronounced a sound critic by Washington Irving.[30]

Although a most deferential admirer of *Mardi,* Jones had a puritanical streak which led him to take time to denounce the smoking and drinking, the "frequent turning up of the calabashes" during the voyage. He hastened, however, to extenuate the author: "While he describes the drinking and smoking as his own act . . . we do not believe that they are in his actual life, though we confess that there

---

to leave New York and meant only that he became a "little more frequent contributor" (*Life and Letters of Bayard Taylor,* edited by Marie Hansen-Taylor and Horace E. Scudder [Boston, 1884], p. 127). Meanwhile he also continued to work as a reporter for the *Tribune* in New York, but on June 28, 1849 sailed for California to over the gold rush for that paper (Albert H. Smyth, *Bayard Taylor* [Boston and New York, 1860], p. 76). Dr. Frederick Taylor, a cousin of Bayard's was Melville's traveling companion to and from Europe in the fall of 1849 and in early 1850 (*Log,* pp. 318, 364).

29. Jones's authorship is suggested by Leyda (*Log,* p. 309), and assumed by Miller (p. 249). The importance of this review had been pointed out years ago by Carl Van Vechten, *Excavations: A Book of Advocacies* (New York, 1926), p. 78.

30. *National Cyclopedia of American Biography.* Jones's reviews and critical papers were issued several times in book form and finally collected in *Characters and Criticisms* (1857), the volume especially praised by Irving. Poe and Bryant also admired Jones as a critic (*DAB*). Stafford, p. 76, describes Jones as "probably the best critic of prose in the period."

is a murkiness of Mardi that smells of the vile weed." Thus spoke a member of that American generation which conceived the prohibition movement, and flourished when "the number of young men who had never tasted alcohol was probably larger than in any previous place or time, unless in some Mohammedan countries at periods of religious revival."[31] Indeed, Melville's glorification of alcoholic delights had annoyed some critics of *Omoo,* and probably all in all did his reputation no good. Then there had been the picture in *Typee* of Fayaway smoking!

Yet few have ever admired more fervently the poetic beauties of *Mardi* than did Jones. Lewis Mumford, with his contempt for those whose shallowness kept them from responding to the vibrant harmonies of a style he called an "orchestra,"[32] was anticipated seventy-five years earlier with truly startling exactitude by Jones, with his scorn for "those who rejoiced in the flute-like music of Melville's *Typee* and *Omoo,* and had not the slightest conception of the meaning of the magnificent *orchestra* [my italics] in Mardi . . . ." Yes, Mumford was thinking rather of *Moby-Dick* than of *Mardi*—one of many instances in which the nineteenth century had its most lavish praise for a work of Melville's other than the one a later century was to honor most— and Jones is not known to have written about *Moby-Dick.* But he did liken those who wanted another *Typee* or *Omoo* to "the man who expects and asks for loaf sugar" and "will not be satisfied with marble though it be built into a palace," thus surely gratifying a young man who felt *Mardi* was so far his finest artifact. The scope of the author's vision, said Jones, was so broad that many would not have seen the world as Melville had: "The fact that Mardi is an allegory that mirrors the world has thus far escaped the critics." (Not Duyckinck, who *had* virtually said it was an allegory, nor the disparaging Ripley and *Examiner.*) Yet surely perceptive was Jones's interpretation of the theme: "In these volumes, youth with its pure, deep love, its fervid aspirations, is personified. The hard rugged world, full of politics trade and theology, and a good many other things quite as real and unlovely, passes in review before our voyager, and everywhere he seeks that the shine of Yillah may fall again on his soul."

31. Fish, p. 266. W. O. Peabody, in reviewing the Reverend Sylvester Judd's *Margaret* (1845), notable for its accurate antiquarianism, in the *North American Review* for January, 1846, declared Judd had besmirched the fair fame of New England by his portrayal of her bibulous past, and expressed special horror of his picture of the heavy drinking at an ordination.

32. "Small wonder," says Mumford, p. 183, "that those who were used to elegant pianoforte solos or barrel organ instrumentation were surprised and repulsed."

Jones protested vigorously against those who made petty strictures upon "the works of genius," who would "pluck the eagle's quills": "We reverence a man when God's *must* is upon him, and he does his work in his own and other's spite. Portions of Mardi are written with this divine impulse, and they thrill through every fibre of the reader with an electric force."

Thus for Jones *Mardi* satisfied one of his main criteria for literary greatness—essential religious inspiration.[33] He saw, however, that *Mardi* projected a conflict between love and Christian love, a conflict that was not fully resolved. The skeptical philosopher Babbalanja was indeed converted to Christianity and settled in Serenia, the isle of Christians, but not so the chief seeker Taji, who was under a compulsion to continue his quest for Yillah instead of remaining there. Jones was right in saying that "With all his humanity Mr. Melville seems to lack the absolute faith that God had a purpose in creating the world."

Yet if Melville did not attain to the basic confidence in Divine wisdom which Jones so admired in as diverse guises as the poetry of Crashaw and the essays of Emerson, he did satisfy another of Jones's criteria of greatness—capacity for seeing religion as deepening man's love and leading to his regeneration:[34] "Whoso wishes to read a romance—a novel of the sentimental or satanic school—has no business in Mardi. . . . But whoso wishes to see the spirit of philosophy and humanity, love and wisdom, showing man to himself as he is, that he may know his evil and folly, and be saved from them, will be reverently thankful for this book. There is an immortality in love. It is indeed the only immortality—and the author, whose heart burns within him like a live coal from God's own altar, need take no care for his fame. Such a one is Herman Melville."

These two criteria were part of the literary creed of Duyckinck also—indeed of Young America.[35] Those with such a religious approach penetrated more deeply into *Mardi,* as will be seen, than did the pagan Fitz-James O'Brien. In that century it was the Hebraist rather than the Hellenist who came nearest to foreseeing Melville's ultimate renown, and also to discovering—if not always with complete sympathy—what Melville was to call the "inmost leaf of the bulb," whose real unfolding surely began with *Mardi.*

33. Stafford, p. 58. Stafford ascribes this review incorrectly to Duyckinck, who in his *Literary World* review did not apply these criteria to any extent.
34. *Ibid.,* pp. 98, 118, 52.
35. *Ibid.,* p. 59.

Since July passed without, so far as I know, any American press comment on *Mardi* besides Jones's high estimate, Melville may have felt enheartened—particularly as in August probably John Sartain (best known as an illustrator) in *Sartain's Union Magazine* was altogether admiring, if brief. Upon finishing the book he decided that since "the 'fabled East' " had been "stripped of its mystery," "Romance as well as empire must travel westward"; that he would not be "at all surprised to see Polynesia, with its myriad islands and bewitching climate, becoming to romance what the 'fabled East' has been for more than thirty centuries"; and that he should "be happy to accompany the author in any future voyage he may make in the same direction." Apparently *Mardi* was for him only a more mysterious yet still pleasing *Omoo*. But the reaction of Frederick S. Cozzens (under the pseudonym Richard Haywarde) in a column in the August *Graham's Magazine* was mixed and exasperated: "Confound the book! there are such beautiful Aurora-flashes of light in it that you can almost forgive the puerilities—it is a great net-work of affectation, with some genuine *gold* shining through the interstices . . ." (Cozzens was the Knickerbocker set's authority on wine).

In September *Mardi* definitely fell on evil times. First was the *American Review,* which began unequivocally: "Mr. Melville, we are sorry to hint, has failed in this book . . . . Vaulting ambition has overleaped itself." It has been assumed that the contributor was Melville's old enemy Peck.[36] Could Peck have so far forgotten that he had two years before dismissed *Omoo* as "tawdry," like a "rickety ill built cottage," as well as "venerous" and "venomous"—epithets he implied clearly applied also to *Typee*—as now to speak of "the praise (we would not say excessive) that the author's *delightful* works [my italics] Typee and Omoo received"? If this reviewer had been the sex-obsessed Peck, he would surely have denounced the temptress Hautia and been fascinated by the pursuit of Yillah instead of totally ignoring both of these females.

This reviewer had a theory as to what had gone wrong with *Mardi,* a book in which although "every page . . . undoubtedly exhibits the man of genius, and facile writer," it "exhibits also pedantry and affectation." What had done the "mischief" was the "astonishment expressed that a common sailor should exhibit so much reading and knowledge of literature": "This was evidently the Author's weak point,

36. Miller, p. 251. Leyda does *not* ascribe this review to Peck (*Log,* p. 315).

and he thereupon (certainly with great ingenuity) contrives a story, the scenes of which are among semi-savages, and in unknown islands, that shall be illustrated on every page by allusions to things historical and literary, scientific, theological, and mythological, of all ages and nations. We half suspect, however, that Mr. Melville intended this as a quiz, but at any rate he has overdone it, and made a tedious book."

Perhaps the most crushing of all the American blows given *Mardi,* because it was so elaborately and specifically adverse, was Henry Cood Watson's[37] attack on September 29 in *Saroni's Musical Times,* though he allowed some incidental merits. Like many others, Watson, English-born music critic of some prominence, was disappointed at not finding another *Omoo,* and his "feelings were anything but gentle toward its gifted author": "We were flattered with the promise of an account of travel, amusing, though fictitious; and we have been compelled to pore over an undigested mass of rambling metaphysics. We had hoped for a pleasant travel ride among the sunny isles of the tropics, instead of which, we were taken bodily, and immersed in the fathomless sea of Allegory, from which we have just emerged gasping for breath, with monstrous Types, Myths, Symbols, and such like fantastic weeds tangled in our vestments and hair . . . the reputation of the author did not prepare us for dull trash . . . its persual has proven to us a most unmitigated 'mortification of the flesh.' "

For Watson everything about *Mardi* had been marred. It began with an "agreeable sea romance," but then plunged into a "cold bath of symbolical ethics, metaphysics, and political economy." The "style" was its "sole redeeming feature," but there seemed to be no plan. Melville "possesses many of the essentials of poetry . . . Nevertheless although so poetic in his prose, he is remarkably unfortunate in his verse." The discourse was sometimes "very pleasing," but sometimes "very prolix and tedious." The "rank vegetation" hid the "roses." The reader "will often have occasion to admire the genius of our

37. This issue of *Saroni's* contains the following statement: "All the Editorial Articles in this number of our paper, are from the pen of Mr. Henry C. Watson, whose services we freely acknowledge. In the future the *Musical Times* will be edited by Mr. H. S. Saroni alone." *DAB* makes it certain that this was Henry Cood Watson (not Henry Clay Watson, who was only eighteen at the time), a prominent music critic, who had been associated with Poe on the *Broadway Journal.* Born in London, he had made a youthful voyage on the Mediterranean before settling in New York.

author; and oftener still, he will painfully realize that—to use Mr. Melville's own words: 'Genius is full of trash.' "[38]

Mardi might have fared much better with the reviewer, probably Simms, in the October *Southern Quarterly Review,* if it had not at one place stepped on sectional toes. Simms comprehended some of the main features: it took "the form of allegory rather than action or adventure"; it was "a fanciful voyage about the world in search of happiness"; "in this voyage the author gives a satirical picture of most of the deeds and doings of the more prominent nations under names which preserve the sound of the real word to the ear, while slightly disguising it to the eye." But alas! "In this progress, which is a somewhat monotonous one, the author gives us many glowing rhapsodies, much epigrammatic thought, and many sweet and attractive fancies; but he spoils everything to the Southern reader when he paints a loathsome picture of Mr. Calhoun, in the character of a slave driver, drawing mixed blood and tears from the victim at every stroke of the whip. We make no further comments." And, so far as I know, that was the last American review of *Mardi.*

Numerically *Mardi* came off very well with the American press during 1849. Out of a total of thirty press notices (counting the two by Duyckinck as two) twenty were entirely good. Of the ten not completely favorable, three were in-between (Briggs, Cozzens, *Palladium*); one other was revealed next year to be hostile (Mrs. Hale); one extolled the literary qualities but condemned it for a sectional reason (Simms). Of the five predominantly adverse articles, two admitted there was wheat though obscured by the chaff (*American Review,* Watson), leaving just three who dismissed the book as utterly unredeemed (Greene, Benjamin, Ripley). It is true that, in the case of *Mardi* more than any of Melville's other books, good notices were hastily penned by busy journalists who assumed that the author of works so successful as the previous books could do no wrong, but who might have changed their opinion if they had examined the new book more carefully. Yet there is no reason for making such an assumption about the seven who proclaimed *Mardi* an advance over *Typee* and *Omoo* (Duyckinck—"bolder invention," more "subtle,"; *Albion;* Willis—"richer"; Newark *Advertiser;* Richmond *Republican; Graham's*—greater "originality"; Jones—"marble" after the "loaf sugar"). At least five other admirers showed real deliberation (*Mirror, Mercury,*

38. Contrast Newton Arvin, *Herman Melville* (New York and Toronto, 1950), p. 100: "If *Mardi* is a mixture of trash and genuineness, however, it is the sort of mixture of which only genius is capable."

Literary American, Bee, Hunt's), leaving five of the favorable items which were admittedly pretty negligible. The allegory was remarked disapprovingly by two (Greeley, Watson), tolerantly by one (Simms), and admiringly by two (Duyckinck, Jones). The condemnations (Greene, Ripley, Watson) were stinging; but the two most thoughtful reviews were extremely adulatory (Duyckinck, Jones). *Mardi* aroused a mixed American reaction, but by no means the total rejection sometimes assumed.

Mardi had been received less well in London than in New York, but there had come a pronouncement from a city as civilized as London, from Paris, that it was a work of real significance. As can be imagined, this statement was eagerly reprinted by Melville's supporters in America. The main concern of the French critic Philarète Chasles was less with Melville's "voyages réels," than with his "voyage fantastique," as was shown by his giving two thirds of his space to *Mardi*.[39] George Duyckinck appended to his translation of Chasles' article in the *Literary World* for August 11, a note to the effect that *Mardi* was a work of a "higher order" than its author's earlier efforts.[40]

Chasles subordinated both his praise and his censure of *Mardi* to his amused wonder at it as a remarkable and significant curiosity. It was "one of the most singular books which have for a long time appeared on the face of the globe"; and Melville was the type of the "caractère anglo-américain," full of crude force, straining after originality, and above all, yearning for hyperbole—in short a curious specimen invaluable to those who wished to study that incredible and enormous phenomenon, America. Chasles' approach was a Gallic intensification of that of some of the British, and was just that which Lowell was to satirize in 1869 in *On a Certain Condescension in Foreigners*: "No entomologist could take a more friendly interest in a strange bug." To Chasles, Melville was at least a pretty big bug. Chasles did call Melville "un Rabelais américain," as has often been noted; but he also said that America had not yet attained to the richness of culture necessary for the production of a true "livre humoriste."

Yet Chasles was much impressed with the political criticism in *Mardi*. His description of the transition between the central and latter parts of the book was a neat one: ". . . du symbolisme métaphysique nous passons à l'allégorie transparente." It was this third part,

39. For the bibliography of the Chasles material, see Chapter II, footnote 73.
40. George had told Joann Miller in a letter of April 11, that Melville had "outdone himself" in *Mardi* (*Log*, p. 297).

in which the countries of the Occident are satirized under the guise of Polynesian islands which most interested the French critic. The European revolutions of 1848 aroused much satisfaction among Americans, who felt that the Europeans were at last coming to appreciate the American example in government.[41] Chasles relished Melville's satiric portrayal of the excited crowds in Northern Vivenza (North America) receiving with loudly expressed joy the news of the spread of the conflagration of revolution from Franko (France) throughout Porpheerio (Europe), as he did also the ridicule of the American self-congratulation over the eternity of republics. He admitted as fair, also, Melville's hits at the eternal French propensity to revolution.

Curiously enough, the delayed American reaction to *Mardi* was less adverse than it was to some of Melville's books which had better beginning luck. Donald G. Mitchell did give it a disparaging mention in the *Lorgnette* in 1850,[42] and it got some side digs in reviews of the later books, for instance from *Knickerbocker,* which, having previously ignored it, rejoiced that the author of *White Jacket* was on the right track again after "the regrettable Mardi." On the other hand, Simms declared that "Wild, improbable, and fantastic as was that allegorical production," *Mardi* more than *Redburn* was "a proof of powers in reserve." Hawthorne described it privately in 1850 as a "rich book" though imperfect.[43] In 1851 came a most romantic tribute in Curtis's popular *Nile Notes of a Howadji,* wherein the Howadji reached for a book and soon "in the hot heat of noon he had drifted far into the dreamy depths of Herman Melville's Mardi": "Mardi is unrhymed poetry, but rhythmical and measured. Of a low, lapping cadence is the swell of those sentences. In more serious moods, they have the grave music of Bacon's Essays. Yet who but an American could have written them?"

That Chasles did consider Melville an author of relatively great importance among Americans was made clear in his book *Anglo American Literature and Manners* (1852), published by Scribners, in which his earlier essay on Melville appeared somewhat condensed as Chapter III. As even then Chasles did not mention any of Melville's books after *Mardi,* his judgment of Melville as an outstanding American writer was due largely to the impact on him of that book. His allotment of twenty-eight pages to Melville in a work which dis-

41. Fish, p. 313.

42. J. O. F. Rowe and H. S. Washburn and friends, about December, 1849, inscribed low opinions of *Mardi* on the last page of their copy (*Log,* p. 356).

43. In a letter on August 29 to Evert Duyckinck (*Log,* p. 391).

posed of Bryant in six and Emerson in less than two did arouse some amazement in America. The New York *International Magazine* in 1852 exclaimed: "To Herman Melville M. Chasles devoted fifty pages, while Mr. Ticknor has not even the honor of a mention. The author of this work is very far from doing justice to American literature and to himself."[44]

By 1853 the first seven of Melville's books had appeared, including *Moby-Dick*, but Fitz-James O'Brien made it clear in his *Putnam's* article that in his opinion only *Typee* excelled *Mardi*. He was fascinated by *Mardi*: his ardent Celtic nature glutted itself on its golden visions. He was strongly attracted by Melville's evocation of a shimmering Polynesian dream world, and equally strongly repelled by his ventures into the world of the mind. "For us," he said, "there is something very charming about Mardi, all the time fully aware of its said defects in taste and style." Reading this "wild book" was like "riding a Tartar steed in the desert." The language was "rich and heavy, with a plating of imagery." Melville had been affected by the singularly "mellifluous and resonant" Polynesian languages, but also by Sir Thomas Browne. "But we find no nonsense in Sir Thomas," and "can't always say as much for Melville." The "philosophical parts" of *Mardi* were the "worst," and O'Brien "did not pretend to understand the system laid down by the author": "When Mr. Melville does condescend to be intelligible, what he has to say for himself in the way of philosophy is so exceedingly stale and trite that it would be more in place in a school-boy's copy-book than in a romance otherwise distinguished for splendour of imagery, and richness of diction. The descriptive painting in this wild book is gorgeous and fantastic in the extreme." It was "a tapestry of dreams, woven with silken threads, dyed in the ocean of an eastern sunset."

If O'Brien did not go below the surface of *Mardi*, at least he got more out of it than he did out of *Moby-Dick*, which he merely mentioned as part of Melville's decline. No one in America was more likely than O'Brien to relish those frequent drainings of the calabashes, and that glittering chatter by which King Media and his party, in their progress through the sunny seas, celebrated their jovial bache-

---

44. An examination of a first edition reveals pages 118-146 devoted to Melville. The book was a translation of *Études sur la littérature et les moeurs des Anglo-Américains au XIX siècle* (1851), Paris. The American translation was also reviewed in *Harper's New Monthly Magazine* (5:856), which declared Chasles' strictures "more acute than profound and convincing"; that it would not take a permanent place as literary history; but that it was vivacious and worth reading.

lor fellowship. Of the would-be Bohemian group at Pfaff's beer cellar in New York, O'Brien was a literary arbiter,[45] where his laugh, said one of his friends "blew care away from the cup of life."[46] No wonder O'Brien turned away from the dark mysteries of *Moby-Dick*, and even from the more troubled parts of *Mardi* to revel in those of its pages that were mere gay phantasmagoria.

The Duyckincks' first enthusiasm for *Mardi* had cooled by the time of their *Cyclopaedia* (1855), wherein they declared that although it was "maimed as a book of thought and speculation by its want of sobriety," it had "many delicate traits and bursts of fancy and imagination." They too were at last most pleased by what it offered merely as a fantasy.

During the four years that followed 1853 O'Brien, as he sat among the beer mugs, read Melville's successive works. Not unexpectedly, in his 1857 *Putnam's* article, he lamented that Melville had drifted more and more toward "metaphysical and morbid speculations." He could admit that it was a "dull critic" who did not "recognize in every page" of "Melville's writings . . . however vague . . . the breathing spirit of a man of genius and a passionate and earnest man of genius": nor was Melville "a dilettante in metaphysics." If he seemed "fantastical," it was "because he wants to say something subtle and penetrating which he has discovered or thinks he has discovered." Yet he exclaimed: "We frankly own here, and now, and once for all, that we have not and never expect to have, the faintest notion of why we took a voyage to 'Mardi'; nor of what we found when we reached 'Mardi,' if we ever did reach it, nor of how we got away from 'Mardi' again, if we ever did get away from that mysterious place."

O'Brien's seem to have been the last American words on *Mardi* for years. The only later comment on it before its author's death I have found was in the *Supplement* (1870) to *Griswold's Prose Writers of America*, wherein it was characterized as "a rambling philosophical romance, with many delicate traits of fancy, but which it will pay nobody to wade through." Somewhat surprisingly, the Harpers reprinted it in 1855, and again 1864, but it was not reprinted again in American until 1923.[47]

45. Paul Fatout, "An Enchanted Titan," *South Atlantic Quarterly*, XXX (January, 1931), 51-59.

46. *The Poems and Tales of Fitz-James O'Brien*, ed. William Winter, (Boston 1881), Introduction, xxi.

47. Hetherington, p. 493.

CONCLUSION

The immediate American reception of *Mardi* was far more favorable than the British, any way the score is added. Melville told Judge Shaw that the American papers had done better by him.[48] On this side of the Atlantic twenty out of thirty press notices during 1849 expressed only satisfaction; over there only one out of fourteen (*Post*) found no faults, as even the publisher's organ demurred a little. Chasles' pronouncement that *Mardi* was important was reprinted three times in America and not once in Britain. The most penetrating positive study was by the American Jones. A similar contrast between the reactions in the two countries seems to prevail until into the eighties.

The reasons for this difference are not altogether clear. Were numerous Americans deterred by defensive patriotism from besmirching the gleaming renown of their successful young author? Perhaps the country which had recently produced Poe and Hawthorne was more receptive to fantasy, to symbol and allegory, to myth, to the supernatural? The odor of transcendentalism, unremarked in the book by the Americans, was a stench in the nostrils of two of the most sympathetic British.

Mardi was not much of a success at the bookstores. Melville wrote to Duyckinck that "a hollow purse makes a poet sink—witness 'Mardi.' "[49] It is true that scrutiny of available statistics does not reveal such a sharp downward sales trend as his complaint implies. For America and Britain together, during its first three years the sales of *Typee* averaged 310 per month, while during its first year, the sales of *Mardi* averaged 215 per month, not such a striking decline after all.[50] Percents of printed copies sold were 76 percent for *Mardi*, 85 percent for *Omoo*, and 92 percent for *Typee*.[51]

A dark picture of the economic fortunes of *Mardi* is indeed given by Richard Curle in his *Collecting American First Editions,* where he says that the Harpers, encouraged by the large sales of *Typee* and *Omoo* "printed a large edition of *Mardi*, which (without any pre-

48. *Log*, p. 300 (April 23, 1849).
49. *Log*, p. 347.
50. Weaver, pp. 253, 273.
51. According to an account sheet, which seems to cover both British and American sales, drawn up by Allan Melville in the fall of 1851, 2291 out of the 3000 copies of *Mardi* printed had been sold, as compared with 5649 out of 6500 of *Omoo*, and 7437 out of 8000 of *Typee* (*Log*, p. 426). At that time *Mardi* had been before the public two years, *Omoo* four, and *Typee* five.

sumption) turned out to be a dismal failure. And that was the fate of all his other books and the publishers never again ran the risk of being left with masses of unwanted copies. And so, even if there had not been a fire at Harpers, *Mardi* would still be his commonest book."[52] That is, of course, among first editions. Naturally in the fire at the Harpers on December 10, 1853, in which all books in stock were consumed, the destruction was greatest of those more recently published, *Pierre, Moby-Dick, White Jacket, Redburn,* and *Mardi.* Both Bentley and the Harpers lost money on *Mardi.*[53]

Were there no special reasons, aside from disappointment at the finances, for Melville's dejection about what had happened to *Mardi?* The three controversies which had been started by *Typee* and *Omoo* were not augmented by *Mardi.* Melville made it clear by his preface and his obvious inventiveness that he was writing fiction. Second, the handling of sex in *Mardi* was, at least apparently, very delicate, abstract, and ethereal. Any psychoanalytic implications of the Taji, Hautia, Yillah triangle, as expounded by modern critics,[54] would have shocked if they had been so understood, as of course they were not, in those pre-Freudian times. Third, there were things in *Mardi* which might conceivably have disturbed a sensitive orthodoxy. The weaknesses of institutionalized Christianity were exposed in the account of Maramma; and the central character, Taji, seems to reject the Messiah in leaving Serenia, the land of the true disciples of Alma, or Christ. On the other hand, Babbalanja, who had been a skeptic, and also the other voyagers do decide to remain in Serenia, and there is in the book neither the censure of the missionaries of the first two books, nor the satire on pretended Christians of *Moby-Dick.* Thus, in both England and America, there were only two objectors to *Mardi* on religious grounds, (*John Bull,* Jones). There was even one praiser of the "gentle religious teachings" (*Mirror*). How different from the vociferous if not wide-spread berating of the report on the missions in the first two books!

Those three controversies which had surged around *Typee* and *Omoo* had been a nuisance to Melville, and had led his publishers to put pressure on him to make revisions he did not approve, and had

52. (Indianapolis, 1930), p. 130. Curle must be referring to the size of editions printed by the Harpers, as, according to Allan's account, more copies of both *Redburn* and *White Jacket* than of *Mardi* were printed by Bentley plus the Harpers.

53. Howard, pp. 128, 133.

54. According to Arvin, p. 96, in *Mardi* "Physical sexuality was charged through and through with guilt and anxiety."

driven him, in his third book, into extravagant romance; yet they had helped to keep the first two books before the public. To a remarkable degree, before *Mardi*, there had been an almost total absence of censure on literary grounds.

Now, however, there was an almost total absence of censure of *Mardi* on any other grounds. The attacks on this book were virtually all on its deficiencies as art, on the confusions in its thought, on the feebleness of its design: that was what galled Melville. This was the first book in which he believed he had tested the wings of his imagination and sought to extrinsify his intellectual quests and emotional yearnings. He had gambled everything on *Mardi* as literature; and he felt that he had lost. It was a bitter anticlimax that such a book should be so assaulted after the universal acclaim of its more pedestrian predecessors as aesthetic triumphs.

The bravado which was in his first comments on the derogatory reviews was quite gone when on February 2, 1850 he sent a copy of *Mardi* to Evert Duyckinck accompanied by a poignant letter in which he expressed hope that his friend's choice library would afford "refuge to a work, which almost everywhere else has been driven forth like a wild, mystic Mormon into shelterless exile." He was exaggerating the hostility of the world's reaction; but the pain he suffered was in that letter, as it was later to be in references to fame in his letters to Hawthorne during the shaping of *Moby-Dick*. Now he told Duyckinck he could dream that *Mardi*, "a plant, now unblown," might possibly "flower like the aloe a hundred years hence." His confidence, however, had been shaken, for he added, "or not flower at all, for some aloes never flower."[55]

The aloe had not flowered by the year of his death, 1891; and yet it was to flower, and somewhat before a hundred years. To paint the blossoming of that aloe is not within my province; yet a few strokes on the canvas may be allowed. There was Carl Van Vechten who in 1926 described *Mardi* as "a wild and brilliant book of the imagination."[56] There was Gorham B. Munson who in 1929 referred to it as "that extraordinary rehearsal of his genius which Herman Melville performed before sitting down to write the greatest work in American literature, *Moby-Dick*."[57] There was Alexander Cowie who said of *Mardi* in 1949: "Yet as one turns its leaves of image, fable, vision, and satire, one is overwhelmed by the sincere fervor of Melville's

55. *Log*, p. 364.
56. *Excavations*, p. 78.
57. *Style and Form in American Prose* (New York, 1926), p. 138.

thought, the prodigality of his invention, the artfulness of his literary borrowings, and his dazzling display of language."[58]

Many of the early admirers of *Mardi,* especially the Americans, got no farther than revelling in it as a "tapestry of dreams." Those who tried to look below the shimmering surface were often baffled, or even repelled, or could speak cuttingly of "some purpose too deep for our plummet to fathom" (Chorley). Yet even in 1849 there were those who continued to adulate as they probed and went beyond a mere accolade for a lusher and dreamier *Omoo.* They perceived "profound reasonings" (*Mirror*); "spirit of humor and love and deep philosophy" (*Sartain's*); "genial humor, philosophy and originality of thought, altogether inimitable" (*Mercury*); "lively, pungent, instructive, and exceedingly clever bundle of thoughts and imaginings" (*Albion*); "glowing rhapsodies, much epigrammatic thought and many sweet and attractive fancies" (Simms). There were also its chief advocates—Duyckinck and Jones. It was almost a little American cult; but it was soon dispersed; and there lingered in the memory of the public, if anything at all, and in the memory of the fabricator of the whimsical voyage, the sting of the cat-o'-nine-tails of Colonel Greene, of Chorley, of formidable "Maga's" Wilson.

58. *The Rise of the American Novel,* p. 375.

Chapter V: REDBURN

"We are glad . . . that the author has descended from his sublime . . . to common and real life. His sailor boy's first voyage . . . is as perfect a specimen of the naval yarn as we ever read."—London *Literary Gazette* (1849), reviewing *Redburn*.

BRITISH RECEPTION

Having found anything but remunerative the experiment of offering his public a voyage frankly fantastic, the now impecunious young author made, with a voyage patently real, a candidly admitted bid for base shillings and dollars. Suggested by Melville's initial sea voyage, as a cabin boy in a merchantman plying between New York and Liverpool, but in many respects not autobiographical, this book was rather hastily put together, and the author's own expectations of favor with the critics were not high. *Redburn: His First Voyage. Being the Sailor-boy Confessions and Reminiscences of the Son-of-a-Gentleman in the Merchant Service* was published in London on September 26, 1849, and, like *Mardi*, by Richard Bentley.[1]

For once the London literary weeklies did not have the first word about one of Melville's books; they were this time anticipated by a London daily newspaper, the *Morning Post,* which on October 1 carried the first known review of *Redburn,* a long and complimentary one. The opening sentence in the *Post,* however, was an apt expression of the main reason *Redburn* aroused less interest than *Typee* and *Omoo*

1. Inserted as an advertisement into the London *Morning Post* on September 26, 1849, was the announcement of a new work "Redburn, etc." as "published this day" by Richard Bentley. But according to an advertisement in the *Morning Chronicle* it was published on September 27. *Redburn* was well advertised in London. It was advertised in the *Morning Herald* on September 8, 10, 12, 15, 17, 18, 19, 20, 21, 22, 24, 25, 26, 27, 28, 29, as well as every day or two throughout October. In the *Morning Post* it was advertised on September 22, 24, 25, 26, 27, 28, 29, on October 1, 8, 9, 10, 11; in the *Morning Chronicle* on October 6, 8, 10, 15, 16, 22.

had and less than *White Jacket* was destined to: it lacked the novelty of subject of the first two, and the novelty in point of view of the third. The *Post's* reviewer began: "The adventures of a sailor-boy during his first voyage in a 'regular trader' from New York to Liverpool, do not, at first thought, seem to prove very rife in novel incident, or rich in descriptive matter." He next epitomized the reason why, nevertheless, *Redburn* was to have a modest success: Melville possessed the "art" of "telling old stories and dressing up old subjects, and presenting old incidents . . . to look . . . fresh enough for the passing entertainment of one who reads for amusement." Such nautical matters readers probably had "heard something of" but would enjoy greatly "hearing described as he describes them" in "a narrative full of interest, and containing many bold portraits of striking individual sea characters, many graphic pictures of life" in a ship, and "some clever sketches of men and manners."

Alone among the British the *Post's* critic showed interest in Redburn's plea for the emigrants: "The details of the horrors aboard such a vessel as the Highlander, when returning to New York with a cargo of poor Irish emigrants are peculiarly deserving of notice: we believe some amelioration has taken place" in the lot "of these live cargoes of human beings, but still the emigrant vessels require to be closely watched."

After pointing out two minor errors[2] and giving extensive extracts, he concluded flatteringly that Melville was "already known" for his "great descriptive power and considerable fancy. . . . 'Mardi' gave high promise . . . fully borne out in 'Redburn,' who, we trust, will ere long give us another yarn as entertaining." Thus the chronicle of the reputation of *Redburn* begins most auspiciously.

On October 20, it was probably editor William Jerdan who, in the London *Literary Gazette*, differing from most of the British, was silent about the lack of originality in the basic materials of *Redburn*. His judgment of this book, unlike his judgment of *Mardi*, was completely affirmative. Curiously enough, he considered not only *Mardi*, but also *Typee* and *Omoo* "allegories,"[3] and rejoiced that Mel-

2. The *Post* objected to an account of a man reading the London *Times* on the score that there was no such paper. (Its name is the *Times*, as I was once tartly reminded by an official of the British Museum), and also to the "incredible" description of the nobleman who had a cornet on his boot sole.

3. I have found no one else who in the nineteenth century took *Typee* to be an allegory; the novel opinion in the *Gazette* is interesting in connection with the contention of Richard Chase (*Herman Melville* [New York, 1949], p. 15) that *Typee* is more interpenetrated with symbolism than any of Melville's other works before *Moby-*

ville had turned to realism: great had been the fame of his "allegories," he said, but "we could not learn so much from *Typee* as from *Gulliver*, from *Omoo* as from *Lilliput*, nor from *Mardi* as *Laputa*." He was "glad, therefore, that the author has descended from his sublime, not to the ridiculous, but to common and real life. His sailor boy's first voyage . . . is as perfect a specimen of the naval yarn as we ever read." He liked its being told "by a mere lad"; and found the last part "still powerful" but "less unified than the first."

Also on October 20, the London *Spectator's* critic, perhaps Thornton Hunt, although he thought the new book lacked the "veracity" of *Two Years Before the Mast* and was inferior to the work of Cooper, still rated it high. This was definitely the most friendly of the reviews of Melville's books in a journal usually pretty hostile to him. It was his restrained realism that especially pleased the *Spectator's* writer. *Redburn* afforded both "information and interest"; the hardships were portrayed without "melodramatic exaggeration." The author left "the filling up to the reader's imagination, instead of painting scenes in detail" as "a vulgar writer would have certainly done. The interest of 'Redburn' arises from its quiet naturalness. It reads 'like a true story.'" The New York scenes revealed that American coast cities were not "much freer from vice and profligacy" or "distress, than the seaports of Europe." Apparently this Briton did not consider Melville's sinister picture of Liverpool overdrawn, for he simply remarked: "At Liverpool many things are fresh to an American that are common to us, or which we ignore without intending it"; and he quoted a passage portraying this city's depravity and destitution.

Redburn reminded the *Spectator's* writer of Marryat, yet seemed no slavish imitation; for although the general idea was in *Peter Simple,* the circumstances were so different "that the story has the effect of originality." The "quiet humor" indeed resembled somewhat Marryat's, which might, however, "arise from the nature of the subject."

John Bull, a week later, on October 27, also thought *Redburn* a great improvement—its author's "faults grow less conspicuous as time runs on, while his excellencies remain undiminished"—but for moral rather than aesthetic reasons: "There was in his earlier works a propensity to portray slippery scenes and to exhibit vice scarcely veiled, for . . . amusement. . . . Of this he has happily steered clear in the present volumes, which in other respects yield to none of his previous works

Dick. This was surely the same contributor as he who in reviewing *Mardi* spoke of its "allegorical theme."

in interest and diversity of narrative, in liveliness of tone, and graphic power of delineation." Like others, *John Bull* was reminded of Marryat, whose "place," however, Melville "bids fair to take."

So far fortune seemed to be smiling on *Redburn*, but now on October 27, the same day it was warmly applauded by *John Bull,* came from *Britannia* the first attack, in the most hostile of the British reviews. As usual, *Britannia* derided Melville's egregious faults as typically American: "The fierce and swaggering exaggeration of the Yankee style is forcibly and, if truth be told, unpleasantly conspicuous in this work." Liverpool appeared "in these pages to be quite as strange and queer a place as any that figure in 'Omoo' or 'Typee.' The author's faculty of representation is similar to that possessed by a bad glass. He distorts whatever he reflects, making every object appear monstrous and unnatural." Here was one Briton who seemingly resented bitterly Melville's depiction of the terrible plight of the Liverpool poor.

In a crushing condemnation, *Britannia* could allow merit to the opening section only: "The first part of the work, relating the childhood of an imaginative and adventurous spirit, is the best, and there are some saltwater passages in the account of the voyage across the Atlantic of great breadth and power. But the staple of the book is so coarse and horrible, mingled, however, with much that is tediously minute, as to leave anything rather than an agreeable impression . . . [illustrated by quoting the death of Jackson]."

In an acidulous conclusion, *Britannia* gave Melville up as hopeless: "The author, from his slap-dash kind of writing, seems to have taken up with the notion that anything will do for the public. . . . In this work as in 'Mardi' his talent seems to be running to seed from want of careful pruning, and unless he pays more attention to his composition in the future, we think it very unlikely that the announcement of a new work from his pen will excite the slightest desire to peruse it."

After *Britannia's* wintry blast, Melville must have been happy to find the London *Daily News* two days later, on October, 29, as laudatory as *Britannia* had been derogatory. The *News,* indeed, detected a technical flaw, which was overlooked by the other reviewers, but has been pointed out recently by Gilman.[4] "There is a discrepancy felt at first between the author and the biographer," said the *News.*

4. William H. Gilman, *Melville's Early Life and Redburn* (New York, 1951), p. 206. Gilman differs from the *News* in stating that the "defect" does not show up until "after the guide book incident" in Liverpool.

"Herman Melville and Redburn are two distinct personages; thus when Redburn does a silly action, we find him enveloping it with rich thought and keen observation. How can we admit the fool in action with the 'wit in mind'?"

Everything else the *News* said was in approbation. Here was "another voice from the forecastle . . . pleasant as Dana's 'Two Years Before the Mast' in its earnestness and simplicity." True there was not the "holiday look of joyous blitheness of Dana," as "Redburn's first voyage is one of hardship and struggling against the difficulties which old seamen put in the way of greenhorns, and is likely to act as a considerable damper to those who, like the hero, feel a vocation for the sea"; but the boy's "original Chattertonian misanthrophy wears off."

The author had "a clear simple style"; and in "the way . . . ship and crew are depicted, and are artfully made subservient to the character and story, one is reminded of Defoe." The picture of Liverpool, said the *News* (apparently not resenting its being so harrowing) was of "Daguerreotype fidelity and freshness." The final words from the *News* could scarcely have been more complimentary: "As in the work of Dana, the forecastle and its inmates afford the richest material to the limner of sea life. Mr. Melville has made the most of their strange and exceptional existence. The story of the man running up the scuttle hole, and rushing over the bows into the sea, in a fit of *delirium tremens* is striking. The conclusion is also fine." Few books contained passages "more striking or more powerfully written." The *News* enjoyed "highly lauding a work so much out of the common."

The next day, October 30, the London *Morning Herald* seemed sympathetic and gave several paragraphs to a synopsis of the story, which was developed "somewhat in the style of" Marryat. There were, however, "some observations which tell strongly against the liberality of the Americans, and the personal freedom which they boast so much of." Redburn's "curiosity is excited by" the "considerate" treatment of the "poor African . . . in this really free country," that is, England. Curiously enough, of a passage in the London chapters, often both then and recently considered unconvincing, the *Herald* said, "The first sight of the metropolis is graphically described." The "paying-off of the crew" was quoted as "one of the best and most amusing" scenes.

Although an encomium was to be expected from *Bentley's Miscellany,* the house organ of the publisher, its contributor's praise was certainly judicious. Satisfaction with the effective realism keynoted his opening comments in the November issue. A book "indebted less for its interest to the . . . fantastical and the ideal, than to the more intelligible domain of the actual and real," it was to be ranked higher than Melville's "earlier productions." In spite of touches of the "wild and visionary spirit" evinced "in its predecessors," *Redburn* was made interesting by its "Dutch fidelity."

Bentley's critic, alone among his contemporaries, seems to have perceived what today is regarded as the major theme:[5] the main interest centered "in the details of the process by which" Redburn was "disenchanted of his pleasant delusions concerning life at sea" and "in the natural development of the feelings of the boy throughout the startling ordeal of his first cruise." The book had for him many other values: The "excitement never flags to the close"; there was "charm" in the "vitality of the descriptions"; the "ship, as in the masterly novels of Cooper and Marryat," acquired "a living interest"; and the author displayed "an intimate acquaintance with the mysteries of seamanship, and a rich graphic power in the use and treatment of them." The London episode was perhaps a "little in excess"; but even the Americanisms only imparted "a congenial flavor . . . which greatly increases that sense of reality which constitutes the paramount merit."

John Wilson, author of the philosophical dialogues *Noctes Ambrosianae*, was very vigorous in body and mind, but irrepressible.[6] As "Christopher North," in the November *Blackwood's Edinburgh Magazine,* of which he was then leading editor, he devoted to *Redburn* fourteen pages, the longest review it received, but next to Chorley's and *Britannia's*, the least favorable in Great Britain. Wilson admitted the book had good points: although less spontaneous and original than *Omoo*, Melville's best, and also than *Typee*, it was at least better than *Mardi*, having a more natural and manly style. Melville had observed Liverpool sharply; Jackson and Captain Riga were "well done"; the depictions of the epidemic, the flaming dead body, and Jackson's death, revealed him on his own ground, telling of things he knew.

5. Gilman, pp. 210, 211.
6. At Oxford Wilson was an athlete, and for his M. A. in 1820 wrote "the most brilliant examination within the memory of man." He explored the Highlands; became, particularly after 1834, the "guiding spirit" of *Blackwood's;* and was later appointed professor of moral philosophy at the University of Edinburgh. He had "a marvelously rich endowment of fine qualities, marred by want of restraining judgment and symmetrical proportion" (Richard Garnett in *DNB*).

On the other hand, Wilson was surprised at Redburn's "precocious misanthropy." He found the characterization slightly inconsistent, since a boy who on shore was "precocious in experience of the world's disappointment" was "converted by the first sniff of salt water" into "an arrant simpleton," whose blunders, though amusing, were "not sufficiently accounted for by ignorance of sea usages." He accused the author of "straining for striking similes, at the expense of truth and good taste." He called the death of the woman in the Liverpool gutter "utterly absurd" and the London expedition "utter rubbish" in the "stalest style of minor theatre melodrama." He considered the details about the coffee "disgusting" and pronounced Harry Bolton highly distasteful as well as inconsistently portrayed.

The first scene between Jones and Captain Riga reminded Wilson "of Marryat, in whose style Mr. Melville would succeed." Melville "must surely have had Peter Simple in his head when describing 'Buttons' at this first deck-washing." Wilson also had some advice: "Mr. Melville is most effective when most simple and unpretending" and should avoid "affectation" and "fancy." And he put Melville in his place: "He will never have the power of a Cringle, or the sustained humor and fancy of a Marryat, but he may do very well without aspiring to rival the masters of the art." (Who was Cringle?)

The condescension of Wilson was undoubtedly intensified by the unfortunate nationality of the new book. He called Redburn's precocity an American quality, and finally said he was always glad to speak "favorably of an American author when we can conscientiously do so." He never again, in the pages of his "Maga," spoke of Melville at all.

Assuming that *Blackwood's* and *Bentley's* came out during the first few days of November, the last British review, the one in the *Athenaeum* for November 10, probably by Henry Chorley, was the most adverse of all, with the single exception of *Britannia's*. The reviewer saw the book as a feeble echo of Marryat: "The humour of the book is borrowed from 'Peter Simple'—the facts are too simple to suggest the notion of their having been borrowed from anyone." Again: "the Peter Simple-ism of Redburn looks, we are bound to say, a little pale in Mr. Melville's imitation of Captain Marryat." He could grant only negative merit: "It wants the novelty of interest and of subject which made *Typee* and *Omoo* popular in their day," but "on the whole it is better written than either." Setting aside the London chapters there was "little in Redburn that is open to the charge of extravagance, either in the matter or manner, and that is itself a novelty in a writer who has hitherto gone on crescendo in the way of mysteries and madnesses of many kinds."

Counting somewhat against *Redburn* in Great Britain was its not-too-original subject. Six of the journalists were reminded of Marryat, their opinions of the relationship between the two authors varying from the two who saw Melville as an inept imitator (Chorley, Wilson) to one who thought Melville would displace Marryat (*John Bull*). The style was generally approved (especially by *Post, John Bull, Spectator, News, Bentley's*), and even by two otherwise mainly hostile (Wilson, Chorley); only one actually condemned the writing (*Britannia*). The sardonic picture of Liverpool was less resented than might have been supposed, as only two took umbrage at it (Wilson, Chorley), and two admitted Melville had only told the truth about that port (*Spectator, News*). A number rejoiced that Melville had returned from the cloudland of *Mardi,* and those who admired *Redburn* did so primarily for its realism, two praising its "fidelity" as "Daguerreotype" (*News*) or "Dutch" (*Bentley's*). Finally, of the ten British reviews of *Redburn* I have found, one was absolutely negative (*Britannia*); two predominantly adverse, including, somewhat fatefully, the longest (Wilson) and the latest (Chorley); two definitely favorable (*Spectator, Herald*); three really commendatory (*Post, Gazette, John Bull*); and two actually enthusiastic (*Bentley's, News*). Thus the British score was by a definite margin in favor of *Redburn.*

It was Melville's own impression, toward the end of the year, that *Redburn* had been a success with the public. From London Melville wrote on December 14 to Evert Duyckinck: "I did not see your say about the book Redburn, which to my surprise (somewhat) has been favorably received. I am glad for it—for it puts money into an empty purse."[7] He was naturally then thinking primarily of the British reaction; and in London he was in a position to scan the British press more completely than has been possible a century later; and his statement certainly suggests that the total tally of reviews may have been even more in favor of *Redburn* than is the tally of the ten I have exhumed.

Melville's letter to Duyckinck continued with the oft-quoted words: "But I hope I shall never write such a book again. Tho' when a poor devil writes with duns around him . . . what can you expect of

7. *Log,* p. 347.

that poor devil? What but a beggarly 'Redburn'!" Thus at the
year's end, Melville was not enhancing his own book's reputation. It
was, however, to be the opinion of another century, that in *Redburn*,
as also in *White Jacket*, he had, as Howard puts it, written better
books than he knew.[8]
The few known British comments on *Redburn* during the next
decades indicate that it was rapidly losing face. In 1851 the London
Morning Chronicle declared it "smacked of reality," but was "in a
lower, less buoyant, and less confident key than the earlier fictions."[9]
In 1853 Ainsworth called it "prosy, bald, uneventful," and parts even
"repulsive," although the "sea scenes were good."[10] The very termina-
tion of good fortune for the poor book—for many years—was signalized in 1856 by the pronouncement of the *Dublin University Magazine*
that *Redburn* was "an abortive work which neither obtained nor deserved much success." This magazine had forgotten there had been
a little blaze of immediate success, even if that was indeed followed
quickly by marked disparagement and oblivion. There were to be
nearly thirty years of silence in the English press about *Redburn*, until
the mariner-author W. Clark Russell, in the *Contemporary Review* in
1884, lauded its blending of realism and fancy and its accurate portraiture of the sailor. It was reprinted in England only once (in
1853), before 1922.[11]

AMERICAN RECEPTION

Once more the faithful *Literary World* printed, as it was to do
again, chapters from a book of Melville's in advance. Now, on November 10, four days before the publication of *Redburn*, the *World*
offered two chapters to illustrate the "attractive manner" of the new
volume. *Redburn* was published in New York on November 14, by
the Harpers.[12]
The first American newspaper to notice the book seems to have
been the Boston *Daily Transcript*, which on November 14, sounded the
keynote of the American reception in saying that the failure of *Mardi*

8. *Herman Melville*, p. 137.
9. In a review of *The Whale*, on December 21, 1851.
10. *New Monthly Magazine*, August.
11. Minnegerode, p. 144.
12. On November 13, the New York *Evening Post* carried the announcement that
the Harpers would publish *Redburn* on November 14, thus showing that the date of
publication was a day or two earlier than Gilman suggests (p. 362).

had not kept Melville from making another bid for the "popularity which his first two books so deservedly won for him" and that a "glance through" the volume showed that he "had succeeded. . . . 'Redburn' would seem to be one of the books."

On November 17 the *Albion* offered a chapter from the new work, the New Bedford *Mercury* a brief note, and the *World* a review. The unsympathetic *Mercury* said that the hero "arrives at Liverpool, and thence goes to London, where, of course, we find him making all sorts of odd comparisons between the hospitalities of civilized and savage life."[13]

Evert Duyckinck, however, in the *Literary World* on the same day, voiced only approbation, emphasizing the verisimilitude and fine style. He began: "The book belongs to the great school of nature. It has no verbosity, no artificiality, no langour. . . . It has the lights and shades, the mirth and melancholy, the humor and tears of real life." Duyckinck quoted the account of the death of Jackson to add: "This is strong writing, and the strength is in the outlook of a man who sees the world and life in their intensity; with no partial exaggeration or morbid feeling, but with a manly sense of actuality." He saw "fidelity of description" in the Liverpool sketches and considered "A Sailor's Boarding House" was "finished in a style worthy of Smollett." Duyckinck found "a simplicity, and ease, which may win the attention of a child," and also "a reflection which may stir the profoundest depths of manhood . . . . This sailor's use of language, the most in the shortest compass may be the literary school which has rescued Herman Melville from the dull verbosity of his contemporaries."[14]

Also on November 17 there were notices in two newspapers by persons who had only sampled the book. Thurlow Weed in the Albany *Evening Journal* was willing to recommend a book by a "writer so graceful and happy," and thus he aided in its soon selling "like hot cakes" in his city.[15] One of the coolest reactions, on the other hand, was that of the Hartford *Courant's* contributor, who said that although many were "very much pleased with Melville's works," he thought they contained "too much truth to be false, and too much fiction to be true" and hence did not "know what opinion to form";

13. Under "New Publications" the Boston *Daily Bee* on November 16 announced *Redburn,* with the remark, "Hereafter we shall speak of them at length," a promise which the *Bee* did not fulfill with respect to *Redburn,* if at all, until after December 31.

14. Miller ascribes this review to Duyckinck (p. 267).

15. Gilman, pp. 274, 304.

but that it could be "no harm for everyone to buy and read for themselves."[16]

The *Sunday Times and Noah's Weekly Messenger* on November 18 came closer to divining Melville's own attitude toward his fourth book than did any other contemporary. Remarking the great success of the first two books, and the partial success of that "riddle" *Mardi, Noah's* guessed that *Redburn* was a calculated bid for popularity (as Melville had told Duyckinck it was), since "it was in the old vein": "It is written for the million, and the million will doubtless be delighted by its racy descriptions of the life of a young sailor. The critics, having worked off their proverbial ill nature on the unintelligible 'Mardi' will be full of praise of 'Redburn,' and our young American author will make the tour of Europe on the topmost wave of transatlantic celebrity."[17]

On November 19 the Springfield *Republican* expressed an unusual opinion in declaring that *Redburn* had "more of an air of reality" than *Typee* and "possibly it may be less interesting in consequence." On November 20 the Norwich *Evening Courier* briefly emphasized the comic spirit. The hero was "a much more innocent and commendable acquaintance than some of his predecessors, being a half-grown youth, of great shrewdness and some simplicity, who tells his tale . . . and makes his criticisms . . . with irresistible humor . . . he will be a great favorite." Up to 1951, even, as Gilman then insisted, modern critics had scarcely done justice to the humor of *Redburn*.[18]

In the same day, November 20, very likely written by the editor, Colonel Greene, the longest and one of the most enthusiastic of the American reviews appeared in his Democratic Boston *Post*. Greene was glad he could praise *Redburn*, for he had feared Melville might write another *Mardi*, an "offspring of that unaccountable insanity" which sometimes "visits minds of undoubted ability"; but *Redburn* had the "Crusoe-like naturalness of his first two books."

Like most, he was delighted with the realism of *Redburn;* he rejoiced that "no glimmer of the levity, coxcombry, affectation, incon-

16. The Washington *National Intelligencer* must have received advance sheets of Duyckinck's article, for on the same date it appeared, November 17, the *Intelligencer* reprinted part of it, together with an excerpt, "Redburn Calls on the Captain."

17. *Noah's* commented on Melville's "remarkable career." He had commenced as a sailor. "Now he has achieved world-wide reputation. He has married into one of the most respectable families in Massachusetts" and was "thought a thorough and sturdy democrat."

18. *Op. cit.,* p. 279.

sistency and hodge-podge[19] of *Mardi* is visible"; that "everything or nearly everything is done properly and in order"; and that although "reared on a basis apparently insufficient"—the "first voyage of a green hand to and from Liverpool"—"the hero and narrator being a sort of American Peter Simple," it was "intensely interesting." The "great charm," however, "is its realness. It seems to be *fact* word for word." Except for "a little that is melo-dramatic and exaggerated in the hero" at first—"the tale is told simply and without the least pretension; and yet within its narrow bounds, are flashes of genuine humor, strokes of pure pathos, and real and original characters. The captain, the mate, Max the Dutchman, the O'Brien and O'Reagan boys, and the story-teller himself, are as well individualized as if volumes had been devoted to each."

He placed the young author in high company indeed, adjudging that "Melville really *excells* De Foe" in character portrayal, though a little inferior in vividness of details. Scott, Bulwer, and Dickens had, he said, developed the art of depicting human nature "even beyond Shakespeare's insight." But Melville, "for great fame, has lived a century too late; and while he undoubtedly equals and in some respects excells the greatest masters in his peculiar work, he must be content with the name of having written some very clever books, and be overjoyed if thereby he put money in his purse." This derogation of the world's latter years involved a strange turn of thinking, though certainly highly flattering to Melville. The Colonel was obviously addicted to extreme statements. Why could not this somewhat extravagant encomium have been reserved for *Moby-Dick?*

On November 21 three newspapers had bits of praise which were little more than remarks that the volume was up to Melville's usual high standards. The Albany *Argus* found it "bears the characteristic marks of its author's genius, and has so much of the simplicity of nature, and so many bright and beautiful passages . . . that it will not want for readers." Likewise the Baltimore *American* the same day said that a new book "from his polished pen" would attract "all readers"; that the "fulness and rich coloring of his writings, with his easy and pointed style, his humor and description of character, have earned for him the name of the Defoe of the sea"; and that hav-

19. An indication that the reviewer of *Redburn* was the same person as the reviewer of *Mardi* is that in both reviews *Mardi* was called a "hodge-podge." In the review of *White Jacket,* its author was accused of "affectation." Thus it is probable this same contributor wrote on *White Jacket* also. There are special reasons for ascribing the *White Jacket* review to Greene, as will be seen.

ing these qualities, *Redburn* would "add much to his laurels." The Worcester *Palladium,* also on November 21, wrote similarly that no writer "plans better," "uses better materials," "gives them better workmanship," or "puts on a more exquisite finish." "His eye is keen to perceive the features of nature, and paint them like one whose pencil has seen no stinted or ignoble service"; whether in "description of natural scenery or a delineation of . . . character . . . there is a freshness, a variety that never fails to attract. The story of Redburn is simple," yet has "that multiplicity of incidents that give attraction to this species of writing."[20]

Of the five journals commenting on *Redburn* on November 24, two were moderately and three enthusiastically favorable. The Richmond *Whig,* though disliking the sea, enjoyed Melville's usual "naturalness of style." The *Whig* approved of the theme of disillusionment, saying that "boys with a romantic conception of the ocean would not like to find the young hero cleaning the pig pen," nor would "the young gentleman who rejoices in a Byron collar" like *Redburn,* because it would "be apt to knock the 'Address to the Ocean' all into prose"; yet to "unpoetical persons like ourselves" who think the sea a "stupid place" it would prove "most readable."

Henry S. Saroni himself,[21] in *Saroni's Musical Times* on that same day, was a little more cordial, like many British reviewers pointing out that although the subject was not novel Melville was "interesting." The beginning of *Redburn* was "particularly lively." The lad's "unsophisticated awkwardness" furnished "opportunities for racy anecdotes of which Mr. Melville has taken advantage with much wit and humor." The account of the "ripening of his greenness" was "extremely entertaining." The hero's impression of England derived "most of its interest" from his "ignorance of British affairs." The scene of the epidemic was "striking . . . painted in the most plain yet vigorous colors. Our talented yet eccentric writer never lapses into sentimentalism when he has something tragical to relate." He concluded tartly: "Now that Redburn has grown wiser from his first voyage let us hope that his next will prove more fertile in incidents."

Though finding the subject unoriginal, the New York *Literary American,* also on November 24, was more complimentary. The new

20. On November 23 the Lansingburgh *Gazette* maintained that "certainly the writings of . . . Melville should be sought with filial interest by the people of Lansingburgh" (Gilman, p. 274).

21. In Chapter IV, footnote 37 is quoted the announcement made on September 29 that from then on Mr. Saroni would do the writing in his magazine.

work "if not as fresh, striking, and imaginative" as his former productions, "was . . . more interesting in its plot, and more nervous in its style." Again the realism scored a hit, for, asserted the *American*, "'Redburn' is all nature": "there are no monstrosities or artificialities about it. [*Mardi!*] It is all life; and shows a power which the author has not before displayed, of drawing the darker pictures, the shadows, of life, with a sombre reality. The dialogues are natural. Mr. Melville is a sailor, and he talks, acts, and writes like a sailor. . . . We cannot but wonder at the interest with which he leads" us "through the ordinary details of a sailor's life." It would surely enhance its author's reputation. Quoting the "Death of Jackson," the *American* asked, "Who will not admit that the picture is drawn in vivid colors, and by a master's pencil?"

Even more flattering was the *Albion's* reviewer, probably Dr. Bartlett, also on November 24, who said that not "even Marryat himself" had "observed the ships more closely or pictures them more impressively." Melville's unflinching realism set his portrayals of sea life apart. Others had painted the "picturesque side of sea life"; but Melville often selected "those views of it which, apart from his clever treatment, would be uninteresting, if not repulsive." He gave us "not stately frigates and pirates, but the whaler and the cabin boy—the Oliver Twists of ocean life, not the Pelhams." Other sea writers presented "heroes," but Melville "characters." This reviewer was surprised at the exceeding gravity of *Redburn*, since "fun and frolic seem, according to custom to be part and parcel of any nautical tale." He revealed his English background in detecting the weakness of the London episode, advising the author to stick to the sea, "his own peculiar element."

No flaws, however, were found by the *Home Journal's* critic, who certainly sounds like the editor, Willis, in the fifth and most favorable of the November 24 reviews. Melville's "Confessions"—this word occurs in the sub-title—"were in simplicity of style, warmth and openness of heart, and in general truthfulness" not inferior to the confessions of Rousseau and Lamartine.

Willis was in the minority in regarding *Mardi* as its author's finest, "which reminded one of the departed great." *Redburn*, however, was not a bit what he had expected. He could have believed the creator of *Mardi* could write a *Tale of a Tub* or a *Pantagruel*, but not *Redburn*, which, nevertheless, was superb in its realism, as well as extremely edifying: "The life-like manner in which every event is brought to the

Herman Melville. This photograph was taken in Pittsfield in 1861 by Rodney Dewey. *The Bettmann Archive.*

Below, Douglas Jerrold. This English dramatist and journalist responded warmly to the portrayal of the social system in Typee Valley as immensely more humane than that in Victorian England.

Above, Margaret Fuller. The distinguished American critic and social reformer ironically recommended *Typee* as reading for the sewing circles engaged in raising missionary funds. *The Bettmann Archive.*

reader is most astonishing. One actually thinks . . . that of these occurrences he was actually a witness, so vividly is the mind impressed
with their truthfulness. . . . The deep feeling which breaths through
the . . . work—the love of home, family affection, that which will be
most admired, can be least described. We feel elevated even when
reading scenes of low life, and we arise from the perusal better and
with nobler intentions." It would be far more popular than the
"previous ones, though it will not perhaps raise the author's literary
reputation from the pinnacle where Mardi placed it."

The New York *Evening Mirror* on November 27 saw the chief
values as not aesthetic but admonitory: "It is a very well-told voyage
of a poor gentleman-born youth, as ship's boy, not deficient in graceful
humor and vivid description. It is not a book, however, to make a
sensation or to deserve one. As a picture . . . by no means too highly
colored . . . of sea-life, we commend it to the dissatisfied boy and the
philanthropist."

Signed "R" and thus certainly by George Ripley, who had been
very hard on *Mardi* in the same paper, was the rather long article
praising *Redburn* highly in the New York *Daily Tribune* for December 1. Ripley declared the new book, although "more self-conscious
than *Typee* and *Omoo,* was still a great relief after the "mystic allegory
and the transcendental, glittering soap-bubble speculation, which he has
'done to death' in *Mardi*." *Redburn* was "a genuine tale of the sea."
"It has the real briny flavor. The writer is equally at home on the
deck and in the forecastle. His pictures of life on the ocean are
drawn from nature. . . . His pages smell of tarred rope and bilge-
water. With some occasional exaggeration, his descriptions have all the
fidelity of a Dutch painting. Nor is he less skillful in his delineations
of a sailor's life in port. The interior of the boarding houses in Liverpool, the scenes of destitution and misery about the docks, the impressions of low life in a commercial city on the mind of an untrammeled
rustic just landing from his first voyage are depicted with a minute
fidelity of touch that is hardly surpassed by the dark and lurid coloring of Crabbe."

Redburn, thought Ripley, would have "extensive popularity." It
was "idle to compare" Melville "with Defoe," or even with some similar
"modern writers." But "he is an artist of unparalleled merit in his
own right. He has the true kind of stuff in him," having "an original
power that will always keep his productions before the public eye."
Ripley ended with what was clearly another blast at *Mardi*: "If he

would trust more entirely to the natural play of his own fine imagination, without goading it on to a monstrous activity, his work would stand a better chance of obtaining a healthy and lasting reputation." Events were to prove that for his own century Ripley was right.

A much lower estimate was placed on *Redburn* on December 3 by the Newark *Daily Advertiser,* which considered it a book for boys: "It is an interesting book for juvenile readers, and others who are much interested in the impulses of boyhood, or the minute incidents of a seafaring life; but the reader who expects another 'Typee' will be disappointed." After a brief summary, the *Advertiser* concluded: "The work is written with commendable simplicity of style, and gives some entertaining and instructive incidents, drawn out, however, with rather tedious minuteness."[22]

Three American magazines of some eminence all praised *Redburn* highly in December, but for very unlike reasons.[23] The longest of the items, probably by John R. Thompson,[24] was in the *Southern Literary Messenger* and echoed the familiar rejoicing at the return to realism: "If this be an imaginary narrative . . . it is the most life-like and natural fiction" since *Robinson Crusoe.* "Melville has made ample amends in Redburn for the grotesqueness and prolixity of 'Mardi,' which we found it impossible to read through. No one can find in this sailor-boy confession any incident that might not have happened—any that has not the air of strict probability. . . . The descriptions of life before the mast, of the sailor boarding houses . . . are well drawn and sometimes remind us of Smollett. . . . Redburn is no ordinary book." Quite unusual, however, was this Virginia critic's dismissal of the adored first two books along with *Mardi*: "We trust Mr. Melville may write many more such and let Polynesia alone in the future, as a field that he has . . . fully exhausted. We have had enough of Babbalanja and the anthropophagi generally, and we regard la belle sauvage as a young lady who has had her day."

That same month, another magazinist, in the *Christian Union and Religious Memorial* found a very different basis for preferring *Redburn*: It was without the licentiousness and almost without the "antireligious temper" of *Typee* and *Omoo*. It possessed, moreover, "the

22. On December 7 the *Long Islander* printed "the graphic description" of Jackson from " 'Welburn' [*sic*] from the pen of Herman Melville." On December 11, the Nantucket *Inquirer* discussed the November number of *Blackwood's,* commenting that *Redburn* was therein "reviewed, not very favorably."

23. On December 23 *Littell's Living Age* reprinted the *Spectator's* review of *Redburn.*

24. Suggested by Leyda, *Log,* p. 355.

merits of naturalness and simplicity; it will be read with interest and
pleasure; the freshness of a youthful experience on the ocean is well
preserved in the autobiography of its hero, whose moral principles and
courage never fail him." Note, not "the autobiography of its author."
To this religious writer *Redburn* was evidently an excellent model
for the young.

Two sentences of the warmest approval were accorded the book,
also in December, by the *Democratic Review,* though that magazine
was then in the hands of Thomas Prentice Kettell, who was supposedly
unsympathetic toward the Young Americans:[25] " 'Redburn,' in the
writer's own peculiar vein, has reawakened the ardor with which
'Omoo' was greeted, and once more Mr. Melville triumphs as the
most captivating of ocean authors. There is a variety of pictures exhibited in 'Redburn,' each drawn with a power and skill seldom
reached, and the humor is of the most contagious nature." Here was
another early reader especially fascinated by the humor. And these are
all the American press comments on *Redburn* in the year of its debut
which I have found.

Six American magazines took cognizance of it during the early
months of the next year, two in January. Charles F. Briggs was editor
of *Holden's Dollar Magazine.* Since he had scored a popular success
with his *Adventures of Harry Franco* (1839), a book based somewhat
on his own experiences as a green hand at sea, and containing some
parallels to *Redburn*,[26] he would surely have wanted to review the
latter book himself in his magazine.[27] He examined the new book
very critically and raised three objections. First, he questioned whether
it was in the main a true story. Some of the incidents, Briggs admitted, must have happened to Melville, who, however, claimed "as
his own" various forecastle traditions familiar to every sailor and thus
tended to "create a suspicion of the actuality" throughout. Second,
Briggs was disturbed by its not belonging to any definite literary
category: "in Redburn we have neither a romance, a satire nor a
narrative of actual events, but a hodge-podge of all three different
kinds of literary composition." Better if he had "confined himself to
a simple record of facts," as in *Typee.* Third, Briggs found serious
faults in the style, which was *not,* he thought, like Defoe's [to which
many compared it]: "The charm of De Foe is his simplicity of style,

25. Miller, p. 47.
26. *Ibid.,* p. 55.
27. Gilman suggests Briggs was the reviewer (p. 277); Miller assumes he was
(p. 267).

and artistic accuracy of description; the author of Redburn on the contrary is, at times, ambitiously gorgeous in style, and at others coarse and abrupt in his simplicity. But his style is always copious, free, and transparent. His chief defect is an ambitious desire to appear fine and learned, which causes him to drag in by the head and shoulders remote images that ought not to be within a thousand miles of the reader's thoughts."

Yet Briggs found the book, for all its defects, interesting. The events might be "commonplace"—he was probably aware that the British had said so—but "clothed in the fresh and poetic style of the author . . . charm us more than novelties would in a less beautiful dress." Had it contained nothing but things like the descriptions of Liverpool—the "most valuable and interesting portions of the book"— and the "incidents that actually befell him, it would have been one of the raciest books of sea adventure with which the English language is enriched." Briggs had a tendency, as he had shown even more clearly in his review of *Mardi,* toward self-contradiction.

When did critics ever agree? It was obviously the same contributor who had in *Graham's Magazine* so warmly acclaimed *Mardi*—almost certainly Bayard Taylor—who now in the January issue of this magazine, found few faults with *Redburn* and approved Melville's having been called the "De Foe of the Ocean": "He has De Foe's power of realizing the details of a scene to his own imagination, and of impressing them on the imaginations of others, but has also a bit of deviltry in him which we do not observe in De Foe, however much raciness it may lend to Melville."

A real Melville enthusiast was Taylor, for he now again showed himself among the minority who admired *Mardi*: "The present work, though it hardly has the intellectual merit of 'Mardi' is less adventurous in style and more interesting." Also it was useful: "The fact that it narrates the adventures of a green hand" would make it "invaluable" to "youthful sailors." He stressed most, however, the fascination of a book which could "be read through at one sitting, with continual delight. . . . The style sparkles with wit and vivacity, but its great merit is a rapidity of movement, which lures the reader along, almost by main force from the commencement to the conclusion of the volume."

Three magazines said something in connection with *Redburn* in February, all being very brief but friendly. *Godey's Lady's Book* had two sentences of praise for this "sensible book . . . that will do more for the author's reputation than ten thousand such as 'Mardi.' Without becoming Munchausenish, it tells some wonderful stories, and the interest is admirably sustained to the last page." *Hunt's Merchant's Magazine* was convinced by a dozen pages that the many "who were so delighted with the previous productions of the author" would like it because "There is a freshness, vigor, and grotesqueness, in Melville's style, that must fascinate equally the old and the young, the grave and the gay." *Sartain's* said nothing specifically about the book but lauded Melville's originality: "His adventures and his descriptions of them are like nothing, living or dead. He imitates nobody; he is evidently a 'law to himself.' Surely it is refreshing in this age of stereotyping and fac-similes to meet with one so unique, so perfectly individual."

It was ominous that the latest of the known American reviews of *Redburn* was also the most completely derogatory, and that, after at least three critics had said explicitly that it was a relief after *Mardi*, this final pronouncement should have stressed its inferiority to that book. Simms, the editor, probably contributed to the *Southern Quarterly Review* for April the article in which he adjudged *Redburn* "cold and prosaic" as compared with *Mardi*, which was "wild, warm and richly fanciful." *Redburn*, indeed, was much more within the "range of the popular sympathies." Redburn as a character, however, was "not symmetrically drawn. He forgets his part at times; and the wild, very knowing bold boy ashore, becomes a sneak and numbskull aboard ship. The portraiture is thus far faulty." Virtually the same point had been made, as will be recalled, by *Blackwood's* Wilson, who, along with Simms, condemned the Bolton episode. The Charlestonian went on to present a judgment to which Melville himself would have been almost willing to assent: "But the truth is, the author has an imagination which naturally becomes restive in the monotonous details of such a career as that of 'Redburn'; and in breaking away from bonds self-imposed, does not suffer himself to see how much hurt is done to his previous labors. The transition was quite too rapid from 'Mardi' to 'Redburn.' Wild, improbable and fantastic as was that allegorical production, it is more in proof of real powers in reserve."

Two eminent American literary men who were interested in *Redburn* made, so far as I know, no public profession of the fact. Lowell possessed a copy;[28] and Hawthorne wrote on August 29, 1850, to

28. Gilman, p. 281.

Duyckinck, "No writer ever put reality before his reader more unflinchingly than he does in 'Redburn' and 'White Jacket.' "[29]

Redburn was perhaps placed under a cloud by the two last reviewers, both so harsh, Wilson in England, and Simms in America. Fitz-James O'Brien, in his 1855 study of Melville's works to date, nearly ignored it, though he praised one of its descriptions.[30] In 1857 he gave it more attention, calling it "an extraordinary mixture of sense and nonsense . . . of exact portraiture and incredible caricature." Melville's picture of the English upper classes was "nonsense"; yet there was also "the freshest and finest writing . . . stories of nautical adventure, told with a grace that Marryat never approached, and fire that Cooper never surpassed." O'Brien said it was then "the least known of the author's works."[31]

Redburn soon virtually dropped out of sight. The Harpers had reissued it in 1850 and in 1855; but after they reprinted it in 1863, nearly sixty years passed before it was again issued in America.[32] In total American sales between 1849 and 1887 *Redburn,* indeed, was a close second to *White Jacket,* and greatly outstripped *Mardi* and *Moby-Dick;* yet during the twenty-three years from 1853 to 1876, *Redburn* sold a total of only a thousand copies in its author's own country. The bottom of the curve of the American fame of *Redburn* was reached in 1876 when the Harpers sold all year a single copy[33]— only one of many indications marking that year as the very nadir of Melville's renown. *Redburn* is not known to have been referred to after 1857 in the press by an American during Melville's lifetime.

Although it must be noted that the total number of American reviews and notices was smaller than had been those of either *Typee* or *Omoo,* the immediate American press reception of *Redburn* had been by a large margin favorable. Of the twenty-seven reviews and notices I have examined, all but eight were clearly positive. These eight consisted of three items noncommittal as to merit, two lukewarm notices, one negative notice, and two essentially adverse reviews. Four critics were reminded of Defoe, one to deny the resemblance. One thought Melville as effective as Smollett, one as Crabbe. Five relished the humor (Norwich *Courier,* Colonel Greene, *Democratic Review,* Saroni, Baltimore *American*). Four found *Redburn* a relief

29. *Log*, p. 391.
30. *Putnam's Magazine* for February.
31. *Putnam's Magazine* for April.
32. Hetherington, p. 494.
33. Gilman, p. 281.

after fantastic *Mardi,* but three considered it good but inferior to *Mardi;* and one, the sole truly hostile commentator (Simms), declared it greatly outranked by *Mardi.* Expressed variously, however, by reference to the "great school of nature," "real life" (Duyckinck); "realness," "fact, word for word" (Greene); "naturalness" (Richmond *Whig*); "all nature" (*Literary American*); "unflinching realism" (*Albion*); "life-like manner" (Willis); "real briny flavor," "drawn from nature" (Ripley); "strict probability" (*Southern Literary Messenger*), a nearly unanimous chorus of American praise greeted *Redburn* for its realism.

CONCLUSION

The first reaction in America to *Redburn* was, to judge from the percentages of positive and negative comments, considerably more cordial than that in England. The British were, on the whole, more disturbed than the Americans about the basic lack of originality of the subject, partly because they were more aware of Marryat's *Peter Simple,* which they mentioned more frequently. The American (Briggs) who said most about the traditional elements in the tale, had a maritime background. Two Americans found the book edifying, one because of its noble sentiments (Willis), one because of the hero's high moral principles (*Christian Union*), and two found it a valuable warning to romantic youth of the hardships of real sea life (*Mirror,* Richmond *Whig*), as did also one Englander (*News*). As in the case of other books by Melville, the British responded less to the humor, only one of them (*Spectator*) praising it, and one thinking the humor borrowed from Marryat (Chorley), as against five professedly amused Americans. In both countries the book was at its debut much admired for its realism, though more generally in America; but in both final contemporary judgments were pretty negative.

Redburn was undoubtedly to a great extent, as will be seen, pushed off the stage by the publication soon of a book more widely acclaimed and generally considered more important, *White Jacket,* on February 1 in London, and on March 21 in New York, in each case just four months and a week after the publication of *Redburn* in the respective cities. The fact that the scenes of *Redburn* lacked the novelty of those of Melville's first two books, tended to make it less popular than they. On the other hand, being without the philosophical lucubrations and experimental writing of *Mardi,* it was better received than that puzzling work.

Gilman has honored the early reviewers of both countries for avoiding the fallacy of most modern observers—that of taking *Redburn* as primarily autobiographical.[34] On the other hand, some moderns, especially Gilman, have found in the book a penetrating presentation of the psychology of a developing adolescent, not only in its comic aspects, which are certainly present, but also in its truly pathetic or even tragic aspects.[35] To this, the main theme, nearly all the early critics were blind, with the sole exception of the contributor to *Bentley's*. Saroni, indeed, said the account of the "ripening" of Redburn's "greenness" was "extremely interesting";[36] he at least did see, as few others did, that there was in the book this process of "ripening"; but for him it was merely comic. Yet Saroni's comment, perhaps even more than the silences of the other reviewers, as contrasted with modern studies of the book, illustrates the difference between that century, and a later one which regards more intelligently and sympathetically, if often too seriously, the complex problems of adolescence.

34. *Ibid.,* p. 279.
35. *Ibid.,* p. 274.
36. In a letter on December 10 to her lukewarm suitor, George Duyckinck, Joann Miller, though a little sentimentally, revealed, more than the majority of the reviewers, a perceptivity of at least one aspect of the central theme: "I am reading Redburn aloud—and it interests me deeply . . . what a picture of a boy's heart he presents to us, terrible in the fidelity with which he paints its suffering . . . This book endears the author to me beyond all he has written, fine as each is in its own way" (*Log,* p. 345).

Chapter VI: WHITE JACKET

"The rattling youngster has grown into a thoughtful man."
—*John Bull* (1850), reviewing *White Jacket*.

BRITISH RECEPTION

Before the autumn of 1849, Melville had finished a book which, in a letter to his father-in-law, he classified with *Redburn* as another job he had "done for money—being forced to it, as other men are to sawing wood." Yet in the same letter he admitted that in neither book had he "repressed" himself "much," but had "spoken pretty much" as he felt. Here perhaps was an admission—partly unconscious —that he realized that *White Jacket,* as well as *Redburn,* had more depth than he was willing to acknowledge.[1] His main intention, according to his preface, was "to paint general life in the navy." He wanted to avoid disturbing elements which would interfere with sales.

When in October he sailed for England, he took the new manuscript with him, and on November 12, a week after he arrived, he got an offer for it, in spite of the uncertain state of the copyright, from Bentley, who would not make a cash advance then, but did so a month later, after Melville had dickered with other publishers, including Murray.[2] So on February 1, 1850, six weeks before it came out in New York, Melville's fifth book was published by Bentley.[3] It was eagerly examined in London, as at least four journals there which had previously evinced interest in Melville, the *Athenaeum,* the *Spectator, Britannia,* and *John Bull,* reviewed it on February 2, the very next day.

1. *Log,* p. 316. On October 16.
2. *Log,* pp. 330, 331, 349.
3. The London *Morning Herald* for February 1, 1850, carried an announcement that "This day is published White Jacket; Or the World in a Man-of-War," by Richard Bentley. The similar announcement in the London *Morning Chronicle* the next day was probably a day behind time.

Two aspects of *White Jacket* called, from the first, for somewhat separate consideration—its attractions as a tale of maritime adventure and its validity as a critique of the United States Navy. Thus, as with *Typee* and *Omoo,* some were more concerned with it as art, others, as document.

In the *Athenaeum* on February 2 Henry F. Chorley,[4] alone among the British reviewers, saw the new book as pure fiction, in which some passages disclosed "close coincidence to the revelations which gave Mr. Dana's *real sea journal* so painful an interest." Confronted, however, with something so much less strange than *Mardi,* which had so strongly repelled him, he regarded *White Jacket*—as fiction—very highly: "Mr. Melville stands as far apart from any past or present marine painter in pen and ink as Turner does from the magnificent artist vilipended by Mr. Ruskin for Turner's sake—Vendervelde. We cannot recall another novelist or sketcher who has given the poetry of the ship . . . in a manner at all resembling his." Cooper's *The Pilot* was "theatrical"; whereas Melville's delineations belonged "to the more dreamy tone of 'The Ancient Mariner.'" A little condescendingly, Chorley found much he could approve heartily, including "new light on the coarse, weather-beaten shapes and into the cavernous corners of a man-of-war"; and "a tone and relish alike individual and attractive." He granted that "With a thousand faults" Melville possessed "more vivacity, colour and energy than ninety-nine out of the hundred who undertake to poetize or prate about sea monsters or land monsters."

On the other hand, the *Spectator's* critic—possibly Thornton Hunt—the same day took it to be a true enough story, and was most interested in it as propaganda; but, in a journal which was always inclined to regard Melville somewhat askance, was among the least sympathetic of the British reviewers: *White Jacket* was only "pretty well done." Granting that the author, in attacking supposed abuses, was "more sensible and sober than most of the British reformers," the *Spectator's* writer was not won over completely. He allowed that it was "often hard to answer his logic," but insisted that "harshness and strictness on points unnecessary in themselves are needed in developing discipline." He believed he had turned the tables on Melville's main argument by pointing out that it was "only necessary to read" his "terrible description of the villainies and vices on shipboard to be satisfied that the 'law's delay' would not do for a man of war."

4. For the identification of Chorley as the reviewer, see Chapter II, footnote 8.

Britannia, also on February 2, true to its name, placed the book in a highly British frame of reference. Accepting it, as did the *Spectator,* as an account of actual experiences, *Britannia* took satisfaction in declaring it valuable as a picture of the "state of discipline in the American navy"—which, as Melville admitted, was more severe than in the British—and evinced smug surprise that under a Republican rule "the commanders in the American navy are not unfrequently brutal tyrants, and the men degraded slaves."

The vigorous attack of *Britannia,* however, centered on the book as an artistic failure, and as such typically American. Americans imagined "everything depends on mental vigor, and nothing on mental discipline," and relied too much on literal transcription, and not enough on art: "The sketches of which this work is composed are worked up with the skill and power of a practiced pen; but . . . the want of continuity of interest is painfully felt as the reader proceeds . . . at present it is sufficient for the instruction of Mr. Melville and other Americans to insist on the principle that even nature to be pleasant must be represented by art, and that the coarse exaggeration which aims at improving nature is but a miserable substitute for that skill which can make it, in its truth and simplicity, the most delightful object of contemplation." Thus *Britannia* made *White Jacket,* as it did other works of Melville, the occasion to lecture Americans on the defects of their literature.

The same day, however, both the literary and documentary values in *White Jacket* greatly pleased *John Bull.* The author had improved and matured: "The rattling youngster has grown into a thoughtful man, who, without any abatement of his rich and sparkling wit, has obtained the mastery of his own fancy." Like *Britannia, John Bull* was gratified to see the British Navy pictured more favorably than the American, relishing especially the point that the English officers, because they were more accustomed to social prestige, were gentler and better liked by the men.

Sympathetic enough with Melville's case against unreasonable regulations, *John Bull* was mainly concerned with the notable aesthetic merits of a book "so minutely graphic that he who has spent a few hours as a reader in this 'World in a Man-of-War' is as much at home in . . . the Yankee Navy, as if had himself served" therein; and said that the "dryness of professional discussion" was "so felicitously palliated by the incidents" that a work essentially "a caustic *critique* upon the American Navy, assumes the form and possesses all the attraction of a first rate sea novel, while it embodies the author's philosophy of life." The characters were wrought into "admirable life pictures" by the "magic effect of a few masterly touches." This British weekly seconded Melville's opinion that required attendance at sermons by a chaplain of a particular denomination was unconstitutional, but regretted to detect in the book "a philosophy which ill accords with the truth of revelation." The last chapter was quoted as poetically admirable but religiously objectionable.

The two London reviews of February 9, in the *Atlas* and the *Literary Gazette,* were both entirely favorable. In his usual vivid style, the *Atlas's* critic declared the book fascinating as the first presentation of the common seaman's side. The mysteries of the seas had been unfolded "minutely" but always from a "quarter deck point of view." Even when a common seaman was the supposed speaker, he had never been permitted to "show a wrinkle of discontent." Melville, however, gave the "forecastle point of view," and the "colouring" was "harsher," and the "resulting impression less pleasant; though we fear, much more true": "We are now admitted behind the scenes; we see the seamy side of the canvas; we can count the tar buckets, the oil lamps, the dangling ropes and grimy workmen, whose services are tasked to form the *tableaux,* that look so agreeable to the spectators standing aft. The captain . . . may pride himself on the tautness of the rigging and the immaculate purity of the decks of his 'tight little frigate.' The foretopman Melville tells us how the mathematical trim of the yards has been secured by remorseless 'coltings,' inflicted on all laggards at the lifts and braces; and how the sleepy sailors were piped out of the hammocks long before it was necessary, in order to spend the chilliest hours of the twenty-four in sloshing, scrubbing, and holy-stoning every plank in the ship."

He of the *Atlas* took great satisfaction in Melville's "partly unconscious admission" that conditions were better in the British Navy. "We believe our navy is *almost* exempt from such disorders" as the "revenges, smugglings and graft" Melville depicted. "Can these stories be true?" Yes, for "His whole narrative is marked by all the sobriety of truth," and, "though enlivened by the sparkling and racy style" of "the author in his happiest moments," is "full of those homely and trivial details which bear with them the conviction that the scene is sketched from life."

Equally approving, though more concerned with aesthetic values, was the contributor to the *Literary Gazette,* probably the editor, genial

William Jerdan, who had liked *Redburn* so much,[5] and for whom *White Jacket* was "a very clever story," wherein "the embellishments which the writer's talents throw in give greater piquancy and effect to the narrative." Portraits, occupations, habits, vices, punishments—"altogether a stirring compound," were "studded with . . . descriptions of sea scenes and with practical observations on" the errors in the "naval discipline of his country." English readers also would find that "Melville's yarn has got such a hold on them that they neither wish to belay or leave it until they have reached the last strand."

The great appeal *White Jacket* had for the London *Daily News* on February 11 was as an important social document. Like other Britons, but even more emphatically, the contributor to the *News* relished Melville's admission that the less onerous discipline in the British Navy was made possible by the very caste system which America had rejected in civilian life. He thought it extraordinary "how the free Americans when they have inherited a bit of hereditary slavery from the mother country, do hug it and improve it. The most striking feature in these pictures of American naval life, which its sons have favored us with, is its rigid and cruel discipline." He said "it should be for the honor of the country which has brought self government on the land . . . to such perfection, to try if some progress of the kind might not be made on board ship."

Another point made by the *News* was the contrast between the writing of the English and American sailor. (The *News* was reviewing *White Jacket* along with *The Petrel: A Tale of the Sea*.) "There is more freshness and spirit, carried even to the verge of vulgarity, in the American. This latter remark does not apply to Mr. Melville. The 'Petrel' is the work of an elegant and refined mind; it is the romance of the quarter deck, with a dive now and then into the hold of the middies. But it ignores the forecastle, in which Mr. Melville lives, and sleeps, and devours his grub." Melville's realism was what appealed to the *News*. *The Petrel* was a "reading cruise for a young lady to embark on of a winter's evening . . . but 'White Jacket' may be put into the hands of any youth, whom his parents would cure of an unlucky hankering after sea life."

The longest British review of *White Jacket* appeared in the London *Morning Post* on February 12. The *Post's* contributor, perhaps

5. Jerdan's editorship—and proprietorship—did not terminate until December 28, 1850 (Frederick Boase, *Modern English Biography* [London, 1892-1921]).

Peter Borthwick,[6] considered the work imperfect, yet eminently worth reading. Along with *Britannia,* he condescendingly pronounced the faults typically American, the faults of youth:

Fresh, bold, original, acquainted with the more striking passages of history, and animated with the spirit of the most brilliant poets, the author brings out the stores of his reading and of his imagination in sudden bursts, without waiting to consider whether the allusion . . . may be far fetched, or the sentiment . . . misplaced. Law, poetry, politics, even theology, take their turns in his pages, without the slightest feeling of doubt as to whether the subject he is treating be worthy of such lofty illustration. The mind of young America, keen, sensitive, but unmatured, lies before us. He has not learned . . . the art of giving to each subject its due weight.

He censured especially three passages: the description of the Bay of Rio, for the combination of poetic beauty with incongruousness; a reference to Christ, for irreverence; and the satiric account of the operation performed by Surgeon Cuticle as full of "disgusting details" and "horrible . . . wit."

The burden of the rest of the long and rather repetitious commentary in the *Post* was that the "excellences" were such as to "atone" fully for the "blemishes." "If the author is extravagant, he is also strikingly original; and whilst he ventures on subjects unsuitable to his pages, he also gives us the genuine outpourings of a vigorous mind." Even if his previous works had not achieved merited fame, this one would have sufficed to show "his superiority over the ordinary . . . writers of the present." The book was not an "ordinary" marine romance: "There is no plot, no hero, and no heroine. The whole is simply a . . . very truthful recital . . . of the scenes . . . on board a man of war. The writer's superiority is the more marked from his not having drawn from his imagination to the usual extent, but having given us incidents of real life . . . in new, striking, and forcible colours." Approving Melville's attack on flogging, and quoting the concluding chapter as, though imperfect, exhibiting "sensibility to what is great and universal in human nature," and "powerfully written," the *Post* strongly recommended the book.

Bentley's Miscellany in March accorded the work "first place among Melville's productions," praising it extravagantly. Other sea writers gave truthfulness, but Melville imparts "the hues of a fanciful and re-

---

6. Whether or not he was the highly literate editor, Peter Borthwick, he was surely the same as he who was later to admire so much *The Whale.*

flective spirit, which gives it the interest of a creation of genius. He is everywhere original, suggestive, and individual. We follow him as if we were passing through an exciting dream. The rainbow dips and plays around us. We see the ship and crew under the influence of enchantment. They are not less real in his pages than we find them elsewhere, but the atmosphere about them is golden and intense, and they glow as they sail on like the points of a reflected sunset." The book "was remarkable for the concentration of qualities—brilliancy and profundity, shrewdness, vivacity, and energy . . . the wild waste of waters is stirred with a spiritual life; while real men and their actions, in constant movement, loom out palpably through the gorgeous mist." There were "great faults," *Bentley's* admitted, but they were "faults of a superabundant fancy and a prodigal genius . . . as much conditions of a peculiar excellence as the rough spots in a piece of old tapestry." Like the *Atlas, Bentley's* remarked that the condition of the sailor was "depicted, not on the quarter deck, according to the common custom, but on the forecastle and in the Stygian depth below." Naturally there probably was some puffery in this rather uncritical review in the house organ of the publishers, but in the same number two other books on Bentley's list were handled quite severely.[7]

The almost completely complimentary London *Globe and Traveller* on March 4 declared that Melville kept within the "alloted range of his subject"; that he proved his knowledge of the American Navy; that he exhibited such "powers of observation" as to "enable him, within so narrow a sphere, and without the introduction" of any "extraordinary" incident "to maintain the interest throughout"; and that he provided "a full and lively picture" of the cruise. Marred by "conceits" and a straining for an "air of smartness," the book yet had some "peculiarly happy descriptions," of which the *Globe* copied two, and also quoted with satisfaction the passage on the greater popularity of the officers of the Royal Navy with their men.

On the same day the London *Morning Herald* carried a brief item, mostly expository, about this "novel, which conveys a lively and, no doubt, accurate description of the mode of life on board . . . very entertaining, and full of such information as could only be afforded by one who has served before the mast." This was the last British review I found.

All in all, *White Jacket* had fared well with its first British commentators. On March 30 the Philadelphia *American Courier* referred

7. These were the *King's Cope* and Janet K. Wilkinson's *Hands and Hearts.*

to the "numerous favorable notices and extended extracts in the London papers of this new volume from . . . Melville." Only two had shown English condescension toward things American; the *Post,* mainly friendly, had found the type of the "mind of young America," "keen," but "undisciplined"; and *Britannia* had thought the "vigor," unchecked by "discipline" and "art," had resulted in an inferior work. *White Jacket,* however, had, as literature, pleased much more than a majority of the Britons of the press.

During the next six years there was more evidence of England's continuing interest in *White Jacket* than in any of Melville's subsequent writings. In its review of *The Whale* in 1851, the London *Morning Chronicle* devoted a long complimentary paragraph to the truthfulness of *White Jacket*: life on a frigate was "elaborated with such daguerreotype exactitude and finish, so swarming with the finest and minutest details, and so studded with little points never to be imagined," that you "must irresistibly conclude" that, "from the first word to the last, every syllable is literal, downright truth." In *Mardi* we were looking through a "telescope," but in *White Jacket* through a "microscope." Yet even in the latter were some touches of "the old fashion of raving."

Ainsworth in his August, 1853, article mentioned *White Jacket* only to refer to the thrill the account of a storm in it "could bring to a quiet landsman." Completely pleased with the book, the London *National Miscellany* in May, 1854, discussed it more fully, stressing its reliability, vividness, and value as "a perfectly reliable and conscientiously written picture" of the American Navy from the sailor's angle, as such having no British counterpart. As "to graphic and appropriate language," there was "no living author" who could "treat such subjects in a style at all approachable to Melville." The *Miscellany* sympathized with his protests about the treatment of the sailor, even his remonstrance about the sixteen hours between supper and breakfast, as the discipline in the American Navy must be much more severe than that in the English or French.

Though Chorley had doubted its literal veracity, the *Dublin University Magazine's* critic, in January, 1856, was the first to maintain that there were some literary sources for *White Jacket.* He "could point out a good many instances . . . where the author has borrowed remarkable verbal expression, and even incidents, from nautical books almost unknown to the general reading public, and this he does without a syllable of acknowledgment." Anderson finds there was much

Nathaniel Parker Willis. The American journalist was one of Melville's most consistently adulatory reviewers. *The Bettmann Archive.*

Below, George Henry Lewes. A gifted English critic, Lewes testifie to the "thrilling" power of *Moby Dick. The Bettmann Archive.*

Above, Horace Greeley. The famous editor of the New York *Tribune* lauded the superb art of *Moby-Dick. The Bettmann Archive.*

truth in this allegation, but insists that Melville could depict an event "so realistically" that accidental discoveries of sources and extensive research have been necessary to prove that it was not a transcript of his own experience.[8] The Dublin critic's final judgment was that, although he suspected Melville's "practical knowledge of seamanship," "his information on all nautical subjects" was most "extensive and accurate" and the book was "an astonishing production" containing "much writing of the highest order." These, the last words in the British press for many years about *White Jacket*, were thus, as had been most of those in 1850, good ones. It was reprinted once, in 1855, in England, during its author's lifetime.[9]

AMERICAN RECEPTION

Symptomatic of the healthy condition of Melville's American reputation in early 1850 was a little flurry in the press of expressions of pleased anticipation which preceded the March 21 publication of *White Jacket* by the Harpers.[10] Five days earlier, on March 16 in the *Literary World*, had appeared the first American review I have found, by Evert Duyckinck—one of the most comprehensive.

Duyckinck made three main points: first, Melville had an ideal combination of literary background and adventuresome life; second, his characters were believable and lifelike; and third, his criticism of the Navy was rational and reasonable. In presenting his first point, he said that it was "this union of culture and experience, of thought and observation, the sharp breeze of the forecastle alternating with the stillness of the library, books and works imparting to each other mutual life," which distinguished Melville's from similar "productions . . . he is not a bookish author nor a tar among books; each character is separate and perfect in its integrity. . . . Your men of choice

8. *Op. cit.*, Chapter XV, and p. 419.

9. Minnegerode, p. 156. During 1857 Melville received a letter from an Englishwoman, Eliza Gordon, praising the book. Her admiration centered especially on the "masterpiece of all God's works Jack Chase" (quoted by Weaver, p. 240).

10. The New York *Commercial Advertiser* carried on March 20, 1850, an advertisement announcing that *White Jacket* would be published on March 21. Before its actual release there had been considerable evidence of interest, aside from Duyckinck's review. As early as February 9, the New York *Evening Mirror* had quoted from the review in the London *Atlas*. On February 15 the Nantucket *Inquirer* reprinted from the *Literary World* an anticipation of finding "an interesting story" and "light on Naval reform" in *White Jacket*. On March 2 the *Albion* had copied a chapter from the new book from "a London newspaper" that "highly commends the forthcoming work." The *Literary World* and the *Home Journal* had printed chapters on March 9 and 16 respectively.

literature and of educated fancy . . . are not likely to acquire the practical experience of the tar-bucket . . . the sailor as man, seen with a genial philosophy and seen from the forecastle has been reserved for our author." In upholding his second point, he found an absence of sentimentality, and of any attempt to "sew finery on the characters," who yet were "interesting . . . as genuine Shakespearean, that is, human personages." In substantiating his third point, he declared: "Melville tests all his characters by their manhood. His book is thoroughly American and democratic. There is no patronage in his exhibition of a sailor any more than in his portraits of captains and commodores . . . . There is no railing, no scolding; he never loses his temper when he hits hardest. . . ."[11] A quaint, satirical, yet gentle humor is his grand destructive weapon . . . a most dangerous weapon if it were not for the poetic element by which it is elevated." In a second article, on March 23, Duyckinck noted again the avoidance of "unmanly, mawkish solicitude" in Melville's attack on flogging and on the fact that so many minor offenses were punishable by death.

The next American review, after Duyckinck's first one, seems to have been in the Troy *Daily Budget,* on March 21. It was entirely favorable. The *Budget* made a point similar to Duyckinck's first: "Writers of sea stories and of nautical journals abound"; yet few, if any, "enter into the very heart of the matter like Melville. His excellence is attributable to the intermingling of his education and his experience." The aesthetic qualities greatly pleased the Troy paper: "His descriptions are strikingly vivid. The whole thing is before us. Whether a wild frolic, a brutal flogging, or a sad burial, every important incident is given . . . and not a single badly chosen epithet mars the consistency and accuracy of the picture. The delineations of character are perfect, and their integrity through the whole trip is preserved unbroken. But the most attractive feature in the book is its reality. It appears like an authentic narrative. The history is simply told with no appearance of labored embellishment, and yet its progress is interrupted by flashes of humor and bursts of genuine pathos, which will command attention or awaken sympathy." Unlike most Americans, the *Budget* could not accept this likeable book as an account of actual adventure.

It was probably the editor, Epes Sargent, dramatist, novelist, and author of the popular song "A Life on the Ocean Wave" and other "sea

11. On March 29 the *Commercial Advertiser* quoted this passage so far.

pieces,"[12] who on March 25 in his Boston *Transcript* rejoiced that Melville had returned from the fanciful realms of *Mardi* to "the forecastle or maintop," where he was "capital company." Seconding the attack on the "flogging and grogging" system, he pronounced *White Jacket* "a very graphic and spirited, and we believe, faithful picture of life on board an American man-of-war." On March 26 the New York *Sun* noted "another charming volume from the pen of that charming writer, Herman Melville"; took it to be "a result of his experience while on board the frigate"; and considered it perhaps more interesting than his previous works. The Boston *Evening Traveller* on March 27 found it spirited, interesting, and instructive, and differing from "most of our glimpses of sea life" in seeing the man-of-war from the forecastle rather than the quarter-deck. On March 28 there was a short item in the New York *Evening Post*: "White Jacket is very popular in England, and is said by many to be his best work"; and one in the Philadelphia *Public Ledger and Daily Transcript*: "The world in a man-of-war is depicted with graphic power and amusing description." On March 29, the New York *Commercial Advertiser* gave two sentences to a book which would "arrest anyone's attention."

Editor Hiram Fuller may have been the writer who, also on March 29, in his New York *Evening Mirror*, regarded *White Jacket* as a reliable revelation of the truth about the navy. It was "not a novel," but a picture of actual life "so evidently valuable, honest, and drawn with a steady hand, for a serious and generous purpose, that . . . it shows the author in a better light than any of his former works." Ranking with *Two Years Before the Mast,* it had an admirably judicious tone: "No appearance of venom or personal spite deforms White Jacket's pictures . . . the sketches of a master, who, by a few bold strokes, can give the whole spirit of a scene, without the temptation to caricature a single feature."

A starred day for *White Jacket* was March 30, when there were no less than four American reviews, of which three agreed that it was an extremely valuable disclosure of real conditions; moreover, the two longest of these concurred in asserting vigorously that the book was not fiction, in approving most of Melville's censure of naval regulations, but, curiously enough, also in strongly objecting to his con-

12. Sargent was editor of the *Transcript* from 1847 to 1853. He was later famous for his school readers (*DAB*). Poe said of his "sea pieces" that he "paints them with skill" ("Literati," *Deluxe Edition of the Works of Edgar Allan Poe* [New York, 1909], . 132). The *Transcript* had carried a two-sentence notice of *White Jacket* on March 3.

demnation of flogging. The March 30 review in *Saroni's Musical Times* was especially cogent, because it was by an old navy man, Saroni himself,[13] who said he too had "done long and grievous penance in a man-of-war." "No fiction, this," he said: "It is this our own experience we find set down in 'White Jacket'; and but for the immeasurable talent displayed, as well as for a few propositions wherein we do not wholly acquiesce, we might think that we ourself had written the book and not Melville. Not that he had written his book in a cynical spirit; for much he has softened down which would have furnished texts for anti-naval harangues. . . . He could have made the picture darker. Let the book be widely distributed to keep foolish youths from being lured to sea by romantic tales. . . . If, after reading 'White Jacket,' they be still bent on 'shipping,' they will then sign the roll with their eyes open." Here was the most convincing of all the pieces of evidence that Melville had indeed told the truth about the Navy. The former sailor then quoted sympathetically accounts of the personal discomforts inflicted on the seamen; he went on, however to say that the abolition of flogging would be "a dangerous experiment." He hoped that steam would "solve the problem by making it unnecessary to have such large and unselect crews."

Long and mainly enthusiastic was the review on the same day March 30, in the *Albion,* probably by the editor, English-born William Young, who saw *White Jacket* as rugged, realistic, plain-spoken, comic unromantic—a book for men, indeed for those who "have not very dainty nerves." (Those delicate females of 1850!) Young claimed that it "was hard to cull a passage for ladies from this clever book." There was, he declared, "no fiction, no allegory in the startling avowals that he here presents to his countrymen." A hundred years later Newton Arvin was to call *White Jacket* "a highly pictorial allegory with a significance that is frankly and unequivocally enforced."[14]

With his British orientation, Young naturally liked a book which aimed "to bring to public notice the oppressive rigor of the laws that regulate the American Navy, and the terrible severity with which they are carried into effect." In enforcing his thesis, however, the author had not "peopled his quarter deck with demons and his forecastle with angels" nor forgotten that there must be considerable discipline at sea. He approved of Melville's condemnation of the regulation

13. For proof Saroni was the reviewer, see Chapter IV, footnote 37.
14. *Op. cit.,* p. 112.

injuring Jack's comfort and health unnecessarily, and quoted passages illustrating the sailor's grievances.

Revealing a limited sympathy with basic democratic philosophy, which set him apart from the book's other American civilian reviewers —no doubt a consequence of his having spent his first thirty years in England—[15] Young launched a tirade, not so much at Melville's opposition to flogging, as at the basis of his attack. He had not expected "in so able, so practical, and so-large-minded an author as Herman Melville . . . to find the 'essential dignity of man,' and 'the spirit of our democratic instiutions' lugged in on such a question as this [flogging]. Is it consistent with the 'essential dignity of man' that one man should sweep the floors of Congress, and another make laws upon it which his countrymen must obey? If the world were big enough, and each man had his desolate island to himself . . . we might keep up this pleasant non-committal delusion, but in the 'world in a man-of-war,' or in the world or out of it, this phantom may be left to the Transcendentalists, among whom our author is by far too good a fellow to be classed." Before two years had passed, that was exactly where some were to class him.

Though at odds with Melville about the turn his thinking about democracy had taken, Young expressed his "unqualified admiration of the touches of humor, pathos, wit, and practical philosophy with which the lighter portions of 'White Jacket' are plentifully seasoned." The "nautical sketches" were "unsurpassed, so pleasantly set off as they are, that one almost forgives the writer for taking away so much of the romance of the sea." He ended handsomely: " 'White Jacket' in its serious portions must draw the attention of serious men. In its lighter pages, it bears those inherent marks of fancy, freshness, and power," which the public expected in every work by Melville.

The third March 30 notice was a single completely complimentary paragraph in the Buffalo *Courier* about "the most admirable thing in its way that has come under our notice for many a year." "From title page to 'finis'," the *Courier* had "read with increasing pleasure and interest. Let those who would obtain accurate knowledge of life on board a man-of-war and of the discipline, conditions and peculiarities of the American Naval Service, buy this book and read. Their money can never be laid out to better advantage."

In the fourth March 30 review the Springfield *Republican's* critic,

15. *Appleton's Cyclopaedia of American Literature.*

probably Dr. J. G. Holland,[16] also found *White Jacket* veracious, and though he was less concerned with the propaganda than with the very pleasing tone, he doubted "whether any more truthful delineator of the vicissitudes of sea life has ever appeared in English literature." Melville was, indeed, superior to his two most noted competitors: "Unlike the broad and coarse narratives of Marryat and the pretending and high wrought romances of Cooper," his "tales bring out the beauties of humble natures, and deal in pictures so pure and simple that while they refresh the searcher after recreation, they leave no stain upon the lip and no bitterness on the tongue."

The next month began well for *White Jacket*. On April 3, the Worcester *Palladium* remarked: "You almost feel the ship toss and rock as you read over his sentences, his narrative seems so life-like." In an impressive article on April 4 on the front page of the New York *Tribune*,[17] George Ripley, signing himself as "R.," dealt with Melville's "glowing log-book of a year's cruise." Ripley was unique among the contemporary critics in perceiving that the jacket was a symbol, though his interpretation was scarcely profound: "The White Jacket is made the emblem and remembrancer of all Mr. Melville's perilous and comic experiences, while immured in the floating prison—to use the mildest term—of a public man-of-war." He objected, however, to Melville's philosophizing: "He here finds ample materials for an entertaining book, and has worked them up into a narrative of power and interest. If he had confined himself to repeating what he had heard and seen, his book would have been more valuable, for the moral and metaphysical reflections which he sets forth in bad Carlylese, are only encumbrances to the narrative, and often become intolerable."

On the other hand, Ripley completely approved of Melville's censure of the navy, and realized that in exposing a most undemocratic institution, the author was a voice of that era of triumphant democratic trends:

Mr. Melville has performed an excellent service in revealing the secret of his prison house, and calling public attention to the indescribable abominations of naval life, reeking with the rankest corruption, cruelty and blood. He writes without ill-temper, or prejudice, with no distempered, sentimental philanthrophy, but vividly portraying scenes of which he was the constant witness and in many instances suggests a judicious remedy for the evils which he exhibits. His remarks on the discipline of our public vessels, are entitled to great consideration and [the italics here

16. See Chapter II, footnote 72.
17. This review was reprinted in *Littell's Living Age* on May 4, 1850.

and below are mine] *coincide with the prevailing tendencies of the public mind.* It is not often that an observer of his shrewdness and penetrating mind is admitted behind the scenes, and still less often that the results of the personal experience are presented in such high-wrought pictures. *A man of Melville's brain and pen is a dangerous character in the presence of a gigantic humbug.*

Ripley's long quotations included a part of the attack on flogging.

Though not entirely adverse, the long review of April 4, the same day, in the New Bedford *Mercury*, was one of the least favorable on this side of the Atlantic.[18] Obviously thinking of *Mardi*, the *Mercury's* contributor did rejoice that the author had "once more put foot on the ratline and donned the trapaulin," and that the "same hand that sketched the cruise of the Julie" and "Dr. Long Ghost . . . is visible in the spirited scenes of White Jacket"; indeed this work was his most "substantial." Still doubting the actuality of Melville's first two tales, he said here was "a matter of fact minuteness of detail that makes the narrative as everyday as the life of a hotel." To the navy what Dana's was to the merchant service, this book was by one "by birth and breeding fitted to comprehend the feelings and sympathies of the quarter-deck, by position and experience part and parcel of the forecastle." Although he could not agree fully with the conclusions about war and flogging, it was "valuable to hear that side of the case."

The New Bedford critic, however, condemned severely the style of some passages: the author "seems to have an unaccountable penchant for fine writing." Melville could be vigorous: "The gale off Cape Horn, and White Jacket at the main mast are hardly to be outdone by anything in the language." But he "will lapse into lavender phrases, whenever the gale or the peril was done." He objected to Melville's "airing his literature from the ready lips of Jack Chase." Indeed he doubted Jack entirely (today we know there really was a "John J. Chase"),[19] even though Dana had disclosed strange and remarkable characters in a forecastle. As for Jack's speech at Rio: "It is hardly credible that any human being, with a rational purpose in his brain, ever addressed another in the style in which Jack sues for and

18. This reviewer was surely not the same who had written in the *Mercury* on Melville's other books, making no adverse remarks whatever. Nor does he sound like William Ellery Channing, Jr., who was to discuss in the *Mercury, Israel Potter* and *The Piazza Tales* (and perhaps *Moby-Dick* also) with unqualified enthusiasm.
19. Anderson, p. 366.

obtains a day's liberty." Interestingly enough, he identified Melville's *Neversink* correctly as the frigate *United States.*

There were two pleasant April 6 items in New York journals. Bryant's *Evening Post* referred to *White Jacket* as "full of piquant and clever sketches," and gave five long excerpts. The *Literary American* printed three quotations and remarked that Melville "seems to have been born for the sea, or rather born for writing about it." The "free and easy style" of the book would "command readers, when more elaborate works will be neglected and forgotten."

On April 10, spread over much of the front page of the Democratic Boston *Post,* in which *Mardi* had been executed, was the century's most hostile article about *White Jacket.* The editor, Colonel Charles Gordon Greene, surely wrote it, for it was full of such umbrage at the anti-militarism and at the enlisted man's point of view in *White Jacket* as might have been expected from Colonel Greene—a man holding an army commission and having the background which led to his appointment as naval officer of the Port of Boston in 1853 by President Pierce, and reappointment in 1857 by President Buchanan.

The Colonel was among a small minority of the reviewers in deploring Melville's censure of the Navy; he asserted that most of them had "considered only" the "literary qualities" of the book (not at all true, as we have seen), which indeed were "high," while its "main aim" was to be "didactic rather than ornamental." Just because a man could produce a "fine romance like Typee" did not mean, in the Colonel's opinion, that he was competent "to discuss the fitness of the Articles of War, flogging, and the whole system of government of the navy." Melville, however, instead of concentrating on particular abuses "overshoots himself by attacking war, the navy, and military glory themselves." These were "part of the human picture and can not be eliminated. . . . His approach is too sweeping and theoretical."

The chapters on flogging, said the Colonel, contained more real argument than all the rest of the book. "But even here he is too abstract. The question is not what is right and wrong, but whether the naval service would be better without it." (This certainly has the ring of the voice of a military administrator.) Differing from most other reviewers, including Ripley, who said that Melville wrote "without ill-temper," the Colonel maintained that "the portions devoted to 'naval abuses' are pursued in a bitter spirit, by one who goes to extremes, and who is thereby liable to prejudice the intelligent reader against even the good there is in him—by one who is more of an enthusiast than a philosopher—by one who better knows how things *ought to be* than how they *can be,* with due reference to the weakness of human nature."

Although not without interesting facts and fine passages, the book on the whole was, the Colonel thought, inferior to all his previous works except *Mardi.* The "most ambitious chapters" were "the greatest failures, because he is incapable of handling his subject didactically, but does not attempt to do it dramatically." It indeed contained a parcel of facts "which anyone might read with profit, but which might as well have been told by a common person as by one of the most brilliant pens that America has yet produced." The Colonel ended very acidly by urging Melville to try his hand at something besides the sea, and by hoping that he would not give us more "autobiographical twaddle": "This constant attempt to be smart, witty and entertaining on no capital, becomes dreadfully tedious to the reader ere he 'achieves' the end of a book of 465 pages. A little of it is very well, but as poured out by Mr. Melville, in his stupid invention of a white jacket, it appears to be a stream of egotism, vapidness, and affectation, with here and there, a fragment of amber on the waves."[20] What will the Colonel do with *Moby-Dick?*

Willis wrote for his *Home Journal* a long and extremely cordial leading front-page article for April 13, not a mere "literary notice." First, as usual bracketing Melville with the greats of literature, he praised the aesthetic achievement resulting from the rare combination of contrasting backgrounds:

Mr. Melville is a literary curiosity. It is quite unusual for one who has acquired his information "before the mast" to possess the ability to present it in a readable form. One might expect the interest of adventure but not taste and high literary ability. . . . The keen perceptions of a man like Melville embrace a world of observation at a glance. . . . He resembles Chaucer and Crabbe, Defoe, Charles Lamb, and Dickens, or rather he is a mixture of all without being a copy of either. Indeed he is

---

20. *Appleton's Cyclopaedia.* He was referred to as "Col. Charles G. Greene," who had won a "National reputation" "as a journalist," in a memorial article on his brother Nathaniel in the Boston *Post* for December 1, 1877. The Greene family was rather Nathaniel in the Boston *Post* for December 1, 1877. The Greene family was military-commission-minded; for according to Nathaniel's obituary in the same issue of the paper, his son "Col. W. B. Greene . . . was graduated at West Point, and during the rebellion was in active service as Colonel of the Fourteenth Artillery Regiment from this State." In view of the Colonel's vociferous attack, Miller (p. 272) is inaccurate in saying that in the chorus of approval of *White Jacket* "though a few advocates of naval discipline grumbled, there was only one dissent of importance," in the *Democratic Review.* The *Post* had briefly mentioned *White Jacket* on April 2.

one of the most original of writers: for notwithstanding his evident familiarity with books, his writings owe little or nothing to others. . . .[21] The great charm of Mr. Melville's books is their vividness and their truthfulness. The thoughts are whole ones; no indistinctness or obscurity is there about them. . . . It is a singular union of gifts, is that clearness of eye and tongue, and . . . there is added a taste which, without being too fastidious, is honest and manly, and a love of humanity, too broad and catholic, to be imposed upon by either convitcion or pretension.

The humor, and then the courageous and telling exposure of abuses, next aroused Willis's admiration. He doubted that "all the incidents" were "intended to be set down as actual occurrences"; this question was "not important for judging the literary qualities" but was in connection with the author's aim to secure reforms. He professed confidence, however, in Melville's testimony as he had used it in his plea. He commended the book to the legislators: "This is no case of mere sentimental suffering, but an exposition of unbounded tyranny and degrading torture." He revealed at length how deeply he had been stirred by the attack on flogging. "Are our free citizens . . . to be scourged like hounds?"

Again, Willis fully sympathized with the book's democratic spirit. He seconded Melville's attack on caste, agreeing that the military system was an anomaly, and that there was indeed a great "gulph" between privates and officers. Our laws had perpetrated in this class distinction a caste system as "imperative and unconditional" as that "of India." The situation was worse in America than in England because there the men in the ranks could not have done better in civilian life. Willis agreed that the refusal to promote officers from the ranks was bad. "There is no symmetry in our institutions while this abominable vestige of feudal barbarity remains." "Finally we heartily commend 'White Jacket' as showing to the world the petty insolence and injustice on the part of officers, the want of attention to the ordinary comfort and health, and the degradation of our seamen: and the demoralized state of our navy consequent on these and other abuses . . . Reform should go deeper than the mere abolition of the cat . . and so construct our army and navy that they may harmonize with our free political institutions and cease to be the foul blot they are

21. Compare Arvin, "Few books of its dimensions have owed so much to books that have preceded them, and few have owed so little" (p. 151). Of course Arvin says this not of *White Jacket* but of *Moby-Dick*. From the twentieth-century point of view, the nineteenth century seemed always to be giving its highest approbation to the wrong item in the Melville canon.

at present, on our national escutcheon." So Willis concluded what is probably the most comprehensively and completely enthusiastic discussion of *White Jacket* ever written. Coming from a journalist with an amazing gift for achieving both popularity and notoriety,[22] it must surely have been widely read.

In brief approbation on April 17 the Baltimore *American* declared that "Brilliant and dashing spirited descriptions" abounded in the volume, which was "in the author's best style, and no modern author ranks higher as a marine painter." Here the "mysteries of life on ship board are revealed" and "the abuses of the service freely commented on." It would "add to his reputation." But on April 24, Donald Mitchell, in *The Lorgnette*, made one of the very few unfriendly American comments: "Peregrine Pickel and Robinson Crusoe" were "safe cures for Redburn and White Jacket."

Melville's appeal for reform elicited on April 25 the hearty approval of the *National Era*, which found in *White Jacket* "reality, not romance." There was "plenty of incident," but "made subservient to the very laudable purpose of exhibiting the condition of our navy": "Facts concerning the use of rum and of the cat-o'-nine-tails are detailed, which must arrest the attention of the nation. The book should be placed in the hands of every member of Congress. It gives a clearer insight into the abuses prevalent in our navy, and a better conception of the necessary remedies, than any work within our knowledge. It entitles its author to the warmest thanks of every American interested in the improvement of the condition and elevation of the character of our sailors."

The leading magazines were now beginning to show interest in the new work. In April the *Democratic Review* admitted its literary merits. There were "inimitable sea scenes" and "most agreeably are sketched the manners and customs of these 'wooden walls.'" Indeed it was "highly interesting and we can afford to wink at the author's weakness," flattering the British for low mercenary reasons: "It is evidently manufactured for the English market—all the seamen heroes are Britons, and all the admirals of England are the oracles and text books. Although the accomplished author thanks God that he is free from national invidiousness, he nevertheless betrays the

22. Beers, pp. 260, 287, 307. Miller (p. 246) dismisses Willis as a "shallow flatterer"; but every item in Willis's praise of this book can be virtually duplicated from modern critics, though not quite such an aggregation of compliments. At any rate, Willis was avidly read, and his *Home Journal* is one of the very few magazines which have survived until today.

fact that London pays him better for his copy-right than New York; and the puffs for English officers, with the left-handed compliments to the American service, doubtless had their value with Bentley." This was hardly fair, for Melville's reasons for admiring the methods of the British Navy were so rational and his book was so full of patriotic fervor for the United States itself and its destiny, even if not for its navy, that he could not rightly be charged with insincere sycophancy of the English; yet the *Democratic* was justified in pointing out the financial advantages to an American writer of pleasing the English. Indeed Bentley may well have anticipated that White Jacket's bouquets for the Royal Navy would please the British reviewers, as we have seen they certainly did. On the other hand, no other American, not even the hostile Colonel Greene, seems to have accused White Jacket of toadying to the British. The editor of the *Democratic*, Thomas Prentice Kettell, disliked the Young Americans,[23] and was quite likely himself this reviewer who seized an unusual chance of making a Young American seem guilty—of all things—of Anglophilism!

Also in April the *American Review*, after reading some chapters thought it would "be one of the most popular books of this world renowned *sea author*." The same month, probably John R. Thompson, in the *Southern Literary Messenger*, approved both its literary and reform aspects. The *Messenger's* reviewer, consistently as enthusiastic about Melville's more realistic books as he was scornful of his more philosophical, wrote one of the most appreciative discussions of the new volume. "As a literary production 'White Jacket' deserves high praise and abounds with the author's peculiar beauties," he said. He quoted the description of the Bay of Rio to comment: "There is extravagance in all this surely, but it is the extravagance of fireworks, ever bursting into new and blazing combinations, and showering around us the lustre of falling stars."

Thompson, or his contributor, lauded the censure of abuses: " 'Redburn' aimed at a reform in the discipline of the merchant service 'White Jacket' directs attention to the subject of 'flogging in the navy. The observant reader will discover . . . how much aloof from the influences of society and moral purpose—how completely without the pale of humanity and foreign to the jurisdiction of the age is the life on board." Like others he emphasized that Melville was the first sea writer with both first-hand materials and culture: "The practical experience

23. Miller, p. 166.

rience from the 'fo'k'sle' uniting with a love of learning and with an educated taste, which Marryat never had, has distinguished Melville from all other writers of his class. . . . It is not often that the stains of the tar buckets and the ink-stand are seen upon the same fingers; and when they are, it is even more seldom that these fingers drive a pen of such graphic and remarkable power."

The fact that the reviewer in the May *Holden's Dollar Magazine* had a good enough nautical background to identify correctly the frigate *Neversink* as the *United States* (unless indeed he merely took without acknowledgement this identification from the New Bedford *Mercury*) makes it virtually certain he was the editor, Charles F. Briggs, one-time sailor.[24] Briggs commended *White Jacket* highly both as entertainment and as a desperately-needed plea: "The descriptions are the finest, most accurate and entertaining of any narrative of sea life that has ever been published" and superior to Cooper's and Marryat's for "fidelity and spirit . . . . The book has two characters and each is perfectly sustained. It is an eloquent, humorous and faithful picture of man-of-war life, and also an exposure of the enormities, defects and evil tendencies of our whole naval system. Much good must result from the circulation of such a book . . . particularly" among "the rising generation." Briggs did not here question the book's being based on real experience, as he had in the case of *Redburn*. Indeed, of the two characters, White Jacket is nearer to self-portraiture than is Redburn; and the other characters on the frigate are nearer than those on the merchantman to being portraits of actual men.[25]

As both literature and propaganda *White Jacket* aroused the enthusiasm of another critic, perhaps Frederick S. Cozzens,[26] in the May *Knickerbocker*. Glad that Melville had escaped from the influence of Carlyle and Emerson which had ruined *Mardi*, he declared that "So strong was the continuous interest that we accomplished its perusal in one sitting. . . . Without . . . much imagination, but with daguerreotype-like naturalness of description . . . MELVILLE has given a volume which, in its evident truthfulness and accuracy of personal and individual delineation, reminds us continuously of that admirable and justly popular work, the *Two Years Before the Mast*."

24. Leyda suggests Briggs was the reviewer (*Log*, p. 374).
25. Compare Anderson, pp. 362-367 with Gilman, pp. 130-131.
26. Leyda suggests Cozzens was the reviewer (*Log*, p. 375). Miller (p. 272) says the reviewer was Lewis Gaylord Clark, the editor, but it seems unlikely that Clark, even willing to be fair to Melville as a littérateur, would have been quite so complimentary a Young American!

He found also a "vein of sly humor" and ability to pun which might have made the author a "Philadelphia Lawyer."

This *Knickerbocker* critic considered the censure of flogging as in harmony with the trend of enlightened opinion, both in and out of the navy. He called "especial attention" to the depiction of "an instance of almost indiscriminate flogging . . . and the consequences of such inconsistent punishment. . . . The force of public opinion, and the example of certain humane officers in the highest rank of the American navy, would . . . indicate that the time is not distant when corporeal [*sic*] punishment, if not . . . abolished, will at least be hereafter less frequently resorted to than formerly, and greatly lessened in its severity."

June brought two superficial but friendly notices. *Godey's Lady's Book* referred to "Another exceedingly pleasant volume, by the renowned author of 'Typee,' 'Mardi,' &c.," liked it "very much," and thought it would be his "most popular" work. The reviewer for *Sartain's Union Magazine* had not yet read "this inviting volume," but thought from the "character of Melville's former volumes" its readers were "destined to rare enjoyment."

Editor Simms may well have done the long review in the *Southern Quarterly Review* for July, quite as favorable as the one in the *Southern Literary Messenger*. He was concerned almost exclusively with the propaganda: "The author's role is that of the reformer." He did not think the satirical portraits exaggerated or the complaints too vociferous. He had a sympathetic ear for the report on the unnecessary petty discomforts and inconveniences in the seaman's routine. Surely it would be easy to remedy those outrageous hours for supper and breakfast, four in the evening and eight in the morning, between which White Jacket had no meals and "no lunches and no cold snacks." He seconded Melville's argument that warriors fighting on such a meal schedule would surely be beaten. He found cogent the attacks on preventing the men from singing at their work; on forbidding the men who had night watches from sleeping during the following day; on the invariable daily flooding of the decks, through which the sailor went barefoot even in zero weather; and on the present impossibility of a seaman's winning a commission. He noticed also the major cruelties, and declared there was "no reason to suspect our author of coloring too highly his complaints of the evil and injustice."

As can be imagined this Southerner quoted with special approbation Melville's contention that quarter-deck authority sat more naturally on those officers who had been more accustomed to social position, and so "the old Virginians were much less severe, and much more gentlemanly in command than the Northern officers."[27] From his final paragraph may be taken a statement which can serve as a sort of epitome of the tone of the American reaction to *White Jacket*: "The author shows himself everywhere, a shrewd, sensible, well informed man, thoughtful and practical." How flatly, a year and a half later, *Moby-Dick* was to cause this reviewer (or another for this magazine) to contradict this statement.

The record of the immediate American reception of *White Jacket* was terminated by high praise from two religious periodicals. The New York *Evangelist* on May 23 regarded with nearly complete approval, for its style, and especially for its strong case for naval reform, what had "every appearance of being a true history of the author's experience as a common sailor on board a man-of-war": "Though the experience was brief, it was instructive, and full of incident which the author has detailed with charming liveliness and graphic power. If it were not a little too ambitious, it would be . . . one of the most able and beautiful pictures of sea life ever drawn. The highest order of descriptive talent is displayed, as well as keen wit and good sense. We can praise, too, very highly the sympathy manifested for the poor sailor. The chief merit of the work lies in this. It opens the secrets of a man-of-war . . . and . . . we trust will awaken sympathy that will not die till the spirit of reform reaches even these grim and secluded abodes of tyranny."

Although greatly irritated by Melville's personality, the reviewer for the *Biblical Repository and Classical Review* for July found his book extremely stimulating reading and a tremendously powerful instrument for effecting reform. Melville seemed more at home in a man-of-war than in the settings of *Typee* or *Omoo*. His year's experience on the *Neversink* as an "ordinary seaman" as here delineated was not only "intensely exciting," but was "really worth something and cannot fail to produce effect in certain quarters": "The volume is brim-full of the author's characteristic faults—a swaggering air, extravagant speech, and outrageous sentiment, profane expressions, mounting at times almost to blasphemy, and a reckless, care-for-nothing manner of life. But as a sketch of the real world on board a naval

27. This Southerner naturally took exception to a reflection on "the Southern slaveholder, as one necessarily more tyrannical than any other class of persons." It must be granted that this "reflection" does seem inconsistent with Melville's compliment to the Virginians as officers.

ship . . . it has wonderful power. The life of a man-of-war is painted with such consummate skill and intense energy of expression, that its horrible features glare upon you like a living being and can never be effaced from the mind. . . . for power in this respect it surpasses any book we ever read . . . As an *exposé* of the wickedness of many of our 'Articles of War' . . . of the bad tendencies and effects of 'Flogging' and 'Grog-rations' in the Navy . . . of the trials, temptations, and hardships of naval seamen . . . it is really withering and often heart-rending." He thought the book would aid potently the efforts then being made to improve the Navy: "Its keen wit, pointed irony, sarcastic humor, biting invective, and fearless exposure of wrong, do prodigious execution, and generally on the right side."

Moved to oratory, he concluded with an elaborate analogy, likening the book to a

seventy-four line of battle ship, in perfect trim, well-manned, and armed to the teeth, fearlessly and proudly ploughing the deep, broad sea of humanity, floating high the banner of Liberty, Reform, and Good-will to the sailor—ready to give battle on any tack, with any craft, on any sea—now slily aiming a solitary thundering death-shot at some ceremonious Commodore, or tyrant Captain, or transcendental faithless Chaplain, or stark mad-with-science heartless Surgeon, which is sure to hit the mark—and now boldly letting off, without warning and without mercy, a whole broadside of hot-shot into the midst of "grog rations," "cat o' nine tails," cruel and murderous "Articles of War," and the whole beleaguering forces of naval iniquity, threatening to sweep the seas, and win a more glorious victory than that of Trafalgar, or Navarino. We commend Melville's "White Jacket" to all the friends of seamen, and to the special regards of our Naval Authorities.[28]

This paragraph suitably terminates the chronicle of the reviews of *White Jacket*.[29] If it were not more cleverly composed, and if its enthusiasm were not even greater than that of most of the reviews, this paragraph might be taken as a composite voicing of the ardent American welcome given in 1850 to *White Jacket,* a round of nearly

28. In its July number *De Bow's Commercial Review of the South and West* printed with expressed approval, a portion of the mainly flattering review in the London *Morning Post.*

29. Out in Hawaii, the *Friend* on August 1 showed some animosity, but rather because Melville had taken "French leave" from "several whalers" [actually from only one: he was legally released from the other two before he "shipped as a sailor on board the United States Frigate 'United States' "] than because it found anything to say against the book itself. The *Friend* indeed then went on to quote the favorable review from the *National Era.*

unanimous applause, since, of the journals which are known to have written about it, only one was completely hostile, and only two even mainly so, out of twenty-eight.

In spite of the general critical enthusiasm which greeted its first publication, *White Jacket* seems in America to have rapidly dropped out of sight. Fitz-James O'Brien did speak of it in 1853, as having less of Melville's "faults than almost any of his works and is distinguished for clear, wholesome satire, and manly style." O'Brien was the first to quote that passage which was to be much admired in a later century, White Jacket's fall from the main-top-gallant-stun'-sail, with this comment: "This is fine. There was never a description like this . . . . Our ears tingle as we read it. The air surges around us as we fall from that fearful height."[30] As O'Brien did not mention the book in his 1857 article on Melville and Curtis,[31] nothing seems to have been said about it after 1853 by Americans for many years. It was reprinted, before Melville's death only once in America, in 1855.[32] It remained in oblivion during the rest of his lifetime.

CONCLUSION

The vote of the British journalists in 1850 was definitely in favor of *White Jacket* as an artistic effort. Only one was actually censorious on aesthetic grounds (*Britannia*—a lack of "art"); one was noncommittal (*News*); one was lukewarm (*Spectator*—"pretty well done"); three objected to certain extravagances in the writing (*Post*—"far fetched" allusions, *Globe*—"conceits," *Bentley's*), but considered these "blemishes" definitely outweighed by the essential excellence; leaving, out of the total of eleven, five who expressed nothing but enthusiastic approval of the style (*John Bull, Atlas, Gazette, Herald*, Chorley).

The proportion of American journalists that year voting for *White Jacket* as a literary success was even greater. Out of twenty-seven, only four said anything about the style which could possibly be considered adverse (Ripley, Colonel Greene, *Mercury*, Mitchell); of these, one, while objecting to the "metaphysical" reflections in "bad Carlylese," still discerned a "narrative of power" (Ripley); only two were purely negative reactions to the manner (Greene, *Mercury*).

The twenty-three other Americans seemed to have read the book (not always carefully) with nothing but pleasure in its form. Of

30. *Putnam's Magazine*, February. For a modern encomium of this passage, see Arvin, pp. 114-117.
31. *Putnam's Magazine*, April.
32. Minnegerode, p. 156.

these, eight may be separated out as special devotees: "not a single badly chosen epithet" (Troy *Budget*); "Nautical sketches . . . un surpassed" (*Albion*); "taste and high literary ability" recalling even Chaucer and Dickens (Willis); "finest and most entertaining" de scriptions of "any sea book" (*Holden's*); "accomplished perusal in one sitting" (*Knickerbocker*); "pen of such graphic and remarkable power" (*Southern Literary Messenger*); "one of the most able and beautiful pictures of sea life ever drawn" (New York *Evangelist*); "wonderful power," "consummate skill" (*Biblical Repository*). Thus the Americans outdid even the British in overwhelming praise.

The comic element in *White Jacket* elicited practically no com ment in England, but a good deal in America, where five enjoyed its "humor" (Duyckinck, Troy *Budget*, *Holden's*, *Albion*, *Biblical Repository*), and one found it "amusing" (Philadelphia *Ledger*). One Briton even sourly described the operation scene as full of "horrible wit" (*Post*). Is this contrast another illustration of the traditional British phlegm, or is the book's humor peculiarly Yankee?

The British gave central, and the Americans only marginal, at tention to the style. Indeed the main difference between the imme diate British and American reactions was that the former concentrated more on the aesthetic aspect and the latter on the humanitarian. The British were comparatively less concerned with Melville's attack on abuses. During 1850, of the eleven British, four ignored his appeals for reform (Chorley, *Gazette*, *Bentley's*, *Herald*); four were sym pathetic (*John Bull*, *Britannia*, *News*, *Atlas*); one condemned the satire on the medicos but approved the attack on flogging (*Post*) and one rejected entirely his case for progress (*Spectator*). Yet five Londoners viewed with great satisfaction a Yankee's commendation of the more humane discipline in the Queen's Navy (*Britannia*, *John Bull*, *Atlas*, *Globe*, *News*).

How much more widespread in the United States was interest in 1850 in the propaganda! True, nine Americans made no comment on the naval abuses, but in all cases but one (Troy *Budget*), theirs were tiny items. Two implied disagreement with Melville (*Mercury Democratic*); only one actually set up a rebuttal (Colonel Greene) Thus only four out of the twenty-eight Americans evinced any real in tention of either disparaging or ignoring Melville's plea for better condi tions. Although two defended flogging (*Albion*, Saroni), these two in other respects, and thirteen more in all respects, strongly approbated Melville's strictures on the Navy (Duyckinck, *Transcript*, *Mirror*

Buffalo *Courier*, Ripley, Willis, *National Era, Southern Literary Messenger*, Simms, Briggs, *Knickerbocker, Evangelist, Biblical Repository*).

Although thus the American press for the most part backed Melville in his case against the Navy, the gold braid no doubt had a very different opinion, to judge from Colonel Greene's review, and especially from a manuscript by Commander, later Rear-Admiral, Thomas O. Selfridge, who as head of naval recruiting in Boston undoubtedly knew the Colonel. The Admiral probably saw in the book a serious obstacle to his own work. Although he evaded many of the main issues, he denounced Melville for opposing flogging, tried to refute many of his minor charges, and declared the book full of "misstatements & inconsistencies . . . improbabilities, false premises & false conclusions." As his manuscript was not printed until 1935, he can scarcely be considered a reviewer.[33]

Some reasons for the much greater American response to White Jacket's appeal for redress of grievances are fairly obvious. The British naturally were less concerned about the problems facing the American Navy. Then, his arguments were based on a democratic philosophy which had less appeal in England.

The actual effect of *White Jacket* on the abolition of flogging is another matter. As the law against flogging in the American Navy was passed by the House on September 25, 1850, and by the Senate on September 28,[34] only six months and eight days after the publication of the book by the Harpers, admirers of Melville have been tempted to believe that his book brought about this statutory action. Two of his biographers asserted the book was the immediate cause of the enactment of the law,[35] the prime piece of evidence being S. R. Franklin's *Memories of a Rear Admiral* (1898).[36] Admiral Franklin who had been a shipmate of Melville's on that cruise of the frigate *United States*, said that the book "had more influence in abolishing

33. Anderson, who discovered this twenty-one page document, analyzes it carefully (pp. 422-423).

34. *Congressional Globe* (The First Session of the Twenty-First Congress), XXI, II, pp. 1907, 2060.

35. Weaver, p. 234; Mumford, p. 117.

36. Many years later Rear-Admiral Livingston Hunt gave Melville credit for having been "one of the chief agents in bringing about the end of this barbarous custom." Hunt's testimony might be thought to be all the more convincing because of his strong dislike of Melville's attitude toward the gold braid; but his only authority seems to be Franklin, whom he quotes. ("Herman Melville as a Naval Historian," *Harvard Graduates Magazine*, XXXIX [September, 1930], 22-30).

corporal punishment than anything else"; that it was "placed on the desk of every member of Congress"; that as "an evidence of the good it did, a law was passed soon after the book appeared abolishing flogging in the Navy absolutely."

As a matter of fact public disapproval of the brutality of naval discipline had been growing for some time and was becoming more insistent late in 1849. The *Democratic Review,* during the last five months of that year, had carried a series of long articles against flogging in the Navy, in the last of which was a statement that the movement to abolish flogging was definitely coming to a head in December, 1849.[37] A resolution for reporting a bill abolishing it was introduced into the House on December 31, 1849.[38] As *White Jacket* was published six months before the law was passed the next September, the book could have been most influential, but it was not mentioned in the long debates which preceded the enactment of the law.[39] It is, of course, not impossible that the book was seen by members of Congress, even though not referred to in the *Congressional Globe* nor in the Executive Documents.[40]

The question of literal autobiographical truth was so overshadowed by the question of the case against the Navy as to attract little attention; in general *White Jacket* was taken to be much more an account of actual adventures than modern scholarship has shown it to be. In England only one critic during 1850 (Chorley), and one later (*Dublin,* in 1856) seemed to regard it as anything other than a real sea journal; in America only three, all diffidently, revealed any doubts (*Argus,* Troy *Budget,* Willis). As the romantic tone of *Typee* had started a debate about its actuality, so the matter-of-fact tone of *White Jacket* silenced all but a few skeptics.

There was some difference between the British and American attitudes toward the religious implications. One Londoner discovered an irreverent reference to Christ (*Post*); and one was perturbed by the presence of a "philosophy" ill-according with "revelation" and by the

37. XXV (Aug., Sept., Oct., Nov., Dec., 1849), 97-115, 225-242, 318-338, 417-432, 538-543.

38. Hetherington, p. 165. The New York *Sunday Times and Noah's Weekly Messenger,* carried on March 3, 1850, this item: "There is to be a public meeting at the Tabernacle on Tuesday, called by the Mayor, and a large body of respectable citizens, to recommend abolishing flogging in the navy." This was seventeen days before the American publication of *White Jacket,* but subsequent to the British publication, February 1.

39. *Ibid.,* p. 168.

40. *Ibid.,* p. 167.

religious theme of the concluding chapter (*John Bull*). In America, however, this same chapter, with its confidence in the wisdom of "Our Lord High Admiral," and its assurance that "Life is a voyage that's homeward bound," was praised (*Southern Literary Messenger*) and quoted approvingly (Duyckinck the Episcopalian). Two American religious magazines, moreover, offered encomiums on the book, only one detecting anything unorthodox (*Evangelist*), though the other did find profanity (*Biblical Repository*). The two British rejoinders seem reflections of a hypersensitive fundamentalism, as *White Jacket* is surely Melville's most Christian book.

Direct testimony to the great popularity of *White Jacket* was not lacking. On April 6, 1850, the *Home Journal* announced that "The first edition of . . . 'White Jacket' was sold as soon as published." On April 20, it again witnessed the book's success: " 'White Jacket' is enjoying universal favor . . . both here and in England, where accurate judges of sea-life and naval discipline abound, and seems by common consent to have taken its place among standard works in the fascinating department of" nautical literature. "Never was a white jacket so famous." *Knickerbocker*, in May spoke of "the universal prevalence of the book."

The considerably smaller total number of reviews devoted to *White Jacket* than to *Typee* make it scarcely correct to speak of 1850 as peak year of Melville's nineteenth-century fame, nor was it so successful financially as the first two books had been; and yet 1850 was his year of serenest relations with his public; in both America and England there was less adverse printed comment on *White Jacket* than on any of Melville's other volumes.

Five reasons may be suggested for the welcome given *White Jacket* in 1850. First was its novelty as the pioneer picture of a navy as seen by an enlisted man. Melville for the first time gave the "forecastle point of view" (London *Atlas*, Boston *Traveller*, London *National Miscellany* in 1854). The related point that he was the first naval sailor-author to unite culture and experience was made by four Americans (Duyckinck, Troy *Budget*, *Mercury*, *Southern Literary Messenger*).

Second was its conventional Christianity and "morality." Even though not pious enough to satisfy an Englishman or two, it contained nothing to arouse the religious and moral tempests that had been stirred up by *Omoo*.

Third was its humanitarianism. Rather than originating the movement for reform in the navy, it rode the crest of the wave of an agitation which was already directed particularly against flogging, and it contributed somewhat, no doubt, to the final victory. How intimately this particular reform was bound up with the general reform tendencies of the period is shown by the fact that immediately after an amendment against flogging was introduced into the House, amendments were moved to abolish the liquor ration for the sailor[41]—certainly not advocated by Melville. When the amendments reached the upper chamber, Senator Hamlin argued that if you refuse the sailors the opportunity of becoming intoxicated, you do "away with a great deal of the necessity for the cat-o'-nine-tails."[42]

Those were years of a rapidly growing interest in the welfare of prisoners;[43] of the successful efforts of Dorothea L. Dix in behalf of paupers and the insane;[44] of strides toward women's rights under the leadership of Margaret Fuller;[45] of the passing, in Maine in 1851, of the first prohibition law.[46] Abolitionism, says Parrington, was only a part of a larger impulse, "a comprehensive program of universal reform."[47]

Fourth, accounting for the book's success in England, was its emphasis on the greater efficiency and humanity in the Royal Navy—which apparently did it no great harm in America, where a sole reviewer registered irritation at it (*Democratic Review*)—and which in England, where the drive for practical reform was weaker, filled a hiatus left by the relative unresponsiveness to Melville's propaganda. Surely his profound admiration for the British sailor, exemplified in his portraits ranging from Jack Chase to Admiral Collingwood, though not noted explicitly by any British commentator, put English readers in a good frame of mind.

Fifth, making for its appeal in America was its trenchant individualism. The vigorous democracy of *White Jacket* must have made it very acceptable in an era pervaded, as no other has been, by the frontier belief in equal opportunity for all. Few boys then "escaped being told that they might become president."[48] A generation

41. *Congressional Globe*, XII, II, p. 1096.
42. *Ibid.*, p. 2060.
43. Fish, p. 259.
44. *Ibid.*, p. 258.
45. *Ibid.*, p. 27.
46. *Ibid.*, p. 267.
47. *The Romantic Revolution in America* (New York, 1927), p. 342.
48. Fish, p. 6.

convinced that the worthy young man could achieve unlimited success, however humble his origin, might well be aroused by Melville's exposure of an institution in which the common sailor, however able, could no longer rise to command. Willis, Simms, and Duyckinck heartily seconded Melville's recommendation that officers be promoted from the ranks, and Willis declared we should so reconstruct "our army and navy that they may harmonize with our free political institutions." Duyckinck said that "a new set of motives and responsibilities among the men" could be brought in by "the advancement of well-approved seamen to office." He called the man-of-war a "floating prison"; the *Evangelist* described naval vessels as "grim and secluded abodes of tyranny."

Melville looked with independent Yankee cynicism upon the pomp and ceremony of Captain and Commodore. He satirized the hateful condescension of the officers on such occasions as the giving of the play in which Jack Chase appeared with such success, a condescension always followed by the "shipping" of their intolerable "quarter deck faces." These thrusts at aristocratic airs surely pleased the admirers of Andrew Jackson. Ripley said, "A man of Mr. Melville's brain and pen is a dangerous character in the presence of a gigantic humbug." For the *Biblical Repository* the book was like a battleship "aiming a solitary death-shot at some ceremonious Commodore, or tyrant Captain."

In *White Jacket* are passages which make it seem a veritable naval "Self Reliance": "Whereas, a seaman who exhibits traits of moral sensitiveness, whose demeanor shows some dignity within; this is the man," says White Jacket, the officers "instinctively dislike." It has been suggested that the optimism and individualism of Emerson were idealizations of frontier characteristics.[49] Ernest Marchand argues convincingly that "Emerson's doctrine of self-reliance is the natural complement of the individualism bred by the frontier."[50] The dominant individualism of the era found embodiment in *White Jacket*, and contributed to its having a success actually greater than it has had during the present century, in which the old individualism has been markedly bridled and tamed.

How well the spirit of *White Jacket* was in tune with the individualistic spirit of those times was shown by the number of American reviews which found the tone of his criticism of the Navy judicious,

49. Lucy L. Hazard, *The Frontier in American Literature* (New York, 1927), p. 195.

50. "Emerson and the Frontier," *American Literature*, III (May, 1931), 149-174.

manly, and calm. A lone dissenter found the discussion of abuses "pursued in a bitter spirit" (Greene). The others found "no railing, no scolding," the avoidance of "unmanly, mawkish solicitude" (Duyckinck); "no appearance of venom or personal spite" (*Mirror*); absence of "ill temper, or prejudice," with no "distempered sentimental philosophy," always proposing "judicious remedies" (Ripley); complaints not "too highly colored," made by a "shrewd, sensible well informed man, thoughtful and practical" (*Southern Quarterly Review*). Finally, an old navy man testified White Jacket was not "cynical" and could easily have made "the picture darker" (Saroni). The appeal of the humanitarianism and individualism of White Jacket was greater in America than in England, although even there the public was ready for a forecastle-man's view of a navy. All in all, though especially for America, it was notably an embodiment of contemporary trends. Ripley said it "coincides with the prevailing tendencies of the public mind." Among Melville's books, it was the one whose success with the reviewers resulted most from its timeliness.

Chapter VII: MOBY-DICK

"Imagination is banquetted on celestial fare, and delight, top-gallant delight."—London *Morning Post* (1851), reviewing *The Whale*.

BRITISH RECEPTION

On June 27, 1850, Melville offered to Richard Bentley a new manuscript, "a romance of adventure founded upon certain wild legends in the Southern Sperm Whale Fisheries, and illustrated by the author's personal experience of two years and more as a harpooner." It would be available "in the latter part of the coming autumn."[1] Evert Duyckinck referred to the new manuscript in August as being "mostly done."[2] Yet the finished proof sheets were not actually mailed to London until September 10, 1851.[3] The long interval, it is now known, was the result of an extensive revision Melville began in August, 1850, better called a total transformation. Several theories concerning the nature of the first version have been advanced: Howard Vincent's that it was a realistic whaling story,[4] Leon Howard's that it was a Byronic tale employing whaling characters and setting.[5] Of the two, Vincent's seems more plausible. But, in any case, it would seem that the book Melville described to Bentley was one he believed had every chance to be popular; and that, in the incandescence of effecting the transmutation, Melville came to care less and less whether or not he was shap-

1. *Log*, p. 376.
2. *Log*, p. 385.
3. Howard, p. 177.
4. *The Trying Out of Moby-Dick* (Cambridge, 1949), p. 22. George R. Stewart in "The Two Moby-Dicks," *American Literature*, XXV (January, 1954), 418-448, expresses conviction there were two versions, which he calls the *Ur-Moby-Dick* and *Moby-Dick*. He is rather inconclusive about the nature of the *UMD*, suggesting it was a "mere whaling voyage" with more "folksy" style, centering about the adventures of Ishmael and Queequeg. Stewart's theory harmonizes with the view above maintained that the first version was on a more "popular" level.
5. *Op. cit.*, p. 164.

ing a production which would please his public. When he had almost finished the book, in the form in which he gave it to the press, he wrote to Hawthorne: "What I feel most moved to write that is banned —it will not pay. Yet altogether write the other way, I cannot."[6] Here were contrasted the two versions, the first, what would pay, the final, what he was moved to write.

Pay it did not, but it was such a book as to impel a British novelist, Viola Meynell, seventy years later, who had chanced upon what was then "a much ignored book," to declare it, in the *Dublin Review* in 1920, "a work of wonderful and wild imagination," and to lead her to confess that "To the present writer Herman Melville satisfies not only every judgment but every inmost preference; so that it seems as if no greatness that has ever been surpasses his greatness." It was such a book, said Howard in 1951, as to force "the world to recognize him as one of the major writers of the nineteenth century."[7]

There has been for me great excitement in turning, in their huge and dusty bound volumes, as carefully as possible, but necessarily rapidly too, the fragile pages of faded old newspapers—of course all unindexed—to see what might be the response drawn from some unknown—or just possibly known—staff member or contributor by a book which was many years later to be so venerated. It was on October 16, 1851[8] that Richard Bentley published in London a book called *The Whale*—fortunately in New York a month later a more imaginative title was found. Melville's reputation was high in October, 1851, though he had certainly not grown rich, but it was a reputation as a writer of popular "romances of adventure." What would the reviewers make of a work which had begun as a "romance of adventure" but had ended by becoming so much more than that? Mostly they had recently read *White Jacket,* but as Richard Chase says, "The abyss which lies between *White Jacket* and *Moby-Dick* is one of the most enormous in the history of letters."[9] It has seemed almost unfair, though fascinating, to pounce upon these early, unsuspecting reviewers, who began to read at "Call me Ishmael" with no knowledge of what a later century was to decree about the achievement in the pages following. There may have been some repetitiousness in the reactions to Melville's five previous books, but the extreme variousness of

6. *Log,* p. 142.
7. *Op. cit.,* p. 150.
8. An advertisement in the London *Morning Chronicle* for October 15, 1851, reads: " 'The Whale' will be published tomorrow, the 16th inst."
9. *Op. cit.,* p. 42.

the impressions the sixth book made on its first readers has made reading the early reviews a perpetual surprise.

It has long been supposed that *The Whale* got off to a terribly bad start, because the first known reviews were the two crushing ones which came out on the same day, October 25, in two of the three British magazines which Poe thought so oppressively influential in America, the *Spectator* and the *Athenaeum*. Recently I have discovered an earlier press judgment in an important newspaper, the London *Morning Herald* for October 20, which may even startle a modern reader who has accepted the idea of the early rejection of *Moby-Dick*:[10]

Herman Melville is on the right track now. His "Omoo," "Typee," and "White Jacket" gave evidence of great and peculiar powers; but the audacity of youthful genius impelled him to throw off these performances with "a too much vigor," as Dryden has it, which sometimes goes near to defeat its own end. But in "The Whale," his new work, just published, we see a concentration of the whole powers of the man. Resolutely discarding all that does not bear directly on the matter in hand, he has succeeded in painting such a picture—now lurid, now ablaze with splendour—of sea life, in its most arduous and exciting form, as for vigor, originality, and interest, has never been surpassed.

What more could Melville have asked than that? But five days later did come the two well-known pronouncements which were so bitterly adverse and which thus illustrated already the extremes in the responses to the new book.

Henry Fothergill Chorley was disdainful of manual occupations, distrustful of new movements, and, as he had grown older, more and more inclined to tincture his criticism with "acerbity,"[11] and his magazine was condescending toward Americans—tendencies all of which he exemplified when on October 25, in the *Athenaeum,* he disposed of *The Whale*. Only he was usually calmer than he was that day. "An ill-compounded mixture of romance and matter of fact," he exclaimed. "The rant and electrical verb might have been permitted if not interrupted by the 'facts of Scoresby and the figures of Crocker.'" His

10. The limitations of previous studies of the reception of *Moby-Dick* are discussed in Hugh W. Hetherington, 'Early Reviews of *Moby-Dick*," *Moby-Dick Centennial Essays* (Dallas, 1953), p. 90.

11. Richard Garnett in *DNB*. William B. Cairns, *British Criticisms of American Writings, 1815-1833* (New York, 1922) says the attitude of the *Athenaeum* was often patronizing toward Americans (p. 18). An *Athenaeum* reviewer—possibly Chorley— of Sylvester Judd's *Margaret* (1845) found in it "that utter lack of artistic taste which is so conspicuous in American works" (March 17, 1849).

final word was: "Mr. Melville has to thank himself only if his horrors and heroics are flung aside by the general reader as so much trash belonging to the worst school of Bedlam literature,—since he seems not so much unable to learn as disdainful of learning the craft of an artist."

Although the *Spectator's* critic, also on October 25, found the purely nautical parts interesting, and the minor, but not the major, characters good, and granted that at some points the author evinced a "vigorous and fertile fancy," the total effect of his article was crushing in the highest degree. "The rhapsody belongs to word-mongering where ideas are the staple; where it takes the shape of narrative or dramatic fiction it is phantasmal—an attempted description of what is impossible in nature and without probability in art," said he, and contended that "a little knowledge is made the excuse for a vast many words," and that "the 'marvelous' injures the book by disjointing the narrative, as well as by its inherent lack of interest."

The real basis for his attack, however, was that the book did not conform to the canons of the novel:[12] "Such a groundwork is hardly natural enough for a regular built novel, though it might form a tale, if properly managed. But Mr. Melville's mysteries provoke wonder at the author rather than terror at the creation; the soliloquies and dialogues of Ahab, in which the author attempts delineating the wild imaginings of monomania, and exhibiting some profoundly speculative views of things in general, induce weariness or skipping; while the whole scheme mars, as we have said, the nautical continuity of the whole. . . . It is a canon with some critics that nothing should be introduced into a novel which it is physically impossible for the author to have known." He then reprimanded the author for shifting the mental point of view. As for the catastrophe, it overrode "all rule," because all, narrator included, sank. (The English edition did not have the Epilogue, in which Ishmael's rescue is explained.) "Such is the go-ahead method." Was this judgment penned by Leigh Hunt's son, a frequent contributor, and later editor?[13]

William Beach Thomas, the historian of the *Spectator,* says that "in the domain of art" it "was afraid of turbulence, resented violence, and disliked being hustled; and this jog-trot progression of its mind is displayed in criticisms of others besides the stormy Brontës. Of Mere-

---

12. Lewis Mumford, p. 177, was still protesting in 1929 against the "conventional critic" who was disturbed because *Moby-Dick* was not a novel. It was better regarded he suggested, as a "poetic tragedy," existing on several planes.

13. *The Story of the Spectator, 1828-1928* (London, 1928), p. 56; DNB.

dith they said that 'if Mr. Meredith intends to cultivate poetry, this overexuberance must be steadily repressed'; and of *Moby Dick* that it was 'rhapsody run mad.' "[14]

From these terrific blows the supersensitive Melville may never have completely recovered. A highly complimentary review two days later, however, should have somewhat consoled him. The only objections raised on October 27 by *John Bull's* reviewer were not aesthetic: he deeply regretted some "worse than heathenish talk" and "occasional thrusts against revealed religion." The rest of his fairly long article contained only praise.

He found three grounds for special commendation. First, he particularly congratulated the author of this "most extraordinary work" for making poetic and significant such an unpromising subject: "Who would have looked for philosophy in whales, or for poetry in blubber? Yet few books which professedly deal in metaphysics, or claim the parentage of the muses, contain as much true philosophy and as much genuine poetry as the tale of the Pequod's whaling expedition." The world of whales was disclosed to be "as brimfull of matters of deepest interest as any other sublunary world." There was charm even though the subject might not "fall within the ordinary canons of beauty," a bit of defense which might have been written by Lewis Mumford. Second, although like the *Spectator's* critic perceiving that *The Whale* was not exactly a novel, he saw in the divergence a mark of superiority. Third, he appreciated the philosophy: "The flashes of truth, too, which sparkle on the surface of the foaming sea of thought through which the author pulls his readers in the wake of the whale ship—the profound reflections uttered by the actors in the wild, watery chase in their own quaint forms of thought and speech,—and the graphic representations of human nature in the startling disguises under which it appears on the deck of the *Pequod*—all these things combine to raise *The Whale* far beyond the level of an ordinary work of fiction. It is not a mere tale of adventure, but a whole philosophy of life that it unfolds."

The big day for *The Whale* in London was November 8. Of the four reviews which came out that day, two elaborate ones, in the *Atlas* and *Britannia,* are almost impossible to categorize as favorable or unfavorable, for they both mingled great disparagement with great adulation. Also both commenced in much harsher mood than they ended, suggesting that in each case, the reviewer, as he approached the last pages, came gradually, even against his will, to submit to Melville's

14. *The Story of the Spectator,* p. 224.

wizardry. Was there collaboration, or had one reviewer seen the other's manuscript? There was, however, no copying, as the approaches were after all quite diverse, the *Atlas* being more impressionistic, *Britannia* more judicial.

The *Atlas* article—as usual brilliantly written—took the form of the most complete summary by far published in the century, satirical at first, but less so toward the end, punctuated with ejaculations. It appeared in two installments, on November 1 and 8, each consisting of six very long columns in small print. The *Atlas* writer kept oscillating between exasperation at Melville and acknowledgment of his power. For example, he ridiculed most of the characterizations, but admired the Ramadan scene. As an illustration of his impatience, take this: "Extravagance is the bane of the book, and the stumbling block of the author. He allows his fancy not only to run riot, but absolutely to run amuk, in which poor defenseless Common Sense is hustled and belabored in a manner melancholy to contemplate. Mr. Melville is endowed with a fatal facility for the writing of rhapsodies . . . once embarked on a flourishing topic he knows not when or how to stop. He flies over the page as Mynheer Van Clam flew over Holland." On the other hand, he could offer such a tribute as finding "the whole written in a tone of exaltation and poetic sentiment which has a strange effect upon the reader's mind in refining and elevating the subject of discourse, and at last making him look upon the whale as a sort of awful and insoluble mystery. . . . In none of his previous works are finer or more highly soaring imaginative powers put forth. In none of them are so many profound, and fertile and thoroughly original veins of philosophical speculation. . . . In none of them, too, is there greater affluence of curious, quaint, and out of the way learning brought to bear upon the subject at hand. In none of them are the descriptions of seafaring and whaling matters so wonderfully graphic, and in none of them is there to be found a more thorough command over the strength and beauties of language."

His conclusion is as fair a sample of his attitude as can be found: "As we close it we feel as if waking from what was partly a gorgeous vision, partly a night-mare dream, but both vision and dream intense, over-mastering in their power, the spell of a magician who works wildly, recklessly, but with a skill and a potency which few, we should think, will be disposed to deny or resist."

The contributor to *Britannia* offered a more systematic study. First, he was greatly disturbed by the failure of *The Whale* to conform to any recognized literary category. It was neither a novel nor a romance. Who ever heard of either "without a heroine or single love scene?" The plot was "meagre beyond comparison," as the whole "might very conceivably have been comprised in half of these interminable volumes." Second, the cetacean chapters might be "important to naturalists or whalers," but not to "the general reader."

But he also found things to admire. He declared first that the character sketches constituted "the principal merit of the work." The crew of the *Pequod* was "composed of mariners of all countries and all colours from the civilized British sailor[15] to the savages and cannibal harpooners of the South Sea Islands. In describing the idiosyncrasies of all these different castes of men our author has evinced acuteness of observation and powers of discrimination which would alone render his work a valuable addition to the literature of the day." Captain Ahab was "well contrasted" with the "commonplace mates." Queequeg was a "most interesting hero," and in the "curious details" of his worship of Yojo, our "author has shown that he has a fund of humor at command." Second, although the action had "halted some in earlier chapters," near the end it assumed "all at once an exciting interest"; the final chase was "most graphically described"; and the concluding paragraphs were "at once so grand, so awful, and so harrowing." Third, "barring a few Americanisms," which sometimes "mar" the style, "the language of the work is appropriate and impressive." Thus, once more, *Britannia's* staff could not write on Melville without giving some expression to a sense of smug superiority to the transatlantic cousins.

Also on November 8, it was the book's magic which, as it had the *Atlas* critic, enthralled George Henry Lewes, in the *Leader*.[16] One

15. This is a curious error—an unconscious revelation of British conceit—as there are no British sailors, civilized or uncivilized, in the crew of the *Pequod*, save only the "Old Manx Sailor," who appears at two moments only, the second time for his ignorant superstitiousness (Chapter CXXVI), and an "English Sailor," who speaks a single line. The crew of the British *Samuel Enderby*, a ship met by the *Pequod*, are quite civilized, and there are some notably civilized British sailors, of course, in *White Jacket*.

16. There is every reason to ascribe this review to Lewes. In 1850 Thornton Hunt had "established the *Leader* in cooperation with George Henry Lewes, who was editor for literary subjects" (Leslie Stephen in *DNB*). According to Lawrence and Elizabeth Hanson, *Marian Evans and George Eliot* (London, New York, 1952), p. 154, Miss Evans, in 1854, knew Lewes "to be a first rate literary and dramatic critic, and she also believed him to be the backbone of the *Leader*; his weekly reviews of books had been one of London's most stimulating journalistic experiences ever since he and Thornton Hunt had begun this radical journal four years earlier." By 1854 she was helping Lewes with his work on the *Leader*, even writing some of his articles (*ibid.*, p. 177), but she had in November, 1851, hardly known him long enough to have aided him with the review of *The Whale*.

of London's best known journalists, he had less than two months ago made the acquaintance of a then obscure woman named Marian Evans, who immensely admired his book reviews. As a critic, says Blanche Colton Williams, Marian's biographer, "he was nobody's mouthpiece."[17] In a short article, but one without adverse remarks, Lewes stressed that the Americans generally excelled in handling the supernatural: "No European pen still has the power to portray the Unseen so vividly as to hush the incredulous"—but to "do this American literature was without a rival." "What *romance* writer can be named with Hawthorne? Who knows the terrors of the sea like Herman Melville?" Uncommon it was in those days for a British critic to find what he considered a typically American characteristic a thing to be admired. What a contrast to *Britannia!* For Lewes, *The Whale* was "a strange wild weird book, full of poetry and full of interest . . . . One tires terribly of ballrooms, dinners, and the incidents of town life! One never tires of Nature, though the imagery often grows riotously extravagant. . . . Then the ghostly terrors which Herman Melville so skillfully invokes have a strange fascination. In vain reason rebels. Imagination is absolute; ordinary superstitions related by vulgar pens have lost their power over all but the credulous; but Imagination has a credulity of its own respondent to power. So it is with Melville's superstitions; we believe them imaginatively." So Lewes revelled in the thrilling pages of Melville's *Whale,* ". . . a strange wild work with the tangled overgrowth of an English park. Criticism may pick holes in this work; but no criticism will thwart its fascination . . . the 'Whiteness of the Whale' . . . should be read at midnight alone, with nothing heard but the sounds of the wind moaning without, and the embers falling into the grate within." This was a tribute indeed: Lewes was the only reviewer to mention what is now one of the most famous of the chapters.

The unqualified acceptance by Lewes was balanced by the equally unqualified rejection by the *Examiner's* critic on that same November 8,[18] who regarded the book with exasperated hostility, and after a very sarcastic synopsis, exclaimed: "We cannot say we recognize in this

17. *George Eliot* (New York, 1936), p. 93. Lewes was "literary editor of the *Leader"* (*Ibid.,* p. 92). Lewes and Hunt were cooperating in more ways than running a weekly, as with their wives then living in one household, in which Mrs. Lewes had borne Hunt two sons. No wonder Lewes turned to Marian.

18. The reviewer may have been John Forster, who had been appointed "chief critic on the *Examiner* both of literature and the drama" in 1833, and was editor from 1847 to 1856. He was notable as a biographer, especially of his friend Dickens. He was also an associate of Landor (Charles Kent in *DNB*).

writer any advance on the admirable qualities displayed in his earlier writings—we do not see that he even cares to put forth the strength of which he has shown himself undoubtedly possessed. If there is not carelessness in the book . . . there is at least so much wilfulness, that our enjoyment is small even of what we must admit to be undeniably clever in it." Here again also was the complaint that *The Whale* failed to conform to the canons of the novel: "But all the regular rules of narrative or story are spurned and set at defiance. . . . Certainly since Tom Thumb, there has been no such tragedy." Consigning it to those curious about whales, a subject not to his liking, he concluded: "Mr. Melville is a man of too real imagination, and a writer with too singular a mastery over language and its resources, to have satisfied our expectations with such an extravaganza as this."

The Whale's destiny to be subjected to alternate damnation and canonization was certainly illustrated when a week later, on November 14, it aroused a reviewer for the London *Morning Post* almost to ecstasy over a "book of extraordinary merit."[19] The dominant note of his long rhapsody was the tale's bewitching potency. True, alone among the British reviewers, he was somewhat worried about the probability. Admitting he had little knowledge of whaling, he queried whether Ahab's quest for a particular whale was not utterly hopeless; and even at times was "disposed to believe the whole book one vast practical joke." But what did that matter in a yarn in which "imagination is banquetted on celestial fare, and delight, top-gallant delight is the sensation with which the reader is most frequently familiar"? "There is a wild and wonderful fascination in the story against which no man may hope to secure himself . . . the spell of genius is upon us, and we are powerless to resist. The author's radiant imagination enthralls us in delicious bondage, and the tide of his animal spirits sweeps all doubts and misgivings triumphantly before us . . . we surrender ourselves without a murmur to the guidance of a companion so fearless, chivalrous, and romantic."

Especially impressive was his gratitude for the intensity of the vicarious experience:

19. The reviewer may have been Peter Borthwick (editor 1849 to 1852), who did much of the editorial writing himself, and who, while at Cambridge, had composed historical dramas. Of aristocratic antecedents, he had been an M. P. The *Post* was "very much an organ of the leisured classes, yet did espouse some liberal causes." It was "possibly the best-written newspaper in England" (Walter Hindle, *The Morning Post, 1772-1937* [London, 1937], pp. 179, 203, 3, 5). At any rate the reviewer was clearly the same as he who had paid such tribute to the imaginative power of *White Jacket* in this paper.

His descriptive powers are so vivid and appealing that we share with him the perils he so graphically pictures, and merge our own identity in his. We keep the night watches with him in savage and solitary seas—we feel the Pequod thrusting her vindictive bows into the cold malicious waves— we stand with him on the mast-head, and sway and swing with him over the writhing waters—we hear the pumps clanking—the blocks creaking— the sails flapping against the masts—the cape winds whistling through the cordage . . . so does the mind of the sympathetic reader yield an unconscious allegiance to the resistless sway of this powerful writer.

The *Post's* critic, furthermore, showed he had caught more than a glimpse of what Rosenberry has recently admired as Melville's "Comic Vision."[20] He was not certain the cetology would find favor with the zoölogists, but "The adventures, whether genuine or apocryphal, are so deliciously exciting—the descriptions are so graphic and pictorial—and the dialogue, like Touchstone's conversation, is 'so swift and sententious,' that we cannot hesitate to accord to Mr. Melville the praise of having produced one of the cleverest, wittiest and most amusing of modern books."

Nearly a month later, on December 16, it was probably Samuel Phillips who in the London *Literary Gazette*,[21] like the writers for *Examiner* and *Britannia,* was greatly exercised over Melville's failure to heed the conventional requirements of the novel: "This is an odd book, professing to be a novel [does it?]; wantonly eccentric; outrageously bombastic; in places charmingly and vividly descriptive." He disliked the use of materials from encyclopaedias "as stuffing"; "bad stuffing it makes, serving only to try the patience of his readers, and to tempt them to wish both him and his whales at the bottom of an unfathomable sea. . . . The story of this novel scarcely deserves the name . . . a preposterous yarn. . . ."

Admitting there were "sketches of scenes at sea, of whaling adventures, storms, and shiplife, equal to any we have ever met with,"

20. Rosenberry, p. 138, says "Thus the comedy which 'mapped the outlines of *Moby-Dick* and shaped its form' is not only compatible with its tragic theme, but essential to it, and the characteristic mixture of the two becomes an organic feature of Melville's profoundest exploration of the ambiguity of life." True, the *Post's* critic said nothing about the tragic depths of the book, but compare with his reference to Touchstone, Rosenberry's statement that "At carefully calculated intervals" Melville "converts" Stubb "into a Shakespearean clown to cast the ironic light of comedy on Ahab and the sombre meaning of his quest" (p. 130). He had said there was "resemblance between Babbalanja and such clowns as Touchstone and Lear's fool" (p. 86).

21. The editor now was not Jerdan, but Phillips (Graham, p. 315), who had reviewed *Typee* and *Omoo* with enthusiasm in the *Times,* and surely wrote this notice of *The Whale,* as it was the sort of thing often said by *Typee* fans.

and quoting an account of an attack on a whale, he concluded: "Mr. Melville has earned a deservedly high reputation for his performances in descriptive fiction. He has gathered his own materials, and travelled along fresh and untrodden literary paths, exhibiting powers of no common order, and great originality. The more careful, therefore, should he be to maintain the fame he so rapidly acquired, and not waste his strength on such purposeless and unequal doings as these rambling volumes about spermaceti whales." Such was the judgment in the *Gazette* on a book which less than a century later Ivor Winters was to describe as "beyond cavil one of the most carefully and sucessfully constructed of all the major works of literature."[22]

Like other Britons, Phillips (or his contributor) reprimanded Melville for drowning his narrator. The Epilogue, not present in the English edition, relates, as everybody knows, that Ishmael alone was "left to tell the tale." Without it, a careless reader might well have failed to observe that the author had in the final chapters accounted for Ishmael's being still alive. The adroit Epilogue, however, is the book's necessary capstone, and its absence understandably aggravated the British puzzlement at Melville's supposed disregard of the "rules of fiction." The earliest British review, the *Spectator's* on October 25, which called attention to this flaw could hardly have reached New York before November 6. As Melville was then in Pittsfield, and the American edition appeared on November 14, it is unlikely that there was time for the writing and adding of the Epilogue. Probably Bentley had received the Epilogue along with the rest of the manuscript, but had carelessly or even deliberately omitted it.[23]

Now, on December 20, came a review in the London *Morning Chronicle,* which took its place, along with those in the *Atlas* and *Britannia* as the third of the elaborate "great faults, great merits" London pronouncements. Because of the strong distaste of the *Chronicle's* writer for the central theme, it should probably be considered the least favorable of the three. Beginning with a veritable panegyric to Melville's first two books, he traced regretfully the growing obscuration of his great gifts by "a tendency to rhapsody," "a constant leaning toward wild and aimless extravagance" (temporarily halted in *Redburn*), culminating in the present work, wherein it ran "a perfect muck throughout," "occasionally soaring into such absolute

---

22. *Maule's Curse* (Norfolk, Conn., 1938), p. 73. Cf. also Arvin, p. 131: "Not many imaginative works have so strong and strict a unity."

23. This surely highly plausible explanation of the fact that only the American edition has the Epilogue was suggested to me by Luther S. Mansfield.

clouds of phantasmal unreason, that we seriously ask ourselves whether this can be anything other than moonstruck lunacy."

Strong words indeed, but he was far from done. For him the work fell sharply into two books, one "very, very bad," but one "very, very good"; and it was hard to say whether he castigated the one or lauded the other more vigorously. The bad, bad book, of which he gave a satirical synopsis, was the main story. It comprised "the jumble of mysticism and rhapsody, with which all that pertains to Captain Ahab is enveloped"; and the failures at characterizations—the shipmates being "phantom-like, inhuman, and vaguely uninteresting," the mates "mere talking shadows," emitting "nonsense," Queequeg, the only bit of "flesh and blood," being "little save an animal."

The good, good book, surprisingly enough for an Englishman, was for him what Vincent has called "The Cetological Center."[24] He declared: "There are very many chapters devoted to the natural history of the whales, containing in our view, some of the most delightful pages in the book. . . . Their appearance, their habits, their manner of swimming, are described in wonderful detail, and with a freshness and picturesqueness of language which brings the mighty animals before us . . . with a bright variety." Really now an *aficionado* of the hunting of the leviathan, as a result of reading what were "certainly the most vivid accounts of whaling ever written," was he of the *Chronicle,* who recounted at length his satisfaction in learning about the process of killing; about the food of the whales; about the great squid, the "kraken" of legend; about the "pleasant details of 'gamming' "; about "the perfect possibility of enjoying a blubber supper"; and finally, illustrated by a long quotation—"a magnificent piece of painting," about the birth of a baby whale. Indeed this last passage was to be one much admired in the next century.

London had given *The Whale* a good deal of attention during the final months of 1851, it will be granted, but it was to provide for it, as far as I could find, one sole review in 1852. *Bentley's Miscellany,* in January, was sure that *The Whale* was the summit of Melville's

24. *Op. cit.,* Chapter IV. The *Chronicle's* reviewer was obviously the same who had reviewed *Mardi,* for he devoted a long paragraph to restating his previously expressed low opinion of that book. Aside from Lewes, the best known of the literary critics writing for the *Chronicle* was Abraham Hayward, who was something of a biographer (Alexander Andrews, *The History of British Journalism to 1855* [London, 1859], p. 278). Internal evidence scarcely indicates that Lewes wrote the *Chronicle* review as well as the *Leader* review; hence it is fairly likely the *Chronicle* review was by Hayward. John Douglas Cook, editor of the *Chronicle,* acted chiefly as an administrator.

achievement. Impressed with the force of the characterization of Ahab, *Bentley's* exclaimed: "Through what scenes of beauty and grandeur that monomania impels him." *Bentley's* went on with cordial approbation: "There are descriptions in this book of un-rivalled force, colored and warmed as they are by the light and heat of a most poetical imagination, and many passages might be cited of vigorous thought, of earnest and tender sentiment, of glowing fancy which . . . show . . . that Herman Melville is a man of the truest and most original genius." The delay of the house organ of the publisher in getting out this review is curious, and whether it makes it more or less of a puff could be debated. That same month, in a "Retro-spective Survey of American Literature" in the *Westminster Review,* Melville got a single but favorable sentence, describing him as "a man of unquestionable genius who struck out for himself a new path in 'Typee,' 'Omoo,' and his latest book 'The Whale.'" Although called the "first and greatest" of American novelists, Hawthorne got no more space than Melville, but Irving and Cooper got much more.

Having swung so far to the right in *Bentley's* review, the British pendulum for *The Whale* swung to the left; from across the Irish Channel came a much severer judgment. The *Dublin University Magazine,* in February, found the book both admirable and defective, was not without relish for the adventures and for the "graphic" scenes of the early chapters, but seemed uninterested in seeking any deep significance. In this last known British review of *The Whale* was made the charge which had been made so persistently in London by the more censorious: "All the rules which have been hitherto under-stood to regulate the composition of works of fiction are despised or set at naught."

It may surprise some to learn that the immediate British reaction to *The Whale* during the three months it was being reviewed, was evenly balanced. The five completely positive reviews (*Herald, John Bull,* Lewes, *Post, Bentley's*) more than cancelled the four completely negative (Chorley, *Spectator, Examiner, Gazette*). That left four harder to classify, of which the *Dublin's* was most adverse; of the three long articles which went to extremes of both praise and censure, in two the former predominated (*Atlas, Britannia*), and in one the latter (*Chronicle*). It was almost an exact tie, with, if anything, a leaning toward the positive.

The ultimate British reaction, however, was absolutely and com-pletely negative. It consisted of the absence for many years of all commentaries except two, both very disparaging. William Harrison Ainsworth, in the *New Monthly Magazine*[25] in July, 1853, admitted that *The Whale* had "much vigorous description, much wild power, many striking details." Yet with amazing violence he denounced the extravagant writing and transcendentalism: "The style is maniacal— mad as a March hare—mowing, gibbering, screaming, like an incurable Bedlamite, reckless of keeper or strait waistcoat." He described the author as "maundering, drivelling, subject to paroxisms, cramps and total eclipse." He considered the book "a huge dose of hyperbolical slang, maudlin sentimentalism, and tragic-comic bubble and squeak," in which the hero "raved by the hour in a lingo derived from Rabelais, Carlyle, Emerson, newspapers transcendental and transatlantic." Among the first reviewers only Chorley had even approached such a fury of derision. The fact that Ainsworth was especially attracted to Irving and Longfellow does lend support to the thesis that more challenging literature was hardly calculated to appeal to the nineteenth-century mind. Transatlantic readers were given little chance to escape Ainsworth's judgment on *The Whale,* for his article, as may be recalled, was twice reprinted in America.

Three years later, a critic in the *Dublin University Magazine,* claiming to be himself a writer about whaling, was only less completely damnatory than was Ainsworth. Melville can hardly have been pleased to find described as a mere earnest what he knew was his best work, and to be told that he had the ability, even the "genius" to do something worth while, if he could get away from "half-insane conceits." The critic added that Melville would rank high if he did not "pervert his lofty gifts," as he had done in *The Whale,* a book which, though valuable for its whaling information, was "eccentric and monstrously extravagant": "The merits are obscured and almost neutralized by the astonishing quantity of wild, mad passages and entire chapters of . . . reckless inconceivable extravagances." Somewhat inconsistently he said that the work was throughout "splendidly written in a literary sense," and that the earlier chapters were "superlatively excellent." What these self-contradictory remarks added up to was somewhat clarified by his saying that *White Jacket* was its author's best work, and that he found "awe-striking sublimity and mystery" and "Shake-

25. Ainsworth, as "Sir Nathaniel," was surveying Melville's work to date. Not much less severe was E. D. Forgues, in the *Revue des deux mondes,* February 1, 1853, who in reviewing *Moby-Dick* said it was time Melville's undeniable power was held in check by "bon sens plus rigoureux" and a "goût plus épuré," and that his work was imbued more than was necessary with the philosophy of Emerson.

spearean" characterization not in Melville but in Cooper, a writer he thought had no faults. His article was reprinted in America.

These two last blows at *The Whale* must have killed British interest; for I have found no references to it in the British press during the next thirty years. Bentley did reprint it in 1855; but it was not again reprinted there until 1901.[26]

AMERICAN RECEPTION

On November 14, 1851,[27] a book was published in New York by Harper and Brothers, which was not quite the same book as had been published a month before in London. First, the book now had the Epilogue, as superb writing as its author ever did, and, it must be admitted, sorely needed; instead of a quotation from Milton, it now had the moving inscription to Hawthorne;[28] it had a more humorous and ironic text because the Harpers had left intact sixty passages which Bentley had bowdlerized;[29] and, best of all, it had been rechristened. Whatever were the circumstances which led to the differences, they were all such as tended to make the American *Moby-Dick* seem more inspired than the British *The Whale*.

The first reviewer of *Moby-Dick* was the great white whale himself. Surely it could have been none other, Melville wrote on November 7 to Evert Duyckinck, than "Moby Dick himself," who had sunk the whaleship *Ann Alexander,* for there was "no account of his capture after the sad fate of the Pequod." The news of this amazing disaster to the New Bedford whaleship off the coast of Peru on August 20 had just reached the United States, perfectly timed to show the public the possibility of the sinking of the *Pequod*. "Ye Gods!" wrote

26. Minnegerode, p. 160. An item not in the *Log* revealing an instance of English interest in the book during its long eclipse may be mentioned. Michael Sadlier in *Excursions in Victorian Bibliography* (New York, 1922) referred (p. 218) to a copy of *Moby-Dick* in which Charles Reade had made extensive notes "maybe with the idea of issuing an abbreviated edition." Reade died in 1884. Leyda says Reade's *Love Me Little Love Me Long* (1859) "Includes a whaling narrative influenced by *Moby-Dick*" (*Log*, p. 606).

27. Or perhaps a day or two earlier (*Log*, p. 433).

28. Minnegerode, pp. 157-158.

29. William S. Ament found that the English editor had carved out sixty passages of from one word to a paragraph or chapter. Every reference to the Bible not strictly reverential in tone was slashed. Profanity and impropriety were equally taboo. Such references as to Queequeg's "skill in obstetrics"—in getting Tashtego out of the sinking whale's head—were omitted. "Most of these," says Ament, "simply serve to flatten out the full flavored ironic humor of the original" ("Bowdler and the Whale," *American Literature*, IV [March, 1931], 39-46).

Melville, "What a Commentator is this Ann Alexander whale. What he has to say is short and pithy and very much to the point."[30]

Two brief advance notices, by persons who had only sampled the book, appeared in the *Daily Evening Transcript* in Boston and the *Evening Journal* in Albany on November 12. The Boston paper had a mere note of welcome for a work which would "be eagerly sought by those who remembered" the author's first two works; and, having "richly" enjoyed those, the Albany paper thought the new book opened "promisingly."[31]

The first American review was, on the very day of publication, boldly flaunted before the world, for it was—a thing almost unheard of those days on either side of the Atlantic—actually signed, and not just with intials, but aggressively, "J. Watson Webb." Glamorous, fiery, duel-fighting Colonel, later General, James Watson Webb, who was to become minister to Brazil after his newspaper days were over, had been for thirty years editor and proprietor of the *Courier and New York Enquirer,* as he was to continue for ten more years until in 1861 he gave up his pen to fight with the sword.[32] His paper, the largest in the city, and one of the chief Whig organs,[33] had not always been friendly to Melville; but now the editor himself came forth most handsomely in militant support of *Moby-Dick,* declaring it definitely his best work and the product of a genius:

His purity and freshness of style and exquisite tact in imparting vividness and lifelikeness to his sketches long since gained him hosts of admirers on both sides of the water. The book has all the attractiveness of any of its predecessors; in truth it possesses more of a witching interest, since the author's fancy has taken in it a wilder play than ever before. It is ostensibly taken up with whales and whalers, but a vast variety of characters and subjects figure in it, all set off with an artistic effect that irresistibly captivates the attention. The author writes with the gusto of true genius, and it must be a torpid spirit indeed that is not enlivened with the raciness of his humor and the redolence of his imagination.

Four American periodicals took cognizance of *Moby-Dick* on November 15. In Hartford the distinguished *Courant* found the book

30. Anderson, p. 62. An account of the disaster was in the Panama *Herald* for October 16 (*Log,* p. 429), from which it was copied in the New Bedford *Whaleman's Shipping List and Merchants' Transcript* on November 4 (Anderson, p. 448).

31. "The Town-Ho's Story," Chapter LIV of *Moby-Dick,* had been published in *Harper's New Monthly Magazine* for October.

32. *DAB.*

33. Mott, *American Journalism,* p. 261. Webb's review was reprinted in *Littell's Living Age* in January, 1852.

pleasant but not very important and echoed the British accusation that Melville had disregarded the rules of the novel: "There is the same want of unity of subject—of a regular beginning and end—of the form and shape of a well built novel which we find in real life. But there is too much romance and adventure of 'imminent perils' and hair-breadth escapes, to be anything but fiction." Yet Melville was improving: "The present story is the most interesting and best told" of his productions, though all showed "abandonment to all the easy slipshod luxuries of storytelling."

The same day the New Haven *Register* printed part of "Stubb Kills a Whale," pronounced the book more "interesting" and "vivid" than the many other accounts of whaling, and predicted for it "a great run." Also on that day Evert Duyckinck, in the *Literary World,* pointed out that by "a singular coincidence" the recent sinking of the *Ann Alexander* by a whale resembled greatly the "catastrophe of Mr. Melville's new work, which is a natural-historical, philosophical, romantic account of the person, habits, manners, ideas of the great sperm whale," but reserved for the next week the most important criticism he had to offer.

The greater outcry in America against the "profanities" and "indelicacies" was obviously caused by the Harpers' brave refusal to sanction such expurgation as Bentley had perpetrated; yet all those who participated in this outcry admitted the book's sparkle and fascination, and—New Yorkers may have been amused to note—resided outside the metropolis.

The Boston *Daily Traveller,* the fourth journal to remark *Moby-Dick* on November 15, though puzzled at its form, worried as to its proportions of truth and fiction, and repelled by its blasphemies, confessed enjoyment of "a new book, from one of the most sprightly and entertaining writers of our day": "It appears to be a sort of hermaphrodite craft—half fact, half fiction. . . . There is so much of caricature and exaggeration mixed with what may be fact that it is not easy to discriminate. Many of Mr. Melville's descriptions are extremely graphic, lifelike and entertaining; he certainly holds the pen of a ready writer; but he indulges frequently in profaneness, and occasionally in indelicacies, which materially detract from the merits of the book, which exhibits much tact, talent and genius."

Shocked protests were elicited from two more provinces in the two following days, but from those who allowed that the book was otherwise a real achievement. On November 17 the New Haven *Daily*

Palladium predicted that the "lively, roving story of Moby-Dick" would be "as popular as any other work of the author"; commended the "thrilling sketches of sea life, whale captures, shark massacres"; but deplored the "irreverence and profane jesting in the colloquies of the weather-beaten jacks," even though true to life. Yet the *Palladium,* evidently not considering it a novel at all, granted it possessed "all the interest of the most exciting fiction," and at the same time imparted much valuable information. On November 18 the Albany *Argus* found the book "the production of a man of genius," abounding in "bright, witty, and attractive things"; worried that the line "between the credible and apocryphal" was not "always very distinct"; and denounced the "irreverence" which would "greatly impair its interest with many who will nevertheless admire its bold and graphic sketches."

The one contemporary to lament the absence of a love interest seems to have been, again in the provinces, the otherwise pleased Springfield *Republican,* on November 17, which in doing so revealed another *Typee* fan: the new book contained "a large and interesting web of narrative, information, and sketches of character and scenery in a quaint though interesting style"—but there was "no Fayaway in it. Alas! fickle and forgetful Melville. . . ."

Now on November 19 there came, from four corners of the provinces, four voices of completely unqualified approval, to make the day one of a veritable chorus of praise. In Boston the *Daily Bee* used few words, but headed its back page with MOBY DICK in largest type; remarked that it was "said to be the best written and most entertaining book" of a "popular and clever author"; and quoted from Duyckinck's comments.[34] In Utica the *Daily Gazette,* employing the same phrases, said it was "pronounced the best written and most entertaining" of Melville's works, "strong praise; for few authors" had produced "stories of deeper interest, narrated in more attractive style." The "hero" was a "whale, to which the one that sank the Alexander was a calf"; and the subject afforded "the finest field for the rich imaginative powers . . . of the author." In Worcester the *Palladium* noticed the new book by a writer in whose manner was "life, elasticity, and freedom from restraint," in whose matter, "originality and freshness": "He has no mannerism which holds him down as an imitator

34. The *Bee* also mentioned the *Ann Alexander* incident; began a long quotation, "Death Scenes of the Whale" from *Moby-Dick,* which it continued as the back page leader again the next day, November 20; and described this passage as "in Melville's best style . . . no ordinary piece of writing . . . ."

of other men; but with tarpaulin and roundjacket he plunges down into the wide world of adventure and jots down whatever there comes within the scope of his vision. 'Moby-Dick' is full of spirit and energy, and will match his previous works in the race for popularity."

The fourth voice in the day's choir came from New Bedford, where the *Mercury* was naturally interested in the whaling aspects. The reviewer—surely the poet William Ellery Channing, Jr.[35]—said he had read many volumes about whaling voyages, but never before one "containing so much natural history . . . nor in so attractive a guise." He forgave Ishmael for shipping from Nantucket rather than from New Bedford, listing without acrimony the reasons Ishmael gave; and averred that "although the whole book is made to serve as a 'tub for the whale,' the characters and subjects which figure in it are set off with artistic effect, and with irresistible attraction for the reader."[36] This praise from the largest of the whaling ports must have especially gratified Melville; for I have carefully searched through the leading papers of three other whaling ports, Sag Harbor, New London, and Nantucket itself, without finding any mention of *Moby-Dick*.

On November 20, in the New York *Evangelist, Moby-Dick* was discussed by a reviewer who was evidently not the same as he who in this journal had denounced *Typee* as irreligious and immoral; for, quite undisturbed over any impieties, he pronounced *Moby-Dick* odd but exciting and artistic. He did begin censoriously, lamenting that Melville had "grown wilder and more untameable with every adventure," had tended more and more to wander from "verisimilitude," and "now in this last venture" had "reached the very limbo of eccentricity"; yet he ended with flattery: "The extraordinary descriptive powers which *Typee* disclosed are here in full strength. More graphic and terrible portraitures of hair-breadth 'scapes we never read. The delineation of

35. Suggested by Leyda (*Log*, p. 456) There is a distinction and continuity in the reviews of Melville's works in the *Mercury* which makes it tempting to ascribe them all to Channing. According to the "One Hundredth Anniversary Supplement" in the *Mercury* in 1912, Channing (named for his more famous uncle) had "some editorial connection with the *Mercury* prior to 1856, the year he took up constant residence in New Bedford and began daily editorial work." He was editor "from 1856 to 1859." But, according to George Harvey Genzmer in *DAB*, Channing was editor from 1855 to 1858. Almost certainly Channing, as editor, reviewed the *Piazza Tales*, and both external and internal evidence point to his authorship of the earlier reviews at least as far back as *Moby-Dick*.

36. Channing (if it was he) promised extracts, which indeed he inserted the next day, November 20. They were from the Chapters "Stubb Kills a Whale" and "The Line." Of the latter he said: "In the lively description of Mr. Melville, even the implements of 'whaling gear' acquire a degree of interest which is almost irresistible."

character, too, is exquisitely humorous, sharp, individual, and never to be forgotten. . . . Father Mapple's sermon is a powerful piece of oratory and passages of great eloquency, and artistic beauty and force are to be found everywhere. It will add to Mr. Melville's reputation . . . a most striking picture of sea adventure." The same day the New York *Observer* pronounced it "a complete exhibition of the art and mystery of whaleology, with graphic pictures of the life and times of whalemen."

So far, in the six days the book had been before the United States public, there had not been a single completely adverse critique, the nearest having been the Boston *Traveller's*. Now came the first real blow, also from Boston, from the *Post*. The hostility to Melville of the notice in the *Post* surely indicates the authorship of the editor, Colonel Greene.[37] Now there was no occasion for him to defend a military institution, as Melville had left behind that subject when he finished *White Jacket*. As the Colonel was a strong Democrat, political bias did not account for his attitude. Deference to a British judgment did influence him this time; yet one cannot help sensing in the Colonel's series of bitter articles on Melville, more than in the case of any other reviewer, some special spite. At any rate, of the new work he said harshly: "We have read nearly one half, and are satisfied that the *Athenaeum* is right in calling it 'an ill-compounded mixture of romance and matter of fact.' It is a crazy sort of affair, stuffed with conceits and oddities of all kinds, put in *artificially, deliberately,* and *affectedly,* by the side of strong, terse and brilliant passages of incident and description." He then settled the matter by quoting the most negative portions of Chorley's negative *Athenaeum* commentary. The Colonel certainly counted his pennies. He ended by declaring the book was not worth $1.50, its price. "Published at twenty-five cents, it might do to buy, but at any higher price, we think it a poor speculation."

There had been three commentators on November 20, and there were four on November 22.[38] Of these the least cordial was the writer, probably William Young, in the *Albion,* who found *Moby-Dick* both an achievement and a failure. Granting that it was "not lacking much

37. Charles Gordon Greene had founded the *Post* in 1831 and conducted it until 1875. He had a reputation as a wit. The *Post* was "the perfect embodiment of" its "founder's standards." He was an active Democrat (*DAB*). The *Post's* long life came to an end on October 4, 1956.

38. Also on November 22 the New Haven *Journal and Courier* printed without comment part of Chapter LXI—the favorite "Stubb Kills a Whale." It is obvious this chapter was being copied from journal to journal.

of being a great work" and defending the possibility of locating a particular whale, he continued: "Not only is there an immense account of reliable information . . . the *dramatis personae,* mates, harpooners, carpenters, and cooks, are all vivid sketches done in the author's best style. What they do and how they look is brought to one's perception with wondrous elaboration of detail; and yet this minuteness does not spoil the broad outlines of each." But the illusion passed away when Melville attempted dialogue; the *Albion's* reviewer lamented "the stuff and nonsense spouted forth by the crazy captain" and maintained that "the rarely imagined character has been grievously spoiled nay altogether ruined by a vile daubing with a coat of book-learning and mysticism; there is no method in his madness; and we must pronounce the chief feature of the work a perfect failure, and the work inartistic." There was "choice reading," nevertheless, for one who could skip "judiciously."

Undiluted praise, however, came from the Philadelphia *American Courier* that day for the latest work of "one of the most spirited, vigorous, good-natured writers in existence"; who is "as sparkling and racy as old wine and sweet as nuts, with a constant flow of animating descriptions and thrilling incidents"; and who has lived "so much upon the mountain deep, that he has become wedded to the wide waters, and yet lives and moves upon the solid earth with all the ease and polish of a finished gentleman." "If there is not enough 'blubber' " here, the *Courier* declared, "to satisfy every 'land lubber,' we shall be exceedingly mistaken and that too, notwithstanding the blunt phraseology which we sometimes meet in Melville. For real, easy pleasant reading, social enjoyment . . . decidedly the richest book out . . . though the 'long yarn' runs out to 683 pages, not a reader will lay down the book without wishing that 'Moby Dick' [Did the *Courier* think that was the narrator's name?] had driven the whale a thousand leagues further, shouting and spinning his yarn as he went. No one can tire of this volume." Melville had been right in feeling gratitude to that first "Commentator," as was shown once more by the *Courier's* saying the reader would be "better prepared to credit" the tale after reading in this journal a recent account of the sinking of the *Ann Alexander.*

All essentially favorable, varying from the qualified commendatory to the rhapsodically enthusiastic, were the four American reviews of *Moby-Dick* which were outstanding for their thoroughness: in the *Literary World, Harper's Monthly,* and the *Tribune,* all of New York, and in the *National Intelligencer,* of Washington. The first two I found years ago, but the latter two, though both of generous length and in important newspapers, remained unknown until I discovered them in 1951. Those in the *Literary World* and the *Tribune* came out on November 22, the other two not until December.

The often-quoted one in the *Literary World* was by Evert Duyckinck, who mixed into his approbation enough censure and even ridicule to make his rather long article the least favorable of the big American four. He expressed the current astonishment at the unusual aesthetic form of the book by calling it "an intellectual chowder," arousing a modern critic to say that "Duyckinck's reference to *Moby-Dick* as 'an intellectual chowder' is preposterous . . . a pigmy phrase for the gigantic undertaking that was *Moby-Dick.*"[39] Duyckinck condemned the "piratical running down of creeds and opinions, the conceited indifferentism of Emerson, or the run-a-muck style" as "out of place and uncomfortable." What a nineteenth-century note was struck in that word "uncomfortable." He was shocked at Melville's having spoken disrespectfully of the angel Gabriel. The "intense Captain Ahab" was "too long drawn out" though "a striking conception."

On the other hand, Duyckinck enjoyed the "vivid narration"; he found the account of the sperm whale "wholly delightful"; he was one of three reviewers who applied the term "allegorical"; he considered the great monster an effective embodiment "in strongly drawn lines of mental association of the vaster moral evil in the world." Thus he was not without real insight into the underlying intentions. Surely this statement was perceptive: "The pursuit of the White Whale thus interweaves with the literal perils of the fishery a problem of fate and destiny." His last sentence placed the book high: "It is still a great honor, among the crowd of successful mediocrities which throng our publishers' counters and know nothing of divine impulses, to be in the company of these nobler spirits on any terms."[40]

Modern Melvillians would surely consider more adequate than Duyckinck's the review on the same day, November 22, in the New

39. Cowie, p. 387.

40. George Duyckinck had sent a copy of *Moby-Dick* to Joann Miller hardly expecting her to appreciate it, as it had seemed tedious to him; she, however, to his surprise, took to it "heartily," as he put it (*Log,* pp. 436, 437, 438). There is a strange pathos in the platonic romance of George and Joann, which seemed to center so much around the books they were reading, especially those of Melville. One guesses shy George never got up the courage to propose before Joann's early death at thirty-six. She was evidently a brilliant woman, and must take rank as one of Melville's most appreciative readers, usually seeming more gifted as a student of literature than George.

York *Tribune,* almost certainly by Horace Greeley. His extended remarks were entirely adulatory. He was one of two reviewers to as-
sign the book to that literary category wherein, according to many
thoughtful moderns, it belongs;[41] referring to the tradition concerning
an invincible whale, Greeley called the book "a 'Whaliad,' or Epic of
that veritable old leviathan," who had laughed at his pursuers.

After an excellent plot summary, Greeley asserted that "the narrative is constructed in Herman Melville's best manner. It combines
the various features which form the chief attraction of his style, and
is commendably free from the faults which we have before had occasion to specify in this powerful writer." (Surely this was Greeley,
here alluding to the stern reprimand which, in his otherwise favorable review of *Omoo,* he had given Melville for telling of his ex-
ploits with liquors and especially with Polynesian girls. It is hardly
necessary to remind the reader of the virtual absence of women in
Moby-Dick.)[42]

Greeley went on to offer a type of defense which has been presented in the present century, by Mumford, Arvin, and others,[43] who
contend that the whaling materials give needed ballast to the symbolism: "The intensity of the plot is happily relieved by minute descriptions of the homely processes of the whale fishery. We have occasional touches of subtle mysticism, which is carried to such an incon-
venient excess in Mardi, but it is here mixed up with so many tangible
and odorous realities that we safely alight from an excursion through
mid-air upon the solid deck of the whaler. We are recalled to this
world by the fumes of 'oil and blubber,' and are made to think more
of the contents of barrels than of allegories." Greeley parted "with this
adventurous philosophical Ishmael, truly thankful that the whale did
not get his head, for which we are indebted for this wildly imaginative and truly thrilling story," which "in spite of its lawless flights,

41. See footnote 69, Chapter VII, below.

42. Since this reviewer refers to a previous review he had written of one of Melville's books, presumably in the *Tribune,* he was one of three: Margaret Fuller, who
had reviewed *Typee,* Greeley, who had reviewed *Omoo,* or George Ripley, who had
reviewed *Mardi, Redburn,* and *White Jacket*—all in this paper. Miss Fuller had died in
1850; Ripley had signed his three reviews "R," and the present review was unsigned;
also Ripley was then or in a few days to be writing his review for *Harper's,* which
had a different approach and no duplications in phraseology. Greeley was, hence, the
probable author.

43. Mumford, p. 164. Arvin, p. 168 says that the "true purpose of the cetological
elements" is "to provide the book with an even intenser literalness than it otherwise
has."

which put all regular criticism at defiance . . . gives us a higher opinion of the author's originality and power" than even *Typee*.[44]

Greeley had relished "a work full of episodes descriptive of strange and original phases of character," such as "the meeting of the author and Queequeg." Queequeg interested also the New York *Commercial Advertiser* on November 28, but only as a basis for regret that Melville was "guilty of sneering at the truth of revealed religion," as it proved by quoting the account of Ishmael worshipping Yojo with his cannibal friend. Although saying "the science of cetology" was "pleasantly interwoven with the legend," the *Advertiser's* brief notice was preponderantly hostile, declaring readers would at first be "repulsed by the eccentricity," as "such a salmagundi of fact, fiction and philosophy, composed in a style which combined the peculiarities of Carlyle, Marryat and Lamb, was never seen before."

Nathaniel P. Willis, consistently an admirer of Melville, surely wrote the entirely approving item on November 29 in his *Home Journal*: Melville had "resolved to combine in the present" book all "popular characteristics, and so fully justify his fame," the result being "a very racy, spirited, curious and entertaining book, which affords quite an account of information, excites the sympathies, and often charms the fancy."

Moby-Dick really received a great deal of attention in America during November; there was some falling off in the number of notices in December. On December 1, however, the New Bedford *Daily Evening Standard* and on December 2 the New York *Evening Post*— Bryant's paper—both reprinted the favorite Chapter XLI. Both praised the vivid writing about whaling. The New York paper said that Melville, "in his new sea-story," described "a marvelous chase by a whaling monomaniac after the 'Moby Dick,' the fabulous leviathan" in which he "probably" lets us "into the realities of actual whaling as minutely and faithfully as any sea-author has ever done." In *Holden's Magazine,* the editor, Evert Duyckinck, reprinted his own *Literary World* review.[45]

Now famous is the remarkable review of *Moby-Dick* in the December number of *Harper's Magazine*. Although only a column and a half long, it was given the place of honor as the first and longest of the "Literary Notices" for that month. As I demonstrated some years ago, to the apparent satisfaction of later writers, it was by George

44. Long extracts were included from Chapters XVII, LX, LXI, and CXXIII.

45. On November 29 and December 6 the Cincinnati *Daily Gazette* printed, without comment, "The Town-Ho's Story."

Ripley,[46] who, eschewing a single touch of disapproval, asserted that the book was the summit of Melville's achievement. Among the reviewers, he was the most explicit in declaring that although Melville had cast his materials in a highly original mold, his success had justified his choice. Ripley pointed out the strange contrasts between the passages of statistical exactitude about whaling and the "weird phantom-like character of the plot." "These sudden and violent transitions," said Ripley, "form a striking feature of the volume. Difficult of management in the highest degree, they are wrought with consummate skill. He has not only deftly avoided their dangers, but made of them an element of power." Ripley enjoyed the "fine vein of comic humor" in the earlier chapters; found the character of Captain Ahab "wonderful"; and extolled the "unique portrait gallery, which every artist must despair of rivalling."

Like Duyckinck and Greeley, he suggested the presence of allegory, saying that "beneath the whole story the subtle, imaginative reader may perhaps find a pregnant allegory intended to illustrate the mystery of human life," and that "the genius of the author for moral analysis is scarcely surpassed by his wizard power of description." The Harpers, of course, were the publishers, and Ripley was writing for their magazine; on the other hand, Ripley, as a Transcendentalist, could be expected to evince sympathetic insight into such a book. His review seems so sincere that it is almost certain he deserves the credit, as "literary adviser of the house,"[47] for keeping the Harpers' edition from being expurgated as was Bentley's.

On December 5, in the Newark *Daily Advertiser,* the sailor turned critic was surely the welcomer of "our old friend," who "fresh and buoyant as ever," "dashes out in another realm of sea life." He valued the book chiefly for the clarity, accuracy, and fascination of its whaling matter: "We doubt if ever the whale has been so scientifically described . . . and his account is worthy to be, and probably will be, incorporated into all future natural histories. It is astonishing that among all the myriads that have frequently seen these monsters of the deep, none, till now, have been able to describe them intelligibly, not to say correctly. A semi-marvelous narrative . . . is the link which connects . . . the various chapters and retains the interest of the reader

46. Hetherington, pp. 217-218. The ascription of this review to Ripley is accepted by Leyda (*Log,* p. 438) and by others.

47. Joseph Henry Harper, *The House of Harper* (New York, 1922), p. 130. His connection with the magazine began with its beginning in 1850 and continued until his death in 1880. At first he was "a writer of the literary notices, but later took more prominent positions" (O. B. Frothingham, *George Ripley* [Boston, 1882], p. 54).

until the last page." The *Advertiser's* critic thought Melville did not repeat himself from book to book; that every character seemed "pictured by a daguerreotype," so "natural" were the features, and so "clear the outlines." Rather curiously he declared that in each "succeeding book" there was "an improvement in the artistic quality," but "in some respects this is not a gain to the general reader"! He also objected to the "metaphysical discussions, half earnest and half banter," a glaring fault in *Mardi,* but little observable in *Moby-Dick*. (!) Was this merely a comment resulting from careless reading, or did this reviewer, like Ripley, really perceive the superior fusion of the ideal and concrete in Melville's greatest work?[48]

In the important Whig paper the Washington *National Intelligencer,* there appeared an extremely imposing review, overlooked until recently, covering almost a whole fine-printed page. It was very likely by William Allen Butler, who had attended the Tetractys Club meetings and had toured Europe with George Duyckinck. Butler had some little reputation as a poetic wit, and, though he avoided politics, was distinguished as a lawyer, later becoming president of the American Bar Association.[49]

He was evidently much excited about *Moby-Dick*. In a very long introduction in which he talked about literary canonization and the blindness of critics to contemporary greatness, he implied he had before him something of immense significance. Even he, however, felt he must complain about Melville's "irreverent wit" and condemn the "ribald orgies" of the forecastle scene. Yet after paragraphs of ecstatic praise of *Typee,* he swung into even more fervid laudation of the present volume, which "presents a most striking and truthful portraiture of the whale and his perilous capture . . . no one can deny it to be the production of a man of genius. . . . The descriptive powers of Mr. Melville are unrivalled, whether the scenes he paints reveal 'old ocean tossed,' or are laid among the bright hillsides of some Pacific island, so warm and undulating that the printed page on which they are so graphically depicted seems almost to palpitate beneath the sun." It was, Butler said, "a prose Epic of Whaling"; thus he was, along with Greeley, the second of the two reviewers who anticipated many moderns, as I shall shortly show, in their definition of the form of *Moby-Dick*.

48. On December 11 in an editorial the New Bedford *Daily Evening Standard* expressed concern lest Melville's "handsome compliment" to the women of New Bedford and Salem [*Moby-Dick,* Chapter VI] might go to their heads (*Log,* p. 440).

49. David Saville Muzzey in *DAB.* My suggestion in "Early Reviews," p. 106 that Butler wrote this review is accepted by Miller, p. 298.

Butler's next passage constituted the most ardent known eulogy given *Moby-Dick* during its author's lifetime:

Language in the hands of this master becomes like a magician's wand, evoking at will "thick coming fancies" and peopling the "chambers of imagery" with hideous shapes of terror or winning forms of beauty and loveliness. Mr. Melville has a strange power to reach the sinuosities of thought . . . he touches with his lead and line depths of pathos that few can fathom, and by a simple word can set a whole chime of sweet or wild emotions into a pealing concert. His delineation of character is actually Shakespearean—a quality which is even more prominently evinced in "Moby Dick" than in any of his antecedent efforts.

Butler enjoyed the comic spirit: the "humor" was "of that subdued yet unquenchable nature which spreads such a charm over the pages of Sterne,"[50] and was found "in irresistible comic passages scattered at irregular intervals"; occasionally he perceived "traces of that 'wild imagining' which throws such a weird-like charm about the Ancient Mariner of Coleridge"; in his detailed and sympathetic summary he stressed the themes—Ishmael's reasons for going whaling, and Ahab's vision of the white whale as the incarnation of all wickedness; and he concluded that "this ingenious romance . . . for variety of incident and vigor of style" could "scarcely be exceeded."

In Greeley's, Ripley's and Butler's critiques, *Moby-Dick* had reached the peak of its American fame during its author's lifetime. In January, 1852, the curve of its reputation was to start a downward turn. Colonel Webb's high praises were reprinted in *Littell's Living Age;* and Ripley culled out and copied in *Harper's Magazine* some of the most flattering sentences from the London *Atlas* article, pronouncing it "one of the most discriminating reviewals we have seen." On the other hand, although eight American magazines noticed *Moby-Dick* this month, of these one only wrote with even qualified favor at any length. This was *Peterson's Magazine,* a women's journal, which preferred the narrative to the philosophical elements, contending that if the work had been "compressed one half and all the transcendental chapters omitted, it would have been decidedly the best sea novel in the language"; but by attempting to combine narrative and philosophy Melville had "spoilt the book." Still, *Peterson's* went on, the "demerit of 'Moby Dick' is only comparative. It is not an indifferent work but a very superior one after all." The whaling scenes

50. For a discussion of Melville's use of "Shandean tricks" in *Moby-Dick,* see Rosenberry, p. 101.

were "powerful," and the "concluding chapters" were "really beyond rivalry," another example of the special American interest in the cetological aspects. Although warmly enthusiastic about the nautical parts, *Peterson's* showed much less approbation of the complete book than had some of the journals in November and December.

During January three magazines paid brief compliments to *Moby-Dick*. *Godey's* of Philadelphia had an amiable note: the work was "a perfect literary whole, and worthy of the pen of Herman Melville, whose reputation as an original writer has been established the world over." *Knickerbocker's* critic, probably Clark, had even less to say, though nothing unapproving: "Melville has taken up this whale [Mocha-Dick] and made him the subject of one of his striking romances. His ocean pictures are exceedingly graphic." *Hunt's Merchant's Magazine* had four guardedly friendly lines, indicating that those who expected to "find an agreeable and entertaining volume . . . will not be disappointed"; that in places it was "rather diffuse, but as a whole will be read with gratification"; and that the whaling scenes were spirited.

On the other hand, the January *Today: A Boston Literary Journal* could find a few facets to approve, but was mainly very antagonistic. *Today* presented what was before long to be the prevailing judgment: *Typee* was fine, but the merit of "Melville's books has decreased almost in the order of their production." *Today* made four adverse points: The valuable accounts of whaling were (1) obscured by "dreamy philosophy and indistinct speculation" and (2) introduced in such a way as to cast doubt on their accuracy. (3) The excellent adventures of Ishmael and Queequeg were ruined by the impiety: "Some of . . . the adventures are narrated inimitably and are almost sufficient to excuse any faults in other parts of the book. Yet the humor of those parts where sacred things are made light of, as for instance, the scene in which the hero joins his pagan friend in worshiping an idol and defends his course by half a page of wretched sophistry is revolting to good taste, and may . . . be dangerous to many . . . who will be likely to read the book." (4) The book should have been pared down. Yet, as if to make some amends, *Today* finally admitted it had its "beauties" and enough fine and valuable passages in it "to amply repay its persual."

In the January *Democratic Review* appeared the most extended American condemnation of *Moby-Dick,* quite likely from the pen of the melodramatic Young American, George N. Sanders, who had just become owner and editor mainly to give political support to Stephen A. Douglas, and who later had a hectic career in Europe as a sort of revolutionist at large.[51] Stirred by distaste for Melville's latest book, he denounced the earlier ones also. *Typee* and *Omoo* were popular, but why were they found on tables from which Byron was prohibited? He went on acidly: "But these were Mr. Melville's triumphs, *Redburn* was a stupid failure, *Mardi* was hopelessly dull, *White Jacket* was worse than either; and in fact, it was such a very bad book, that, until the appearance of *Moby-Dick,* we had set it down as the very ultimatum of *weakness* to which the author could attain. It seems, however, that we were mistaken. In bombast, in caricature, in rhetorical artifice—generally as clumsy as it is ineffectual—and in low attempts at humor, each of his volumes has been an advance upon its predecessors." Like *Today,* he viewed Melville's efforts as resulting only in a sharply descending achievement curve.

Sanders—if it was he—became more personal, and accused Melville of an "immeasurable vanity": "From this morbid self-esteem, coupled with a most unbounded love of notoriety, spring all his rhetorical contortions, all his declamatory abuse of society, all his inflated sentiment, and all his insinuating licentiousness." He ended with a final fling at the style: "But if there are any of our readers who wish to find examples of bad rhetoric, involved syntax, stilted sentiment and incoherent English, we will take the liberty of recommending to them this precious volume of Mr. Melville's." Much good Melville's Democratic party affiliations were doing him with the reviewers! And Sanders a Young American!

Now came the lowest blow of all, from Democratic Charleston. The *Southern Quarterly Review's* critic, also in January, did grant the book had merits, but then stabbed it even more violently than had the *Democratic.* Characteristically American was his admitting that the whaling sections were "interesting and instructive" and that "in all the scenes where the whale was the performer or sufferer, the delineation and action are highly vivid and entertaining." "In all other

51. Merle E. Curti, "George N. Sanders, Patriot of the Fifties," *South Atlantic Quarterly,* January, 1928. Sanders denounced "Old Fogydom," preached American capitalism to the world as an antidote to tyranny, and in Europe actively encouraged Kossuth, Mazzini, and Garibaldi. The *Democratic's* reviewer of *Moby-Dick* was obviously a different one from its reviewer—probably Kettell, then the editor—who had lauded the power and humor of *Redburn;* and had objected to *White Jacket* as Anglophile, but had granted it was very well written. According to Stafford, Sanders was the most "outspoken leader" of the more political aspect of the Young America movement in the fifties (*op. cit.,* p. 18).

respects," he announced, "the book is sad stuff, dull and dreary, or ridiculous." The "Quakers are the wretchedest dolts and drivellers, and his Mad Captain . . . is a monstrous bore." His last crushing sentence declared that the captain's "ravings, and the ravings of some of the tributary characters, and the ravings of Mr. Melville himself . . . are such as would justify a writ *de lunatico* against all parties." I have always wanted to believe it was not editor Simms who wrote these words.

If Melville's political connections had ever affected his literary reputation, they obviously meant nothing now, unless obversely. The Young Americans were divided, Butler enthusiastic, Duyckinck less so, Sanders bitterly contemptuous. But it was the Whigs who were for his book and the Democrats who were against. No one had lauded *Moby-Dick* more warmly than those very active Whigs, Webb and Greeley, in their Whig papers, the *Courier* and the *Tribune,* or than Butler in the Whig *Intelligencer.* From three Democratic journals, the Boston *Post,* the *Democratic Review,* and the *Southern Quarterly Review,* had come the most vicious of the American attacks. Thus at the end of January, 1852, thanks largely to the kind efforts that month of Melville's own political party, his book's fortunes were at low ebb.

In February, however, in the widely-circulated *Graham's Magazine,* a critic came nobly to its support, with almost entirely adulatory remarks centering admiration on the style:

This volume sparkles with the raciest qualities of the author's voluble and brilliant mind, and whatever may be its reception among old salts, it will be sure of success with the reading public generally. It has passages of description and narration equal to the best that Melville has written, and its rhetoric revels and riots in scenes of nautical adventure with more than usual glee and gusto. The style is dashing, headlong, strewn with queer and quaint ingenuities moistened with humor, and is a capital specimen of deliberate and felicitous recklessness, in which seeming helter-skelter movement is guided by real judgment.

Melville's teeming fancy sometimes led him to excessive use of analogies, but "The joyous elasticity and vigor of his style . . . compensates for all faults, and even his tasteless passages bear the impress of conscious and unwearied power. His late books are not only original in the usual sense, but evince originality of nature, and convey the impression of a new individuality, somewhat composite, it is true, but still giving to the jaded reader of everyday publications, that pleasant shock of surprise which comes from a mental contact with a character at once novel and vigorous." Differing from many, he saw in Melville's later work evidence of onward development. His was the last known American review; and so, after all, the immediate American press reaction came to an end with an isolated piece of hearty applause.[52]

Moby-Dick was ignored by its author's more distinguished American literary contemporaries—unless these are regarded as including Ripley, Greeley, Willis, and Simms—except Longfellow and Hawthorne. In his journal, Longfellow had written of reading it "all evening" and finding it "very wild, strange, and interesting."[53] From two famous letters Melville wrote, one to Nathaniel, one to Sophia Hawthorne, the lost letter Hawthorne had written him before November 17 can be partially reconstructed. For Melville, Hawthorne's letter had been "joy-giving," because he "had understood" and "praised" the "pervading thought" and "soul" of the work. And to the surprise of Melville, who thought women would not care for his book, it had greatly pleased Sophia.[54] There is, furthermore, evidence that Hawthorne might have written a review of it if Melville had encouraged him.

The immediate reaction of the American press to *Moby-Dick* had been, by a considerable majority, a positive one. Nine friendly notices were so slight as to give little evidence of being based on actual reading of the book; but there were twelve reviews which were clearly favorable and revealed real perusal of the text, including the four longest (by Duyckinck, Ripley, Greeley, and Butler). Five are best classified as lukewarm, leaving only six that can be fairly called negative. An ominous indicator of the way the wind was blowing, however, was the fact that three of the most hostile came in early 1852, as the ultimate American judgment was to be most emphatically negative.

The Duyckincks in their *Cyclopaedia* (1855) did repeat Evert's approval as expressed in the *Literary World*. To judge, however, from O'Brien's first essay about Melville, in 1853, *Moby-Dick* made practically no impression on him; for he mentioned it only once in this long critique: "Typee . . . was healthy; Omoo nearly so; after them came Mardi with its excusable wildness; then came Moby Dick, and Pierre, with its inexcusable insanity." Apparently O'Brien did not

---

52. Ripley, in the March, 1852 *Harper's Magazine*, inserted a paragraph from Lewes's favorable *Leader* review.

53. *Log.*, p. 434. The entry was for November 15.

54. *Log*, pp. 435, 443.

think *Moby-Dick* even worth the time involved in a direct fling at its sanity.

Four years later, in his second essay on Melville, O'Brien gave the book some attention, but only in scorn. Now he confessed he could not understand *Moby-Dick*. He exclaimed: "What . . . did Mr. Melville mean when he wrote 'Moby Dick'? We have a right to know, for he carried us floundering on with him after his great white whale . . . now perfectly exhausted with fatigue and deafened with many words whereof we understood no syllable, and then suddenly refreshed with a brisk sea breeze and a touch of nature kindling as the dawn." O'Brien did apply the word "genius" to Melville, but lamented loudly that here was a man who distorted "the flowers of his fancy; a man born to create who resolves to anatomize; a man born to see who insists on speculating." O'Brien made it perfectly clear that for him the author's "flowers of fancy" were most fragrant in *Typee*. However complimentary he may have been to Melville's power in general, he rejected what today is considered the chief manifestation of that power. Curiously enough, he preferred *The Confidence-Man* to *Moby-Dick*, but he did not think highly of that book either; it was simply better than Melville at his worst, his worst being *Moby-Dick*.

After O'Brien's 1857 article, in America, for many years, the rest was silence, perhaps not complete silence about Melville, but silence about *Moby-Dick*. As early as 1852, the Boston *Daily Transcript* could begin a note on *Pierre* thus: "The author of 'Typee' here wholly forsakes the sea and . . . ," with no mention of *Moby-Dick*. The widespread condemnation of *Pierre* tended to destroy interest in its author and to cause many to read back into *Moby-Dick* the despised qualities of the next book. The fact that there was more awareness than has generally been realized of *Israel Potter* (1855), the *Piazza Tales* (1856), and *The Confidence-Man* (1857) merely served to make more deafening the silence about *Moby-Dick*. Reviewing the *Piazza Tales* the New Bedford *Mercury* commenced: "The author of Typee and Omoo is so well known . . . ," again with no reference to *Moby-Dick*. Melville's publishers themselves did not consider it worth mentioning that he had written such a book. The Harpers advertised *Pierre* in the New York *Evening Post* on August 27, 1852 as "By Herman Melville, Author of 'Typee,' 'Omoo,' 'Redburn,' etc."[55] In the same newspaper three years later G. P. Putnam advertised *Israel Potter* as "By Herman

55. This advertisement was repeated on August 28, and September 2 and 6. Many additional examples of striking ignorings of *Moby-Dick* could be given if space permitted.

Melville, Author of 'Typee,' 'Omoo,' etc. etc." These advertisements were eloquent in their omissions.

The record of the sales of *Moby-Dick* in America provided further proof that while the immediate reaction was almost a kind of acceptance, the delayed reaction was a virtual rejection. By November 25, 1851, according to Melville's accounts with the Harpers, the sole American publishers of the book during his lifetime, 1,835 copies had been sold; and by February 7, 1852, 471 more. These were respectable figures for the times; but during the whole next decade only 1,236 copies, or an average of only 123 a year, were sold; and between 1863 and 1887, the year of the twenty-seventh and last account with the Harpers, only 555, or an average of only 23 a year. The total number of copies of *Moby-Dick* printed and sold in America up to and including 1887 was thus 3,797.[56] On the other hand, during less than three years Wiley and Putnam had sold, up to January, 1849, 6,392 copies of *Typee*.[57] The lack of new editions or even reprintings over many decades provides further evidence of the nature of the ultimate nineteenth-century judgment on *Moby-Dick* up to the end of its creator's lifetime. In America there was only one reprinting between 1851 and 1892, by the Harpers in 1863.[58]

During the single year 1887 were sold 200,000 copies of *Ben-Hur* (1880), and during 1888, 290,000 copies.[59] The sales of *Moby-Dick* were, of course, as nothing to those of Susan Warner's *The Wide Wide World* (1850) or Mrs. E. D. E. N. Southworth's *The Curse of Clifton* (1852).[60] Mott points out that *Moby-Dick* "was a very poor seller [comparatively] indeed when it first appeared," and won its right to be included in his list of "Over-all Best Sellers" only by the distribution of "more than a million copies" in the United States between 1921 and 1947.[61]

CONCLUSION

There was a great contrast between the immediate and delayed reactions to *Moby-Dick*. The later opinion was so adverse that it in-

---

56. These figures are from the accounts of Melville with Harper and Brothers in the Melville papers in the Houghton Library at Harvard.

57. Weaver, p. 253.

58. Minnegerode, p. 159. Cowie says justly: "Charles Anderson asserts (*Melville in the South Seas*, p. 439) that 'The popularity of . . . Moby-Dick has been consistent all along,' but he admits (on the same page) that there were no editions of it in the 1870's and 1880's. A book not reedited for twenty-nine years can scarcely be designated as 'popular' " (*op. cit.*, p. 815).

59. Frank Luther Mott, *Golden Multitudes: The Story of Best Sellers in the United States* (New York, 1947), p. 173.

60. *Ibid.*, p. 124, pp. 136-139. 61. *Ibid.*, p. 132.

vites scrutiny of the primary response, preponderantly favorable, at least in America, yet still curiously ambivalent, for the seeds which could grow into an ultimate rejection. A composite picture of the attitudes in the reviews—they ceased after three months—toward five aspects of the book may be revealing.

First, much more in the United States than in the British Isles, the cetology tended to make *Moby-Dick* acceptable. That it portrayed the pursuit of the leviathan counted for it in a country where whaling was so important economically and so appealing to arm-chair adventurers, as shown especially by four Americans (Newark *Advertiser,* Channing, New York *Observer, Peterson's*). It is difficult to imagine an American complimenting the author for making such an unattractive subject fascinating, as did an Englishman (*John Bull*). Exceptional as one of the most ardent admirers of Melville's cetology was one Londoner (*Chronicle*).

Second, the characterization aroused less interest than might have been expected. It had its highest eulogy from a Briton (*Britannia*), was especially commended by three Americans (*Evangelist,* Butler, Ripley), but acidly condemned by one (*Albion*). The appreciations of the humor seemed to illustrate the proverbial English deficiency, for it was enjoyed particularly by only two Englishmen (*Post, Britannia*), but by four Americans (Webb, Butler, *Graham's,* Ripley). It was, indeed, an especially American brand, Constance Rourke has insisted.[62]

Third, by two Englishmen (*John Bull, Chronicle*), and by seven Americans (*Traveller,* New Haven *Palladium, Advertiser,* Butler, Duyckinck, Albany *Argus,* and with special virulence, *Today*), Melville was charged with impiety. The English edition, it will be recalled, was expurgated. Of these, three (*John Bull,* Butler, and to some extent Duyckinck) admired the philosophy.

Fourth, the problem of the aesthetic form created considerable discussion. There was repeated insistence that Melville had failed to conform to the accepted canons of the novel. Six Britons (Chorley, *Spectator, Examiner, Gazette, Britannia, Dublin Magazine*) and three Americans (*Traveller, Courant, Commercial*) reprimanded him on this score. There were, however, four actual defenses of the unique form,[63] two British (*John Bull,* Lewes), and two American (Greeley,

62. *American Humor* (New York, 1931), p. 196.
63. John Erskine contends that the book is a poem rather than a novel because its art lies, not in picturing exterior life, but in preparing our minds for an effect of emotion, for a catharsis (*The Delight of Great Books* [Indianapolis, 1928], p. 233).

Ripley). One American clearly implied approval of the pattern (Butler); one was puzzled rather than repelled (Duyckinck).

Fifth, the main intention was ignored by many, including professed advocates, but also elicited a whole spectrum of comment, ranging from bitter scorn, through mere bewilderment, to ecstatic encomium. Moments of "lunacy" were found (*Chronicle*); the book was disposed of as mad (Chorley, his sycophant Colonel Greene, *Southern Quarterly*); the "metaphysics" were wished away (*Peterson's*); but significant and profound "allegory" was discovered by two Americans (Duyckinck, Ripley), and the allegory was shown to be effectively extrinsified in the realistic whaling tale (Greeley); the "power to reach the sinuosities of thought" delighted another American (Butler); "the original philosophical fancy" was admired by one Briton (*Atlas*); and "a whole philosophy of life" was perceived in it by another (*John Bull*). Thus some, but not all, recoiled from Melville's deeper soundings.

Finally, as for judgment of general merit, *Moby-Dick* came off a good deal better on this side of the Atlantic, with three friends to one enemy in America and one to one in the British Isles. True there were only six completely adverse reviews, three British and three American; but there were only three British as against sixteen American notices which contained no censure whatever (of which, however, only six American can be considered certainly based on a reading of the book).

The response was hardly of the sort to be elicited by a merely commonplace production. There was a marked tendency for reviewers to go to extremes in approbation and derogation, sometimes in the same article. Although the majority failed to grasp its greatness, surely at least three Britons (*John Bull*, Lewes, *Post*) and three Americans (Greeley, Butler, Ripley) showed adequate enough apperceptions of the unique genius revealed in *Moby-Dick* to satisfy the modern Melvillians. And four confessed (*Atlas*, Lewes, London *Post*, Butler) they were enthralled by its "potent magic spell."

If, however, the immediate reactions were so varied that it is possible, as has been done, to build up a case for an acceptance[64] or for a rejection,[65] the delayed reaction was unequivocally a rejection. After its peak of good fortune in early December, 1851, in the follow-

---

64. John C. McCloskey, "Moby-Dick and the Reviews," *Philological Quarterly*, XXV (October, 1946), 20-31.

65. By John Freeman, F. O. Matthiessen, Alexander Cowie, Howard P. Vincent, and somewhat more cautiously, Newton Arvin.

ing January a strange reversal was already setting in, and before long it was only too evident that if Melville was considered important at all, it was not as the author of *Moby-Dick*.

The final verdict that his chief work must be consigned to the dungeon of annihilation may have been enough to cause Melville to project into *Pierre* the implication that *Moby-Dick* had failed, though no record exists that he said so directly. Yet it seems to me as it seems to Arvin,[66] that even in the immediate reaction, ambiguous as it was, there were elements which might well, for Melville, have poisoned the honey which was undeniably present. It was not for Melville to have the satisfaction of hearing a leading professor of American literature proclaim as one did seventy-six years after its publication, that *Moby-Dick* was "among the few really great books of the nineteenth century."[67]

The brave speaking out at first of critics who were adulatory, even ecstatic, even respectfully perceptive of some of the main themes, makes the complete contemptuousness or thorough obliviousness of the final voices Melville was to hear for three decades not less, but more, dramatic, and perhaps inexplicable except on the basis of such denunciation of nineteenth-century timidity and blindness as flared out in the Melville Revival. True, a few watchers joyously announced in 1851 the new planet which many were to believe had not been discovered until seventy years later. But in that century it was not the praise of the prophets ("language in the hands of this master becomes like a magician's wand," "a unique portrait gallery which every writer must despair of rivalling," "the gusto of true genius," "the subtle imaginative reader may . . . find a pregnant allegory," "It must be a torpid spirit indeed that is not enlivened with the raciness of his humor and the redolence of his imagination," "celestial fare") that lingered in the mind. It was always the snide phrases of the Pharisees ("disdainful of learning the craft of an artist," "rhetorical artifice clumsy as it is ineffectual," "morbid self-esteem," "insinuating licentiousness," "stuff and nonsense spouted by the crazy captain," enough to "justify a writ *de lunatico* against all the parties"), and the conclusion of Colonel Greene's "review" ("not worth the money asked for it, either as a literary work or as a mass of printed paper") that stung the public's memory and soon induced amnesia.

66. *Op. cit.,* p. 200.

67. Fred Lewis Pattee, "Herman Melville," *American Mercury,* X (January, 1927), 32.

As to why the nineteenth century for many years let it go at that, the modern who has gladly embarked with Ishmael has his theories. One could say that it was not for that century but for another to find in the language of *Moby-Dick* "so vibrating a life," "an energy of verbal inventiveness ... it is hardly too much to call Aeschylean or Shakespearean."[68] One could recall what a stumbling block in that century was the question of whether the book was a legitimate novel that has now been proclaimed as belonging, in its use of the stuff of an "heroic" age, in its superb Homeric similes, among the true epics[69] and as having, also, a quite unique organic or dynamic unity.[70] One could note that its stature has been raised many cubits by the critics who have defined its mode as not the medieval, rigid, and sterile one of allegory, but the new, flexible, and fructifying one of symbolism.[71]

Its reappraisals of conventional values are far less disturbing today than they were in that age of optimism. The depth psychologists have provided keys which have opened doors in its labyrinths which were then locked.[72] There were then those protests about "thrusts against revealed religion"; now W. H. Auden finds Ahab the most compelling portrayal since Shakespeare of the "Christian Tragic Hero," who is led by the sin of pride to defy God, and to rush into deserved and catharsis-providing, though splendid, doom.[73]

Yes, Melville's contemporaries wanted escape, but most of them got just enough in journeying to his valley of the cannibals, and drew back from his tale which offered a path to seas more perilous. As they said loudly, *Moby-Dick* was a "wild" book; but a hundred years later it was extolled as a "wild Everest of art."[74] Harold Nicolson, in accounting both for the vogue of Tennyson and for what Tennyson's audience did to him, spoke of the Victorian "distrust of the absolute

68. Arvin, p. 164.

69. *Ibid.*, pp. 156-157. For a poet's view that it is an epic, see Padraic Colum, "*Moby-Dick* as an Epic," *The Measure* (March, 1922), 16-18, reprinted in *A Half-Day's Ride* (1952), pp. 175-179. Ivor Winters, p. 73, says *Moby-Dick* is "less a novel than an epic poem." Mumford, p. 193, says "The best handbook of whaling is also . . . the best tragic epic of modern times." For Van Wyck Brooks also it is an epic ("From a Reviewer's Notebook," *Freeman*, VII [May 16, 1932], 238-239).

70. Walter Bezanson, "*Moby-Dick*: Work of Art," *Moby-Dick Centennial Essays*.

71. Matthiessen, *American Renaissance*, p. 250. Arvin, p. 165. Henry Reed, "Allegory and Symbolism," *New Statesman and Nation*, XXXIII (May, 1947), 397. W. H. Auden, *The Enchafed Flood* (New York, 1950), p. 65.

72. Henry A. Murray, "In Nomine Diaboli," *Moby-Dick Centennial Essays*. See also Chase, *op. cit.*

73. "The Christian Tragic Hero," *New York Times Book Review*, December 16, 1945, p. 1.

74. *Pierre*, ed. Henry A. Murray (New York, 1949), Introduction, p. xiii..

imagination." "It is important," he says, "to realize how deep and how universal was the current suspicion of the wilder flights of the imagination, how general was the yearning to find in poetry that simpler sweeter dream world which their jangled nerves desired."[75] What a candidate to please such a taste was the portent of the albino leviathan, though he was at last to be accepted, in a time of bolder concepts of the province of art as, though terrifying still, "godlike in his beauty too."[76]

To that later era *Moby-Dick* was to seem not merely baffling and confused—but complexly profound—a work which would scarcely yield even part of its capacious store of King's treasures except after some such careful probing as Arvin's "fourfold interpretation" of its "planes of significance"—the "literal, the oneiric or psychological, the moral, and the mythic."[77]

It was not so much that the reviewers withheld approbation as that they lacked vision. A surprising number did approve, and a few did catch glimpses of the book's true meanings and importances. Yet their praises were not enough to win for it the status of a classic which it was at last to achieve.[78] Not only did the nineteenth century, the twentieth century would say, in so eulogizing *Typee,* honor its author for the wrong book; but the nineteenth century honored his master-piece, in so far as it did honor it, not for the opulent pavilion it was at last declared to be, but only for certain facets of that pavilion that came within its own prudently circumscribed perspective.

75. *Tennyson* (Boston, 1923), p. 237.
76. Arvin, p. 167. See also Mumford, p. 127.
77. *Op. cit.,* p. 167.
78. Russell Blankenship, *American Literature as an Expression of the American Mind* (New York, 1931), p. 386, says, "*Moby-Dick* has more compelling power than any other book in the whole field of American literature."

Chapter VIII: AFTER MOBY-DICK

"He has added satire to his repertory, and as he uses it scrupulously, he uses it well."—George Henry Lewes (?) (1857), reviewing *The Confidence-Man*.

PIERRE: AMERICAN RECEPTION

Once more Melville commenced a new book with the idea of aiming at sales and acceptance. He had begun all the others to provide men with the vicarious excitement of nautical adventure—both the four in which he had stayed within the confines of what the public supposedly wanted, and the two in which he had rebelled against such restraint—*Mardi* and *Moby-Dick*. Now it occurred to him there was another potential audience, the women; and he wrote to Sophia Hawthorne—surprised that she had enjoyed pursuing the white whale—to promise that he would not send her another "bowl of sea water," because the "next chalice" he would "commend" would be a "rural bowl of milk."[1]

He tried to have his new book offered first to the English readers, as his other six works had been. Thus, although the Harpers had in February, 1852, accepted it for publication, he was, on April 16, sending the proof sheets to Bentley, promising to delay the American publication until he had made "some satisfactory negotiation in London."[2] To persuade the obviously reluctant Bentley to bring out his new book in England, he described his completed manuscript as if it were indeed the "bowl of milk" he had originally envisioned, and he made clear the implications of that metaphor—which he did not now employ, though it was clearly in his mind. It would be "a regular romance," with a "mysterious plot," "stirring passions," pre-

1. *Log*, p. 445.
2. *Log*, p. 449.

senting an "elevated aspect of American life." He seemed to think
an artisocratic love story would appeal especially to the ladies.

Pierre; or the Ambiguities had become in its final shaping anything but a country idyl for feminine readers; and it was strange indeed if Melville really believed this most mordant of American books,
was, as he told Bentley, "very much more calculated for popularity"
than his previous works.[3] Bentley did not think so, and on May 5
agreed to take the book only if Melville would consent to expurgation: "If you will give me permission to make or have made by a
judicious literary friend such alterations as are absolutely necessary
to 'Pierre' being properly appreciated here, I would undertake this;
and I will add that you will have no reason to regret this course."[4] Evidently Melville refused, and *Pierre,* instead of being published by a
prominent English house, as his other books had been, made in London a very lame debut, merely as an issue of the American sheets
under the imprint of the Harpers' London agent, Sampson Low, Son,
and Company, and not until November,[5] three months after the Harpers had brought it out on August 6 in New York.[6]

Three brief notices and a review antedated this American publication. The first two noticers pleasantly observed that Melville had
found a new province. On August 2 the Boston *Evening Transcript*
remarked that "The author of 'Typee' here wholly forsakes the sea
and ventures upon a regular story of life and love and personal adventure," with what success it did not know until it found "leisure to
read" it. The Lansingburgh *Gazette* on August 3 said that the
author had "chosen a new field wherein to give rein to his vivid
imagination. . . . The book is full of sterling incident and abounds
in numerous fine passages. . . . Frailty and vice are delineated with
energy and acuteness, and in the most glowing language." Would
Melville "find more admirers ashore than afloat?" The Hartford
Courant, on August 4, displayed indecision and bewilderment. A
"slight examination" revealed the work to be "very exciting"; but,
the style was "strange . . . not at all natural and too much in the
myopic, transcendental vein that characterizes some of our best writers," such as, "we suppose, however, belongs to the new era of progress,
and so we must submit to it."

3. William Braswell, "Melville's Opinion of *Pierre,*" *American Literature,* XXIII
(May, 1951), 246-250, argues convincingly that Melville's April 16 letter to Bentley,
which contained this statement, was ironic.
4. Quoted by Bernard R. Jarman, p. 307.
5. Howard, p. 198.
6. According to an announcement by the Harpers in the New York *Mirror.*

The first review on either side of the Atlantic, then, came on August 4 from Melville's old enemy, the Democratic Boston *Post*. The contributor was probably, once more, Colonel Greene. Not having the *Athenaeum's* Chorley to fall back on, he now produced comments of his own, ten times as long as those he had bestowed on *Moby-Dick*, to show that *Pierre* was a gifted writer's miscarriage. By now he had decided that *Typee* was Melville's only work of any merit, which he had offset by producing "a score of trashy and crazy volumes," including "such stuff as 'Mardi' and the 'White Whale.'" He had hoped Melville "had sown his wild literary oats, and had now come forth the vivid and brilliant author he might be if he chose to criticize himself and lop off the puerility, conceit, affectation and insanity which he had previously exhibited." But, no: "'Pierre; or the Ambiguities' is perhaps, the craziest fiction extant. It has scenes and descriptions of unmistakable power. The characters, however false to nature, are painted with a glowing pencil, and many of the thoughts reveal an intellect the intensity and cultivation of which it is impossible to doubt. But the amount of utter trash in the volume is almost infinite—trash of conception, execution, dialogue and sentiment. Whoever buys the book on the strength of Melville's reputation, will be cheating himself of his money, and we believe we shall never see the man who has endured the reading of the whole of it." Again the Colonel's shrewd Yankee concern, real or pretended, for his pocketbook outweighed his Democratic party loyalty.

Greene then offered an essentially correct synopsis, calling attention to the fact that the proof that Isabel is Pierre's sister is "Just nothing at all." "But even this string of nonsense is equalled by the nonsense that is strung upon it, in the way of crazy sentiment and exaggerated passion. What the book means, we know not. To save it from utter worthlessness it must be called a prose poem, and even then, it might be supposed to emanate from a lunatic asylum rather than from the quiet retreats of Berkshire. We say it with grief—it is too bad for Mr. Melville to abuse his really fine talents as he does." It would have been "a thousand times better" if he had stopped with *Typee;* for "he has produced more and sadder trash than any other man of undoubted ability among us, and the most provoking fact is, that in his bushels of chaff, the 'two grains of wheat' are clearly discernible."

Even Greene's deadly assault[7] did not keep the newspapers from burbling along cordially. The Boston *Daily Advertiser* on August 7

7. It was reprinted on August 28 in *Littell's Living Age.*

merely noted the new field, the "hero from the very highest aristocracy of the country, so high one hardly knows where to look for it," and the "scene entirely on land." The New York *Atlas* the next day had not found time to read it, but had "faith in its interest and excellence," as had "the reading public," who were "ready to receive" anything of Melville's. On August 10 the Albany *Argus* had read "enough to discover . . . the most unmistakable signs of superior genius." There were "some things" the *Argus* did "not like," but there was a "grace and power in many of its descriptions, and often an originality of conception, that almost startles one with delight." Those were the kindest words the book got. Probably it was Dr. Holland who in the Springfield *Republican,* on August 15, was less favorable though sympathetic: "Of mist-caps, and ravines, and sky-piercing peaks, and tangled underwoods, and barren rocks of language . . . the book is made." Melville had "changed his style entirely," and was "to be judged of as a new author," regrettably, for "while the new Melville displays more subtleness of thought, more elaborateness of manner (or mannerism) and a higher range of imagination, he has done it at a sad sacrifice of simplicity and popular appreciation."

The Boston Daily *Evening Traveller,* on August 17, was puzzled, and handled the book gingerly, trying to weigh the good and bad. The author had "forsaken the South Sea islands" and the ocean for a region "more real to most readers"—"But his work is even more unnatural and improbable than either [*sic*] of his previous productions, whilst the interest is extremely disagreeable and tragical in character. The plot is complex and involved, but on the whole skillfully managed. The characters, though exceedingly unnatural and bearing but little resemblance to living realities, are held in a firm grasp; and throughout the book bears the marks of the writer's unquestioned genius. Still we have not been much interested in it; and we think it will add little if anything to Mr. Melville's previous reputation."

Two reviewers in August concurred in seeking to annihilate *Pierre.* One, in the *Literary World,* was probably George Duyckinck (as Leyda suggests), whose partial estrangement now from his friend Melville can hardly account entirely for his treatment of *Pierre.* He had perused it more carefully than had any other reviewer, except perhaps, as will be seen, Peck. He was strongly repelled by what he took to be its ethical theme. He exclaimed: "The combined power of New England transcendentalism and Spanish Jesuitical casuistry could not have more completely befogged nature and truth than this confounded Pierre has done." He saw the purpose as an illustration of the possible antagonism of a sense of duty to all the recognized laws of social morality. "The most immoral *moral* of the story, if it has any moral at all, seems to be the impracticality of virtue. . . . Mr. Melville's chapter on 'Chronometricals and Horologicals,' if it have any meaning at all, simply means that virtue and religion are only for the Gods and not to be attempted by man. But ordinary novel readers will not unkennel this loathsome suggestion." Duyckinck's analysis of the philosophy of Plinlimmon, the author of "Chronometricals and Horologicals," was fair enough; and his theory that Melville's implication was that Pierre's tragedy resulted largely from his trying to be a "Chronometrical" or adherent of a too lofty and absolute morality, though probably erroneous, has been advanced in the twentieth century.[8] More convincing have been the recent critics who have argued that Melville approved neither of Pierre's conduct nor of Plinlimmon's theory.[9]

Inhibited George (or was it Evert?) denounced Melville's failure to treat sex with reverence. "We cannot pass without remark the supersensuousness with which the early relations of the family are described. Mother and son, brother and sister are sacred facts not to be disturbed by sacrilegious speculations . . . and the horrors of an incestuous relation between Pierre and Isabel seem to be vaguely hinted at."

He finally turned on the book where it was indeed vulnerable. "A literary mare's nest," he declared it was, "alone intelligible as an unintelligibility." He censured, as have others, the frequent coining of nouns by the addition of the suffix "ness." He made a curious prediction, which the event proved to be entirely erroneous, of a vulgar success: "All the male characters of the book have a certain animal

8. Weaver, p. 225, says *Pierre* is planned to show the impractibility of virtue. S. Foster Damon, "Pierre the Ambiguous," *Hound and Horn*, II (January 7, 1929), 118, says its ultimate purpose is to prove impossible both the Pagan and Christian systems of salvation. Mumford, p. 216, assumes Plinlimmon is a spokesman for Melville.

9. Tyrus Hillway, "Pierre the Fool of Virtue," *American Literature*, XXI (May, 1949), 216, contends that Pierre's tragic fate comes, not because it is impossible to carry out the precepts of Christ in this world, but because his character is flawed by pride, and his motives tainted by sensuality. Matthiessen, p. 471, says Melville's "heart was not in Plinlimmon's doctrines." William Ellery Sedgwick, *Herman Melville* (Cambridge, 1944), p. 161, says Melville "had no stomach for Plinlimmon's doctrine," and that Melville cautions us not to take Pierre's views for his own. Murray, in his Introduction to his edition of *Pierre*, p. lxxvii, contends that Plinlimmon's pamphlet is a summation of the ideas of Hawthorne rather than of Melville himself.

force and untamed energy which carry them through their melodramatic parts—no slight duty—with an effect sure to bring down the
applause of the excitable and impulsive." So he joined the chorus
of those hoping to meet Melville again in the "hale company of
sturdy sailors . . . telling a traveller's tale."

Equally derogatory, also on August 21, was the reviewer in the
Albion, the same who had tolerated *Moby-Dick,* surely editor William
Young. He pronounced *Pierre* "a dead failure." Errors of unknown
writers could be passed over hastily, but one must be "explicit" when
"public favorites go astray." A sarcastic summary of the plot gave him
occasion to say of Isabel that he could not "determine whether she
be more ridiculously sublime or more sublimely ridiculous"; to lament
the "influence of Eugene Sue"; to decry the "heaping up horrors and
trash"; and to "regret to add" that "ambiguities are still further
thickened by hints at that fearfullest of all human crimes" intimated
by the "Cenci portrait."

Young condemned the dialogue. He remembered that "in noticing
that bold, original work 'Moby Dick,'" he had shown that Melville
"never could make his characters talk." It was the same here. "Almost every spoken word reminds you of the old Greek Tragedies"—
a remark intended, I suppose, derisively.[10] Mr. Falsgrave was the only
character whose dialogue was not "absurd to the last degree." Would
that Melville would "wash out the remembrance" of this "crazy
rigamarole" by writing "a fresh romance of the Ocean."

Not completely pejorative, though harsh enough, was a commentator, perhaps editor Hiram Fuller, of the New York *Evening
Mirror* on August 27 in a front-page article. Quoting at length from
Duyckinck's review, he added he had read "these 'ambiguities' with alternate feelings of pleasure and disgust." The book contained "a good
deal of fine writing and poetic feeling," but the "metaphysics" were
"abominable." "The whole tone of the work, from beginning to end is
morbid and unhealthy; and the action, as well as the plot, is monstrously unnatural." Indeed Melville should feel "almost as much
ashamed" of it as he had a "right to be proud" of *Typee.* He con-
ceded it was "marked by great intellectual activity; while some of
the descriptive portions are transcendently beautiful." Yet "It reminds
one of a summer day that opens sweetly, glittering with dew drops

10. Compare Carl Van Vechten, *Excavations,* who likens *Pierre* (in praise, of
course) "with its ingeniously subtle theme" to a "Webster and Tourneur melodrama."
Van Vechten defends the "Gothic dialogue" on the basis that Melville wanted it to
"lack contemporary feeling" (p. 82).

redolent of rose-odors, and melodious with the singing of birds, but early clouded with *artificial* smoke, and ending in a terrific display of melodramatic lightnings and earthquakes. There is no sequency in the accumulated misery that overwhelms every character in the tragedy. Insanity, murder and despair sweep their Tartarean shadows over the scene; and we close the volume with something of the feeling, and just as much of benefit as we experience in awakening from a horrid fit of the nightmare."

The severe though dignified attack by a writer in the *Southern Literary Messenger* in September centered almost entirely on the moral perversity. It may have been by John R. Thompson. He began by lamenting that Melville had been writing under "an unlucky star" since *Typee,* and as for the *Ambiguities,* it was "the most aptly titled volume" met with for years. The critic's statement of the ethical theme was almost identical with Duyckinck's: "The purpose of the *Ambiguities* (if it have any, for none is either avowed or hinted) we should take to be the illustration of this fact—that it is quite possible for a young and fiery soul, *acting strictly from a sense of duty,* to erect itself in direct hostility to all the universally received rules of moral and social order. . . . And our sympathies are sought to be enlisted with Pierre for the reason that throughout all his follies and crimes, his sense of duty struggles with and overcomes every law of religion and morality. It is a battle of the virtues, we are led to think, and the supreme virtue prevails." To illustrate the absurdity of Melville's purpose, "supposing him to have one," he gave a devastatingly satiric synopsis. He admitted it was laudable in Pierre to wish to treat Isabel kindly and to cover up their father's shame; yet "to accomplish it, Pierre is led to do things infinitely worse than it would be to neglect it. He not only acts like a fool in severing the most sacred ties and making the dearest sacrifices to purchase what he might have obtained at much lighter expense, but he justifies his conduct by a sense of duty, false in the extreme. . . . The truth is Mr. Melville's theory is wrong. It should be the object of fiction to delineate life and character as it is around us, or as it ought to be. Now Pierre never did exist, and it is very certain that he never ought to exist. . . . Mr. Melville has deviated from the legitimate line of the novelist. But badly as we think of the book as a work of art, we think infinitely worse of it as to its moral tendency."[11]

11. It may be said that Pierre did indeed at first believe he was acting from a sense of duty, but later came to realize the taint of incest in his thoughts. Elinor May Gaggy, *Pierre: Key to Melville's Enigma,* Unpublished Dissertation, University of Wash-

Another aspect of the failure of *Pierre,* its ridiculousness, was the burden of the review, also in September, in the Toronto *Anglo-American,* in the form of a satirical dialogue. Rather surprisingly, one of the interlocutors said he would welcome a new work from the "author of *Mardi.*" The "Doctor," however, told him he would be a fool to spend his money on *Pierre,* which was a "gigantic blunder" about a hero who was a "dreamy spoon, alike deficient in heart and brains"; and the book was a "New York Werther, having all the absurdities and none of the beauties of Goethe's youthful indiscretion!"

Of the three reviews in October, the one in *Graham's Magazine* was by no means entirely hostile. *Graham's* commentator saw the work as a penetrating study in psychology, but unpleasant and a failure as a novel. He admitted: "None of Melville's novels equals the present in force and subtlety of thinking and unity of purpose. Many of the scenes are wrought out with great splendor and vigor, and a capacity is evinced of holding with a firm grasp, and describing with a masterly distinctness some of the most evanescent phenomena of morbid emotions." On the other hand, the "spirit is intolerably unhealthy," and it was a "provoking waste of talent." "Pierre, we take it is crazy, and the merit of the book is in clearly presenting the psychology of his madness; but the details of such a malady as that which affects Pierre are almost as disgusting as those of the physical disease itself." This was the nearest any reviewer came to anticipating what Dr. Henry A. Murray has found in the book; but this modern psychiatrist does not regard the details as "disgusting," has a new vocabulary, and is less concerned with insisting that *Pierre* is insane than with pointing out that Melville has achieved a remarkable depiction of the "anima," a largely subconscious phenomenon of the mind.[12]

The October review of *Pierre* in *Godey's Lady's Book* was for that magazine's staff an unusual exertion, as they had usually offered little beyond a pleasant enough nod at Melville's works. Now, however, *Godey's* critic had an original idea. After modestly saying that he "really" had "nothing to add to the severity of the critical notices"

ington, Abstract, *University of Washington: Abstracts of Theses,* Vol. 10 (1945-46), says, "Melville does not indicate anywhere that he considered Pierre's sacrifice anything but quixotically mistaken" (p. 23).

12. Murray says, "It is astonishing that two generations before Jung, Melville, unaided by the findings of depth psychology, should have described with such fidelity, subtlety, and beauty, all the significant features of the first phase of the anima experience" (*op. cit.,* p. liv).

which had surely been enough "to satisfy the author" and the public that he had made a bad mistake in leaving his "native element the ocean" for these "ambiguities," this critic advanced an engaging theory: "It may be, however, that the heretofore intelligible and popular author has merely assumed his present transcendental metamorphosis, in order that he may have range and scope enough to satirize the ridiculous pretensions of some of our modern literati. Under the supposition that such has been his intention, we submit the following notice of his book, as the very best off-hand effort we could make in imitation of his style. . . ." The "notice" was composed chiefly as a parody of the "ness" mannerism in *Pierre,* which has been objected to by both early and recent critics. That in *Pierre* Melville was creating a satirical transcription of the popular sentimental novel has been recently argued cogently by Braswell and Miss Yaggy, and partially accepted by Thorp, Matthiessen, Howard, and Rosenberry. Braswell contends that Melville wrote with tongue in cheek to show how extravagant his style could be; and that he "bequeathed his immortal curse to the world" to provoke deliberately the bitter criticism he received.[13]

The hostile reaction to *Pierre* was yet to reach its crescendo, in blasts from Charleston in October and from George Washington Peck in November. So far, the commentators had at least refrained from calling *Pierre* the product of a maniac; but it was obviously the same reviewer who had in the *Southern Quarterly Review* (was it really Simms?) made out a writ of lunacy against the author of *Moby-Dick* who now proffered a similar charge against the author of *Pierre*: "That Typee, Omoo and other clever books should be followed by such a farrago as this of Pierre was surely not to be predicted or anticipated. . . . That Herman Melville has gone 'clean daft' is very much to be feared; certainly he has given us a very mad book, my masters. His *dramatis personae* are all mad as March hares. . . . The sooner this author is put in ward the better. If trusted with himself, at all events give him no further trust in pen and ink till the present fit has worn off. He will grievously hurt himself—or his very amiable publishers."

There was a bitter ironic fitness in the fact that the last American review of *Pierre* was from the pen of George Washington Peck, in the

13. "The Satirical Temper of Melville's *Pierre,*" *American Literature,* VII (January, 1936), 424-438. "The characters in *Pierre* were all satires on those in popular sentimental fiction; tyrannical parents, weak clergy, romantic hot-headed young gallants, sensitive' blond and brunette heroines. . . ." Although Pierre reached some understanding of reality, he "lived and died by the romantic code" (Yaggy, p. 23). Howard speaks of "Melville's obviously satiric attitude toward his hero" (p. 189). Rosenberry considers it a "latent parody" of the popular sentimental novel (p. 159).

American Whig Review, although the faults he detected in it were certainly very different from those he had found in *Omoo.* Like the man from Charleston, Peck scented evidences of madness in the author of *Pierre,* particularly in the style, and devoted nine pages to annihilating the book. He pronounced the dialogue of Lucy and Pierre "insane rhapsody," yet those passages were "deprived by the 'thee's' and 'thou's' of the only recommendation that can palliate insanity, and that is simplicity." He called the style "the most extraordinary thing that an American press ever beheld." It was "precisely what a raving lunatic who had read Jean Paul Richter *in a translation* might be supposed to spout under the influence of a particularly moonlight night."

With great diligence Peck set out to discover the lurking secret of the diction. "Carlyle's compound words and Milton's latinic ones sink into insignificance before Mr. Melville's extraordinary concoctions." The essence, he found, of this "great philological reform consists in 'est' and 'ness' added to every word to which they have no earthly right to belong." He provided a table of examples of these "concoctions," with page references. His hunt from page to page of *Pierre* to determine the meaning of the recurring impossible word "instantaneousness" ended only in his ironic disappointment. That there was some justice in this phase of Peck's attack can hardly be denied.

Peck seems to have been oblivious of *Moby-Dick,* which he is not known to have reviewed. In pronouncing *Pierre* Melville's "worst and latest work," he said "Pierre aims at something beyond the mere records of adventure contained in Mardi and Omoo," with no mention of *Moby-Dick.* Was it so utterly contemptible as to be unworthy of even a passing reference from Mr. Peck?

He gave much attention to the insidious immorality, as he saw it, of *Pierre.* He appeared to resent analysis of the psychology of sex, and to imply that Melville sought to palliate incest:[14] "Pierre entertains toward this weird sister feelings which Mr. Melville endeavors to gloss over with a veil of purity but which even in their best phase can never be anything but repulsive to a well constituted mind. . . . When he strikes with an impious, though happily weak hand, at the very foundations of society, we feel it our duty to tear off the veil with which he has thought to soften the hideous features of the idea, and warn the public against the reception of such atrocious doctrines. . .

14. E. M. Benson says Melville "approached the subject with ulcerous contempt" ("Pierre," *Outlook,* CLII [June 19, 1929], 211).

Nor has any man the right, in his morbid craving after originality, to strip these horrors of their decent mystery." Peck's various objections were perhaps best summed up in his passing "sentence" on *Pierre* as having "a repulsive, unnatural and indecent plot, a style disfigured by every paltry affectation of the worst German School, and ideas unparalleled for earnest absurdity." The accusation of Germanism was current coin among the American critics of the time, and was used to demolish writers as different as Emerson and Poe.[15]

A paragraph in the *National Magazine,* a New York Methodist organ, in November, was a fair enough summation of the prevalent contemporary reaction: "The papers secular and religious, are very severe on Herman Melville's last work, called 'Pierre; or the Ambiguities.' A Boston paper pronounces the volume 'abominable trash—an emanation from a lunatic rather than the writing of a sober man.'" This magazine, however, had not yet done with *Pierre*. In January its editor, Abel Stevens, in his "Editor's Table," lamented the "morbid propensity for morbid characters" which he saw developing in "our national literature," Hawthorne being the prime offender. "Poe's best poems and his prose tales are rife with it . . . 'Pierre, or the Ambiguities,' the late miserable abortion of Melville is another. In the name of all that is good or beautiful, why should art of any kind be prostituted to such moral deformities? As well might the sculptor reproduce the horrors of Dupruyten's Pathological Museum." Stevens sought to show, by quoting from the London *Atlas* an attack on Hawthorne's unhealthiness, that the whole American tendency was derived from "a bastard French school." So France as well as Germany was held a source of poison.[16]

In Fitz-James O'Brien's survey of Melville's writings to date in the February, 1853, *Putnam's Magazine,* he naturally gave *Pierre* much attention because of its recentness. He said that he had at first believed it a hoax, but that he was no longer under that delusion. He preferred *Mardi,* in which the extravagances and improbabilities were, because of the exotic setting, not unacceptable. But suppose Melville had placed Babbalanja and Media and Yoomy, as he had placed Pierre,

15. F. L. Pattee, *The Development of the American Short Story* (New York, 1923), p. 127. Murray says that *Pierre* is indeed pervaded by German romanticism (*op. cit.,* p. xciv).

16. *Albion,* in reviewing *Pierre,* had exclaimed: "Would that Mr. Melville had hit upon a less Frenchified mode of . . . plot development. . . ." Stevens was distinguished as a historian of the Methodist Church (William W. Sweet in *DAB*).

in Fifth Avenue! "Pierre has all the madness of Mardi without its vague, dreamy poetic charm. All Mr. Melville's many affectations of style and thought are here crowded together in a mad mosaic. . . . Pierre transcends all the nonsense-writing that the world ever beheld. Thought staggers through each page like one poisoned. Language is drunken and reeling. Style is antipodal and marches on its head."

The "moral was bad," O'Brien said, without being explicit as to what the moral was. But he was sure the book was vicious: "Everybody is vicious in some way or other. The mother is vicious with pride. Isabel has a cancer of morbid, vicious, minerva-press romance, eating into her heart, and licks the dust beneath Pierre's feet viciously. Delly Ulver is humanly vicious, and in the rest of the book, whatever of vice is wanting in the remaining characters, is made up by the superabundant viciosities of style."

O'Brien could not understand *Pierre*: "The Rosetta stone gave up its secret, but we believe that to the end of time Pierre will remain an ambiguity." He evidently felt he had disposed of *Pierre* once and for all in 1853; for in his 1857 article on Melville he made no mention of it. This sentence of his from his earlier article may be offered as a fair summation of the generally held opinion: all of "Melville's books have had their share of success, and their own peculiar merits, always saving and excepting Pierre—wild, inflated that it is."[17]

Comments of the American press on *Pierre* fell into four groups: first, there was the rather tentative sole suggester that it was a satire (*Godey's*); second were the amiable but superficial little greetings from newspapers; third were five who thought that in it considerable or even brilliant potentialities had been partially (Springfield *Republican, Traveller*) or hopelessly (*Graham's*, Greene, *Mirror*) spoiled; and fourth was the greater number of scornful and utter condemnations (Duyckinck, the two Southerners, the *Anglo-American*, Peck, Stevens, O'Brien). Its immediate American reception was far nearer to a total rejection than had been that of *Moby-Dick*. The consensus was that it was morally vicious, stylistically monstrous, incomprehensibly transcendental, and violently mad.

Strangely enough, the Harpers reprinted *Pierre* in 1855; but it was not again reprinted in America until 1922;[18] and after receiving a few

17. It is truly remarkable to find the *Berkshire County Eagle* on August 26, 1853, referring to "HERMAN MELVILLE, author of 'Pierre,' 'Moby-Dick,' and those witching tales of the Marquesas."

18. Minnegerode, p. 162; Hetherington, p. 147.

highly derogatory passing remarks in reviews of Melville's subsequent prose works, it seems to have remained unmentioned until the latter date.

PIERRE: BRITISH RECEPTION

Whether a consequence of its unimpressive London advent, without the promotional machinery of an important British publisher, or merely the result of the seeming repulsiveness of the book itself, *Pierre* got, so far as I know, only two British reviews. One was in the *Athenaeum,* on November 20, probably by the indefatigible Henry F. Chorley, who had been so hard on *The Whale.*

"Germanism" was one of the chief crimes of which Chorley accused the author of *Pierre,* which he denoted "a would-be utterance of Young Yankee sentimentalism." It had, however, nothing characteristically American about it, but read "like the upsetting into English of the first novel of a very whimsical and lackadaisical young student at the U—niversity of Gottingen." "Diffuse transcendentalism" was present: "When he sat down to compose it, the author evidently had not determined what he was going to write about. . . . As for the style it is a prolonged succession of spasms, and the characters are a marrowless tribe of phantoms, flitting through dense clouds of transcendental mysticism. . . . We take up novels to be amused—not bewildered—in search of pleasure for the mind—not in pursuit of cloudy metaphysics." Although unlike the Americans, as has been seen, Chorley revealed no horror at the daring probings into the foundations of morality, his was a bitter assault.

The other review was in the *London Men of the Times,* in which the book was disposed of as "An unhealthy, mystic romance . . . a decided failure," according to Minnegerode.[19] I have not been able to examine this review. In 1853 Ainsworth refused to speak of Melville's last and worst production, 'Pierre.'" So the British had done with *Pierre.* It was not reprinted in England until 1922.[20] A hundred years after its appearance, a Spaniard, perhaps the greatest painter then living, was to say there was only one American book worth reading, Melville's *Pierre.* The painter's name was Pablo Picasso.

ISRAEL POTTER: AMERICAN RECEPTION

For the second time, prior British publication of a book of Melville's did not materialize. Probably he had now discovered that the im-

19. *Op. cit.,* p. 162.
20. Hetherington, p. 499.

mediate monetary rewards of serial publication in an American
magazine outweighed the financial advantages of a first London appearance in book form. At any rate, on June 7, 1854, Melville offered
to George Palmer Putnam a story called *Israel Potter,* to run for an un-
stated number of months in his new magazine. Once more Melville
made a resolution, as he had often done before when commencing a
book, to give his public what it wanted. Now he assured Putnam
that this story would "contain nothing of any sort to shock the fastidious . . . little reflective writing . . . nothing weighty." It would be
"adventure."[21] Melville had a new compulsion to check-rein his
Pegasus—the tastes of magazine readers. Essentially this time he carried out his promise. Putnam accepted the tale, no doubt with little
hesitation, as Melville had, since the failure of *Pierre,* begun successfully a new career as a magazinist; indeed he was the best-paid regular contributor of prose to *Putnam's Monthly Magazine.*[22]

The first chapter of *Israel Potter* was in the July, 1854, issue of this
magazine, the last in the March, 1855, issue. Its serialization was followed with continued applause by several newspapers, and as far as
I know, by no hisses. The Berkshire *Eagle,* on July 7, adjudged the
"literary matter" in *Putnam's* to be "of superior merit," and was sure
that Melville's "Berkshire story"—Melville represents Israel as being
born in Berkshire—would be of special local interest. In early August
the *Morning Courier and New York Enquirer* declared that the author
had "effected a sudden and great improvement in his style, which in
this tale is manly, direct, and clear." On August 25, the *Eagle* noted
that Israel was "still an exile from Berkshire, continuing his European wanderings, amid all sorts of strange adventures, with much result of poetical thought and eccentric comment." On August 29 the
Courier was glad to report that the story had preserved "the direct
simplicity of style," and on September 30, that it was "continued with
unflagging interest." The New York *Citizen* remarked on September
2, "Melville is reaping fresh honors in his 'Israel Potter'"; on December 30, "Gladly we . . . plunge into a continuation of 'Israel Potter'
. . . a stirring narrative; so that if you begin it you must finish it"; on
February 3, 1855, " 'Israel Potter' is good, as usual." The Boston *Daily
Advertiser,* on March 7, came the nearest to an unfriendly comment:
"Israel Potter is brought to a conclusion, satisfactory doubtless, to those
who have kept the run of it."

21. *Log,* p. 488.
22. Howard, p. 225.

By March 10 *Israel Potter* had been made by G. P. Putnam and Company into a book.[23] The first review known to have greeted it in its new guise was on March 12, in Melville's old friend, the New Bedford *Mercury,* and surely by William Ellery Channing, Jr., who was then the editor.[24] Readers of *Putnam's,* he said, would be glad that "this very pleasant 'autobiography' " had been given a permanent form: "Mr. Melville's works are unequal, but none of them can be charged with dulness, and he is especially at home on his native soil, with a keen sense of the rugged but abounding picturesqueness and beauty of its scenery, and of the peculiarities of the Yankee character of the revolutionary period. Among the famous, Benjamin Franklin and Capt. Paul Jones have a part to play in this veritable history, which is a mixture of fun, gravity, romance and reality very taking from beginning to end. It will take its place among the best of its predecessors and may certainly be said to belong to American literature." This paragraph underlines a chief reason for the book's appeal, its patriotic motif, and negates the notion that nobody in the fifties considered of permanent importance any creation of Melville; but it was not *Moby-Dick* which Channing declared belonged "to American literature."

The longest of the contemporary American reviews was an entirely favorable one in the New York *Norton's Literary Gazette* on March 15. The *Gazette's* critic said that those who had been following "the fortunes of this redoubtable hero" would undoubtedly be glad to peruse them in one connected story," as it afforded "rich and novel entertainment, not excelled by anything" which Melville had written before. He offered a brief but quite adequate summary of this "simple story of a plain honest Yankee of the sturdy race who fought for their liberties in 1776"—a man who exhibited "the unmistakable characteristics of a true son of New England." He declared "the interest of the story is intense. The reader is carried along . . . now admiring the quiet beauty of some bit of description, and owning, it may be, its truthfulness; now laughing at the Yankee shrewdness that is never outwitted, now filled with horror at the mad passions of fighting men, and taking as real each shifting scene that comes before him. But with . . . 'Typee' and 'Omoo' in mind, and some knowledge of the power of Mr. Melville's imagination, we believe we are more indebted to him for this eager interest than to Israel's autobiography [that is, the source book]." It was indeed, to use Melville's own

23. The date it was deposited in the Clerk's Office in New York (*Log,* p. 499).
24. See Chapter VII, footnote 36.

words, "a dilapidated old tombstone retouched." He predicted a "large sale." Thus the glorification of American traits and deeds pleased more than one Yankee critic. Although typical of 1855 in thinking of Melville as the author, not of *Moby-Dick*, but of his first books, the *Gazette's* critic certainly accorded his literary powers a very high rank.

Colonel Greene, editor of the Boston *Post*, had been able to stand nothing by Melville since *Redburn;* surely it was he who, also on March 15, wrote for his paper a conspicuous back-page review of *Israel Potter*, which he found tolerable. Melville's earlier books had "placed him high among our writers of fiction," said the Colonel, but "his late works have been unsatisfactory, not to say ridiculous." Giving a short synopsis of the new one, he rejoiced that this author was improving and had now "made a most interesting book"—"a book not great nor remarkable" but having "a curt, manly, independent tone, dealing with truth honestly, and telling it feelingly. Its *Paul Jones* and *Benjamin Franklin,* to be sure, are not without a spice of Melville's former 'humors,' as they used to be called; but on the whole its style, sentiment and construction are so far above those of 'Pierre' and some of its predecessors, that we dislike to say one word against it. It is a reasonable book, with passages and descriptions of power. We trust its successor will be quite as sensible, but be of wider scope and a larger subject."[25]

On March 17 three New York journals all praised *Israel Potter* more highly than had the Boston critic. The *Morning Courier* was delighted with its effective narration:

This very simple yet graphic recital of interesting adventure is republished in attractive form from the pages of Putnam's Magazine, its appearance in which we have noticed with more or less favor for many months past.[26] As a literary performance it is equal to anything which Mr. Melville's pen has produced, although it is in quite a different vein from that in which he has hitherto worked with so much success. Its style is remarkably manly and direct, and is in this respect a pleasant contrast to that of . . .

25. On April 5, the *Post*, reviewing *Westward Ho!,* compared Kingsley's *Amyas Leigh* with *Israel Potter* as examples of historical fiction in the form of "supposed biographies." The American book was more "truth-like, pithy, vigorous and readable than the English," which, however, was "far superior to 'Israel Potter' in scope, in brillancy, in tone, and in character."

26. My search through the *Courier* from January 1, 1855, to March 17 resulted in the discovery of one noncommittal mention only. It had complimented the book in 1854, as has been noted.

Pierre. It is occasionally coarse for the refinement of our day; but so are *Robinson Crusoe* and the *Pilgrim's Progress.*

Melville had promised Putnam not to "shock the fastidious," but that was the nineteenth century! What in *Israel Potter* could the *Courier* have possibly imagined needed this bit of defense?

On the same March 17 it was doubtless British-born editor William Young who in his New York *Albion* liked the book's vitality: "A downright good book. . . . There is in it a masculine vigor, and even a certain fantastical ruggedness, that separate it from the herd of smoothly written tales, and give it . . . a distinctness and raciness of flavor . . . Franklin and Paul Jones are admirable sketches of character; but our author, as we know of old, is in his own special element when he deals with the sea and its belongings. The fight between the *Serapis* and the *Bonhomme Richard* is a masterpiece of writing; albeit some may deem its imagery too fanciful and far fetched. Perhaps it is —but it it helps the description wonderfully."[27] He quoted from the account of the battle; and then recalling that *Albion* was aimed at British-American subscribers, said: "Of course the Revolutionary War, in its principle, as in the details . . . is not touched up to the exact taste of some British readers." But even though Melville "could be plain spoken about England, he could admit that America was 'civilized in externals but savage at heart.' "[28] Also on March 17, the New York *Evening Post,* after a brief synopsis, said that the "story is delightfully told by . . . one of the most popular writers of our country in his peculiar department, and portions of the history of several of the remarkable men of the revolution, such as Paul Jones and Ethan Allen, are interwoven with the narrative."

The New York *Commercial Advertiser* on March 21 presented a very high estimate of the book, saying that it would "be ungracious . . . not to express once more the pleasure we have derived from its perusal." (Apparently the *Advertiser* had carried favorable notices, which have not been located, of the installments as they had come out). It declared *Israel Potter* "an original and extremely graphic story of our revolutionary era"; "thoroughly saturated with American sentiment"; "quite equal in a literary point of view to any of its author's

27. Compare Mumford, p. 241, who says that *Israel Potter* contains, "one of the best accounts of a sea-fight." Sedgwick praises both the sea fight and the sketch of Franklin (p. 181), in what he describes as a "brilliant historical novel" (*op. cit.,* p. 80).

28. Young contrasts Melville's broadmindedness with the hypocrisy America showed at the recent famous Ostend Conference.

previous works"; and "much superior to some of them in other respects."

The two March 22 reviews were completely and warmly commendatory, and were both in religious organs which had for years shown no bigotry in their comment on Melville. The Boston *Puritan Recorder*[29] summarized the plot sketchily, but said: "The material out of which the book is made is deeply interesting; but it is moulded with so much skill, that it has all the effect of a most thrilling romance. We should be at a loss where to look for anything more exquisitely beautiful in the way of description, than the account of the old exile's coming back to the spot where he was born, and being unable to find a solitary individual who remembered him." On the same day, the New York *Evangelist*,[30] which had found more fine artistry than flaws in *Moby-Dick,* now virtually eulogized this "spirited Revolutionary story" from "the accomplished pen of Herman Melville," as "in some respects the best thing he has ever done." "It abounds in sharp delineation of character, stirring incident, and rich historical allusion. It is a work of unquestionable literary merit."

The only review during the whole next month I have found was on April 5 in the Newark *Advertiser*. Short but sweet, it was probably by the contributor with the nautical background who for years had been applauding Melville in this paper. *Israel Potter* was for him "a most charming tale, and one which, as it came out monthly in *Putnam's Magazine,* we have often praised." It was "one of the most genuine of the author's numerous works, and will be, for its patriotic interest, most popular in the community." He was "sorry to see the work hastened so rapidly to its close," and inclined "like little Oliver" to " 'ask for more.' "

Two magazines took cognizance of the book in their May issues. The remarks in *Putnam's Monthly* were anything but a puff. Apparently Melville had again confused some of his readers about the matter of the proportion of truth and fiction, and *Putnam's,* eschewing aesthetic judgment, sought to set them right. It made three points: first, that in the dedication Melville explained whether he was writing a romance or an actual narrative ["it preserves, almost as in a

---

29. The editors were given, as for this date, as "Rev. Parsons Cooke, Rev. Samuel H. Riddel."

30. "Wm. Bradford and Henry M. Field" were given as editors "with the aid of six D. D.'s and numerous correspondents in this country and Europe." On a clipping dated April 30, probably from an Albany paper, it was stated that "Melville often, with a few words, gives us a finer and more life-like description than most men create out of long chapters and thick books" (*Log,* p. 501).

reprint, Israel Potter's autobiographical story," were his words];
second, that the original was "not as rare" as he thought—"We have
a copy"—; and third, that he departed "considerably from his original."[31] Also in the "Editorial Notes" was a very cool *bon voyage,*
ending with the wish that the book "be everywhere received according
to" its "deserts"—again certainly not a puff.[32]

The paragraph that month in Abel Steven's *National Magazine,* a
New York Methodist organ, was, despite a slight reservation, very
favorable: "Israel Potter . . . is a story of the revolutionary times,
written in a half-comic, half-patriotic vein, yet withal exceedingly attractive, and not a little instructive . . . vividly recalling many of the
scenes of the period. . . . The Yankee character is well sustained, in
its hero's adventures by sea and land. A tinge of obscure sarcasm
pervades the book, most apparent in its dedication to the Bunker Hill
Monument."

So came to an end the interest of the early American reviewers in
Israel Potter. It was the silences which had been ominous. The
Literary World had ceased in 1853, and so Duyckinck was less likely
to find a mouthpiece. But what of Willis, Greeley, Ripley, Butler,
Graham's, who had all professed to admire *Moby-Dick?* The lack of
studies of any length, the diminution of the total number of reviews
and notices in the case of *Israel Potter,* also boded no good for its
author's ultimate reputation. Yet from those who had shown in
print their awareness of it had come nearly unanimous approbation.
Least enthusiastic had been the publisher's own organ; the only other
praise that was not essentially whole-hearted was from Colonel Greene,
who had eyed Melville askance for years, and even he admitted a
tremendous improvement over *Pierre.* All the rest had liked *Israel
Potter* very much. Again it was one of Melville's less daring books
which pleased the public. Putnam reprinted it twice in 1855.[33]

31. According to *Putnam's,* Israel was neither born in the Berkshires nor acquainted
with Paul Jones.

32. *Putnam's* averred in this "note" that it was proud of its literary children who had
gone into the world to set up for themselves. "The youngest of the tribe is named
'Israel Potter,' the earnest, indomitable, free-hearted Israel, who having just made his
bow to his highness, the Bunker Hill Monument, is about to take a patriotic progress,
like a new President, over the nation."

33. Minnegerode, p. 170, quotes from the Hartford *Republican* on *Israel Potter:*
"The descriptions with which it abounds are among the finest in the language. Such
splendid writing rarely issues from the press." And the Reading, Pennsylvania, *Gazette*
is quoted in an advertisement inserted by the publishers on March 15, 16, and 20 in the
Commercial Advertiser as saying it was "Melville's best book." These two reviews
seem to have been favorable.

Yet, as had happened before, it was again the destiny of one of his books to be neglected or regarded with more distaste as the years passed. The Duyckincks in their *Cyclopaedia* as early as the end of the year 1855 said that *Israel Potter* had not met "with deserved success." The last known word about it in a newspaper or magazine during the century came two years later from Fitz-James O'Brien, who gave it a few lines in his 1857 article in *Putnam's*. It was comparatively reasonable, he thought, with "considerable clearness and force" but lacked "animation." He considered two of its chief characterizations hardly successful. Franklin was pictured as "one of the prosiest possible old maxim-mongers, though at the epoch he was living brilliantly in Paris"; and Paul Jones was a mere "hero of melodrama."

O'Brien's judgment in *Putnam's*, harsher than had been passed by any reviewer, undoubtedly made more impression on the public than a passing allusion—some comfort to Melville surely —by Hawthorne in *Our Old Home* (1863) to the "excellent novel or biography of 'Israel Potter.'" There was no American reprinting of the book after 1855 until 1922, although in 1863 there came out a kind of pirated edition under the title *The Refugee*.[34]

ISRAEL POTTER: BRITISH RECEPTION

The exact date of the G. Routledge and Company publication of *Israel Potter* in England is unknown. It was surely six weeks or so later than the early April publication by Putnam, for it was very unusual for English literary periodicals to wait two months before reviewing a book with a London imprint—if they were going to cover it at all—and the first British review was apparently on May 5, in the London *Leader*.[35] A mature piece of writing, it may have been by Lewes, who had only three days before settled in East Sheen with Marian Evans after returning from eight happy months spent with her in Weimar and Berlin. They had been in England since the middle of March, and he had a fortnight before received "a few commissions from the *Leader*,"[36] for which both he and Marian were soon writing. She might possibly, indeed, have written the review, but Lewes, who had lauded *Moby-Dick*, is the more probable author.

34. *Ibid.*, pp. 165-169. Hetherington, p. 498.
35. Before I realized the probability of the later English publication, I had scanned a large number of British newspapers and magazines through March and April of 1855 for references to *Israel Potter*, but without results.
36. Hanson, *Marion Evans etc.*, p. 180. Blanche Colton Williams says of Marian that "Before the end of May she had delivered several articles for the *Leader*" (*George Eliot*, p. 111).

After reading the first half, which showed "vigor, freshness, artist-like skill," he "felt disposed to rank *Israel Potter* as incomparably the best work that Mr. Melville had yet written." After that, he thought it began to decline, because, first, it centered around Jones, the "least successful" character; and second, Melville ceased to be particular and became general to get his story into one small volume. "If he had left his hero's life in London and death in America for a second volume, and crossed out half the sea scenes in which Jones figures" he would have given us "not only his best book, but the best book that an American author has written." Also the interviews between Potter and Franklin and Potter and King George III were excellent. It was, indeed, "a curiously unequal book," the work of an "original thinker," but "damaged by want of art."

The review in the *Athenaeum,* on June 2, had all the earmarks of Henry Chorley, who now, after *Moby-Dick* and *Pierre,* was thoroughly out of patience: "Mr. Melville's books have been from the outset of his career somewhat singular—and this is not the least so of the company. . . . Whether Israel Potter be man or myth, he is here set in a strange framework. Mr. Melville tries for power and commands rhetoric,—but he becomes wilder and wilder, and more and more turgid in each successive book." A curious opinion indeed, that this book was more untamed than *Pierre.* Chorley illustrated the wildness of Melville's style by quoting his very unflattering description of the Thames—"one murky sheet of sewerage. . . . Fretted by the ill-built piers . . . shot balefully through the Erebus arches, desperate as the lost souls of harlots, who, every night, took the same plunge." Chorley continued:

Benjamin Franklin, it is true, is painted in less peculiar colors than those employed to blacken the "City of Dis" London. But the philosophical printer, however available for the purpose of such a nice observer and delicate delineator as Mr. Thackeray, retains neither bone, nor muscle when dealt with by such a proficient in the "earthquake" and "alligator" style as Mr. Melville. He [Franklin] is selfish in his prudence, and icy in his calmness. Such, we take it was not the real Franklin. On the other hand, Paul Jones is a melodramatic caricature—an impossible mixture of a Bayard and a bully; and in a book where scene painting has been tried for, we have encountered few scenes less real than the well known attempt to burn Whitehaven, and the descent on St. Mary's Isle as told in "Israel Potter." Mr. Melville, to conclude, does not improve as an artist,—yet his book, with all its faults, is not a bad shilling's worth for any railway station reader, who does not object to small type and a style the glories of which are nebulous.

This was both the longest and the most adverse of the early reviews. Pure Chorley were the earthquake-and-alligator touch and the planned anticlimax of the deadly bit of faint praise at the end. I know of no other British comment in print on *Israel Potter*[37] during the century.

It would seem that the British reaction to *Israel Potter* was far less favorable than the American. Of course, a generalization based on two specimens is shaky, but the more widespread silence in England points to the same conclusion. In America Melville still had his articulate admirers in 1855, including those who thought his latest work as good as (*Mercury*) or even better than (*Evangelist*) his previous productions. It is only too easy to invent a hypothesis to account for the contrast in the impacts made by a book "thoroughly saturated with American sentiment" (*Commercial Advertiser*). The amateur psychoanalyst cannot help noting that Chorley selected to exemplify the vices of Melville's style a passage from his portrayal of London as Hades; and that both British critics disliked the American national hero who was so adept at annoying and making ridiculous the British.

THE PIAZZA TALES

The only collection of his stories Melville brought out was the *Piazza Tales*. Written as a preface and not previously published was "The Piazza"; the other five tales had appeared in *Putnam's Monthly Magazine*,[38] but had elicited only two press comments which I have located. The sole known mention of "Bartleby," had been in the *Literary World* on December 3, 1853, and was quite flattering, describing it as "a Poesque tale, with an infusion of more natural emotion." "The Encantadas" was followed with great enthusiasm by the *Berkshire County Eagle,* which pronounced it, on March 10, more mature writing than *Omoo* or *Typee,* for here Melville had combined "the excellencies of his early and later styles to the advantage of both";

37. It was reviewed at length in July in the *Revue des deux mondes* by Émile Montégut, who saw it as a patriotic democratic legend, involving sublimation of humble facts so that Israel became a symbol of democracy in an aristocratic country.

38. "Bartleby, the Scrivener: A Story of Wall Street," in November and December, 1853; "The Encantadas or Enchanted Isles," in March, April, and May, 1854; "The Lightning-Rod Man," in June and July, 1854; "The Bell-Tower," in August, 1855; and "Benito Cereno," in October and November, 1855.

on April 7, "a work of genuine talent"; and on May 4, "a charming series of articles." Lowell was reported to have said of "The Encantadas" that "the figure of the cross in the ass's neck brought tears into his eyes, and he thought it the finest touch of genius he had seen in prose."[39]

About May 20, 1856, *The Piazza Tales* was published in New York by Dix and Edwards.[40] The first review was in the *Berkshire County Eagle* on May 30, probably by J. E. A. Smith. It was the "most readable" thing by Melville since *Omoo*; the tales were "graphic"; "less striking" than *Moby-Dick,* they were "more uniformly excellent" and "more free from blemishes than any of" his later books. "Bartleby" was "from life" and "one of the best bits of writing which ever came from" his pen. The next day the New York *Criterion* commented on each of the tales: "Bartleby" was "quaint"; "Benito Cereno" was "thrilling" and "powerful"; "The Lightning-Rod Man" was "indifferent"; "The Encantadas" was "charming"; "The Bell Tower" was "memorable."

The book received at least ten American notices in June. The Boston *Daily Evening Traveller,* on June 3, contained the longest of the contemporary discussions of "Bartleby": "a splendidly-told tale, which in itself renders the volume of value." Indeed, the *Traveller* had "no hesitation in saying that for originality of invention and grotesqueness of humor, it is equal to anything . . . of Dickens, whose writings it closely resembles, both as to the character of the sketch and the peculiarity of the style," and followed with a synopsis. As for the other tales, though five of them were "gorgeous in their way," they were so "deeply tinged" with the mystic as scarcely to be "appreciated or understood." On June 4 the Boston *Post,* surprisingly enough, had nothing hostile: the stories were all "readable and forcibly written."

The highest praise *The Piazza Tales* received in that century, so far as I know, was in the New Bedford *Mercury* on June 4, surely from William Ellery Channing, Jr. Expectations of "something good,"

39. Charles F. Briggs, first editor of *Putnam's* reported this comment in a letter to Melville (*Log,* p. 487). On April 10, 1854, the *American Phrenological Journal* mentioned "The Encantadas" as notable (*Log,* p. 486). In the spring of 1855, J. H. Dix, then editor of *Putnam's,* sought advice about "Benito Cereno" from George William Curtis, who liked it but objected to the "statistics" near the end of the tale.

40. On that day the book was deposited for copyright at the Clerk's Office in New York. It was released to the public between May 24 and 31. (Merton M. Sealts, "The Publication of Melville's *Piazza Tales,*" *Modern Language Notes,* LIX [January, 1944], 56-59).

aroused by the name of the "author of Typee and Omoo," were realized in the present volume, with its pleasant introductory sketch, and its "tales of all descriptions"—

tales of the sea and of the city, some of which are told with due gravity, like that of "Benito Cereno," and others, such as "The Encantadas" with that copiousness of fancy and geniality of imagination, which resemble Melville more nearly to Charles Brockden Brown, the great novelist than to either of our other American story-tellers. Hawthorne is more dry, prosaic, and detailed, Irving more elegant, careful and popular, but MELVILLE is a kind of wizard; he writes strange and mysterious things that belong to other worlds beyond this tame and everyday place we live in. Those who delight in romance should get the Piazza Tales, who love strong and pleasant sentences, and the thoughtful truths of a writer, who leaves some space for the reader to try his own ingenuity upon—some rests and intervals in the literary voyage.

Indeed, as can be seen from his comments on this book and on *Israel Potter,* more than anyone else in 1856, Channing envisioned Melville as a writer of really permanent importance.

Contributors to two Boston newspapers enjoyed looking at the book the next two days. All of the tales were, according to the *Puritan Recorder* on June 5, "characterized by a singularly graphic power"; according to the Boston *Transcript* "the numerous friends of Mr. Melville will peruse this volume with great pleasure"; for the "author's great powers of description" appeared "to admirable advantage." It would "have wide circulation in cultivated circles, and be a favorite book at the watering places."

The *Hampshire and Franklin Express* found, on June 13, "peculiar charm" in the *Piazza Tales,* as in "all of Melville's writings," as well as "a style of great beauty" and "graphic description." The characters were "life-like," and "the portraiture natural and beautiful," in "this work of an entertaining and highly cultivated writer."[41] In the Newark *Daily Advertiser* on June 18, the ex-sailor who had now for years been following Melville's career was surely the welcomer of a book "in the real Omoo and Typee vein," rejoicing that he had "laid his rhapsodizing aside, which savored too much of Swift, Rabelais and other such works, as suggests they were the fruit of his reading rather than his imagination." This book, however, evidenced "that he has neither 'run out' nor been overpraised, for the same freshness, geniality, and beauty are flourishing as of old."

41. Sent to me by Jay Leyda. "Toby" wrote on June 16 to Melville of reading the *Piazza Tales,* evidently with satisfaction (*Log,* p. 516).

After so many encomiums, the book received considerably cooler treatment on June 23, in the New York *Tribune*. The "peculiar traits" of the author's "genius" were found in *The Piazza Tales* in a "less decided form." There was here "something of the boldness of invention, brilliancy of imagination, and quaintness of expression" and "not a little of the perversity and self-will." "Bartleby" was "the most original," and "as a curious study of human nature" possessed "unquestionable merit." "Benito Cereno" and "The Encantadas" were "fresh specimens of his sea romances, but not improvements on his earlier ones." The other two tales were "ingenious rhapsodies."

The book was then noticed by two Salem newspapers, of which the *Gazette* on June 24 was the more approving. "Everything from" Melville's pen was "eagerly sought by his numerous admirers"; and of the six tales, three were "fine specimens of the author's widely recognized power as a story teller." The "first part of the story of the scrivener has a singular fascination, which it was impossible in the nature of things to keep up"; "The Encantadas" was "more in the vein of the wondrous traveller's tales, the sober telling of which won" his reputation; and "The Bell-Tower" was "a happy emulation, though not an imitation, of the style of Poe." (The preferences of the *Gazette* do seem peculiar). The *Register,* of the same town, on June 26 perhaps intended its single sentence to be less sarcastic than it sounds: "The characteristics of Melville's style, and the peculiar turn of his mind are known to a multitude of readers, who will recognize in these tales their true paternity."

The reviewer for the *Southern Literary Messenger* for June, probably John R. Thompson, had never heard of *Israel Potter* (it was some distance from New York to Richmond), for he referred to Melville's "last appearance as an author, in 'Pierre'"—"rather an unfortunate one," in his opinion; but he found in *The Piazza Tales* "much of his former freshness and vivacity." The best was "The Encantadas," for in that "he conducts us again into that 'wild, weird clime, out of space, out of time,' which is the scene of his earliest and most popular writings." A "very flat recital," unworthy of Melville, however, was "The Lightning-Rod Man."

In July *The Piazza Tales* seems to have attracted less attention, though what was written continued to be mainly complimentary. Mrs. Ann S. Stephens in her *New Monthly* that month could "heartily recommend them" as "fine reading." It was probably William Young who in the *Albion* on July said that the "brilliant and erratic" Melville showed in these tales, "imperfect as they are," that he was "brimful of talent." He listed them all, but commented specifically only on "The Bell Tower," as a "fine conception, rather bunglingly worked out." But the Springfield *Republican's* critic, perhaps Dr. Holland, like Channing, ranked the stories with those of Hawthorne: "Marked by a delicate fancy, a bright and most fruitful imagination, a pure and translucent style, and a certain weirdness of conceit," they were "not unlike, and seem to us not inferior to, the best things of Hawthorne." Rather disappointingly, however, he singled out for praise only "The Piazza,"—"one of the most graceful specimens of writing we have seen from an American pen."

I have found one August notice only. "The Bell Tower" on August 8 appealed to the Berkshire County *Eagle* because it was "a picturesque and arabesque tale well fitted to inspire an artist, as it did one in New York who has made four striking sketches from it." The *Eagle* thought the author, now in his prime, would go on to even better achievement.[42]

September brought a little flurry of renewed interest, as the volume was looked at by three prominent American magazines. But *Godey's Lady's Book* was definitely chilly. Melville had "numerous admirers, and perhaps his writings render him worthy of them," *Godey's* said, but "we cannot read his productions with much satisfaction. His style has an affectation of quaintness which renders it, to us, very confused and wearisome." But his admirers would "not think worse of him after reading this book." Clark, in the *Knickerbocker,* though brief, was complimentary, declaring that the stories, "though partaking of the marvelous, are written with the author's usual felicity of expression, and minuteness of detail," and—something the modern reader has probably been waiting for—had commendation for "Benito Cereno" as "most painfully interesting" so that "in reading it we became nervously anxious for the solution of the mystery it involves." Something of a left-handed compliment, perhaps, but that was the one tale singled out by Clark for mention. "The book will repay a perusal," he concluded.

The *Democratic Review* dealt handsomely enough with the volume in general—"a collection of tales upon which he seems to have lavished even more than his usual care, and all of which exhibit the peculiar

42. The comment in the *Eagle* was a postscript to the article "A Trio of American Sailor Authors," which it reprinted from the Dublin *University Magazine* (*Log*, p. 519). Leyda identifies the artist as "Webber." There was an inconsequential mention of the book in the August *Putnam's* (*Log*, p. 518).

richness of language, descriptive vitality, and splendidly sombre imagination which are the author's characteristics." It referred particularly to three: "The Lightning-Rod Man," which "excited great attention when originally published"; "Bartleby," in which admirers of Poe might see an "imitation of his concentrated gloom"; and "The Bell Tower," wherein there was "a broad tinge of German mysticism, not free from some resemblance to Poe." The *Democratic* said nothing, however, about "The Encantadas" or "Benito Cereno." Yet, its final word was that "the tales are perfect in themselves, and would each form the feast of a long summer's noon."

So the day of *The Piazza Tales* with the American reviews was over. What were the statistical results? "Bartleby" was the favorite, with three votes for first prize, besides the encomium it received when it was just a magazine item; and for one critic it was worthy of Dickens (*Traveller*).[43] Next was "The Encantadas," with two firsts.[44] "The Piazza" got one "Oscar." "The Bell-Tower," three honorable mentions; and "The Lightning-Rod Man" two booby prizes. Of the fifteen notices only one was really negative (*Godey's*), two cool, and twelve completely positive. Thus statistically the book was a decided success with the press.

In the volume was "Benito Cereno," which Edward J. O'Brien was to place first in 1928 in his list of "The Fifteen Finest Short Stories";[45] and of which in 1947 Stanley T. Williams was to say that only then were "we beginning to realize the perfection of its form and the subtleties of its meaning," and that as the work of a "great novelist" it had "indescribable beauty."[46] Only three of the first reviewers even mentioned it, of whom one found it "painfully interesting" (Clark), and another described it as "thrilling" and "powerful" (*Criterion*). Yet the inadequacy of the reactions, and, even more, the silence of the great majority about this tale seem woof of the same cloth of which the warp was the increasing obliviousness to *Moby-Dick*. Melville was getting a fairly good income from his magazine contributions, but the critical disregard of those tales and sketches which were in the magazines but not collected in book form—especially "I and My

43. Arvin, p. 244, does place "Bartleby" first. More representative of modern opinion is Howard, p. 220: "Neither *Moby-Dick* nor *Pierre* had been so completely and pervasively charged with provocative implications" as "Benito Cereno."

44. Briggs, as editor of *Putnam's*, wrote Melville: "The only complaint that I have heard about the Encantadas was that it might have been longer" (*Log*, p. 488).

45. *Forum*, LXXIX (June, 1928), 906-914.

46. "'Follow Your Leader': Melville's 'Benito Cereno,'" *Virginia Quarterly Review*, XVIII (Winter, 1947), 61-79.

Chimney"—tales and sketches which have during the last ten years been studied so intensely,[47] was another indication that the America of 1856 had no real conception of the significance of his work.

Fitz-James O'Brien, in 1857, did extoll (with justice, surely) "The Encantadas": "Mr. Melville balances the charm, truth and hazy golden atmosphere of 'Las Encantadas' against the grotesque absurdity and incomprehensible verbiage of the 'Lightning-Rod Man'"; but he did not mention "Benito Cereno" or even "Bartleby." The anthologists of the later nineteenth century exhibited a curious predilection for selecting as representative specimens of Melville's prose the lesser of *The Piazza Tales*.[48] The book itself was never reprinted; nor was there a new edition until 1924.

The Piazza Tales had not done too badly in America, but when it crossed the Atlantic, it had to face the energetic and relentless Henry F. Chorley. In London it was issued from the American sheets, rather than actually published, by Sampson Low, Son and Company, in June.[49] It contained "delightful stories," said the London *Atlas*;[50] but on July 26 Chorley, in the *Athenaeum,* consigned it to—he could imagine no worse destiny—the adolescents. Americans—Irving, Poe, Hawthorne—excelled in the short story, he granted; and Melville might "deserve to be added to the list," but here he had given us "merely indications, not fulfillment." Was it really cricket to make no mention of "Bartleby," "Benito Cereno," or even "The Encantadas," and give most of his space to an attack—with quotations—on "The Bell-Tower," a work he pronounced "barely intelligible"? Melville would have to put up with a "very young public"; adults would "lay by the rhapsody and raving in favor of something more temperate," Chorley declared, and concluded: "The legends have a certain wild and ghostly power; but the exaggeration of their teller's manner appears to be on the increase." That Melville was getting "wilder and wilder," as Chorley had said in reviewing *Israel Potter,* was now with him a fixed idea. Surely his was an erratic reading of *The Piazza Tales,* so much more

47. For example, Chase, pp. 163-167, 168-175.
48. Melville was represented in Rossiter Johnson's *Little Classics* (Boston, 1875) by "The Bell-Tower." In the Stedman and Hutchinson *Library of American Literature* (New York, 1899) the only selections from Melville were "The Bell Tower" and a few poems from *Battle Pieces.* "The Lightning-Rod Man" was included in a collection entitled *Capital Stories by American Authors* (1895). Chase thinks even "The Lightning-Rod Man" worth two pages of discussion, but gives ten to "Benito Cereno."
49. *Log,* p. 517.
50. Minnegerode, p. 172, quotes from the notice in the *Atlas.*

disciplined, modern critics would say, than *Pierre*.[51] From other British journals, and for the rest of the century, there was only silence for Melville's book of stories.

THE CONFIDENCE-MAN: AMERICAN RECEPTION

No external evidence has been found to help determine to what extent *The Confidence-Man* was wrought with the aim of satisfying the average reader; internal evidence points to its author's having been mainly concerned with saying what he wanted to say. *The Confidence-Man: His Masquerade* was published in New York by Dix, Edwards and Company on April 1, 1857.[52] The first press mention seems to have been in the Boston *Evening Transcript* on April 3, and was a mere remark that the volume would be "warmly welcomed" by Melville's admirers, and that it was commendable "as a unique affair." The Boston *Daily Advertiser* on April 8 noted that the scene was a western steamboat; declared that the "confidence man" succeeded in getting the passengers' money with "rather more facility than is quite natural"; offered a fairly good statement of the theme: "... that the world is full of knaves and fools, and that a man who ventures to believe what is told him, necessarily belongs to the latter class"; but did not venture any general judgment.

The Boston *Evening Transcript* on April 10 copied from the *Knickerbocker Magazine* the most favorable of the American reviews,[53] whose author was much pleased with Melville's original and effective use of fresh American materials. "One of the indigenous characters who has figured long in journals, courts, and cities," he said, was "the Confidence Man," whose "doings form one of the staples of villainy, and an element in the romance of roguery." "Countless are the dodges attributed to this ubiquitous personage, and his adventures would equal those of Jonathan Wild." No wonder "the subject caught the fancy of Herman Melville—an author who deals equally well in the material descriptions and the metaphysical insight of human life. He has added by his 'Confidence Man' to the number

51. Chase, p. 149 says that "the Melville who wrote *Bartleby* and *Benito Cereno*, and even *Billy Budd*, was an authoritative and efficient artist"; and p. 150, "On the aesthetic principles of unity, coherence, and style *Benito Cereno* is one of the best single pieces Melville ever wrote." Matthiessen, p. 373, calls the latter "one of the most sensitively poised pieces of writing Melville ever produced."

52. *The Confidence-Man*, ed. Elizabeth S. Foster (New York, 1954), Introduction, p. xxxi.

53. At the end of this review was this: "—*Knick*."

of original subjects—and achievement for the modern raconteur, who
has to glean in a field so often harvested."

In his article on Melville in the April *Putnam's Monthly*, Fitz-
James O'Brien revealed measured fondness for *The Confidence-Man*,
but did not regard it as its author's worst; it belonged to the "metaphysical and Rabelaistical class" of his writings, but in it he "is more
reasonable, more respectful of the probabilities, possibilties, and the
weak perceptions of the ordinary mind than he usually is when he
wraps his prophetic mantle about him. The 'Confidence Man' is a
thoroughly American story." It was perhaps O'Brien also who exhibited the rather cool approach in the "Books of the Week" column
in the New York *Evening Times* on April 11. He thought this Confidence-Man almost "as ambiguous an apparition" as Pierre, who was
"altogether an impossible and ununderstandable creature." In the
new book, however, there "was no attempt at a novel or romance";
and as the author had "not the slightest qualifications for a novelist,
. . . he appears to much better advantage . . . than in his attempts at
story books" in this "Rabelaisian piece of patchwork without any of
the Rabelaisian indecency." Yet he could admire the style almost as
much as the British were to: "The oddities of thought, the felicities of
expression, the wit, humor, and rollicking inspiration are as abundant
and original as in any of the productions of this most remarkable
writer."

Melville's sister Augusta wrote on April 15, "Today's mail brought
us several highly complimentary notices of Herman's new book 'The
Confidence Man,' "[54] a statement that suggests the possible existence
of early April favorable reviews I have not found. The very next
day, April 16, the Boston *Puritan Recorder* was briefly flattering according to its lights: "This book was got up for amusement, and in
that view it is no failure. Its reading may be very useful to dyspeptics."
This was not the only case of a nineteenth-century reader taking the
book more lightly than have recent scholars.

The Worcester *Palladium* in April balanced faults and merits,
finding a little preponderance of the former. "A great deal of material
in the work" deserved "better setting than the author has given it,"
and was "not worthy of him." Unusual was the *Palladium's* judgment that the "careless rambling style . . . would seem to have been
easier for the author to write than for his readers to peruse." There

54. *Log*, p. 572. There would not, of course, have been time for the April 11 ones,
discussed below, to cross the Atlantic.

were "bright flashes in it; scintillations of poetic light, and much common sense well expressed, but the book as a whole is somewhat heavy." Still there were "minds with which it will chord; and as it pictures nineteenth century notions it will command attention." The central figure was a character type we see "every day, and often in the same light as does our author."

The technique but not the underlying implications appealed to the Springfield *Republican's* reviewer, perhaps Dr. Holland. He declared it "the oddest, most unique, and the most ingenious thing" Melville "has yet done. . . . The book is very interesting, and very well written, but it seems to us like the work of one not in love or sympathy with his kind. Under his masquerade, human nature—the author's nature—gets badly 'cut up.' "

Most adverse of the American opinions was that in the Newark *Daily Advertiser* on May 23. Was the one-time sailor, who in this paper had for years shown such a liking for the sailor author, disappointed to find him on such a tack? Or was this a different contributor? Whoever he was, he was now sour enough: "Melville, certainly a man of great talent, manages to write the most unreadable books. The one before us is a manifest improvement upon the last; for a certain class of persons, those who read police reports, will relish this record of trickery and deceit. It seems as if Melville was afraid to write as well as he can, or else he has the dyspepsia. Nothing else can account for such vagaries."[55]

Evidently resentful of the enjoyment the *Saturday Review* had got out of Melville's satire on the American pursuit of the dollar, the *Berkshire County Eagle* quoted on June 19 from that London magazine to add, "We need not say to those who have read the book that as a picture of American society it is *slightly* distorted."[56]

In the June *Mrs. Stephens' Illustrated New Monthly*, Mrs. Ann S. Stephens herself wrote on *The Confidence-Man*. How typical of the times she was in lamenting that Melville "seems now to be bent upon obliterating his early successes," and that he "appears now to be merely trying how many eccentric things he can do." His style, she admitted, had "become more individualized—more striking, original, sinewy, compact," and in the new book the "philosophizing was sharp, comprehensive, suggestive, and abundantly entertaining." Yet for her

55. On April 25, *Porter's Spirit of the Times*, a New York newspaper, had this item: "We have not read this book, but the announcement of the author's name is a guarantee of its interest and literary merit."
56. *Log*, p. 580.

it added up to a baffling futility, because "the object of this masquerade" was not evident. "The book ends where it begins. You might, without sensible inconvenience, read it backwards."

The American jury had been almost evenly divided about *The Confidence-Man*. Three comments were completely favorable, of which only one could be considered a review (*Knickerbocker*); one was almost entirely approving (Dr. Holland's paper); one was in-between (*Palladium*); one entirely negative (Newark *Advertiser*); two thought the style felicitous but the total effect a failure (O'Brien, Mrs. Stephens). There was still to be a British review in July, much more commendatory than hers, but Mrs. Stephens' was the last American review of a prose work by Melville I have discovered. If after that month, any American, before 1921[57] wrote about *The Confidence-Man*, I have no knowledge of it.

THE CONFIDENCE-MAN: BRITISH RECEPTION

The Confidence-Man, curiously enough, fared much better across the sea. Melville achieved for it an English publication only two days after the American, on April 3 by Longman, Brown, Green, Longmans and Roberts,[58] under the same title it bore in America. Melville had probably been in London about November 1,[59] the previous fall, and had then opened the way for its acceptance by the London firm. The influence of Hawthorne, then Consul at Liverpool, had no doubt helped. The firm did a good job of advertising it in the London *Morning Herald* and *Morning Post*.[60] No book of Melville's since *The Whale* had been introduced to the British public under such impressive British auspices; and no book of his since had created such a stir as it was to create in London intellectual circles; for within a week after its publication it was, on April 11, reviewed by no fewer than four of the leading London literary periodicals, in each case with some thoroughness.

Of the four Londoners who wrote on *The Confidence-Man* on that April 11, the *Spectator's* critic, perhaps Thornton Hunt, was the most adverse; indeed he had not one good word to say. Long unfriendly

57. Weaver, even in 1921, gave it short shrift (p. 348).

58. According to an advertisement by the publishers in the London *Morning Herald* on Wednesday, April 1, 1857, *The Confidence-Man* would "be published" on "Friday next"—April 3. Foster, p. xxv, gives the date as April 8.

59. *Log*, pp. 526, 531. The agreement with the English publishers was signed in March by Hawthorne acting for Melville (*Log*, p. 560).

60. It was advertised by Longman, etc., in the *Morning Herald* not only on April 1, but also on April 6, 7, and 8; and in the *Morning Post* on April 6 and 8.

to Melville, the *Spectator* had been terribly hard on *The Whale*. Now in the new book "the precise design" was "not very clear"; "Satire on many American smartnesses, and on the gullibility of mankind which enables these smartnesses to succeed is indeed an *evident object* of the author," an object poorly enough achieved, the reviewer declared (after some summary of the plot), because of "the defective plan and the general flatness of execution." Besides, Melville had allowed "too great success on the part of the rogues"; and, he insisted—curiously enough—that the cruelty to the poor could not be as bad in America as Melville pictured it. He summed up: "He stops short of any continuous pungent effect; because his plan is not distinctly felt, and the framework is very inartistical," and for the English reader at least, a difficulty was the "local allusions."

Only a little less harsh was the *Literary Gazette* on the same day. It granted there were some gleams of subtle thought, and the substance had value; but the form made it seem "the composition of a March hare." The reader would experience "dizziness in the head"; for it certainly was not an achieved novel (nor had been *Moby-Dick,* according to the *Gazette's* review of that work). Now the *Gazette* did not want to be "confounded with the cold unimaginative critics, who could see nothing in our author's earlier fictions"—*Mardi,* with its "lovely descriptions" and "glittering reaches of vivid nautical narrative"—"the conception of 'The Whale,' ghostly and grand as the great gray sweep of the ridged and rolling sea." "But these wild beauties were introduced to us with a congruity of outward accompaniment lacking here." All had been excused by those exotic settings; but here we had a Mississippi steamboat! There might be a "method in all this madness"; the author might have had "a plan, which must needs be a very deep one indeed. Certainly we can obtain no inkling of it." There were "bright bubbles of fancy"—"the greater the pity to see these good things so thrown away." He gave evidence of "much latent genius, which, however, like latent heat, is of little use either to him or to us." We could welcome him "as the prose poet of the ocean," but "he has ruined this book, as he did 'Pierre' by a strained effort after excessive originality." When would he discover that "standing on the head makes not either for ease or dignity"?

But there were two other reviews that day, the big surprise being the one in the *Athenaeum,* for it could scarcely have been more favorable. There are arguments both for and against its having been written by Henry F. Chorley. After his successive execution of each of

Melville's books since *White Jacket,* it is difficult to imagine his finding any good in Melville, who, he said, had been "getting wilder and
wilder." On the other hand, the depreciators of *The Confidence-Man,*
and there are such even today, may think it a peculiarly ironic gesture
for Chorley, after having so harmed Melville's reputation, to offer to
him this valedictory of lauding to the skies this most difficult and
sardonic of his works. At any rate, the reviewer, probably Chorley,
delighted in this "morality enacted by masqued players." He did think
the sequel might be needed before one could be sure "as to the lucidity
or opaquencess of the author's final meaning." But hear this: "Mr.
Melville is lavish in aphorism, epigram, and metaphor. When he is not
didactic, he is luxuriously picturesque, and although his style is one,
from its peculiarities difficult to manage, he has *now obtained mastery
over it, and pours his colours over the narrative with discretion as
well as prodigality* [the italics are mine]." No such favorable judgment was passed on the book, even in the early years of the Melville
revival. In 1949, however, Chase said that in *The Confidence-Man*
Melville employed "a style unique among his writings for its leanness,
nimbleness, and jaunty vigor."[61] The characters, said Chorley, all
"enrich the colloquy," and are "a little world of persons mutually interested, generally eccentric, but in no case dull." After a sympathetic
listing of these figures, and excerpts chosen as specimens of excellent
writing, he concluded: "Full of thought, conceit, and fancy, of affectation and originality, this book is not unexceptionally meritorious, but
it is invariably graphic, fresh, and entertaining."

The praises in the *Athenaeum* were outdone by those in the *Leader,*
also on April 11. Probably the critic was Lewes, admirer of *The
Whale* and *Israel Potter,* who was still contributing to this magazine.[62]
He took the central philosophical issue in *The Confidence-Man* to be
the question "Are men to be trusted?" This was worked out so that
"festoons of exuberant fancy decorate the discussions of abstract problems" on a background of "vivid, natural Mississippi landscape. . . .
The narrative is almost rhythmic, the talk is cordial, bright American
touches are scattered over the perspective." In the Pacific stories, Melville had used an Indian pencil: "His books were all stars, twinkles,
flashes, vistas of green and crimson, diamond and crystal." Now he

---

61. *Op. cit.,* p. 185.

62. B. C. Williams, p. 143. A possible argument against his being the contributor
is that he and George Eliot were then on the Scilly Isles, where, however, they were
continuing their literary work, though less strenuously. "Wherever we are, we work
hard," Marian wrote from there to a friend (Hanson, p. 196).

has used "neutral tints"; and "he has added satire to his repertory, and as he uses it scrupulously, he uses it well." Lewes had one demur: "His fault is a disposition to discourse upon too large a scale, and to keep his typical character too long in one attitude on the stage." But Lewes's conclusion was highly adulatory: "The charm of the book is owing to its originality and to its constant flow of descriptions, character-sketching, and dialogue, deeply toned, and skillfully contrasted."

Not so enthusiastic, yet definitely favorable, were the comments four days later on April 15 in the London *Critic*: "Herman Melville, hitherto known to us as one of the brightest and most poetical word-painters of places, here adventures into quite a new field, and treats us, under the form of a fiction, to an analytic inquiry into a few social shams. The machinery of the story, or drama, as it may perhaps be more accurately called, is simple enough; it is in the filling up that the skill and ability are apparent." There had been in his other books also "a vividness and an intensity about his style which is almost painful for the constant strain upon the attention," and *The Confidence-Man* was "of all his works" the one "which readers will find the hardest nut to crack." The *Critic* was not sure it had cracked it; there might be a "meaning hidden," as a "dry vein of sarcastic humour" perhaps implied. Yet more acceptable than any other contemporary's would seem to be the *Critic's* cracking of the nut thus: There was not enough real confidence in the world, but a great deal of imitation confidence: yet confidence was the foundation of happy human intercourse. The confidence man himself, however, might be "an arch imposter."

On April 18, the London *Examiner* had a friendly notice: "Mr. Herman Melville, a clever American author, whose Marquesas Island story no reader can have forgotten, has published a fanciful work which he calls a 'Masquerade.'" The *Examiner's* brief summation of Melville's satiric theme revealed real perusal of the book; "We are only ready with a blind trust in the man who has raised mists of self-interest before our eyes. We have not much confidence in any man who wants to borrow money with his honour as security." (Forster was no longer editor of the *Examiner*.)

John Bull,[63] who had been, all in all, a staunch supporter of Melville through the years, was loyal as ever on May 11, if somewhat less complimentary than Lewes. Melville, said *John Bull*, made "an ex-

___

63. On April 12, 1856, *Britannia*, which had shown a good deal of interest in Melville, had been incorporated with *John Bull*.

cellent master of the ceremonies, rushing hither and thither among the motley crowd, with no ostensible object saving that of making himself agreeable to everybody, and turning everybody to account for his own jaunty purpose."[64]   Indeed there was not much of a story "to tie together the pen-and-ink sketches of American life with which the volume is crowded." Yet there was "a vein of philosophy that runs through the whole," and the conflict between the feeling of trust and distrust "of which every human breast is . . . the perpetual battlefield, has not often been so forcibly as well as amusingly illustrated as it is in the incoherent ramblings of 'the confidence man.' "

A critic in the *Saturday Review,* to which George Eliot and also Lewes were contributors,[65] on May 23 scolded Melville severely for his "irreverent use of Scriptural phrases," yet had for the most part enjoyed the book immensely. He cautioned against taking the book seriously. It was "an Autolycus, or Falstaff, or Flibbertigibbit" among books. Of course such books were "quite wrong—there are other people in the world besides those who cheat and those who are cheated—all pleasant folk are not rogues, and all good men are not dull and disagreeable." The truth was the opposite, and if Melville were serious, he should be gravely condemned. Obviously, however, all he wanted to do was "to entertain," and this aim "has been fully attained in the volume before us"; for the characters "are all wonderfully well sustained and linked together," and the scene gave scope for Melville's "satirical pencil." The China Aster story might be a valuable warning to borrowers of money. There was "considerable power" in Melville's severe attack on "the pretended philanthropical, but really hard and selfish optimist school."

The appeal of the unflattering picture of American life to British readers was evident in his conclusion, but he had the grace to admit the portrayal was not inapplicable to England: "The money-getting spirit which appears to pervade every class of men in the states, almost like a monomania, is vividly portrayed in this satire, together with the want of trust and honor, and the innumerable 'operations' or 'dodges' which it is certain to engender. . . . We are not much behind the Americans in this vice . . . and we gladly hail the assistance of so powerful a satirist as Mr. Melville in attacking the most dangerous and debasing tendency of the age."

64. Recall that Chase describes the style as having "jaunty vigor."
65. "The first of the year [1856] found all talents, as Marian put it, engaged on the new *Saturday Review*" (Williams, p. 119).

The last of the known reviews came in July, in John Chapman's *Westminster and Foreign Quarterly Review*.[66] Although not the most favorable of the London critiques, it still was basically a recognition of *The Confidence-Man* as a meritorious production. It showed Melville in "a new character"—"that of a satirist, and a very keen, somewhat bitter observer. It required close knowledge of the world, and of the Yankee world, to write such a book and make the satire acute and telling, and the scene not too improbable for the faith given to fiction. Perhaps the moral is the gullibility of the great Republic when taken on its own tack." The *Westminster* did raise an objection: there was a certain hardness, an absence of humor, of kindliness, "too much of the spirit of Timon," a lack of "the colors that exist in nature"; yet the last sentence showed the judgment to be after all a positive one: "Few Americans write so powerfully as Mr. Melville, or in better English, and we shall look forward with pleasure to his promised continuation of his masquerade. The first part is a remarkable work and will add to his reputation."

The last prose work Melville published thus received from the British a reception amazingly cordial[67] after their ambivalent reaction to *The Whale* and their hostility or indifference ever since. As George Eliot was a contributor not only to the *Saturday* but also to the *Westminster,* as well as a friend of Dr. Chapman, its editor, three of the essentially affirmative reviews—including the one probably by Lewes—had come from her circle, though there is no proof she wrote any of them. Of the nine British reviews, only two were really negative, if both rather violently so. Of the others, one had confessed some puzzlement (*Critic*), one had recoiled a little at the Timonism (*Westminster*), but at least three were completely positive (Chorley, *Leader, John Bull*), out of the seven which were basically tributes to the book as a powerful, brilliant, and entertaining satire.

The British, furthermore, were much more pleased with it than were the Americans, as well as much nearer to understanding it. An obvious explanation of the contrast would be Melville's derogatory picture of American morals and manners. One American did express resentment at this (*Eagle*); yet the text of only one British article (*Saturday Review*) supports such a theory; and almost the most

---

66. The editor, John Chapman, M.D., (who had just received this degree) may have written the review, but there were many other contributors to this then influential magazine.

67. The Pittsfield *Sun* reported on May 22 that *The Confidence-Man* "is critically noticed in most of the London literary papers" (*Log,* p. 569).

censorious of the Londoners thought American conditions could not be so bad as pictured (*Spectator*). Subconsciously, British satisfaction and American irritation at the spectacle of cozzening on the Mississippi steamboat may have had an effect; but one cannot help suggesting that the British journalists were more sophisticated connoisseurs of satire. Yet, even in England, as Elizabeth Foster pointed out, there was "confusion about the central intention," "almost complete failure to detect the underlying pessimism," and inability to realize that "religion itself is weighed and found wanting on every page of the book."[68]

Not until the later nineteen forties was a strong attempt made to win recognition for *The Confidence-Man*. Melville's only English biographer could pass over it in 1922 as "an abortion."[69] By 1944 Sedgwick was lauding it;[70] but it was Chase's belligerent advocacy of it as a "supreme achievement," and Elizabeth Foster's scholarly edition of it in 1954 that gave it at last a certain recognition.[71] Why this bitter book was welcomed more cordially in Victorian England than in the supposedly disenchanted nineteen twenties and thirties is something of an enigma. A partial explanation is the failure of the reviewers to perceive the true depths of its disillusionments.

68. *Op. cit.*, p. xxv.

69. John Freeman, *Herman Melville* (New York, 1926), p. 144.

70. *Op. cit.*, p. 187.

71. Dan G. Hoffman says, "Thanks to the recent efforts of Richard Chase, *The Confidence-Man* is at last beginning to gain recognition as Melville's 'second best book'" ("Melville's 'Story of China Aster,'" *American Literature*, XXII [May, 1950], 137). For another high estimate, see John W. Schroeder, "Sources and Symbols for Melville's *The Confidence-Man, PMLA*, LXVI (June, 1951), 363-380. Critics can be found who are still not converted, however.

Chapter IX: "DEAD LETTERS"

"On errands of life, these letters speed to death."—"Bartleby the Scrivener: A Story of Wall Street" (1853).

PITTSFIELD: A WRIT *DE LUNATICO*

In his correspondence Melville more than once commented explicitly on the vanity of fame. For example, writing in 1885 to his English admirer James Billson about their mutual admiration for the author of "The City of Dreadful Night," he said, "As to his not achieving 'fame'—what of that? He is not the less, but so much the more, and it must have occurred to you as it has to me, that the further our civilization advances upon its present lines, so much the cheaper sort of thing 'fame' becomes, especially of the literary sort."[1] More cogent, however, were his moldings of the relationship of the writer to publisher, critic, and public into brilliant satire in *Pierre* and "Bartleby the Scrivener."

Whatever may be the defects of *Pierre,* those are sparkling pages in which Melville recounts the fatuous adulation the public poured upon Pierre's juvenile efforts, particularly "Tropical Summer: A Sonnet." This title inevitably recalls *Typee,* the object of almost equally undisciplined praise. Of course, neither is this trivial poem an exact image of a book which, after all, has power and originality; nor is the general reaction to it a precise duplicate of that to the book. To make the satiric point, the worth of the production is minimized, the abjectness of the adoration maximized. What is said about "Tropical Summer: A Sonnet" approaches what would have been said about *Typee* if its authenticity had not been doubted, and if it had not contained chapters which aroused accusations of "voluptuousness" and of shaking the foundations of western Christian culture. Even so, there were reviews of *Typee* perilously close to what the "mighty

1. Metcalf, *Herman Melville*, p. 270.

Campbell clan of editors of all sorts" said as they "spoke in high terms" of Pierre's "surprising command of language"; as they "begged to express their wonder at his euphonious construction of sentences"; and as they "regarded with reverence the pervading symmetry of his general style." From their flattery of Pierre emerges vividly the simulacrum of the Melville he felt his own audience wanted him to be. One, "in an ungovernable burst of admiring fury," says Pierre's manner is "characterized throughout by Perfect Taste." Another eulogizes Pierre as one who "never permits himself to astonish; is never betrayed into anything coarse or new; is assured that whatever astonishes is vulgar and whatever is new must be crude"; and declares "it is the glory of this admirable young author, that vulgarity and vigor—the two inseparable adjuncts—are equally removed from him."

How completely this Pierre would have satisfied that critic whose judgment nearly always—least so for *The Confidence-Man*—turned out, despite some presumptuous heretics, to be the judgment that was to prevail through Melville's three score years and ten; whose voice seems to have been the most heeded of the voices from Albion! According to Marchand, it was Henry Fothergill Chorley who "mirrored more truly the average opinions of the majority of the readers . . . than did almost any other [*Athenaeum*] critic";[2] because he felt "on the whole . . . more at home with the common English virtues and solid Victorian moralities";[3] and because, unmoved by personal or political considerations, he insisted only that literature should not be too disturbing. Chorley's promptly-made decisions that certain of the books of the Melville canon were worth preserving and others were for the burning remained virtually unchallenged up to the day Melville was buried. Chorley had a fatal gift for writing not for eternity but for time. I am afraid he is the villain of my chronicle.

The response of Pierre's readers, if not of Melville's, is tremendous. Wonder and Wen, who have recently abandoned tailoring for publishing, propose bringing out a collected edition of his works bound in "Russia leather." He receives bushels of albums from young ladies who want each inscribed with a bit of original verse and his autograph. He is invited to lecture at "Zadockprattsville." At first Pierre is gratified by all this, but it becomes more and more distasteful. What he particularly resents is the insatiable demand for information about his private life, for first a portrait of oil, then a daguerreotype for the

2. Marchand, p. 193.
3. *Ibid.*, p. 192.

"Captain Kidd Monthly," then for intimate details, such as "the precise texture and hue of the first trowsers he wore." Pierre at last rebels and takes an "ample parcel" containing the "Biographico Solicito Circular" and many silly fan letters he has received and sees it "eternally quenched in the fire." Like Neil Paraday in Henry James's "The Death of the Lion," Pierre discovers the heavy burdens of those who have become "contemporaries," and would have fully agreed with the narrator and Miss Hunter in that scintillating tale as to the deadly vulgarity of the biographical curiosity about the "lions."

When, however, Pierre produces his great book, on which he labors with an intensity and exaltation which recall for most readers Melville's writing *Moby-Dick,* he is never to have the chance to exhibit that "pyramidal scorn . . . for the whole infinite company of infinitesimal critics" he has built up in himself, because the book is rejected by his publishers after they earlier accepted it and actually began the printing.

Out of financial difficulties with publishers, out of resentment at expurgations forced on him while his books were going through the press, out of bitterness at certain critiques of *Moby-Dick,* Melville forged the satirical masterpiece, the letter to Pierre from his publishers, "STEEL, FLINT & ASBESTOS": "Sir: You are a swindler. Upon the pretense of writing a popular novel for us, you have been receiving cash advances from us, while passing through our press the sheets of a blasphemous rhapsody, filched from the vile Atheists, Lucian and Voltaire. Our great press of publication has hitherto prevented our slightest inspection of our reader's proofs of your book. Send not another sheet to us. Our bill for printing thus far, and also for our cash advances, swindled out of us by you, is now in the hands of our lawyer, who is instructed to proceed with instant rigor." Melville's actual relations with his publishers had never reached quite such an impasse; and the legality of the case of STEEL, FLINT & ASBESTOS against poor Pierre is more than questionable; but Melville had told Bentley that *Pierre* was intended to be a popular novel; and Bentley had demanded permission for "judicious . . . alterations" before publishing it, which Melville refused.

"Bartleby the Scrivener: A Story of Wall Street," a tale of apparent simplicity, is actually a potent portrayal of the artist's problem in a world of economic restrictions—a problem projected with a kind of masked yet specific utilization of certain facets of the situation

which then confronted Melville.[4] It has been shown that he was
to employ a similar technique in other tales in 1854 and 1855, especially "I and My Chimney." How could "Bartleby" have been a
satire on Thoreau, as Egbert S. Oliver has contended,[5] since *Walden*
was not to be published until eight months later?

One day Bartleby arrives unannounced to apply at the office of a
Wall Street lawyer for a position as a scrivener. He is hired, and at
first works with exemplary and even excessive diligence; but after
only three days, he announces that he "prefers not to" do proofreading;
and after a few weeks he decides that he "prefers not to" do copying
either. It would seem that he can no longer bring himself to perform
the duties of scrivener, who writes only what he is told to write (the
artist cannot endure to write on demand, without any possibilty of
self-expression).

Bartleby's lawyer employer, the narrator, is a sort of composite of
those men in Melville's life representing the practical or commercial
realm: his father-in-law Justice Shaw, and his uncle Peter Gansevoort,
who were both lawyers and both contributors to his financial support;
his brother Allan, who often served as his business manager and ac-
countant, was also a lawyer, and like the lawyer in the tale had his office
in Wall Street; and his publishers. Bartleby's employer is known, he
boasts, as an "eminently *safe*" man. Indeed he is virtually Bartleby's
publisher, as he gives to his clients the documents Bartleby "writes."
Toward Bartleby he—like Melville's lawyer relatives and his pub-

4. Probably first perceived by Mumford (p. 238), who, however, suggested only a
few general aspects of the projection. Leo Marx, "Melville's Parable of the Walls,"
Sewanee Review, LXI (Autumn, 1953), 620-627, says that " 'Bartleby' is a parable of
Melville's fate as a writer . . . who forsakes conventional modes because of an irresistible
preoccupation with the most baffling philosophical questions," the latter symbolized by
the wall Bartleby gazes at. This thesis seems plausible, but Marx misses the satiric implications of the other characterizations, which are brilliantly outlined by Chase
(p. 147).

5. "A Second Look at Bartleby," *College English*, VI (May, 1945), 431-439.
Oliver's theory was attacked by Alfred Kazin in "Ishmael in His Academic Heaven,"
New Yorker, XXII (February 12, 1949) on sound but mainly intuitive grounds. A
good part of Oliver's case is invalidated by the simple fact that *Walden* was published
after "Bartleby." Since, however, "Civil Disobedience" did appear in 1849, and Oliver
makes much of the fact that both Bartleby and Thoreau were put in jail, a few vital differences may be pointed out. Thoreau was jailed for non-payment of taxes, in protest
against imperialism; Bartleby for vagrancy, certainly involving no political protest.
Thoreau said he enjoyed being in jail; Bartleby merely drooped. Thoreau relished the
companionship he found there; Bartleby remained disconsolately solitary. Thoreau ate
hungrily his breakfast of "chocolate and brown bread"; Bartleby went on a hunger
strike. Thoreau emerged from jail defiant and rambunctious; Bartleby languished there
into silent death.

lishers—feels a sense of responsibility, along with alternating moods of deference and exasperation. If Bartleby won't write, he must get out and do something else. Much good to a lawyer is a non-writing scrivener; much good to a publisher is a non-writing author! Yet the narrator is kind, and might have let Bartleby linger in the deserted office, if his professional friends had not begun to make sinister insinuations. Lawyer and publisher alike must consider their professional standing.

Now this writer Bartleby tends to take on in a number of ways the contours of Melville himself in 1853. The health of both Bartleby and Melville posed a problem. During the spring of that year, Melville's family were greatly concerned about the strain he had been under, and his eyes had given trouble for years.[6] Bartleby's employer says, "I looked steadfastly at him, and perceived that his eyes looked dull and glazed. Instantly it occurred to me, that his unexampled diligence in copying by his dim window for the first few weeks of his stay with me might have temporarily impaired his vision."

Surely for Melville there was a joy in aesthetic creation; yet there is abundant evidence that for him the mechanics of writing were torment. He could not spell;[7] his handwriting was execrable. His insecurity about his ability to punctuate is illustrated in a note which accompanied the corrected proofs of *The Piazza Tales*: "There seems to be a surprising profusion of commas in the proofs. I have struck them out pretty much; but hope that someone who understands punctuation better than I do, will give the final hand to it."[8] Unlike many professional writers, Melville had never undergone an apprenticeship, in news office, print shop, or college, which helped to make the mechanics of writing a matter of course. His excruciating sufferings over proofreading were undoubtedly reflected in the reaction of Pierre to his sheets, which "were replete with errors": "preoccupied by the thronging and undiluted, pure imaginings of things, he became impatient of such minute, gnat-like torments; he randomly corrected the worst, and

6. *Log*, p. 468. As early as 1847 Melville's wife was writing, "He does not use his eyes but very little by candlelight" (quoted in Weaver, p. 266). Agonized passages about the aggravation of Pierre's optical difficulties by his "incessant application" are commonly taken as autobiographical (*Complete Stories of Herman Melville*, ed. Jay Leyda [New York, 1949], Introduction, p. xv).

7. To Duyckinck he wrote on December 12, 1850: ". . . my cousin—was crossing the R. R. track yesterday . . . in his slay—*sleigh* I mean—and . . ." (Metcalf, p. 96).

8. March 24, 1856. In the Melville papers in the Houghton Library at Harvard University.

let the rest go; jeering at the rich harvest thus furnished to the entomological critics." In such a state of mind was conceived the case of Bartleby, a man condemned to what seemed to Melville at the time the greatest of possible sufferings—to earn his living by copying and proofreading. Bartleby is able to stand the copying longer than the proofreading.

Perhaps Melville had a fear that he might be driven to subsist by a clerk's menial tasks, by literal copying. Copying and proofreading as an occupation is, however, essentially a reduction to absurdity of the occupation into which the publishers, as echoers of public opinion, seemed to be trying to force Melville. About a year before this, Bentley had made his position clear: he had written to Melville, "If you had restrained your imagination and written in a style to be understood by the great mass of readers—nay if you had not sometimes offended the feelings of many sensitive readers you would have succeeded in England."[9] The only criterion of excellence in the profession of scrivener is the precision of the copying—the exactitude of conformity to what the lawyer wants written. Hand, eyes, brain are wearied—to no ideal purpose—only to the receiving of a small stipend. So Bartleby "preferred not to."

Melville had not ceased entirely to write, but during the fourteen months between the appearance of *Pierre* in August, 1852, and of "Bartleby" in November and December, 1853, he had completed and published, besides "Bartleby," only one story, half as long, "Cock-a-Doodle Doo." He might have created, but did not, a "Tale of Agatha," which he urged Hawthorne to write, and which, after Hawthorne declined, he struggled with himself. Two short stories in fourteen months were not much for a man who was trying to make a living by writing.[10] For fourteen months he had fought against some psychological blockage until he found a way of getting going again by the catharsis achieved in the devising of the haunting tale of the scrivener who "preferred not to" write.

Particularly in the spring of 1853, Melville's family and friends had made in vain great efforts to secure for him a consular appointment, believing he needed desperately a relief from the toil of incessant composition; but he himself had shown little initiative in seeking such a position. His mother lamented that in his absorption

9. May 5, 1852, quoted by Jarman, "With Real Admiration," p. 312.

10. Another might-have-been book of this year was a work on tortoises, for which the Harpers actually made him an advance payment (*Log*, p. 482).

in a "new work" [Agatha?], he had "not taken proper and necessary measures to procure this earnestly wished for office."[11]

After it becomes clear that Bartleby will neither work nor quit the office, the lawyer urges him to get another job. Again Bartleby "prefers not to." He rejects the idea of a clerkship in a store as involving "too much confinement"; nor is he enticed by the prospect of employment as bar-tender, bill-collector, or companion for a young man going to Europe. So, as a vagrant, Bartleby is put in jail, where he prefers not to eat—and thus not to live. Lawyer Allan Melville "was particularly energetic in seeking out all possible sources of political influence," says Herman's granddaughter, Mrs. Metcalf,[12] but the plot to get Herman a consulate collapsed. It is not difficult to imagine the members of the family then urging Herman to try various other forms of employment.

As an artist, in the Berkshires at the end of 1853, Melville was isolated as he had not been for years. Of the three author friends who had afforded him the greatest stimulus and support, one of the two Duyckinck brothers had only too clearly signalized his defection by his review adjudging *Pierre* "loathesome" and "unintelligible"; and Melville had not, as he had the two previous summers, invited the Duyckinck brothers to visit at Arrowhead. Hawthorne had left the Berkshires two years before, and his friendship with Melville was never again to flourish as it had during the writing of *Moby-Dick*.[13] After the joy which the glowing letters of Nathaniel, and of Sophia too, about *Moby-Dick* had given its author, their silence about *Pierre* must have loomed up as a great vacancy. The friendless Bartleby "seemed alone, absolutely alone in the universe."

Now since "Bartleby," though it surely has deeper levels of psychological and universal significance, is on a surface level, full of strikingly definite allusions to Melville's personal situation in 1853, there may also be allusions, equally specific, to the contemporary scene, perhaps to the literati of New York, of Boston, of Charleston, and of London.

When Bartleby shows the first symptom of his growing negativism —refusing to participate in the proofreading—the lawyer turns to get from the other members of his staff their opinions of their recalcitrant

11. On April 20, 1853 (Metcalf, p. 147). His mother was convinced that the "constant In-door confinement" to which his "occupation as an author compels him, does not agree with him."

12. *Ibid.*, p. 146.

13. Arvin's summation of this controversial subject seems sound (p. 206).

co-worker. Chase's description of the other scriveners, Turkey and Nippers, as representing "middle-brow culture" is sound, at least as a starting point. He says they have sold out to commercial interests; that they stand for the "compromised artist," suspicious "toward Bartleby, their acknowledged superior as a scrivener—the attitude of the uneasy middle-brow toward the genuine artist."[14]

Is there not in the implications of these portraits of the two other scriveners a more circumstantial contemporary reference? Are they not, since they are writers of sorts, the *voices of* "middle brow culture," in other words, the critics, the reviewers?[15] These inferior and "compromised artists" have sold out to commercial interests by turning to magazine work, especially to book reviewing, for a living. Many of the early reviewers were novelists, dramatists, biographers, historians, poets, essayists, a few more "successful," but the majority less "successful," than the "Author of *Typee*," and the producers of extensive lists of works long since forgotten. Some of them may have been jealous. Melville knew these gentlemen. He had his opinion of them, but to present it explicitly would have been ineffective, as well as hardly chivalrous. But he has given it to us most suavely and powerfully under a not too opaque allegorical veil.

Turkey and Nippers are both subject to extreme and regular alternations of mood, oppositely timed: Turkey is civil and bland in the morning and rash and energetic in the afternoon; Nippers is edgily nervous in the morning and harmless in the afternoon. (Was it not so with the breed of reviewers, with their veering whims, their opinions depending often on nothing more profound than the time of day? Perhaps also here was an over-all summation of the notices to date of all Melville's books, half good, half bad). These two scriveners also have in common an egregious lack of discipline in their violent phases.

They, however, are also contrasted. Turkey is English; he is old; he is pursy; he drinks so much beer that his face flames. (John Bull!) He is phlegmatic, but erratic and insolent when aroused; and

14. *Op. cit.*, p. 147. Chase's view that "there is a profounder level" on which Melville partly identifies himself with the lawyer, whose qualities were a part of his personality, seems quite acceptable; as does also Arvin's theory that there is also a metaphysical level revealing men as "at once immitigably interdependent and immitigably forlorn" (*op. cit.*, p. 243).

15. Alexander Eliot in "Melville and Bartleby," *Furioso*, III (Fall, 1947), 11-21, sees in the tale Melville's portrayal of his rejection by his "readers." Marx, p. 621, says the "other scriveners" were "the writers society selects, and though not too lavishly, rewards."

in his exascerbated phase much given to making blots (stupid attempts at censure?) on his copy. The lawyer finds that in his excited phase he is ceasing to be an asset, and tries to get rid of him for the afternoon only, but the scrivener insists that if he is useful in the morning he must be useful in the afternoon also. The lawyer then tries to get Turkey to wear a coat of the lawyer's own, the scrivener's being so greasy; he accepts the gift but continues to be obstreperous in the afternoons. (Were publishers not often trying to control reviewers?)

Nippers is American; he is young; he is sallow; he is very temperate (Prohibitionist Horace Greeley?), but he has a built-in brandy supply in the nervousness of his temperament. He is the victim of ambition and indigestion; he seems impatient of being a mere scrivener, as is shown by his unwarranted drawing up of legal documents. (Many of the reviewers were trying to succeed as authors.) He is something of a "ward politician," having seedy visitors he calls his "clients." (Some reviewers were supposedly biased by political considerations.)

The first time the lawyer seeks to get from his other scriveners their reactions to Bartleby's refusal, it is morning and "Nippers' ugly mood was on duty, and Turkey's off." Hence Turkey merely says blandly that his employer is justified in requiring Bartleby to continue; Nippers, however, says "I think I should kick him out of the office." (Melville must do what the publisher abetted by the reviewers wants him to do—produce limpid sea stories without disturbing overtones— or else—.) The next time the lawyer interrogates them, it is afternoon, and their moods are, of course, reversed. Turkey now offers to black Bartleby's eyes (by means of a bad review); but Nippers gently replies that it is for the lawyer to decide: "I think his conduct quite unusual, and indeed, unjust, as regards Turkey and myself. But it may be only a passing whim." (Melville might come to his senses. "We strongly advise the author in the future to confine himself to more real and practical subjects," said *Britannia* in reviewing *Mardi*.)

The lawyer also quizzes Ginger Nut, surely the least qualified of all to offer an opinion, for he is just the janitor and office boy and only twelve, although "his father was a car-man, ambitious of seeing his son on the bench instead of a cart." Ginger Nut's reply is, "I think, sir, he's a little *luny*." (From the reviewer who was most immature and had the poorest background, although indeed his father was ambitious for him, came this most crushing of the judgments.)

Moby-Dick was "trash belonging to the worst school of Bedlam literature" (Chorley); its style was "maniacal . . . like an incurable

Bedlamite" (Ainsworth). *Pierre* was "a literary mare's nest (Duyckinck, the traitor!); it had "all the madness of Mardi, without its . . . charm" (O'Brien); its author had gone "clean daft," and "the sooner he was put in ward the better" (Simms—?). Forms of the word itself—*luny*—had been used more than once. *Moby-Dick* at times seemed nothing but "moon-struck lunacy" (London *Chronicle*). *Pierre* was a book such as "might emanate from a lunatic asylum" (Colonel Greene); it was "what a raving lunatic" might "spout" (Peck). Ahab's "ravings" and "the ravings of Mr. Melville himself" were "such as would justify a writ *de lunatico* against all the parties" (Simms—?). *Luny,* though not a Latin word, is italicized in Ginger Nut's answer in the tale, surely as a verbal guide back to the odious Latin phrase *de lunatico,* and to its English derivatives in those reviews which had seared most deeply. But how sane is a "Nut"? As for the other two scriveners, they are victims of an incipient manic-depressive psychosis, quite precisely delineated here by Melville, who has been credited by a prominent modern psychiatrist with anticipating many of the findings of depth psychology.[16] How deftly Melville, out in Pittsfield, has turned the "writ" against the reviewers!

On December 10, 1853, on a Saturday afternoon, according to the New York *Tribune* for the following Monday, a "destructive conflagration" broke out and "within a few hours the immense Book Publishing House of Messrs. Harper and Brothers . . . was a mass of smouldering ruins." The Harpers had been Melville's American publishers since *Typee,* and hundreds of unsold copies of his books were burned.[17]

In those days the modern custom of dating the issues of magazines as for the month subsequent to their actual publication had not been devised, and often many days of a month had passed before the number bearing the date of that month was really ready. For example, in 1846, Melville, though then in Lansingburgh, less than one hundred and sixty miles from New York City, had not by May 23 received his May number of the *Knickerbocker*.[18] It is highly probable that on December 10 the December number of *Putnam's Monthly,* containing the second half of "Bartleby," was not yet off the press, and that after the fire there was time for Melville to write and to submit to be added the two remarkable paragraphs, which were separated from the main body of the tale by a row of asterisks in the text as

16. Murray, p. xxvi.
17. Minnegerode, p. 97.
18. See Chapter II, footnote 42.

printed in the magazine (shown in my photostatic copy). The final paragraph consists only of the exclamation "Ah, Bartleby! Ah, humanity!" The preceding added paragraph intimates the cause of Bartleby's strange behavior. The lawyer had, like Pierre's fans, tried unsuccessfully to probe into Bartleby's biography (Murray had asked Melville for "documentary evidence" that he had been in the South Seas); but after Bartleby's interment, the lawyer had heard a "rumor" he passes on: Bartleby had been a "clerk in the Dead Letter Office at Washington, from which he had been removed by a change of administration." The lawyer exclaims: "Dead Letters! does it not sound like dead men? Conceive a man by nature and misfortune prone to pallid hopelessness, can any business seem more fitted to heighten it than that of continually handling those dead letters, and assorting them for the flames? For by the cart load they are annually burned." There is no mention of the dead letter office or the burning of letters in the portion of the story before the asterisks.

A stage in the disillusionment of the artist beyond that represented by Pierre, whose ambitious effort at self expression had been rejected by the publishers, is represented in Bartleby. He had found out what was the destiny of many letters—documents in which human beings, blunderingly or adroitly, try to say what they want to say, and which have, in the act of mailing, a virtual publication. In *White Jacket,* young Lemsford, a sailor poet, hides his manuscripts in one of the big guns. After the frigate arrives in Rio, the gun is fired, and Jack Chase declares, "That's the way to publish."[19] Even though the last two paragraphs of the story may possibly have been written before the fire, the dead letters still seem to represent some of Melville's books.[20]

Not all poems are published by being fired out of cannons; not all letters go to the dead letter office. Some of Melville's "letters" had reached their addressees: he was "the Author of *Typee.*" As for England, Bentley, thinking in terms of finances and disregarding the critics' welcome for *Redburn* and *White Jacket,* had written him shortly before the Harpers published *Pierre* that all his books had "with exception of Omoo and Typee proved failures."[21] As for

19. *White Jacket,* Chapter XLV.
20. Richard Chase takes the "dead letters" to be all of Melville's books, but it would seem that those of his books which had found fewer readers and far fewer comprehending readers were more appropriately called "dead letters" than *Typee* and *Omoo,* still popular in 1853.
21. Bentley informed Melville that by *Mardi* he had lost £68, by *Redburn* £76, by *White Jacket* £173, by the *Whale* £135. In a letter quoted by Jarman, p. 135.

America, if the books destroyed in the fire be arranged in increasing order of the number of the copies burned, this is the sequence: *Typee, Omoo, White Jacket, Redburn, Moby-Dick, Mardi, Pierre,* giving a plunging unpopularity curve as indicated by lack of sales.[22] Nor did that tell the whole story, as there had been of *Typee* three American reprintings, of *Omoo* four, of *Redburn* one, of the other four none. Thus, in comparatively large numbers, copies of his more daring books—*Mardi* and *Pierre*—and of his greatest book, had failed to be delivered to those perceptive readers he had hoped existed somewhere. The delayed critical reaction to *Moby-Dick,* moreover, had been very adverse in both countries. The books he thought his best had not been wanted; they had missed their destination; they had been in tall piles consumed in the "conflagration." Weren't the books he most cared about "dead letters," destined for the burning?

BARTLEBY TO BILLY BUDD

During the last part of Melville's life a legend arose that after *Moby-Dick* he soon lapsed into silence and oblivion. It persisted into the next century, especially during the early years of the Melville Revival, the twenties, and was not completely exorcised until near the end of the forties. There was no truth in the notion about the silence; but as for the oblivion, his reputation was indeed, at the time of "Bartleby," very near necrosis.

His moribund fame was only a little reanimated by *Israel Potter* and *The Piazza Tales,* accepted as pleasant but by few as really important; and not at all, at least in America, by *The Confidence-Man,* so fumblingly handled on this side of the Atlantic. The more cordial British discussion of that book made no impression over here, but may have had repercussions in England.

Standing as valedictory until thirty years had passed were the opinions of the *Dublin Review* critic in 1856 and of Fitz-James O'Brien in 1857, the last to assess Melville's total efforts to date. They concurred in completely deflating *Moby-Dick.* There was validity in O'Brien's report on the change that had been coming over Melville: "His life . . . has been excessively introverted. Much as he has seen of the world, and keen as his appreciation is of all that is true and suggestive in external life, he has turned away habitually, of late years, at least, to look upon his own imagination." Wherein a later century was to differ in its judgment, as expressed by Dr. Murray, that "extraordi-

22. Minnegerode, p. 97.

nary and portentous were the penetration and scope, the sheer audacity
of the author's imagination," especially in *Moby-Dick*,[23] which to the
Irish Irishman in 1956 and the American Irishman in 1857 was a
closed book.

Nor did Melville much enhance his renown by his four volumes of
poetry. Of these the first, *Battle Pieces* (1866) won the most favor
probably because, as a book of Civil War poems, it had topical appeal.
Of the nine notices or reviews it received, four were clearly positive.
It was declared to contain the "most stirring lyrics of the war" (*Harper's Monthly*); indeed, these "war lyrics" were "full of martial fire . . .
sometimes really artistic in form" though the "thought" was "too
vaguely expressed" (*Evening Post*—William Cullen Bryant?); they
were "not inappropriately rugged" (New York *Herald*); they "doubtless" would "find many admirers" (*Godey's*). By others *Battle Pieces*
was severely handled: no "real grasp on the causes and purposes of the
struggle"; none of the poems was "absolutely bad," but many "cannot be called good" (F. B. Sanborn, the abolitionist, in the Springfield
Republican); the book was "epileptic" (*American Literary Gazette*);
"Nature did not make" its author "a poet" (the *Nation*—Charles Eliot
Norton?); it was unreal, unconvincing (*Atlantic Monthly*). The
lukewarm ninth critic was no doubt correct in regarding it as "on
the whole . . . not adding to the reputation Mr. Melville has won by
his rich poetic prose" (Channing, in the New Bedford *Mercury*).

Clarel (1876), a poem in two volumes, totaling 571 pages, based
on Melville's travels in the Holy Land, received seven American reviews, of which the only one which was not crushing did find "the
verse flowing and musical" (*Library Table*). But it was elsewhere declared a "puzzle," with a "vein of earnestness . . . singularly at var-
iance with the carelessness of the execution" (New York *Daily Tribune*—Edmund Clarence Stedman?); the descriptions were good, but
"work of art it is not in any sense or measure" (The *World*—Richard
Henry Stoddard?); it was "sadly uninteresting" (The *Galaxy*—Arthur
C. Stedman?); and two concluded it should have been written in
prose (New York *Times, Lippincott's*). For America, the matter was
well enough summed up in a statement that his "literary reputation
will remain, what it has fairly become, a thing of the past—for all
that his new book will do for it" (Springfield *Republican*).[24]

23. "In Nomine Diaboli," *Moby-Dick Centennial Essays*, p. 5. See also Introduction
to *Pierre*, p. xiii.
24. Quoted by Leyda, "Another Friendly Critic for Melville," 247.

During these darkest decades in the story of Melville's fame, a much higher valuation was placed on his work in England than in his own land, as has been seen in the case of *The Confidence-Man*; and now, standing out in sharp contrast with the American cold dismissal of *Clarel*, was the almost amazingly warm encomium given the poem by the London *Academy*, on August 19, 1876, which, after summarizing its plot, pronounced it "a book of very great interest, and poetry of no mean order." The *Academy* declared that the "form" was "subordinate to the matter" and that "a rugged inattention to niceties of rhyme and meter here and there" seemed "deliberate rather than careless":

In this, in the musical verse where the writer chooses to be musical, in the subtle blending of old and new thought, in the unexpected turns of argument, and in the hidden connection between things outwardly separate, Mr. Melville reminds us of A. H. Clough. He probably represents one phase of American thought as truly as Clough did one side of the Oxford of his day. We advise our readers to study this interesting poem, which deserves more attention than we fear it is likely to gain in an age which craves for smooth, short lyric or song, and is impatient for the most part of what is philosophic or didactic.[25]

Since the other two volumes of verse, *John Marr* (1888) and *Timoleon* (1891) were issued in editions of only twenty-five copies of each, it is not surprising that there seems to have been only one review of the first and none of the second. The review was by Richard Henry Stoddard, probably in the *World*. He spoke highly of Melville's poetry in general, declaring "Sheridan at Cedar Creek" the "second best cavalry poem" in the language, but was noncommittal about the volume at hand.[26]

What the publication of *Billy Budd* (unpublished until 1924), which Melville was working on in the very year of the end of his life, might have then done to his fame can only be conjectured. Probably its scalpel-like ethical probing would have been only painful and bewildering to the Age of Innocence.

LEICESTER: CULT OF BABBALANJA

In June, 1881, James Thomson left the "City of Dreadful Night" to spend a holiday in Leicester. There he fortunately met John W.

25. Quoted, *ibid.*, 247.
26. *Log*, p. 811.

Barrs, who "quickly became one of his trustiest and most intimate friends," was soon "Jack" to him, and invited him to be a guest of him and his sister at their home, Forest Edge, four miles out of Leicester. He accepted and stayed at Forest Edge from about June 21 to July 25.[27] It was the happiest time in the latter part of Thomson's life, so happy indeed as to result in a diminution of his pessimism in the poems of the one year of life he had left.[28] He played tennis, listened to Barrs quote the whole of "The Rubáiyát"; and surely it was then that he introduced to Jack and his sister and their friend James Billson, who often came over from his own nearby country place, Bird's Nest, some books by an American they had never heard of, Herman Melville. Thus a tiny votive flame was kept burning in England.

It was probably Thomson who aroused the interest of the Leicester group in Whitman, too. Six years earlier, during the very nadir of Melville's fame, Thomson had tried to tell the British about him, in an article in the *National Reformer* for August 30, 1775, on Whitman, wherein he had said that he knew but "one living American writer" who approached Whitman "in his sympathy with all ordinary life and vulgar occupations, in his feeling of brotherhood for all rough workers, and at the same time in his sense of beauty and grandeur, and in his power of thought"—Herman Melville.

The seed planted by Thomson continued to grow after his death, for three years later—it was summer again at Bird's Nest—Billson, exhibiting some bashfulness, wrote to Melville to assure him that "here in Leicester your books are in great request." The "rapidly increasing knot of 'Melville readers' " had with difficulty obtained copies of his works, and were not satisfied to possess only *Mardi, Typee, The Confidence-Man, The Piazza Tales, Omoo, Redburn, Moby-Dick, Israel Potter,* and *Pierre.* What else had he written?[29]

Melville, although somewhat inclined to draw back in those years from visits of *aficionados*, responded warmly to this young correspondent, and wrote him nine charming letters. The Leicester group then thought of the perfect gifts for Melville, volumes of Thomson's poetry and criticism. It was a clever choice, for it greatly pleased

27. Henry S. Salt, *The Life of James Thomson*, rev. ed. (London, 1914), p. 120 (original ed., London, 1889).

28. *Ibid.*, p. 132.

29. Metcalf, p. 267. Billson cherished the letters, and made copies of them to send to Mrs. Metcalf (*ibid.*, pp. 267-271). He also printed them in the *Nation and Athenaeum*, XXIX (August 13, 1921), 712-713.

their American idol, who in thanking them wrote "your friend was a sterling poet if ever one sang," and sent them as a present *Clarel.*[30]

Possibly by Billson was an article in the London *Daily Telegraph* early in 1885, though if so, he had perhaps slanted it for popular consumption by omitting any discussion of his favorite *Mardi* and by declaring that "we owe those fancies of beauty, of peace, of waftings of aromatic sunlit air which possess the mind when the islands of the Pacific are named" to *Typee* and *Omoo.* Later that year Billson sent Melville a copy of Robert Buchanan's poetic tribute to Whitman in the *Academy* on August 15, in which he showed he was also fascinated by the "sea-magician" Melville, whose wand had evoked Leviathan and Fayaway. *Moby-Dick* seemed at least as important as *Typee* to Buchanan.

Acquainted with the Leicester group, from whom, if not directly from Thomson, he caught the spark of interest in Melville, was Henry Stephen Salt,[31] who had been a master at Eton, who was a friend of G. B. S., and who completed in 1889 his biography of Thomson and at almost the same time began to be active in keeping Melville's renown alive. He published late that year in the Edinburgh *Scottish Art Review* a supposedly comprehensive study of Melville's works, which he divided into two periods, the "Practical" and the "Phantasies," obviously preferring the former. For Salt *Typee* was still the work which "took precedence of all his other writings in merit no less than in date." At least better than *Mardi* was *Moby-Dick,* for in it the "extravagances" were more harmonized with the plot. He admitted that in the concluding scenes the author "rises to a sort of epic dignity and intensity." Yet he gave more space to *White Jacket* than to *Moby-Dick,* which actually seemed to horrify him. Where his heart lay was shown clearly a year later when he wrote to Melville proposing to get out a new edition of *Typee,* a project blocked by Murray.[32] Three years later in *The Gentleman's Magazine,* in a revised version of his earlier article,[33] Salt did evince a somewhat higher opinion of *Moby-Dick*: " 'The Whale,' faulty as it is in many respects, owing to the turgid mannerisms of Melville's transcendental

30. Metcalf, p. 269.

31. Salt said in *Company I Have Kept* (London, 1889), "I was brought into touch with Herman Melville through my biography of . . . Thomson. He was a great admirer of Melville." According to *Herman Melville: Representative Selections,* ed. Willard Thorp (New York, 1938), Introduction, p. cxxvii., it was Sidney Dobell, editor of Thomson's poems, who got Salt to read Melville.

32. Salt in 1892 edited *Typee* and *Omoo.*

33. Reprinted in the New York *Eclectic Magazine,* April, 1892.

mood, is nevertheless the supreme production of a master mind; let
no one presume to pass judgment on American literature unless he
has read, and re-read, and wonderingly pondered the three mighty
volumes of 'The Whale.'" A little comfort this might have been to
Melville if he had then been still among the living. Salt was, however,
careful to say again that *The Whale* was less important than *Typee,*
his attitude being shown only too clearly in the title of this second
article "Marquesan Melville."

Jack Barrs, at the request of "my friend Mr. H. S. Salt," sent Melville a copy of Salt's *Scottish Art Review* article, protesting vigorously
that he had not done justice to *Pierre* (according to Salt the "*ne plus
ultra* . . . of metaphysical absurdity"), which he had "always liked"
—the kindest words Melville ever heard about that book. Evidently
the Leicester group fostered a little cult of *Mardi,* for Barrs continued,
"I have a very deep rooted fondness for Babbalanja & consequently resented the way Salt dealt with the 2nd and 3rd volumes of Mardi."[34]
Billson had told Melville back in 1884, "I have liked the Mardi best."
They at Leicester were definitely not mere *Typee* addicts.

In his second article Salt mentioned that "among those who appreciate his work are William Morris, Theodore Watts, R. L. Stevenson, Robert Buchanan, W. Clark Russell." As for Stevenson, however,
he seemed aware only of *Typee,* and his attitude toward that was
quizzical. Salt told in *Company I Have Kept* (1889) of hearing
William Morris "quoting *Moby-Dick* with huge gusto and delight."[35]
Havelock Ellis, moreover, in 1890, revealed that he regarded Melville
as a "distinguished" writer.[36]

THANET: ONE FOR MOBY-DICK

There was another Englishman—the only one after 1851 of whom
Melville was to have any knowledge—who came out boldly and openly
for *Moby-Dick.* He was W. Clark Russell, one-time sailor, now successful author of sea tales. His article "Sea Stories" in the London

34. Metcalf, p. 278. Barrs continued, "I once read to Philip Bourke Marston the
chapter Lombardo & his Costanza to his great delight and altho' Marston was not
more than one of our best minor poets he was a true critic—He was so interested that
he obtained for reading all yr books accessible to him . . ."

35. Quoted by Thorp, p. cxxvii. English admirers not hereinabove mentioned but
listed by Thorp were Edward Carpenter, Louis Becke (who edited *Moby-Dick* in 1901),
James M. Barrie, John Masefield (much later), Augustine Birrell, and Sir Alfred Lyell.

36. Ellis wrote to Melville for information about his ancestry in connection with
studies he was making about the heredity of "distinguished English and American
poets and imaginative writers" (*Log,* p. 825).

Contemporary Review for September, 1884, is one of the most striking items in the whole chronicle of Melville's fame.[37]   What made it gleam, a star in the dark, was Russell's unequivocal declaration— "Whoever has read the writings of Melville must I think feel disposed to consider 'Moby Dick' as his finest work,"—followed by cogent reasons for this judgment.   It was not a mere nautical narrative like Cooper's and Marryat's novels.   The thread that strung together "a wonderful set of fancies and incidents" was "Ahab's revenge": "Melville takes this vessel, fills her full of strange men, and starts her on her insane quest, that he may have the ocean under and around him to muse upon, as though he were in a spacious burial ground, with the alternations of sunlight and moonlight and deep starless darkness to set his thoughts to.   'Moby Dick' is not a sea story . . . it is a medley of nobly impassioned thoughts born of the deep, pervaded by a grotesque human interest, owing to the contrast it suggests between the rough realities of the forecastle, and the phantoms of men conversing in rich poetry, and strangely moving and acting in that dim weather-worn Nantucket whaler."   The Forecastle chapter "might truly be thought to have come down to us from some giant mind of the Shakespearean era . . . full of extraordinary thoughts, yet gloriously coherent."

Furthermore, Russell declared that among the "poets of the deep," whose names could be "counted upon the fingers of one hand . . . I rank him first."   Dwelling on the limitations of the others, Russell went on to praise for their truthfulness, Dana and Melville, the latter especially in the works preceding *Moby-Dick*.

The article was twice reprinted in America;[38] and it led Melville— incidental testimony, if more be needed, to its uniqueness in those years—to initiate a correspondence with Russell.   Melville had responded cordially to the overtures of the Leicester circle, but had not been the prime mover.   Now in the late spring of 1886 he seized the gracious pretext of a mutual admiration for Dana to write to Russell. Nor was he satisfied with the mails, coldly impersonal, perhaps unreliable, but prevailed upon the artist Peter Toft, who had recently been his admiring visitor, to carry the letter in person to Russell at St. Lawrence-on-Sea, Thanet, in easternmost Kent.   He would run no risk of this being a dead letter!   It was a truly remarkable gesture for

37. Russell was reported in the New York *Herald* the previous December to have written a letter to magazinist A. A. Hayes suggesting that the latter write a life of Melville (*Log*, p. 783).

38. In the Philadelphia *Times* for June 21, 1885, and in the weekly Harper's *Handy Series* on December 25, 1885, in expanded form.

a man who so shunned publicity and the overtures of the American literati, and explainable on the basis of his satisfaction—not merely in finding another "sea brother"—but in discovering that a certain copy of *Moby-Dick* had been no dead letter, but had been delivered to one of its true addressees, at St. Lawrence-on-Sea. For thirty years there had been no such validated delivery.

Russell, as it can be well imagined, replied delightedly; letters quick with life crossed the Atlantic in both directions; and so grew a friendship which came nearer than any other—at least in the sunset years—to being to Melville what had once been that with "The Man of Mosses." It culminated in a pair of dedications, of *John Marr* to Russell in 1888, and of *An Ocean Tragedy* to Melville in 1889. Russell had preceded his dedication of his romance by only a month with an article in January, in the weekly Chicago *American,* reaffirming his faith in the supremacy of *Moby-Dick*: "I am sure there is no name in American letters that deserves to stand higher for beauty of imagination, for accuracy of reproduction, for originality of conception, and for a quality of imagination that in 'Moby Dick,' for instance, lifts some of his utterances to such a height of bold and swelling fancy as one must search the pages of the Elizabethan dramatists to parallel."

In his letters to Melville Russell tended to picture his American friend's British reputation in rosier colors than he did in published articles. In his 1884 article Russell had said "For one who reads Melville and Dana, thousands read Marryat. . . ." Two years later, in his first reply to Melville, he said, "Your reputation here is very great," and that it was "hard to meet a man whose opinion as a reader is worth having" who did not place "your works" above those of many "renowned English writers." Of course there could be truth in both statements; yet there is also in both obvious slanting. In Salt's second article, in April, 1892, he said the news of Melville's death "excited but little interest on this side of the Atlantic." Barrs' remark in his 1890 letter, representing a more median opinion, may be taken as a fair enough summary of the situation, "Notwithstanding the inadequacy of the recognition of your books on this side, they are not without warm admirers."

The record of reprintings would indicate that the books could hardly have been widely read in England. After "Bartleby" there were in England, of all Melville's books, before his death only the following reprintings: four of *Typee,* four of *Omoo,* one of *White Jacket,* and one of *Israel Potter.*[39] The English Melville enthusiasts

39. Hetherington, pp 491-497.

told of their great difficulties in securing copies. According to Clarence Gohdes, during the last two decades there was a great deal of issuing of American books in England, but there were fewer of those by Melville than by Poe, Lowell, Irving, Cooper, Holmes (seventy), Hawthorne (ninety), Emerson, Bryant, Whittier, Howells, or Mark Twain. There were even twenty each of Whitman and Thoreau; but only nine by Melville.[40] From the printers' records, the published articles, and the correspondence emerges the picture in England during Melville's last years of a small if ardent group of readers—and general neglect.

NEW YORK: CULT OF THE CANNIBALS

Three decades of virtual American silence about *Moby-Dick* were briefly interrupted at the end of the first two by a rather left-handed compliment when the Springfield *Republican* in 1876 spoke of the "masculinity, the rich imagination, the singular picturesqueness of 'Omoo,' 'Typee,' and 'Moby Dick,'" and said that "Melville lives in his novels a sort of posthumous life . . . yet they are worth reading, particularly the last, with those preposterous heroes, the White Whale, and Captain Ahab."

Ten years passed, and then, about seven years before Melville's death, in September, 1891, a few sporadic flickerings of response to *Moby-Dick* began to appear. Writing in 1900, the artist Peter Toft, who had, like Melville, been a sailor in a merchantman, a whaler, and an American man-of-war, described interviewing Melville in 1886. Toft remembered that as a young mariner he had been "fascinated" by "weird" *Moby-Dick* and declared—an opinion he claimed to have had at the time of the interview—that Melville "was the most original genius America has produced."[41] As Thomas Beer recalled years later, highly literate Senator Cushman Davis, who in 1886 began his war on the lawless corporations, was fond of *Moby-Dick,* and in 1900 likened tycoon Senator Mark Hanna's diabolical pursuit of idealistic Senator Richard Pettigrew to Ahab's chase of the white whale.[42]

In 1887 "The Death of the Whale" chapter was included in Lippincott's *Half Hours with the Best American Authors,* edited by Charles Morris.[43] In 1888 the *Nation* alluded to the whaling scenes as "de-

40. *American Literature in Nineteenth Century England* (New York, 1944), p. 46.
41. New York *Times,* March 17, 1900.
42. Review of Mumford's *Herman Melville,* New York *Herald Tribune,* March 10, 1929, and Beer's *Hanna* (New York, 1929), p. 232.
43. *Log,* p. 804.

scribed with wonderful power and felicity" in that "classic story of whaling adventure."[44] That year Julian Hawthorne gave it measured praise as being, unlike Melville's earlier books, for men rather than for boys.[45] The next year the Harpers put five pages from *Moby-Dick* in their *Fifth Reader,* which helped to give the tale currency, but was no doubt the seed of the notion—never breathed by an early reviewer whether friendly or hostile, but persisting later for a long time on certain cultural levels—that it was just a boy's book.

Late in 1889 Melville received evidence of a recognition of the excellence of *Moby-Dick* in a letter from Professor Archibald Mac-Mechan of Dalhousie University in Halifax, over a thousand miles northeast of New York, who had "read and re-read" it "with increasing pleasure" and regretted that its "unique merits" had not "received due recognition."[46] As he mentioned no other of Melville's books, I suppose he was implying the superiority of *Moby-Dick;* but he did not get his opinions into print until 1899.[47] Much earlier than that, yet too late to enhearten Melville, there appeared in the Springfield *Republican* on October 4, 1891, six days after he had been laid in his grave, an encomium, glaringly unusual among the obituary notices, which expressed the most glowing American praise given to *Moby-Dick* during the whole half century after the end of 1851, and proclaimed it unequivocally the "crown" of its author's achievement and a book looming among the "small realists and fantasts of the day" as "Hercules among the pigmies." Funeral flowers![48]

Also during these seven last years of Melville's life there had been two items in the press from Americans, who, though they ignored *Moby-Dick,* did envision Melville as genuinely important. In 1886 was

44. *Log,* p. 807.
45. *Log,* p. 810.
46. Metcalf, *op. cit.,* p. 276.
47. "The Best Sea Story Ever Written," *Queen's Quarterly,* VII (October, 1899), 120-130, reprinted in *The Life of a Little College* (Boston, 1914). I have no churlish desire to withhold from Professor MacMechan what honor is due him, but V. L. D. Chittick's extravagant claims for him as the "discoverer" of *Moby-Dick* ("The Way Back to Melville: Sea Chart of a Literary Revival," *Southwest Review,* XLIX [Summer, 1955], 238-248) are invalidated by (1) his unfortunate misdating of MacMechan's *Queen's Quarterly* article as 1889 instead of 1899 and (2) his ignoring of the fact that Russell had in 1884 in a *published* article explicitly stated *Moby-Dick* was Melville's "finest work" five years before MacMechan's much less explicit words came to Melville—and in letter form only. MacMechan's article appeared eight years after the Springfield *Republican* item and other items ignored by Chittick.
48. In the fall of 1890 Horace Scudder, editor of the *Atlantic Monthly,* almost commissioned George Parsons Lathrop to do an article on Melville: Lathrop was cooperative; but then Scudder decided to wait until Melville was dead (*Log,* p. 826)!

published a report—under the heading "A 'Buried' Author"—of a
New York meeting at which Professor J. W. Henry Canoll read a
sketch of and poem in tribute to Melville, whose "keen microscopic
mind" he "relished," though of Melville's works he referred only to
Clarel.[49]   In 1890 a columnist in the Boston *Post* protested against
Melville's being thought a mere describer of the South Sea islanders
(evidently unaware of how vigorously, even viciously, in this very newspaper Colonel Greene had once striven to establish precisely that
notion); alluded to the poems and *The Confidence-Man;* and insisted
that his best work was "unsurpassed in its way in English literature."[50]
Both commentators were obviously conscious of being voices in the
wilderness.

These were vocal moments amid the general silence.   Charles D.
Cleveland had left Melville out altogether from his *A Compendium of
American Literature* (1859), but left him out in good company along
with Thoreau and Whitman.   The compilers of the *Supplement* to
Griswold's *Prose Writers of America* (from which Melville had been
completely omitted in 1849) in 1871 gave Melville the same space as
Holmes and also as Sarah Jane Lippincott, dismissing him because of
his "incorrigible perversion of his rare and lofty gifts."[51]

Melville did not help his fame by such gestures as refusing to assist
in the founding of the Authors' Club in 1882 when asked to do so.[52]
The British Robert Buchanan reported in 1885 that he had hunted
everywhere in vain in New York to locate "the one great imaginative
writer" fit to stand with Whitman "on that continent."[53]   One
"Stylus" told in the *Literary World* that year of his youthful delight
in *Omoo, White Jacket,* and *Moby-Dick* too, but summed up thus:
"Had he possessed as much literary skill as wild imagination his works
might have secured for him a permanent place in American literature."[54]   In 1886 the New York *Commercial Advertiser* remarked that
Melville's "name would not be recognized by the rising generation";
and that "although his early works are still popular, he is generally
supposed to be dead."[55]   Edwin P. Whipple in his essay "American
Literature" in *American Literature and Other Papers* (1887) inserted

49. *Log,* p. 797. In the New York *Commercial Advertiser,* January 18.
50. *Log,* p. 827.
51. *Supplement,* p. 666. The phrase quoted above was lifted without acknowledgement from the *Dublin University Review's* 1856 article on Melville.
52. Howard, *Herman Melville,* p. 316.
53. In the *Academy,* August 15, 1885.
54. *Log,* p. 794.
55. *Log,* p. 796.

this misinformation: "Herman Melville, after astonishing his public with a rapid succession of original novels, the scene of which was placed in the islands of the Pacific, suddenly dropped his pen as if in disgust of his vocation." Charles Richardson in his *American Literature* (1889) put Melville in his place among "The Lesser Novelists"; one in whose works "fact" and "fancy were mingled by the nervously impatient author, in the proportion desired by his immediate public," and who thus produced "sprightly but now forgotten improvisations." His books were surely poorer, averred Richardson, than his conversations which so charmed the Hawthornes.[56] Albert H. Smyth in his *American Literature* (1889) gave Melville half a page devoid of any critical comment.

In November, 1890, Edward Bok declared in his syndicated column that there were "more people today who believe Herman Melville dead than there are who know he is living."[57] He was once famous —but now—"Busy New York has no idea he is even alive." The Boston *Post* columnist who admired Melville countered that he would not have been so forgotten if he had lived in Boston. Both of the participants in this little battle of the cities were so poorly informed about him as to believe he was still in the Customhouse, from which he had resigned five years before.

Publishers' records suggest that, during these years before his death, Melville was somewhat more widely read in America than in England. In America, after "Bartleby" in 1853, and before 1891, there were five reprintings of *Typee*, three of *Omoo*, two of *Mardi*, and one of *Redburn*, one of *White Jacket*, one of *Moby-Dick*, one of *Pierre*, and two—including a kind of pirated edition—of *Israel Potter*.[58]

Yet in the United States he had during his later life no such little devoted group as those James Thomson inspired to study him, no such perceptive and vigorous advocate as Russell. As for the New York literati of the day, neither Richard Henry Stoddard nor Edmund Clarence Stedman, though they were interested in Melville, really regarded him as a writer of stature. Stoddard, indeed, in reviewing *John Marr* (1888) called *Moby-Dick* "probably his greatest work," but in a memorial article on October 8, 1891, in the New York *World and Express,* gave Melville a humble rank in saying that early in his career his countrymen, "less literary in their tastes and demands than at present, were easily captivated by stories of maritime

56. P. 404.
57. *Log,* p. 827.
58. Hetherington, pp. 491-498.

life like 'Omoo,' and 'Typee,' and 'Moby Dick.'" Stedman perhaps valued Melville more highly; in trying—not his fault that he tried in vain—to interest the members of the Authors' Club in Melville in 1890, he described him as "one of our strongest geniuses."[59] Robert Buchanan reported that in 1885 he heard from "Mr. E. C. Stedman, who seemed much surprised in his interest in the subject" that Melville was still alive.[60] How disappointing to find that Stedman chose to represent Melville in the Stedman and Hutchinson *Library of American Literature* (1899) by only a few poems and "The Bell-Tower."[61]

Melville had been omitted from all the gift books and annuals; he had been named by none of the "Academies";[62] and literary dictator William Dean Howells is not known even to have mentioned him. Indeed Howells seemed to be passing him by pointedly in writing that "if we put aside the romances of Hawthorne and the romantic novels of Cooper," we could hardly find much American fiction of "scope and import before the Civil War." It was thus not surprising that an egregiously inaccurate obituary could appear in no less a paper than the New York *Times* entitled "A Tribute to the Late Hiram Melville."[63]

If the book now universally regarded as his masterpiece was cherished by a mere handful, chiefly British—including indeed some choicer spirits—; if those who had the power to shape general literary opinion ignored him or gave him humble status; if while living he was widely believed dead; he still had been issued, particularly by his own countrymen, a ticket of admission of sorts to Literary Valhalla—which read "The Author of *Typee*."

He had foreseen it, even before he had finished *Moby-Dick*: he had written to Hawthorne, "What 'reputation' H. M. has is horrible"; for "'Typee' would be given" to the "babies" of the next generation

59. *Log*, p. 823.
60. "Imperial Cockneydom," *The Universal Review*, May 15, 1889. According to Buchanan, Cockneydom had spread even to Chicago, preventing the recognition of Whitman and Melville.
61. William Sharpe, in reviewing this production in the London *National Review*, March, 1891, made no mention of Melville, but declared Poe, Emerson, and Hawthorne "great literary artists."
62. Allen Walker Read, "The Membership in Proposed American Academies," *American Literature*, VII (March, 1935), 145-165. According to Read, in 1884 a straw vote in the *Critic* resulted in a list of "Forty Immortals" living, which included Holmes, Henry James, Julian Hawthorne, George Parsons Lathrop, but not Melville. Holmes, Lowell, and Whittier got the highest votes.
63. See my study of the incredible inadequacy of the obituaries, followed by a small wave of protest at this inadequacy, in "A Tribute to the Late Hiram Melville," *Modern Language Quarterly*, XVI (December, 1955), 325-333.

"perhaps, with their gingerbread."[64] Why was he so galled at the prospect? Because he knew that to gain real stature in the world of letters he must show there was a deep originality in his vision of life that was not merely a fruitage of his years of exotic voyaging.[65] I have shown in Chapter II how, by the time of "Bartleby," *Typee* had become a part of the national legend; and in Chapter VII how within a few months after its publication even *Moby-Dick* had been eclipsed by the remembrance of *Typee*. Except for a half-dozen voices—including those from Leicester, from Thanet, from Halifax—nearly all coming from places far from the "insular city of the Manhattoes," though fortunately heard by Melville at 104 East Twenty-sixth Street in that city, he was for most of those who knew of him at all, "The Author of *Typee*."

Thus his Uncle Peter Gansevoort had described him as early as 1853 in a letter begging an influential friend to commend Herman to President Pierce for a consular appointment.[66] In a letter from Pittsfield in 1858, George Duyckinck, who had never liked *Moby-Dick* too well, alluded to "your friend Typee Melville."[67] In 1859 Titus Munson Coan and John Thomas Gulick, Williams College undergraduates and sons of Hawaiian missionaries, visited Melville in Pittsfield. Coan complained that "in vain I sought to hear of Typee and those Paradise islands," for Melville insisted on talking about Greek philosophy of which they had "quite enough at . . . Williams."[68] It was the same farther west. Merton M. Sealts's thorough investigation of the lecture tours which in 1857-59 took Melville as far west as Milwaukee reveals that he was for the newspapermen almost exclusively the author of *Typee* and *Omoo*. The only exceptions were, early in 1858, two mentions without comment of *Moby-Dick,* one in Detroit and one in the Cincinnati *Enquirer,* which did also speak with patience of *Pierre* and with derision of *The Confidence-Man;* and in the Cleveland *Morning Leader* a reference, also without remark, to *Mardi* and to a book it called Maybe Dick![69]

In 1868 *Putnam's Magazine* reported receiving a letter from "Herman Melville, Esq., author of 'Typee.'"[70] In 1876 *Lippincott's Magazine,* reviewing *Clarel,* remarked, "If Melville has written anything

64. *Log*, p. 413.
65. Rosenberry, p. 172, substantiates this point by quoting from *Pierre*.
66. *Log*, p. 470.
67. *Log*, p. 549.
68. *Log*, p. 605.
69. *Melville as Lecturer* (Cambridge, 1957), pp. 36, 44, 31.
70. *Log*, p. 694.

since the three captivating books Omoo, Typee, and Mardi, we do not know." Titus Munson Coan in his *Life in Hawaii* (1882) referred to the "gifted author of Typee and Omoo." In 1886 the St. Louis *Globe Democrat* said that Melville, "once renowned," though "seldom mentioned of late," published *Typee* and *Omoo,* and that "He wrote other clever books, but none of them won so much reputation as his two first."[71] Jack London in the *Cruise of the Snark* (1911) told of reading *Typee* about 1886, which stirred in him a desire to go to Typee Valley, as indeed he did, only to find the Marquesans sadly degenerated.[72] In 1889 the Boston *Post* declared that "Moby-Dick, which followed Omoo and Typee, did not come up to the high standard established by those delightful books."[73] In 1890 Edward Bok in his column mentioned only Melville's "most famous tale, Typee."[74] That year the New York *Critic* seemed to be able to recall only *Typee,* which "had a deserved success here and in England forty years ago," and whose author was "not entirely unknown."[75] Henry Adams tried to find the calabooza of *Omoo* in Tahiti, but said nothing about the pursuit of the white whale.[76]

And so it came about that, in a paper no less important than the New York *Tribune,* the very first of the obituaries which followed Melville's death on September 28, 1891, contained this gem: "He won considerable fame as an author by the publication of a book in 1847 entitled 'Typee.' . . . This was his best work, although he has since written a number of other stories, which were published more for private than public circulation." What unconscious accuracy! The "other stories" had indeed a "private circulation" among a small and scattered band who would to a later era seem to have been the true lovers of the Muses. Not quite all the copies of the "other stories" had turned out to be "dead letters." A few had been delivered to those who had opened them as if they were veritable "sugred Sonnets" for his "private friends." Yet for the most part, Melville's worst fears had been realized. He had gone down to posterity, as he had written forty years ago in that letter to Hawthorne he supposed he would, as a "man who lived among the cannibals."

In that letter there was a curious qualification: "When I speak of posterity, in reference to myself, I only mean the babies who will

71. *Log,* p. 816.
72. Pp. 154-177.
73. *Log,* p. 816.
74. *Log,* p. 827.
75. *Log,* p. 828.
76. *Log,* p. 832.

probably be born in the moment almost immediately ensuing upon my giving up the ghost." He may have been merely modestly indicating that he feared his fame would terminate with that "ensuing" generation. But could he have been prophesying that there would be a different reaction after they were gone? By 1920, the beginning of the widespread renewed interest in his work, those "babies" were nearly thirty. Many of them were still young enough to be able to receive, along with their children, new light in which Herman Melville would no longer be seen as the author of the tale of sojourn among kindly maneaters but now of a work immensely more incandescent, wherein there "floated one grand hooded phantom, like a snow hill in air."

INDEX

DATE DUE

DEC 0 1 1997	